MW00415032

Jihad in Islam

Sayyid Abul A'la Maududi

Translated by

Wing Cmdr. Syed Rafatullah Shah

Book: Jihad in Islam

Author: Sayyid Abul A'la Maududi

Translator: Wing Commander Syed Rafatullah Shah

Editor: Syed Firasat Shah

First Edition   2017

Dedication

This translation work is dedicated to Mr. Syed Nusrat Shah (Late) and Mrs. Hayat Uzzia Nusrat (Late), the parents of both the translator Wing Cmdr. Syed Rafatullah Shah (Late) and the translation project Coordinator/Editor Syed Firasat Shah. May Allah grant them peace in the afterlife and this work of their sons may become sadqa al jariyah (a charity for perpetual reward), AMEEN.

Contents

Publisher's Note

In the name of Allah, the Most Gracious, the Most Merciful

The author started writing this book at the age of 23 and completed this work in three years time. The first edition of this book was published in 1930 through Dar ul Musannifeen, Azamgarh, Uttar Pradesh, India. When the book first became public, Allama Iqbal made the comment about this book and said, "On the topic of jihad, such a profound research work with unapologetic content has neither been published in Urdu nor in any other language." In 1926, following the murder of Swami Shardhanand, there was severe criticism of Islam from all over India and Islam was being bashed from all directions. One day, Maulana Muhammad Ali Johar said in one of his speeches, "I wish there would be a servant of God who would write such a book on the topic of jihad in Islam, which will repel all the criticisms and blames and clarify the real concept of jihad for the world." The author was present in this gathering and heard the Maulana's words and wondered in his heart that why not he be this servant of God. Therefore, he immediately started working on this project. The level and the vastness of the academic research and the level of intellectual acumen put into this work will become apparent to any reader of this book.

We are presenting to our readers the English translation of the book Al Jihad fil Islam, translated by Wing Commander Syed Rafatullah Shah and edited by Syed Firasat Shah. The Urdu edition that was used for translation is that version which was reviewed by the author himself to correct the errors that were present in the earlier editions.

Khalid Farooq Maududi
Head of the Idara Tarjuman ul Qur'an
Urdu Bazaar, Lahore, Pakistan
8 Rabi ul Awal 1437 AH (21 December 2015)

Foreword

In the Name of Allah, The Most Gracious, The Most Merciful

As has happened many times in its history, the Muslim Ummah (nation) is once again going through a very important and testing period. Based entirely on the historical evidence, it can be said with confidence that it will come out of this situation intact and back on track. This phenomenal aspect of the Muslim Ummah to rejuvenate after each testing period is due to the two main sources of guidance available to Muslims, the teachings of the Holy Qur'an and the traditions of Prophet Muhammad (SAW), that have remained uncorrupted throughout its history. These two sources have continued to guide the Ummah out of difficult situations at various times in its History. However, it is also true, that in such difficult times there have been attempts to redefine the Islamic teachings in order to find compromised ways out of such desperate situations.

The Islamic system of life does have the built-in flexibility and adaptability to adjust itself according to circumstances. However, in times of degeneration there have been and are tendencies even within Muslim scholarship, to cross the limits of allowable flexibility and tamper with the fundamental teachings of Islam. At one such juncture in history, during the British Rule in the Subcontinent, there was severe criticism by non-Muslims of the fundamental teachings of Islam, particularly on the subject of Jihad. This was the time following the murder of a Hindu leader of the Shudhi Movement (a movement with the mission to reconvert those to Hinduism who chose to convert to another religion), reportedly by a Muslim. A measured and balanced response to that criticism of Islamic teachings came from Sayyid Abul A'la Maududi through his book Al Jihad Fil Islam.

A similar campaign, however one that is more intense, widespread, and well organized, exists today with respect to the criticism of Islamic teachings, that they are supposedly responsible for radicalizing the Muslims. This is in response to some acts of violence against civilians, committed by or attributed to Muslims. The Muslim response to this negative propaganda against Islam ranges from denial of the original concept of Jihad as if it was not part of Islamic teachings, to aggressive responses legitimizing such actions under the pretext of Jihad that are not permitted in the Islamic teachings. There is a need today to revisit the balanced approach presented by Sayyid Maududi. We are presenting to our readers the English translation of the marvelous research work Al Jihad Fil Islam by Sayyid Maududi, explaining the original concept of Jihad in Islam.

For the sake of keeping the originality of the work, it was decided to present just the translation without any addition, omission, detailed explanations, or synthesis of this research work. Therefore, the reader will find references up to World War I, after which the original book was written, and not from a later, more recent period of history; at some places where these older references are given in the text, we have inserted highlighted comments as reminder flags for the reader. These reminders are intended to invite the reader for a simple intellectual exercise, to find striking similarities in the contemporary history, and to notice how history is repeating itself. For the ease of identification, *a bold italic font* has been chosen for such notes. At some places, the writer Sayyid Maududi has himself added some thought provoking comments in the later edition of the book to invite the reader to think of what was written years ago, have manifested itself again in the events that occurred around the world in later years.

The haziness created due to the dust generated by the so-called war on terror was settling down and the vision was becoming clearer 14 years after 9/11, when the incident of Paris killings happened and we are back to square one, a similar situation has again been created where truth has become hard to perceive. Until very recently, the United Nations, the highest international body, is debating over the issue of defining terrorism. On the other hand, thanks to the media portrayal of Islam in the recent years, Islam is taken by many today as synonymous with terrorism. The events of the current times, ranging from the murder of a Dutch filmmaker to the Palestinian struggle for freedom, are all being branded as Islamic terrorism. Terms like 'jihadist' are introduced and ill informed, uncareful and those with ulterior motives against Islam use them as if they are synonyms to terrorists, to unintentionally or intentionally malign Islam and its esteemed doctrine of Jihad. This book will provide an opportunity for the readers to analyze what qualifies within the Islamic concept of Jihad, and will provide an opportunity to see the comparative teachings of other major religions of the world and the modern Western thoughts in relation to wars and conflicts.

Apart from praying for my elder brother Wing Commander Syed Rafatullah Shah (died March 20, 2003) for his efforts in translating this important work in English, I would like to extend my thanks and acknowledge the support of many who had helped me in this effort through their valuable suggestions and encouragements. The English translations of the Qur'anic verses used in this book are taken from Marmaduke Pickthall. The readers, who may not be familiar with the Islamic terminology used within this book, are requested to refer to the glossary of Islamic-Arabic terms at the end of the book. I seek forgiveness from Allah for any errors that may have been left unattended in the translation. I also ask the reader for any feedback for future improvement in the manuscript.

Translation Project Coordinator/Editor

Syed Firasat Shah

Email: firasatshah@gmail.com

Phone: +92-322-2907448

Note: For any comments, corrections and suggestions for improvement, as well as to obtain additional copies, please contact me at the above email/ phone number.

Preface

In the name of Allah, the Most Gracious, the Most Merciful

In the modern age, for political reasons, Europe has levelled false accusations against Islam. One accusation is that Islam is a bloodthirsty religion and teaches spilling of blood to its followers. If there would have been any truth to this claim, it would have happened at the time when the sword of the followers of Islam had shook the world and indeed the world could have considered that these conquests are the results of some violent training that the followers of Islam have been put through. The surprising fact is that this blame game started much after the shining sun of Islam had already sat long ago. This concept was concocted and floated at the time when the sword of Islam had already been rusted, however, the swords of the orchestraters of this blame, the Europeans, were being reddened by the blood of many innocent humans and they were swallowing the weak nations of the world like a python snake swallows small animals.

If the sense would have prevailed in the world, question would have been raised, that the people who are the biggest enemies of peace; who have reddened the face of the earth by repeatedly spilling the blood of innocent people; who were robbing the small nations of the world; how in the world do they accuse Islam and level a charge on it that in actuality is appropriate for themselves? Is the real reason for what they did was that the flood of criticism, which was coming towards them, its tides would turn towards Islam? Nevertheless, this is a weakness of men, that if he is weak in the battlefield, he becomes weak at centers of learning as well. The one from whose sword he is defeated, he also loses the power of the pen to compete with that dominant one. This is the reason why the prevailing philosophies and opinions of the world are always those, which are written by the hands that are holding the sword at the same time. It is for this reason that Europe was successful in its Islam bashing campaign. Nations of the world with a slave mentality accepted the propaganda of Europe with such an acceptance that may exceed the level of acceptance of heavenly tablets.

In the previous and in the current centuries, so much had been written on the topic under discussion, that it appears like an outdated and a battered topic. However, I have noticed this flaw in the writings in defense of Islam, that the writers are often overwhelmed by the opponents and put themselves in the defendant's box and start replying to the accusers as if they are convicts. Due to the overwhelming influence of their critics, some of the writers have gone to such extents as to modify the teachings and codes of Islam to suite the liking of their critics. They tried to remove from the historic record such elements that they thought were dangerous, and they would not like the opponents to have a peek into them. The people whose writings are free from such problems, even those are not explicit enough in their works to encompass all the relevant details of jihad and warfare in Islam, one still feels thirsty after reading such works and many questions remain unanswered.

To dispel the misconceptions around the subject under discussion, there is a need to address the topic of Jihad Fe sabeel-illah and that of battling for the prevalence of the right. Therefore, it is a requirement to present the teachings of Islam and its laws without any addition or subtraction, exactly as they are described in the Holy Qur'an, the Hadith, and the books of Islamic jurisprudence. Such works should be in accordance with the bounds associated with the original spirit of Islam.

Not a single issue of this world enjoys a total consensus, rather, each party keeps its own opinion dearer. According to the Holy Qur'an, *each party is happy with what it has.* Therefore, no matter however much we taint our opinion with that of the others, it is impossible that the people holding a variety of opinions would like our faked position, and the difference of opinion could be bridged. Therefore, the better approach would be to present our own belief system, commandments, teachings and codes, and put forth arguments in support of them, following that, leave it on the intellect of the others to accept or reject them. If they accept our argument fair and good, if not, we should not bother much about these disagreements. This is the correct approach to outreach and spreading the message of Islam. As this is the way of the people of great determination and the way that prophets of Allah had adopted.

I have been planning for some time to embark on this work, but luxury of time was required to undertake such a gigantic task, but for people associated with newspaper journalism, free time is a commodity rarely available to them. However, in 1926 there was an incident, which prompted me to commit myself to this work. This incident was of the murder of Swami Shardhanand, a leader of the Shudhi movement. The incident provided another opportunity for the ill informed and shortsighted people to spread wrong information about the teachings of jihad in Islam, as unfortunately the person who was arrested and accused of the murder was a Muslim man. The newspaper reports associated his motives to the animosity against men of other faith, and that he was expecting entry into paradise through this act of his. The truth is known to Allah, however, what came forth were these details. Because of this incident, the enemies of Islam became paranoid. Despite the clear declarations by Muslim scholars and the consensus explanation in magazines and by renowned leadership of Muslims, instead of keeping this incident within the physical limits of the act, the entire Muslim nation and even the teachings of Islam were regarded as being responsible for the act. The Qur'anic teachings were openly criticized and portraid as the source for producing blood thirsty followers and murderers. It is said that these teachings are against peace and a danger for security and calm of the society, its teachings have produced such prejudice in its followers that they regard every non-Muslim liable for killing and they hope for Paradise by killing non-Muslims. Some people with rotten minds even suggested that until the teachings of the Qur'an are present in this world, it is not possible to have peace and security, therefore, all mankind should strive for getting the world rid of these teachings. These rubbish thoughts were propagated on such a large scale that even people of reason also became confused, a person like Gandhi, who was the greatest man of opinion among the Hindus, under the influence of anti Islamic propaganda, repeatedly stated the following views:

"The advent of Islam was in such an environment that in it ultimate power of decision was with the sword and it remains with the sword."

Although, these opinions neither were based on sensible research nor on any academic discourse, rather, were being repeated like a parrot who repeates the same words once taught to him by his master. However, one unusual incident has filled-in colors of reality in a concept, which was otherwise full of mystery, with which ignorant people can easily be deceived. Although, such popular misconceptions prove as big hurdles in the way of spreading the message of Islam, however, at such times the need to present the correct teachings of Islam is even more intense, so that the mist is removed and the sun of reality rises with its full glitter.

Considering this, instead of waiting for free time to become available to me, I used the little time that was available to me after my routine engagements with the newspaper publication, and started writing and compiling material for this work. Along with it, I started publishing parts of this study as columns in the Daily Jamyah. Initially my intention was to write a brief article on the subject, however, once the work started, so many avenues related to the subject began opening for me, that it became difficult to contain the topic in small columns of the newspaper. Therefore, after writing about two dozen columns in the newspaper, I stopped writing further episodes. Now, after completing the work, I am presenting it in the form of a book. Although, this work has covered most of the important aspects of the topic, I still feel that at places, I just restricted myself to a few sentences where full chapters could only have done justice for complete explaination of certain aspects of the topic.

I have made a deliberate attempt to stay away from my own or someone else's opinions and restricted myself to the point of view extracted from the Qur'an, for all major and miner topics of the work. Wherever I felt the requirement for further explanation, I refered to the hadith and the authentic books of jurisprudence, so that the reader can be assured that the writing is not influenced by what is in the fashion today. Rather, whatever is presented is based on the words of Allah, His Prophet and the great scholars of Islam.

I appeal to all those non-Muslims who do not keep any grudge against Islam based on blind rivalry, to study the teachings of Islam regarding warfare and then spell out if there is any objection they have on these teachings. Even after doing so, if someone has some remaining doubts, I will try to clarify such doubts.

Abul Aala

Delhi, 15 June 1927

Preface to Second Edition

This book was not available in the market for quite some time. Firstly, it was difficult to publish such a hefty book during the time of war, secondly, the intention behind holding out on its second publication was to include a chapter covering the changes that were happening in the international law, during the course of the World War II. Unfortunately, I fell ill during this time and it was difficult for me to continue the work of research and writing. Now this book is being published with only some nessessory changes and with correction of some errors. If Allah will grant me the strength, the planned chapter will be included in the next edition of this book.

Abul Aala

14 Ramadan, 1366 Hijrah (31 July 1947)

Chapter One

Facts about Jihad in Islam

Respect for Human Life

Civilization has for its primary basis, the respect of human life. The first right that man has on civilizations is his right to live and his first civilized duty is to let others live. This right is embodied in all religious and other codes of law-that, which does not recognize this right, can neither claim to be the religion nor code of law of human beings, nonetheless people living under its influence can hope to live peacefully. One can judge for oneself, whether it would be possible for men to live together; where life has no value and there is no arrangement for its security, where there can be no peaceful mutual interaction. In the absence of the essential prerequisites; commerce, industry and agriculture cannot be established or sustained. Hence, civilized pursuits such as; earning money, making and keeping abodes, travel and tourism and leading a meaningful life in general, would be impossible. Let us set aside the utilitarian aspect and consider only the humane aspect of the proposition. If a fellow human can take the life of another human with impunity, this would be the ultimate in heartlessness and savagery, and under such circumstances, there can be no social progress and even maintaining any degree of humanity would be impossible.

Worldly laws and codes seek to enforce value-systems through threats of punishment and force. The object of a true religion however, is to instill the respect for life and blood which would thus be inviolable even in the absence of worldly law and the ability to enforce it. From this standpoint, the validity, correctness, and effectiveness of the Islamic teachings have no match whatsoever.

The Holy Qur'an has sought to instill this respect and value-system, by a variety of means. Surah Al-Maidah (Chapter 5 of the Holy Qur'an), relating the story of the two sons of Adam (AS), one of whom murders his brother, states:

> "For that cause, We decreed for the children of
> Israel that whosoever killeth a human being other
> than (the one guilty of) manslaughter or corruption
> in the earth, it shall be as if he had killed all
> mankind, and whoso saveth the life of one, it shall
> be as if he had saved the life of all mankind. Our
> messengers came unto them of old with clear proof
> of (Allah's sovereignty), but afterwards, lo! Many
> of them became prodigals on earth"
>
> (Al-Maidah: 32)

Allah, speaking of the qualities of the pious and righteous,
states,

> "And those who cry not unto any other god along
> with Allah, nor take the life which Allah hath
> forbidden save in (course of) justice, nor commit
> adultery-- and whoso doeth this shall pay the
> penalty" (Al-Furqan: 68)

At another place, Qur'an states:

> "Say: come I will recite unto you that which your
> lord hath made a sacred duty for you: that ye ascribe
> no thing as partner unto Him, and that ye do good to
> parents, and that ye slay not your children because
> of penury----- We provide for you and for them-----
> and that ye draw not nigh to lewd things whether
> open or concealed. And that ye slay not the life
> which Allah hath made sacred, save in the course of
> justice. This He hath commanded you, in order that
> ye may discern" (Al-Anam: 151)

The prime addressees of these verses were those who held
human life of little value and who in the interest of petty personal
gain, would murder even their own children. For this reason the
Prophet Mohammad (SAW) used to always preach of the sanctity
of life in the most effective manner. The books of hadith are
replete with the sayings of the Prophet (SAW), stressing, that
shedding of innocent blood was the worst kind of sin, some of
these are quoted below:

Anas bin Malik states that the Prophet (SAW) once declared:

"Of the graver sins the major ones are, holding anything or person partner to God, killing a person, and telling lies".

Ibn Umar relates the following saying of the Prophet (SAW): "A believer remains acceptable in the eyes of his religion, till he sheds human blood without due cause".

A hadith from Nisai quotes the Prophet (SAW) as saying: "The first thing that a man will be questioned about, on the Day of Judgment, will be the account of his prayers and the first thing to be settled between men will be claims of blood".

In reply to a question, as to what is the gravest of sins, the Prophet (SAW) stated, that it was holding someone equal to Allah. The next in gravity is the murder of one's own children, for fear that one may have to share one's food with them, and the next was fornication with the neighbor's wife.

Moral Impact of the Islamic Teachings on the World

Respect for life that Islam propagates are not the result of the thinking of any philosopher or teacher of ethics, that its effects would remain confined within the covers of books or to universities. It is the teaching of Allah and each word of it became the fundamental part of every Muslim's faith. The effect of this teaching on the savage and fearsome Arabs was such that they were transformed into a peace-loving people, who had the greatest respect for human life. This, to the extent that after the passage of only a quarter of a century, a woman could travel alone, in their land, from Qadisyah to Sanaa in complete safety, where earlier, big and well guarded caravans could not travel without fear. Then, when half of the civilized world came under the sway of Islamic Law, like many other ills and wanton practices, disrespect for human life was also corrected. Today the status that respect of life is given, in the accepted and respected laws of this civilized world, is the magnificent result of this great Islamic Revolution.

On the eve of the revelation of the Holy Qur'an, life had little value. The world is well aware of the Arab savagery and disregard for life, but even among those nations, which were considered highly civilized and cultured, with established centers of learning and wisdom, the conditions were not much better. The stories of the events in the Roman coliseums are well known. Multitudes of men became victims of gladiatory for the entertainment of the gentry. Savage killings of men by beasts, having them slaughtered like animals, arranging spectacles of men burning to death just for the entertainment of friends, were neither uncommon nor looked upon with disdain. In many nations of Europe and Asia, torturing and killing prisoners of wars as well as other prisoners and slaves, by different means was a common practice of that time. The great men of learning and philosophy of enlightened Rome and Greece were proponents of such human killings under various circumstances. Even philosophers of the eminence of Aristotle and Plato, condoned the removal of the female womb, hence, premature abortion of pregnancy was not considered illegal or immoral. The father had right to a son's life, and the Roman lawmakers were proud of this legal and unlimited parental potent. Suicide was not a wrongful act in the eyes of the rulers and stoics; it was rather, appreciated and sometimes performed in gatherings specially arranged for the purpose, even people of the wisdom of Aristotle, did not consider it worthy of any disdain. For a husband, killing his wife was of the stature of killing a pet animal.

In India, among Hindus, the custom of human sacrifice was common, to the extent that cremation of the living widow on the dead husband's funeral pyre was a legal act, even stressed upon and highly recommended by their religion. (It could be said that widows volunteered for the sacrifice, but the fact is that there were so many social pressures on her that she was well nigh forced into the suicide).

The life of one from the 'Shudr' caste was of no great moment, only for the reason that the poor chap was 'born from the feet of the god, Brahma' (sic); his blood was not inviolate for one of Brahman caste. If he (the Shudr), happened to hear the recitation of the holy 'Vedas', killing him by pouring molten lead in his ears was not only permissible but obligatory. 'Jal Pradha', was a popular Hindu custom, according to which the parents cast their first-born into the river Ganges, the parents used to consider this a sublime act.

In these dark times, Islam gave birth to the concept of the 'sanctity of life'. Shedding of human blood, per its concept, was prohibited unless absolutely justifiable. There was strength in this, the strength of being in conformity with nature and unlike contradiction of it like 'Parma Dharma' and 'Ahinsa'. That was the reason for its acceptability and rapid spread to every corner of the globe. It apprised man of the true value of his life. Whether any nation accepted its call or not, it had the quality that none could withstand its effects, at least to some extent, on its socio-cultural life. No fair and unbiased scholar will deny the effect of this call, on establishing the sanctity of life was paramount and greater than the effects of the 'Sermon of the Mount' or of Hindu 'Parma Dharma'.

Rightful Killing

Consider carefully, where Qur'an teaches us of the sanctity of life; it does not merely say that life cannot be violated under any circumstance. If this alone had been stated, the concept could have been considered defective. No code of law of the world is bereft of the proviso for enforcement. Human nature dislikes restraints, it is not possible that man would always be disciplined and law-abiding. It is in man's nature that he is capable of doing both good and bad. Where it is possible that he can be disciplined, he is also capable of the grossest indiscipline. Therefore, to control the unruly and undisciplined aspect of his nature and compel him towards discipline, it is necessary to have laws and rules, which are explicit in specifying the punishment for their violation and for disregard of prohibitions. Only stating, "Do not create strife in the land after it has been set aright" or "Do not shed blood that has been declared sacred ", is clearly not enough. Man has to be told what his punishment would be if he is found guilty of the major sins of spreading strife or of bloodshed. Such oversights are possible in manmade laws, but they are not, where divinity is the author; divine law is explicit on the inviolability of life, lest it be forfeit per its legal injunctions. The inviolability is relevant only within lawful bounds. Whenever man crosses these bounds or limits, spreads strife or when he threatens others' lives without warrant, the sacredness of a man's life turns into a burden for society and he loses his right to live, in his death alone is the life of humanity. Taking of a human life is indeed a big evil, but worse is spreading strife and disorder, so states the Qur'an. When a person is guilty of this bigger crime, it is far better for the world that his ability to do so again is curbed.

The Holy Qur'an states, "You have been ordered that the death of the murdered be avenged". Thus the systematic discrimination between high and low status among men, imposed by nations gone astray, has been eliminated. The Holy Qur'an states, "by virtue of their being human, all men are equal". Therefore, it is not possible that the rich may take the life of the poor or the master of his slave and go Scot-free. By virtue of being human, they are all equal. Killing can only be avenged by taking the guilty one's life, whether he be rich or poor. In order to remove the element of horror from this killing for punishment, the Holy Qur'an states,

> "O, you wise people, do not consider this punishment (qisas), the death of a man, but a lease on life has been given to society, by removing a dangerous ulcer, from its body".

Prophet Mohammad (SAW) explained this philosophy of lease on life, by virtue of a death by 'qisas'. He stated in this regard, "Help thy brother, whether he be oppressed or the oppressor". People asked him as to how indeed the oppressor could be helped? He replied, "by holding his hand and preventing him from committing a foul act". In fact, any tribulation caused to an oppressor is but a kindness to him and indeed, is an aid to the oppressor. This is why instructions regarding establishment of the bounds of Allah are strict. The act of establishing Allah's bounds is greater than, 'the prosperity brought by 40 days of rain'. The prosperity brought by rain is that it lends fertility to the soil, which increases the produce of the land, which brings prosperity to the dwellers. The prosperity due to the establishment of Allah's bounds is that strife, disorder and oppression have their roots severed, and His creations can live in peace and harmony, the essentials for progress of civilization.

Rightful Killing Versus Wrongful Killing

The restrictions on shedding blood of the innocents are severe and equally strict are the instructions in Islam, to shed blood in the rightful cause. Thus Islam points to the middle path, the path between oppression and docile tolerance. On one side is the transgressor who holds human life of little value and considers it right to shed human blood to satisfy his lowly desires. On the other side is the misguided group that holds the mistaken viewpoint that life is sacred and inviolable, whatever the circumstance maybe. The Islamic law negates both these wrong schools of thought. It holds that human life as neither inviolable like the honor of the Holy Kaaba or that of one's mother or one's sister, nor is it so valueless, that it maybe sacrificed to satisfy one's ego or emotions. It teaches us that the human life is not so cheap, that one may enjoy the spectacle of seeing it writhe in pain in dungeons, ending it painfully by burning or torture or in ending the life if found obstructing one's desires or to satisfy ones base and carnal desires. Life is not for sacrifice on the altar, on some wrong pretext for carrying out some false traditions. Definitely, shedding blood for such unholy and filthy purposes is not only intolerable, but is most emphatically prohibited. Islam also teaches us that there is something of more value than human life and that is the cause of righteousness. When shedding blood is the requirement of the cause, it is not only correct to do so, but is obligatory. To refrain from shedding blood under such circumstances is prohibited.

Until one maintains the sanctity of truth and justice, one's life remains sacred, but when one insists on violation of bounds, one makes one's own life valueless, rather a burden for society.

Unavoidable Killing

Although, rightfully depriving someone of his life, as punishment for wrongful killing, is also bloodshed, it is unavoidable. Without this, peace cannot be established in the world; strife and violence cannot be uprooted; pious cannot be protected from the evils of the impious; rightful cannot get their rights; freedom of conscience is not possible and transgressors cannot be kept from transgressing. Hence, Allah's creation cannot enjoy any degree of physical, mental, and spiritual peace. If Islam is accused of this kind of bloodshed, it has no compunctions about accepting it. But, the question is, which society is innocent of such rightful and necessary bloodshed? Buddhism's 'Ahinsa' holds it wrong, but it was forced to make a difference between spirituality and necessity. Ultimately, assuring salvation (Nirvan) for a little group, the rest of the Buddhists were provided skeletal spiritual instructions and given leave to follow 'Grahast Dharam', the law of necessity, for the pursuit of such occupations as politics, criminology and war. Similarly, Christianity, despite its professed and total abhorrence for war and bloodshed, had to ultimately accept its necessity. When Roman atrocities became unbearable, the Christians occupied the throne and subjected the empire to such bloodshed, which far exceeded the limits of 'unavoidable bloodshed'.

In the Hindu religion, its authors also suggested the philosophy of 'Ahinsa' and 'Parmu Dharam', which totally forbid bloodshed of any creation of God and proclaimed taking of human life a major sin. However, Mannu, a contemporary man of law and religion, was asked for a ruling as to what was to be done if someone made advances towards their women or plundered their belongings or insulted their religion. He replied that such a person, no matter whether he be a 'guru' or a scholar or of the Brahman caste or an old man, should indeed be put to death.

The objective of this discussion is not to argue the necessity of unavoidable killings by comparison of the relevant aspects of various religions, that is a different subject; it will be discussed later, where it will be seen that those religions that considered war as heinous, were practically unable to avoid it. Here our aim is only to demonstrate that all nations, no matter what heights their philosophies and ideologies may have achieved, must ultimately rely on practical solutions to address their worldly problems, and that the world compels them to combat reality with workable practicality. It was not God's intention that the world be given such pleasing and delectable regulations as can be found in 'Ahinsa' or the divinity of such revelations would have dumbfounded the world's intellect. The intent was not philosophical exhibitionism; rather He intended to give His creatures a correct, clear, and precise code of conduct, following which would put their world and Hereafter, in good order. Despite the consideration that without the provision of the clause, "Without just cause," merely instructing man, "Thou shalt not kill", would not have sufficed. And despite seeing that man deserved the chastisement, "Why do you preach, that which you do not practice", it was not possible that The Divine, The Unfaltering, would continue accepting that man continue professing 'Ahinsa' and 'Parmu Dharam' and that He would at the same time condone the wielding of the sword. It was in his wisdom that the Lord instructed man not only to hold life sacred, but also prescribed taking of it as punishment for causing death. In this way, He rationalized the use of strength, which could hence be utilized effectively for furthering the concept of 'sacredness of life'.

Collective Evil

Individuals and also groups or nations are liable to the law of punishment for death. Just as man individually can get unruly, so can the groups or nations. Like individuals, groups or nations can succumb to temptation and greed and go beyond all bounds to satisfy themselves. Individuals can be kept under control and their desires for trespass under check, either by punitive or by preventive means. Similarly, for curbing a group's or a nation's tendency for evil, war becomes unavoidable. Except the manifest enormity of effects, there is no difference between individual and collective evil. The effects of individual evil and mischief are confined within a particular restricted circle, only a limited number of people in its sphere of influence are affected adversely and a little bloodying of the soil can cure the problem. Strife caused by a group however, can have effects that are unlimited and catastrophic. Because of it, for many people, existence can become a burden. Nations in their entirety have their lives jeopardized, even the entire system and organization of civilization can face tumult and turmoil. The end of such strife cannot be affected, without the flow of streams of blood.

When nations stoop to arrogance and indiscipline, the unleashed strife adopts many forms. Many satanic powers become part of the upheaval and thousands of calamities arise as the logical result. Some such nations have greed as their factor of motivation and for this reason they indulge in loot and plunder of weaker and poorer nations. The trade of overpowered nation is usurped, its industry is destroyed. On one pretext or the other, the aggressors, by virtue of their military might alone, continue to fill their coffers with the hard earned wealth of the weaker. All this while the object of this vile attention, the rightful owners, the already impoverished, diseased and famine stricken nations continue having their problems further aggravated. Success often goes to the heads of the conquerors, fanning their egocentricity to the extent that some do not desist even from laying claims to god-head. The poorer people's rights are easily violated; the existing justice, law and value systems are trampled down; the standard of cruelty and wickedness is raised. The pious, God-fearing and noble of the land are crushed and the vile and wicked scum of the earth are raised in their place. The influence on the conquered nations is such that in time, the springs of virtue, nobility and charity dry up and in their place, ensue gutters of distrust, vileness, cruelty, immodesty, lawlessness, and other equally heinous attributes of society.

Some such aggressors are propelled by their deep and unholy compulsion for conquest for the sake of conquest and for subjugating humanity or a big part of it, to their over-lordship. Then, such a person or nation starts subjugating all weak and defenseless nations, depriving them of their freedom and laying waste their lives and lands to satisfy the thirst for power. The world soon becomes strife-stricken and humans are effectively forced into slavery of other humans. That in time becomes the root cause of social upheaval. In certain cases, there is the assumed perception that conqueror's beliefs can also be forced on the conquered nations. Religious freedom becomes a fatality and the desire to follow their own religion rather than that of the conqueror becomes worthy of punishment. The situation definitely is calamitous then.

War, Social and Moral Obligation

Under the above stated circumstances, war is not merely allowable, it becomes a moral imperative. At such a time the biggest service to humanity is to redden the earth with the blood of these cruel aggressors. This is to free the weak and the oppressed from the satanic usurpers of land and to protect them from the strife and unbearable oppression being meted down to them. Such usurpers, who are none other than the disciples of Satan, unleash unspeakable moral, spiritual and physical hardship on the children of Adam. They are indeed the foremost enemies of humanity, they deserve no sympathy. The true kindness to them would be to eliminate their mischief and their capability thereof. They themselves forfeit their right to exist, as do those who help their mischievous cause. They are in fact that part of the body, which is deeply infected and the vile affluence gathered in that part is such that there is a likelihood of it fatally infecting the rest of the body. Under these circumstances, it is necessary that the defective and infected part of the body be surgically removed and cast away. It is possible, that there is an intellectual or a scholar who even considers the elimination of such people or groups a sin and is deeply horrified at the prospect of their bloodshed. Such a scholar however, cannot cause a corrective change in the society. Such a person can definitely can exist in the jungles or on mountains, as a hermit, in the pursuit of mental peace or in intellectual concentration but he can never succeed in removing evil and cruelty from the world nor will he be a participant in promoting world peace. Such a person may succeed in forming a group of like-minded people, who along with others will be willing to share the torments unleashed on them, but he cannot hope to establish a group of determined humans who would be capable of uprooting evil and persecution from this world, and reating for God's creations, a place, where peace and harmony flourish and men are unencumbered in pursuit of the higher aims of humanity.

Practical ethics, the aim of which is the establishment of the correct order of things in civilization, is that branch of philosophy in which one may not indulge in pursuit of pleasurable mental and intellectual sensuality. The object of medicine is not to seek satisfaction in the pursuit itself, rather, it is to actually find remedies for physical maladies, whether the remedy is bitter or sweet. Similarly, the goal of ethics is not to seek sensual pleasures but to reform the world, be it through harsh or lenient measures. A true ethical reformer can neither rely solely on the sword nor on the pen alone, to reform the society; most solutions need the involvement of both. Until the time that preaching and prohibitions are sufficient to hold in check an unruly and boisterous congregation of men and to keep them within bounds of ethics and humanity, the use of the sword is not merely impermissible, it is prohibited. However, when the mischief and transgression become so deep-rooted and rampant that no counseling and advice will have an effect, using force against them may be the only option. If they refuse to refrain from violating other's rights, attacking other's character and self-respect or from intruding into other's moral, spiritual, or physical life, then all rational members of the society must stop the transgressors by force. They must continue this struggle, unabated, untill such time that rights of the Lord's creation are restored.

The Wisdom of War

Keeping in consideration, the wisdom and necessity of war, as seen in the foregoing, Allah, The All Wise and All Knowing, states,

> "Had it not been for Allah's repelling some men by means of others, cloisters and churches and oratories and mosques, wherein the name of Allah is oft mentioned would assuredly have been pulled down" (Al-Hajj: 40)

In this blessed verse of Qur'an, not only mosques are mentioned but also churches, cloisters, and oratories are mentioned. The word used in the verse for church is 'Sawame' which envelops both the Christian church and the Jewish synagogue. After using these multi-faceted words, He has chosen using the word 'salat', which covers all forms of prayer to the Lord. The word 'masajid' (mosques) has been used last of all. The verse states that if God had not chosen eradication of the evil at the hands of the just, from time to time, even places of worship that cannot be regarded as a place of danger by any, would not have been safe. The verse points out that the worst form of aggression and conflict is one in which even places of worship are not safe. In a very subtle way, He also warns man of the divine plan, according to which, if a group becomes capable of such wanton behavior, He will make another group a means of bringing it to task. The wisdom and necessity of war have also been illustrated in the verse relating the death of Goliath at the hands of Prophet Dawood (AS).

> "If Allah had not repelled some men by others the earth would have been corrupted. But Allah is a Lord of kindness to (His) creatures"
>
> (Al-Baqrah: 251)

At another place, the Qur'an, speaking of conflict between nations and mutual enmity, states,

> "As often as they light a fire for war, Allah extinguisheth it. Their effort is for corruption in the land, and Allah loveth not the corrupters"
>
> (Al-Maidah: 65)

Jihad in the Way of Allah

This is the conflict with strife and turmoil, greed and avarice, malevolence and enmity, discrimination and prejudice, for containing which, Allah has instructed the good and the faithful to raise their swords,

> "Sanction is given unto those who fight because they have been wronged; and Allah is indeed able to give them victory; those have been driven from their homes unjustly, only because they said our Lord is Allah" (Al-Haj: 39-40)

This is the first of the verses of Qur'an on this subject. In this verse, those against whom war has been made permissible are not those who have very fertile lands or are highly successful in commerce or those who have a different creed, rather, these are those, whose crime of cruelty and of committing atrocities is clearly obvious. They drive innocent people from their homes and are so discriminatory that they subject the oppressed to hardships and pain, just because they (the oppressed) say their lord is Allah. Against such people, war was not ordered only for defensive purposes, but also in aid of and in defense of the weak and defenseless, who are suffering such atrocities.

> "How should ye not fight for the cause of Allah and of the feeble among men and of the women and children who are crying: Our Lord, bring us forth from out this town of which the people are oppressors! Oh, give from thy presence a protecting friend! Oh, give us from thy presence a protector!"
>
> (Al-Nisaa: 75)

A war waged in self-defense or for the protection of the weak, helpless and oppressed, Allah has declared, is not in the cause of his subjects, but in His own cause. It is not for achieving any mortal aim, but to elicit His favor. It has been commanded that such a war should continue till the oppression and aggression ends. In this context the Holy Qur'an states, "Continue fighting till the mischief continues", till War itself surrenders, there is no sign of conflict left, and there is no need left for combat. It has also been stated that if such a fight is abandoned, considering it an unnecessary bloodshed or in consideration of own losses of life and material, it can have devastating results on the society.

Defining the Bounds of Right and Wrong Causes of War

Allah did not stop at instructing man on the wisdom and necessity of war, but went on further to elaborate the instructions as follows,

> "Those who believe do battle for the cause of Allah and those who disbelieve do battle for the cause of idols (In the cause of oppression and arrogance). So fight the minions of the devil. Lo! The devil's strategy is weak" (Al-Nisaa: 76)

This is the deciding factor, which has established the bounds of the rightful and wrong causes. Those who fight in the cause of oppression and cruelty are devil's friends. Their aims are to deprive the rightful of their rights and the owners of their possessions and to create difficulties for the believers indeed fight for a wrong cause. Allah has nothing to do with it and it is not for the people of faith to participate in such fights. However, those who fight such tyrants in the cause of the oppressed, with intent to rid the world of tyranny and turbulence and to establish law and order in its place, their intent is to suppress the tyrants and provide for the Lord's creations an environment of peace, tranquility and opportunity to strive for the higher aims of humanity; these are indeed 'mujahids' they fight in the way of Allah. They do not aid the oppressed, but indeed, Allah Himself does, Allah's promise of success is undoubtedly for such people.

The Prudence and Excellence of Jihad

Pages after pages of Holy Qur'an are filled on the subject of prudence and excellence of 'Jihad in the cause of Allah'. To stress on its excellence and prudence the Qur'an says,

> "O, ye who believe! Shall I show you a commerce that will save you from painful doom? Ye should believe in Allah and his messenger, and strive (do Jihad) for the cause of Allah with your wealth and lives, if you did but know" (Al-Saf: 10-11)

Of those who take part in such 'Jihad', the Qur'an states,

> "Lo! Allah loveth those who battle for his cause in ranks, as if they were a solid structure" (Al-Saf: 4)

The high station and stature accorded to 'Jihad', has been so acknowledged in the Holy Qur'an:

> "Count ye the slaking a pilgrim's thirst and attendance of the inviolable place of worship as equal to the worth of him who believeth in Allah and the Last Day, and striveth (does Jihad) in the way of Allah? They are not equal in the sight of Allah. Allah guideth not wrong doing folk. Those who believe and have left their homes and striven with their wealth and their lives in Allah's way are of much greater worth in Allah's sight. These are they who are triumphant" (Al-Taubah: 19-20)

This is the war in the cause of the right. A night's wakefulness in such cause has been declared better than a thousand nights of prayer and worship at home, hellfire has been forbidden to touch the eye that so keeps awake and the feet have been declared safe from the hellfire, which in the cause get soiled with dust. Along with this, those who choose to ignore the call and although feeling uneasy about it, prefer the comfort of their homes, have been very severely chastised and warned:

> "Say: If your fathers, and your sons, and your brethren, and your wives, and your tribe, and the wealth ye have accumulated, and the merchandise for which ye fear that there will be no sale, and the dwellings ye desire are dearer to you than Allah and his messenger and striving (Jihad) in His way; then wait till Allah bringeth his command to pass. Allah guideth not the wrongdoing folk" (Al-Taubah: 64)

Reasons for the Excellence of Jihad

Consider why Jihad has been awarded such a high status and praise, why have those taking part in Jihad been told time and again that their status is indeed very high? Why have those who avoid it and stay home, been so severely chastened and warned? If you seek the answer to these questions, please go through the verses that proclaim its high status and recognize the triumph of those who participate in it and the foulness of those who run away from it. In these verses, nowhere has success been shown to mean the amassing of wealth and treasure or the establishment of empires and sovereignty. Unlike the pronouncement (according to Hindu belief) of Krishna to Arjun, that if he succeeds in the grand war of' Mahabharat' he would gain the over-lordship of the world (Geeta 37:6), the Holy Qur'an has nowhere enticed the Muslims with gains of treasures or sovereignty. Only the hope for Allah's approval, forgiveness, and blessing has been kindled.

Among the Arabs, the responsibility for the provisioning of water for pilgrims, performing 'Haj' or 'Umrah' was considered a matter of great influence, importance and pride; it was also a source of great income. Islam, however, decreed a higher status for those who leave their abodes in order to fight in Allah's cause. Apart from this, there is no mention of any reward for such people. At another place there is mention of trade in connection with Jihad; this may lead the reader into thinking that there might be a consideration of worldly wealth. On a little study, it will become clear, that trade in this context is the expending of wealth and even life for gaining Allah's favor. Even though victory could have meant gathering of much wealth, increase in commerce, rights to the magnificent palaces of the conquered and much prestige, people have not been enticed into Jihad by promises of such gains. Rather, those people have been scolded who, out of consideration of their family, trade, fortune and luxury of their homes, chose to stay away from Jihad.

The question is, that if the object of this bloodshed is not the acquisition of worldly gains and sovereignty, what does Allah intend for His creatures to gain from it? Why does He makes promises of such high favor to those who participate in it? Why indeed has He granted such favor to even the feet, dust soiled, in its pursuance? What is so triumphant in this dry and unsavory struggle for those who participate in it?

The answer can be found in the part of the Holy Qur'an, which states that Allah does not want that mischief and oppression should spread on His earth; that His creatures are troubled and exterminated without due cause; that the strong swallow up the weak; that people's peace and tranquility are usurped; their moral, spiritual and material lives are destroyed. He does not tolerate that the world becomes a home of misdeeds, cruelty, murder and oppression. He does not want His creatures to be in bondage of others, stripped of all human respect.

Can any be more deserving of Allah's clemency than the group which sets out in the way of Allah, without thought of recompense and without consideration and temptation of any material gain, just for the purpose of clearing the world of mischief, cruelty and oppression and to establish in its place, justice and the rule of law? Who indeed is more deserving of His favor? Then who can say that he has not achieved! Or, that he is not triumphant! Indeed for such triumph, even death on the battlefield would be like the blissful embrace of an ardent lover. This is the very reason for the high status accorded to Jihad, just after 'iman bi Allah' (Faith in Allah).

On careful consideration, one will come to the conclusion that this is the very spirit behind all virtuous deeds. Human desire, that he will not tolerate evil in any condition and for establishing virtue he will sacrifice anything, are the noblest of his attributes and his success in life is dependent on this spirit. If one tolerates evil in respect of others, this moral weakness will ultimately compel him to accept ill against himself and when this toleration becomes a part of his psyche, he descends to the level that Allah terms as a 'scourge'. In this state, man does not accept only physical bondage, but is actually a psychological slave as well. He becomes incapable of distinguishing the right from wrong and good from evil. He falls to such depth of inhumanity from which it is almost impossible for him to get out. On the contrary, the man who has the moral courage to consider evil as evil and continues to struggle to rid the human brotherhood of it, he is an honest man of a very high stature. His existence is a blessing for humanity. Although, such a person desires no recompense in this world, despite its inherent ingratitude, humanity will not fail to acknowledge that, that servant of humanity is its true leader. This illustrates the words, of Holy Qur'an, that proclaim that the God fearing and pious will be the inheritors of this world and the words that declare them are, "these are the triumphant ones".

The Importance of Jihad in the Scheme of Civilization

After understanding the real meaning of Jihad it will be easy to gauge its importance in the lives of nations and its necessity in keeping the development of civilization on an even keel. Today if there was a force of goodness that contained evil and struggled against oppression and transgression, that brought the oppressors to their knees before goodness, then the development of civilization would not have been so uneven and lopsided. In reality, today humanity is divided between oppressors and the oppressed, between masters and slaves. The moral, ethical, and spiritual destruction of the entire human civilization is at hand, somewhere due to enslavement and oppression and somewhere due to oppression and toleration.

The willingness to resist wrong and bow its head down in acknowledgment of the right and the just is the hallmark of respect and dignity for any nation. Let alone the defense of others, against the forces of evil; if a nation is awake to the necessity of its own defense and is willing to sacrifice all, be it wealth, fame, luxury or life itself in the cause, it would have earned respect in the community of nations. It is necessary that, even if actively championing the cause of others is not possible, it should be firm, at least, in the defense of its own right and justice for itself. If it fails to enforce even this minimum standard of justice and if the spirit of sacrifice is at such low ebb; then when forces of evil attack it, instead of combating them or dying in the effort, it accepts a subservient existence. A life of disgrace would be its lot; its life would definitely be worse than death. To make us understand the gravity of the situation, Allah in His book of wisdom has time and again mentioned of the nations, who in consideration of the price they may have had to pay, avoided Jihad and ultimately accepted the dominance of the forces of evil. Such nations forever had become losers and non-achievers. Allah terms them as cruel, they had brought oppression upon themselves by their misdeeds. Indeed they were destroyed by their own cruelty. At one place in the Qur'an it is stated,

> "Hath not the fame of those before them reached
> them-- the folk of Noah, Aad, Thamud, the folk of

> Abraham the dwellers of Madain and the disasters (which befell them)?Messengers (from Allah) came to them with proofs (of Allah's sovereignty). So Allah surely wronged them not, but they did wrong themselves. And the believers, men and women, are protecting friends, one to another; they enjoin the right and forbid the wrong" (Al-Taubah: 70-71)

In these verses Allah relates to us of nations who were victims of cruelty to themselves. He goes on to state that the qualities of believers are, that they help each other and enjoin doing right and forbid wrong. The object here is to tell us, that the nations long extinct had stopped imposing the right and noble way and opposing evil. This indeed was cruelty they did to themselves, which ultimately destroyed them. At another place, speaking of the cowardice of the Children of Israel and their disinclination to fight in His cause and its dire consequences, Allah tells us of the time when Musa (AS) having chastised them by saying that Allah had made them the keeper of the Holy Land and instructs them to enter it and not to retreat, because those who show their backs achieve nothing. But, the Children of Israel who were mortally in fear of the enemy replied,

> "O! Musa! Lo! A giant people (dwell) therein and lo! We go not in till they go forth from thence. When they go forth, then we will enter (not till then)" (Al-Maidah: 22)

Then two stalwarts of the Children of Israel, who feared Allah and with whom Allah had been gracious, spoke out and tried to encourage them into entering the land, and promised them that victory would be theirs, if they but put their faith in Allah. But they ostentatiously replied:

> "O Musa we shall never enter (the land) till they are in it. So go thou and thy lord and fight! We will sit here" (Al-Maidah: 24)

The Lord punished them for this cowardice, and they had wandered on the earth for forty years, not finding a home anywhere.

"(Their Lord) said: For this, the land will surely be forbidden them for forty years that they will wander in the earth, bewildered" (Al-Maidah: 26)

At another place, Qur'an relates in detail the self love and cowardice of the Children of Israel, and their fear of death, because of which they were not ready to fight and had to face the possibility of extermination,

"Bethink thee (O Mohammad) of those of old, who went forth from their habitations in thousands, fearing death, and Allah said unto them: Die, and then He brought them back to life. Lo! Allah is a Lord of Kindness to mankind, but most of mankind give not thanks" (Al-Baqarah: 243)

Later, the Muslims were given the instructions to fight, in very unambiguous words,

"Fight in the way of Allah and know that Allah is Hearer, Knower" (Al-Baqarah: 244)

Later still, speaking of another group of the Children of Israel, He says:

"Bethink thee of the leaders of the Children of Israel after Musa, how they said unto a Prophet whom they had: Set up for us a king and we will fight in the way of Allah. He said, would you then refrain from fighting if fighting is prescribed for you? Yet, when we prescribed fighting for them, they turned away, all save a few of them: Allah is aware of evildoers" (Al-Baqarah: 246)

There are many other examples like that of the Children of Israel in Holy Qur'an, which explain the truth, that for the establishment of good, the most necessary, is the readiness to defend it, whatever the sacrifice maybe. The nation that loses this spirit will soon succumb to the forces of evil.

Chapter Two

Defensive Warfare

It must have become quite obvious from the foregoing discussion that the Qur'anic teachings seek to instill in its followers, such an indomitable spirit that neither there would ever be an inclination in them to bend before oppression nor would they accept such dominance. According to the teachings of Holy Qur'an, the worst form of human depravation is that he would accept bondage of the oppressor rather than fight, owing to his disinclination to put at stake his luxuries, worldly possessions and his kin. This disinclination and fear do not have their basis on physical weakness but rather they are products of the weakness of heart and faith. If this weakness develops into a national characteristic, that nation loses its dignity and self-respect, it would not only be disinclined and unable to raise a finger in favor of a cause that is generally just and right but would become unable to uphold its own moral values as well.

Human bondage is not merely a physical phenomenon in isolation. It is preceded by the acceptance of spiritual and mental subservience as well, while the physical attribute is just the donning of the spite and indignity of physical slavery. This final manifestation of human indignity is only observable in a nation that has lost all semblances of self-respect and dignity. The nation, which on account of its cowardice and weakness cannot find itself equal to the task of defending its rights, will see evil and mischief more powerful and is ready to accept its subservience. Such a nation will also never find itself equal to the task of defending its values, culture, laws or religion and morality, nor will it be able to keep its system. If right and wrong cannot coexist, it is not possible that the suppressed will be able to maintain their own value-system, while in the mental and physical bondage of others, who have a different value-system.

The nature of truth and justice is unique. This is not possible for it to accept the comradeship of falsehood and oppression. Therefore, the people who wish to follow the path of truth and justice; it would become incumbent on them to give up following dictates of evil and oppression and would have to cast off the chains of all other subservience.

The Holy Qur'an, which is actually a compilation of nature's dictates, clearly teaches the acceptance of the above principle. In the same context, it has prescribed only two paths for achieving its fulfillment: accomplishment or death in the process. There is no compromise solution, though some of its followers, owing to their weakness of faith or lack of determination, have accepted compromise as a way of life. This way of life has been termed as human indignity and the weakness of heart, the incapability to combat evil. The Holy Qur'an tells us that this is the sinister quality of those, who due to their cowardice, abandoned the way of the Lord and invited upon themselves His wrath. It further states that the acceptance of this undignified way of life is cruelty to oneself. The Holy Qur'an, chastising those who lead such a life of indignity and non-fulfillment states:

> "Lo! As for those whom the angels take (in death) while they wrong themselves, (the angels) will ask: in what were ye engaged? They will say: we were oppressed in the land (the angels) will say: was not Allah's earth spacious that ye could have migrated therein? As for such, their habitation will be hell, an evil journey's end" (Al-Nisa: 97)

This verse was addressed to those people, who at the time of 'hijrah' (migration of the Muslims from Makah to Madinah) chose to stay behind in Makah. They were unwilling to give up their worldly possessions, their commerce and the comfort of their homes, accepted a life under the unholy influence of the idolaters. Here they were unable to live in accordance with the Islamic tenets. Because of the oppression, they also had to follow many of their (idolaters') customs. To the extent that some of them even had to become a part of the army of non-believers, which fought against their Muslim brethren at Badr, the first battle the Muslims fought against non-believers.

Consider carefully this lesson of national pride and honor. Here those who deem themselves weak and accept subservience of the unrighteous, have been said to have committed brutality to themselves. Their excuses of weakness and disability being unacceptable are being questioned as to why, if they were weak and unable to resist, did they not migrate to another place. In the end, they are cast in that pit of human degradation, hell and there is no worse place than that.

Religious Compulsion of Defensive War

Islam stresses forbearance, in all our dealings except in the defense of religion or when there is a threat of another religion or system being imposed on Muslims. The Qur'an expressly instructs the Muslims that, if anyone tries to usurp their rights or property, oppresses them, hinders the following of their faith and the dictates of their conscience, disrupts their communal system and is bent on their persecution, just because of their being Muslim irks him; then showing humility and meekness towards him is forbidden. One must oppose him with one's full capability and strength.

> "Fight in the way of Allah those who fight against you, but begin no hostilities. Lo! Allah loveth not aggressors. And slay them wherever ye find them, and drive them out of the places whence they drove you out, for persecution is worse than slaughter. And fight not with them, at the inviolable Place of Worship until they first attack you there, but if they attack you (there), and then slay them. Such is the reward of the disbelievers. But if they desist, then lo! Allah is forgiving, merciful. And fight them until persecution is no more, and religion is for Allah. But if they desist, let there be no hostility except against wrongdoers. The forbidden month for the forbidden month and forbidden thing in retaliation[1]. And one who attacks you; attack him in like manner as he attacked you. Observe your duty to Allah, and know that Allah is with those who ward off (evil) (Al-Baqarah: 190-194)

---

[1] This means that the sacredness of the Holy month and of the Holy place must be duly observed, as long as the enemy also observes their sanctity.

These orders for the protection of Islam and for the defense of a Muslim homeland are so strict that whenever an attack either is expected or takes place, one is expected to set aside whatever one is doing and proceed for the defense of Islam and the Islamic system. Then, one is to continue the struggle, unabated, until the defense has been successfully accomplished. Hence, all books of 'fiqh' (Islamic jurisprudence) are unanimous in stating that in the event that the enemy attacks the Muslim State; its defense becomes the duty of every individual Muslim. In severity, this duty is equal to that of the offering of the daily compulsory prayers or of fasting. The well-known book of 'fiqh' 'Bidae wa Sanaya ', speaks on the subject and states:

> "When the general announcement is made that the enemy has attacked a Muslin land, Jihad becomes a 'fard' (compulsion). Everyone in his individual capacity and whoever has the required means and ability, has to answer the call for Jihad. When the call for Jihad is given, then compliance of obligation becomes effective and all in their individual capacities get ready for war. At such a time, compliance becomes as obligatory as answering the call for prayers or fasting. The slave does not have to seek permission of the master for such compliance or the wife from her husband. They are exempt from complying with the orders of the husband or the master, as in the case of mandatory prayers or fasting. Similarly, parental permission is not necessary for a son going for Jihad".

The words of 'Bidae wa Sanaya' negate the possibility that Jihad is mandatory only when the cause is ideological i.e. when the enemy on account of its religious fervor seeks to destroy or harm Islam. On the contrary, it clarifies that when an Islamic state is attacked, for whatever reason, its defense becomes mandatory.

For existence of Muslims as a nation, the qualities of courage, aggressiveness, determination, and perseverance are necessary pre-requisites. When a Muslim nation loses its independence, not only does it lose its ability to serve humanity-its major objective, but also the ability to uphold Islamic value-system and order. It will therefore be just as mandatory to defend its geographical and political frontiers as the ideological ones. If a Muslim state is attacked, it will be as if the attack is on Islam itself. Under the condition, the mandatory nature of jihad is not only in reference to one's own country but extends to other beleaguered Muslim nations as well, who do not have the capacity to defend themselves. This is very clearly stated in the preceding quotations. Similar instructions are available in other books of 'fiqh' as well. The authors of 'Al-Nihaya' and 'Al-Zakhira' two other well-known books of 'fiqh' are unanimous in the statement. The author or of Al-Nihaya paraphrased the details from Al-Zakhira in the following words:

> "The fact is that after the general announcement, jihad becomes mandatory on all who may be close to or engaged in confronting the enemy; it is also conditionally mandatory (fard kifayah) on those, not in the immediate neighborhood of the conflict. This means that when their participation is not really necessary, they may stay away. But, when their need arises, whether it is on account of the inability of the area residents or their reluctance, this participation then becomes as mandatory as the performance of compulsory prayers or fasting, foregoing which is not excusable under any circumstance.
>
> The degree of compulsion of jihad, is directly proportional to the vicinity of the area of conflict, i.e. it is extremely mandatory on the area residents; the degree of compulsion decreases as the distance from the area of conflict increases in all directions. The situation can be illustrated by the instructions regarding the death of a person. If a person dies and the near ones or the neighbors are restrained, for whatever reason, from undertaking his burial, it becomes one's duty wherever one may be, to make the necessary arrangement. "The same situation prevails, where jihad is concerned."
>
> (Shami: v3, p240)

The importance of jihad in Islam can be judged from its

mandatory nature and from the fact that undertaking it is a compulsory religious rite, of the status of offering the compulsory prayers or fasting. The stress on it can be fathomed from the verses of 'Al-Taubah', which were revealed at the time of the battle of Tabuk. These verses indicate that when a force attacks Muslim areas, in order to harm Islam or Muslims, jihad becomes a test of the effected Muslim's faith. Therefore, speaking of those who had on one pretext or another, sought excuses for not taking part in the jihad against the mighty Romans and taking into account the weakness of their faith, had been permitted to stay back, the Qur'an states:

"Allah forgives thee (O Muhammad)! Wherefore didst thou grant them leave ere those who told the truth were manifest to thee and thou didst know the liars? Those who believe in Allah and the Last Day ask no leave of thee lest they should strive with their wealth and their lives. Allah is aware of those who keep their duty (unto him). They alone ask leave of thee who believe not in Allah and the Last Day, and whose hearts feel doubt, so in their doubt they waver" (Al-Taubah: 43-45)

The Many Faces of Defensive Warfare

From the imperative nature of the commandments for defense, it becomes apparent that the most important of the duties assigned to man, is the duty of defense of his religious and national existence against the forces of mischief and evil. War, however, has more faces than merely its proclamation and thereby vanquishing or enslaving the vanquished and obstructing their freedom. In order that personal opinion is kept out of the discussion, we shall gather all the Qur'anic verses relevant to the subject and from them try to understand the different forms that such wars can take.

1) Response to Brutality and Aggression

According to Qur'anic scholars of renown, the following was the first verse revealed on the subject of warfare:

"Sanction is given unto those who fight because

they have been wronged; and Allah is indeed able to give them victory. Those who have been driven from their homes unjustly only because they said: Our Lord is Allah--For had it not been for Allah repelling some men by means of others, cloisters, churches, oratories and mosques, wherein the name of Allah is oft mentioned, would assuredly have been pulled down. Verily Allah helpeth one who helpeth Him. Lo! Allah is strong almighty--"

(Al-Haj: 39-40)

Another verse, that Allama Ibn Jariar and others claim was the first, states,

"Fight in the way of Allah against those who fight against you, but begin no hostilities. Lo! Allah loveth not aggressors. And slay them wherever ye find them and drive them out of the places whence they drove you out, for persecution is worse than slaughter" (Al-Baqarah: 190-191)

In these two verses, following commandments have been given:

a) When war is waged on Muslims and they are oppressed and brutalized, war in self-defense is permissible.

b) Against those who plunder and loot the homes and property of Muslims, war should be waged.

c) When Muslims are being persecuted because of their religion and beliefs, they are permitted to wage war against those responsible.

d) If the enemy, having overpowered the Muslims, forces them off their lands, depriving them of its sovereignty, they (Muslims), whenever they gather sufficient strength, must try to regain what they had lost.

2) Defense of the Truth

One of the reasons given, under which war against the non-believers is ordained is:

"Lo! Those who disbelieve, spend their wealth in

order that they may debar (men) from the way of
Allah. They will spend it, then it will become
anguish for them, then they will be conquered"
(Al-Anfal: 36)

Later, speaking of the Battle of Badr, in which, Allah intended
that, with his help, truth should prevail and mischief and
oppression should be subdued, says,

"Be not as those who came forth from their
dwellings boastfully and to be seen of men, and
debar (men) from the way of Allah, while Allah is
surrounding all they do" (Al-Anfal: 47)

Chapter Al-Taubah again contains the commandment to do
battle against those who disbelieve:

"They have purchased with the revelations of Allah
a little gain, so they debar (men) from His way. Lo!
Evil is that which they want to do" (Al-Taubah: 9)

Later still, war has been ordained against the 'People of the
Book'. Their crime and sin is stated as,

"O ye who believe. Lo! Many of the (Jewish) rabbis
and the (Christian) monks devour the wealth of
mankind wantonly and debar (men) from the way of
Allah" (Al-Taubah: 34)

Speaking more specifically on the subject, the Qur'an says:

"Now when ye meet in battle those who disbelieve,
then it is smiting of the necks until, when you have
routed them, then making fast of bonds; and
afterwards grace or ransom till the war lay down its
burdens That (is the ordinance). And if Allah willed
he could have punished them (without you) but
(thus it is ordained) that he may try some of you by
means of others, and those who are slain in the way
of Allah, He rendreth not their actions in vain"
(Muhammad: 4)

From the quoted verses, it becomes clear that war has been
ordained even against those who obstruct the Muslims from
following the 'path of Allah'. The phrase 'path of Allah' has the

same meaning as 'straight path' mentioned several times in the Qur'an. Here it means the act of pursuance of religious duties. Therefore, there is no doubt that placing hindrances in the path of those who follow Islam is in fact obstructing Islam itself.

If we consider carefully, a person's path can be impeded in three conditions:

> -When a man is following one path, his efforts to adopt another are thwarted.

> -When one is already on a particular path and is forced to abandon his chosen path.

> -There are many impediments, both physical and through threats, put in his way, making following his chosen path impossible.

The words 'debar' (men) from the path of Allah encompasses all three meanings. Here they either mean that a person is obstructed from accepting Islam or that the person has already accepted Islam and efforts are made to make him give it up and revert to his old ways, or it is made difficult for Muslims to lead their lives according to their beliefs. If the 'path of Allah' is obstructed the moral and ethical duty of a Muslim, is to remove all such obstructions, physically if necessary and by use of force if necessary.

3) Punishment for Treachery and for Violation of Agreements

Surah Al-Anfal gives another circumstance when it becomes necessary to wage war:

> "Lo! The worst of beasts in Allah's sight are the ungrateful who will not believe; those of them with whom thou madest a treaty, and then at every opportunity they break their treaty, and they keep not duty (to Allah). If thou comest on them in the war, deal with them so as to strike fear in those who are behind them, that haply they may remember. And if thou fearest treachery, from any folk, then throw back to them (their treaty) fairly. Lo! Allah loveth not the treacherous" (Al-Anfal: 55- 58)

A similar verse in Surah Al-Taubah with a little more severity:

> "Freedom from obligation (is proclaimed) from Allah and his messenger towards those of the idolaters with whom you made a treaty: Travel freely in the land four months, and know that ye cannot escape Allah and that Allah will confound the disbelievers" (Al-Taubah: 1-2)

This refers to the four months, for which the non-believers were granted respite and during which the Muslims were forbidden to make any attack on them.

Of those who follow the terms of the treaty faithfully, it has been instructed that none should violate it while its term runs. However, of those who frequently violate the terms of the treaty the Qur'an says:

> "Then when the sacred months have passed, slay the idolaters, wherever ye find them, and take them (captive), and besiege them, and prepare for them each ambush. But if they repent and establish worship ('salat') and pay the poor- due (zakat), then leave their way free. Lo! Allah loveth those who keep their duty" (Al-Taubah: 5)

Later in the same surah, it is stated of the faithless and perfidious idolaters:

> "How can there be a treaty with Allah and His messengers for the idolaters save with those with whom ye made a treaty at the inviolable place of worship? So long as they are true to you, be true to them. Lo Allah loveth those who keep their ditty. How (can there be a treaty for others) when if they have the upper hand of you, they regard neither pact nor honor in respect of you? They satisfy you with their mouths the while their hearts refuse. And most of them are wrong doers" (Al-Taubah 7-8)

More is said of these deceitful people in the same verse, later:

> "And they observe towards a believer neither pact nor honor. These are they who are transgressors. But if they repent and establish worship (salat) and

pay the poor- due (zakat), then they are your brethren in religion. We detail our revelations for a people who have knowledge. And if they break their pledges after their treaty (hath been made with you) and assail your religion, then fight the heads of disbelief--Lo! They have no binding oaths--in order that they may desist. Will ye not fight a folk who broke their solemn pledges, and purposed to drive out the messenger and did attack you first? What fear ye them? Now Allah hath more right that ye should fear him, if ye are believers. Fight them! Allah will chastise them at your hands, and he will lay them low and give you victory over them, and He will heal the breasts of folk who are believers"

(Al-Taubah: 10-14)

On careful study of the verses quoted above and the circumstances under which they were revealed, the following instructions become apparent:

a) War should be waged on those who enter into treaties with Muslims and then violate them. This also covers those of the infidels, who pledge allegiance and then did mutiny against the Islamic State.

b) There are some with whom treaties exist but, the hostility of their attitude and actions are such that there is always a danger that Muslims or Islam itself will come to harm on their account. Such should be given notice that their attitudes and actions amount to 'contravention of treaty' and then they should be adequately punished for their temerity.

c) There are others, with whom treaties exist, but they often violate these and are always scheming against the Muslims, and in their desire to harm them, stoop below all levels of morality and ethics. Against such, continual war is specified. Pacts and treaties with them are permissible only on the condition of their conversion to Islam and in the presence of adequate proof of this conversion. Otherwise, to keep Islam and Muslims safe from their misdoing, killing, besieging, and arresting them and other such like actions are necessary.

4) Suppression of the Covert Internal Enemy

Apart from the manifest external enemy, no Islamic nation is devoid of some not so obvious internal enemies. These, despite their apparent friendliness have, cutting of the roots of Islam as their major objective. These are referred to, in Qur'an, as hypocrites. About such, it states,

> "O Prophets strive against the disbelievers and the hypocrites! Be harsh with them. Their ultimate abode is hell, a hapless journey's end"
>
> (Al-Taubah: 73)

At another place, it states:

> "The hypocrites and those in whose hearts there is a disease, and the alarmists in the cities do not cease, we verily shall urge thee on against them, then they will be your neighbors in it but a little while. Accursed they will be seized wherever found and slain with a (fierce) slaughter" (Al-Ahzab: 60-61)

Surah Al-Nisa states in these regards:

> "They long that ye should disbelieve even as they disbelieve, that ye may be upon a level (with them). So choose not friends from them till they forsake their homes in the way of Allah; if they turn back (to enmity) then take them and kill them wherever ye find them, and choose no friend or helper from among them" (Al-Nisa: 89)

Later it states:

> "Ye will find others who desire that they should have security from you, and security from their own folk. So often as they are returned to hostility they are plunged therein. If they keep not aloof from you nor offer you peace nor hold their hands, then take them and kill them wherever ye find them. Against

such We have given you clear warrant"

(Al-Nisa: 91)

These verses indicate that sin of the congregation of infidels, by virtue of which, they have been declared deserving of the penalty of death. However, to clarify the concept further, some more verses of the Qur'an are quoted which will clearly indicate the type of folks, these non-believers are. Surah Al-Nisa states:

"And they say: (it is) obedience; but when they have gone forth from thee a party of them spent the night in planning other than what thou sayest. Allah recordeth what they plan by night. So oppose them and put thy trust in Allah. Allah is sufficient as trustee". (Surah Al-Nita: 81)

Surah Al-Taubah states:

"Had they gone forth among you they had added to you naught save trouble and had hurried to and fro among you, seeking to cause sedition among you; and among you there are some who would have listened to them. Allah is aware of evildoers. Aforetime they sought to cause sedition and raised difficulties for thee till the truth came and the decree of Allah was made Manifest, though they were loth" (Al-Taubah 47-48)

Al-Taubah further states:

"And they swear by Allah that they are in truth of you, when they are not of you, but they are folks who are afraid. Had they but found a refuge or caverns, or a place to enter, they surely had resorted thither swift as runaways" (Al-Taubah 56-57)

The same 'surah' further states:

"The hypocrites, both men and women, precede one from another. They enjoin the wrong, and they forbid the right, and they withhold their hands (from spending for the cause of Allah). They forget Allah so He hath forgotten them. Lo! The hypocrites, they are transgressors" (Al-Taubah: 67)

Speaking of the same group, Surah Al-Ahzab states:

> "And when the hypocrites, and those in whose hearts is a disease, were saying: Allah and His messenger promised us naught but delusion, and a party of them said: O folk of Yathrib! There is no stand (possible) for you; therefore turn back and certain of them (even) sought permission of the Prophet, saying: Our homes lie open (to the enemy). And they lay not open. They but wished to flee. If the enemy had entered from all sides and they had been exhorted to treachery, they would have committed it, and would have hesitated thereupon but little" (Al-Ahzab: 12-14)

Surah Al-Munafiqun states:

> "When the hypocrites come unto thee (O Mohammad), they say: We bear witness that thou art indeed Allah's messenger, and Allah beareth witness that the hypocrites are speaking falsely. They make their faith a pretext so that they may turn (men) from the way of Allah. Verily evil is that which they are wont to do" (Al-Munafiqun: 1-2)

These verses point to the group among the hypocrites that cannot be treated as Muslims, even for the sake of appearances. Typical of such a group is that it outwardly professes Islam, at the same time also openly speaks heresy, or it may openly profess Islam, but is always a thorn in the sides of Muslims; it seeks continually to cause them harm; keeps in good contact with the enemy and passes on official secrets of the Muslim state to them. It seeks to weaken the faith of the Muslims and tries to create differences between them. Material and moral support are readily provided to the enemy by it, and when Muslim defenses are in need of its support, it is seen supporting the enemy instead.

Such a group of hypocrites is certainly more harmful for Islam than the external, obvious enemy. Therefore, those affiliated with such groups, when discovered, should be shown no leniency. These social ulcers are candidates for the severest corrective surgical expulsion from the body of Islam.

5) Defense of Peace

One form of the enemy seeks to create strife and disorder amongst the residents of a Muslim country. Robbery, murder, and arson are some of its tools, by which it seeks to destroy the internal peace and security of a Muslim state or to overthrow a legitimate Islamic government through such terrorism. The Qur'an speaking of such, states:

> "The only reward of those who make war upon Allah and his messenger and strive after corruption in the land will be that they will be killed or crucified, or have their hands and feet on alternate sides cut off, or will be expelled out of the land. Such will be their degradation in the world, and in the hereafter theirs will be an awful doom; save those who repent before ye overpower them. For know that Allah is forgiving, merciful"
>
> (Al-Maidah: 33-34)

The wordings of the verses quoted above may mislead some of the unlettered to believe that the subject of these verses is that group, which is openly at war with an Islamic nation. Whereas, the words, "Who make war upon Allah and his messenger" stand for those who create strife and disorder in an Islamic state. Similarly, in the Indian penal code (referring to British India), the words used, are 'waging war against the king' in connection with those who create internal strife and disorder and indulge in acts of terrorism for the purpose of creating internal strife and disorder. In the Islamic jurisprudence however, the phrase embodies two meanings. It can stand for causing the state to be destabilized through murder, arson, robbery, and terrorism in general; on the other hand, it can stand for disrupting and destabilizing the Islamic state for ultimately overthrowing the legal Islamic government, in power at the time. The circumstances, under which the verses were revealed, also indicate that the words are used in relation to those involved in armed uprising against peace and constitution.

Anas bin Malik (RA), states that some people from the tribe of Oraina, came to the Prophet (SAW) and after conversion to Islam, made their abode in Madinah. However, the climate did not suit them. They soon became extremely sick. The Prophet (SAW) advised them that if they lived among the camels, drank their milk, and used their (camels) urine as medicine, they could be healed. Hence, they started living in a camel pasture in the outskirts of Madinah. After sometime when their health improved, these people of Oraina murdered the camel attendants and stole the camels. On instructions of the Prophet (SAW), they were captured and as punishment for their crime, their hands and feet were chopped off; they were blinded and left in the open to die. Sahih Muslim, a book of authentic hadith (sayings or teachings of the Prophet) states on the authority of Anas bin Malik's narration, that these people of Oraina were blinded because they had blinded the camel attendants who had attended them. Abdullah bin Umar (RA), a companion of the Prophet (SAW) is said to have stated that the fore-quoted verse of the Qur'an was revealed in connection with these very Orainians. Other prominent scholars disagree with this and state that this verse was revealed in connection with those who spread strife and terrorism in an Islamic state. They claim that intensity of punishment prescribed has a direct bearing on the degree of severity of the crime. An account of this incident can be found in authentic books of 'hadith', including Sahih Muslim and Sahih Bukhari.

6) Aid of the Weak and the Oppressed

Another state of defensive warfare, in which the use of the sword have been permitted for Muslims, is in aid of a group of Muslims who, due to its weakness, finds itself in the clutches of non-Muslims and does not have the strength to get out of it. In these circumstances, Muslims who possess the might and means, have an obligation to help their Muslim brethren in order to get rid of the oppressive enemy. The Holy Qur'an states in this regard:

> "How should you not fight therefore in the chosen
> cause of Allah and of the feeble among men and of
> the women and the children who are crying: Our
> Lord! Bring us forth from out this town of which
> the people are oppressors! Oh, give us from thy
> presence some protecting friend! Oh, give us from
> thy presence some defender" (Al-Nisa: 75)

At another place, the need for such support is emphasised:

"And those who believed but did not leave their homes, ye have no duty to protect them till they leave their homes; but if they seek help from you in the matter of religion then it is your duty (to help) except against a folk between whom and you there is a treaty. Allah is seer of what ye do. And those who disbelieve are protectors, one to another--if ye do not so, there will be confusion in the land, and great corruption" (Al-Anfal: 72-73)

In this verse, the nature of relationship that can exist between Muslims of an independent state and those living under the sovereignty of a non-Muslim State, out of choice or compulsion, has been explained in detail. Firstly, after mentioning "Those who believed but did not leave their homes," it is explained that there cannot be any mutual political or civil interaction between the two. Meaning thereby that neither there can be intermarriages between them, nor are they entitled to a share of each other's inheritance and so forth. The Muslims of non-Muslim states are not entitled to any monetary aid from other Muslims nor are they allowed holding a position of any importance in the governance of a Muslim state, unless they prefer to migrate to such state. However, even after all other relations have been severed; the relations of faith, assistance, and preservation have been left intact. The words, "but if they seek help of you in the matter of religion", clearly indicate that the connection of faith, assistance and preservation is still intact, till such time that the person remains a Muslim, whatsoever corner of the globe he may be living in.

A group or a person, whose religious beliefs and practice are endangered or become a target of oppression, has a right to ask other Muslims for help and they are duty bound to provide it, if they possibly can and if no treaty exists between them and the power against which help is being sought. Sanctity of a Muslims is of utmost importance, however, no help can be provided even to a brother Muslim, until the treaty is enforced. Apart from the provisions of this clause, the need for support and assistance to and for sponsoring other Muslims has been stressed in the verse. Muslims have been warned that, in view of the unity between the non-Muslims when dealing with them, despite their mutual internal differences, there is a likelihood of great discomfort, strife and a possibility of annihilation, if they (Muslims) are not ready to provide the necessary assistance, when required.

The Purpose and Aims of Defense

If we consider the various forms of defensive warfare, discussed above, we will find one factor common in all of them, i.e. Muslims under no condition should allow their religion and their national existence to be dominated by the forces of evil and mischief. Whenever such evil makes its entrance whether from the outside or from within, they should be ready to spot it and crush it. For the accomplishment of the task that Allah intends for them to undertake, they should remain politically, a force to reckon with. For the purpose, they should make themselves safe from such evil and mischief.

Muslims should be able to protect themselves and should be alert to the mischief of evil, both internal and external, if they are not, they invite on themselves the wrath of God, and calamity as the past, extinct generations did. It is necessary that Muslims remain viable, in order that they accomplish the mission that God in His wisdom intends them to carry out. Thus, if they endanger themselves, they commit a cruelty not only to themselves but also to the entire humanity.

Enemies of Muslims have clearly been those, who have been in the past, responsible for their downfall. They have been instructed to crush these trouble-mongering evil powers, lest they extinguish the light of divine guidance from this world and become an obstruction in the path of universal reforms. The instruction for the use of force against them is of course conditional to their raising their heads, but it entails the necessity of keeping the ability for the purpose, in absolute readiness. This, to the extent that the enemy is aware of the indomitable nature of the forces of Islam and the respect of its capability is such that it would lack the will to raise its head.

> "Make ready for them all thou canst of (armed) force and of horses tethered, that thereby ye may dismay the enemy of Allah and your enemy, and others beside them whom ye know not. Allah knoweth them. Whatsoever you spend in the way of

Allah it will be repaid to you in full, and ye will not
be wronged" (Al-Anfal: 60)

The need for a well-equipped standing army for a Muslim state
is paramount. Reliance cannot and should not be placed on hastily
raised units of militia that owe their existence to a particular
military situation. In the above verse, the word 'force' has been
used to cover all forms of weaponry, from old time canons to the
present-day missiles. For keeping the military force well equipped
would of course mean 'with the latest and most sophisticated and
effective weaponry', if a nation can afford to do that, it should, but
failing that, it is not exempt from maintaining an army at all. The
clause, "all thou canst," clarifies that the state will just have to arm
them as best as it can.

The verse then puts forward the concept of 'strategic
preparedness'. The idea stated is that, when a well-equipped force
is kept all the time in a state of readiness, it enkindles an element
of fear in the enemy and in the situation, where the enemy has the
intention to attack, would hesitate in doing so. In time, this fear is
substituted by respect. Due to this respect, the Muslim State gains
friends. Where these very friends, finding the Muslim army weak
and unprepared would not have hesitated in taking advantage of it,
now do not even consider it an option and continue being friends.
Later, the verse states that the wealth spent in keeping the state
defense well equipped and alert pays its dividends, as by keeping
the oppressive forces at bay, the ensuing peace and security
provides opportunities that would compensate for the wealth thus
spent. The words, "it will be repaid to you in full, and ye will not
be wronged," explain that, there is compensation for the wealth
thus spent both in this world and in hereafter. This is also an
absolute fact that what is good for the Muslim in this world is also
to his advantage in the next.

Chapter Three

War of Reforms

Let us consider now, what the necessity was, for the preservation of the Muslims as a nation through allowing them defensive warfare. Did Allah intend the Muslims to accomplish some special mission for Him, that preserving them from strife and evil was necessary? In the previous pages, it has been oft repeated that Muslims, after losing their national strength, will not be able to accomplish the special task that Allah has ordained for them. Herein, in fact is the answer to the above question. Let us now examine what that special task is.

The Qur'an, which addresses each facet of life, explains the 'special task' as follows,

> "Ye are the best community that hath been raised up for mankind. Ye enjoin right conduct and forbid indecency; and ye believe in Allah" (Al-Imran: 110)

This verse addressing the Muslims, states that they have been created to serve humankind in general, not any particular segment of it. The supreme service that they are to render to humanity is that they instruct and insist people to do good, and that they forbid evil. One nation would have as its object in life, the service of the entire humanity; a normal person brought up in circumstances, where nationality and statehood are the very zeniths of conceptual thought, cannot be expected to understand its real meaning. Though, many will be familiar with terms such as 'allegiance', 'fealty' and 'fidelity', these would be in relation to a particular geographic and social division. However, to part from these concepts and consider that an entire nation will have as its aim, service to the entire humanity, is perhaps an idea too farfetched, for them to grasp its meaning. Therefore, in the interest of better understanding, let us first examine the term, 'Service to humanity'

The Ethical Concept of Universal Obligation

If we analyze desires of man, we will find that there is none among these that differ from the basest of animals. Just as man desires delicious food, a horse desires plenty of green, juicy grass; like man feels great satisfaction in the display of his manly prowess and exploits, so a ram feels satisfaction, if it can ram others of its species, out of a fight; just as man makes the best possible arrangements for his defense, so the smallest insect does. The only difference is that while for an animal, fulfillment of its desires is the aim of its life. For man, this fulfillment is but a necessary step in achieving some higher objective; if it so happens, someone's aims are no higher than achieving satisfaction of his desires, and he uses his God given intelligence, only for that purpose, then such a person can of course become no more than an animal of a high degree. He would be far from being a human worth any consideration.

In the interest of his self-preservation and well-being, man has many compulsions. He is compelled to earn money, for if he did not, he would die of hunger; to protect himself from the elements, he has to build a home; similarly, he has to wear clothes and undertake other such actions for his protection. It is also a compulsion for him that he defends himself against enemies, for if he neglects this defense, he may get into trouble. However, obviously this defense is not the aim in itself, rather it is a means to achieving something higher, the achievement of which is the purpose of man's life.

A good human being is one, who fulfils his own natural desires, for the purpose that he may remain better able to fulfil his duties to society and to Allah. The true achievement of man is just the recognition of his duties and obligations and their fulfillment to the best of his ability. Man has been made duty-bound to fulfil duties to himself, for if he is not able to do so, he will also be unable to do his duty towards others, while the latter also being his obligation.

If it is true of an individual, that his true achievement is his ability to recognize his obligations and to fulfill them to the best of his ability, then the same must be true of any congregation of individuals. By becoming a congregation or a group, the humanness of the individuals that make up the group does not increase or decrease. Therefore, the collective level of virtue of the group should be the same as that of the individuals who make up the group. If an individual's aim in life is only the satisfaction of his baser instincts, he can be considered no more than an unintelligent animal. It follows that a group, made up of such individuals can be no more than a bunch of barely civilized animals. Their effort would likely be directed towards their own well-being, their prosperity, and their own peace; there would be no concern for the well-being of others.

If a person is found to be very active and concerned in putting out the fire that his home has caught and is always foremost in defending his rights, honor, life and property however, when he witnesses another's abode on fire, another's life, honor, and property endangered or someone else's rights violated, does not move a finger in his aid, could we call him a fine and virtuous man? Nay, In fact we could hardly call him a man at all. Then if it is a nation, which shows the greatest alacrity in putting out the fire of its own home and in the defense of itself and whatever is its own, and is ready to go to any lengths for the purpose, however, is not ready to aid any one also who it finds in need of help, how can such a group or nation lay its claims to greatness or virtue? As the individual has obligations, apart from himself, towards his kith and kin and towards God, a nation has its duties in relation to God and humanity. It would have to strive towards fulfilling its duties.

Defense of its own independence, unity, and standing against aggression, oppression and vice directed toward it, is the first duty of a nation, but that is not all. Its real duty lies in using its strength and prowess in aiding the entire humanity in achieving its salvation and in removing obstacles in its (humanity's) path, that hinder its ethical, material and moral progress. It is duty-bound to continue striving until the world is free of all strife, evil, suppression, oppression, and turbulence.

Instructions of Islam Concerning the Collective Duty

It is unfortunate that the bigoted and narrow-minded 'Gurus' of the world have not even tried to comprehend the high significance of collective virtue. The few, who think on these lines, unfortunately, do not have the required depth of perception. When they speak of individual ethics and morality, they talk not only of duties towards human beings and are not restricted from enumerating these, even towards the smallest particle of dust. However, on the question of collective human life, their comprehension appears too small to house the enormity of the concept of humanity and duty towards its entirety. Collective duty from their perception is relegated to reflect national or racial colors. This in time forms the foundation of racial and national loyalties, which with little doing, acquires the form of discrimination.

These narrow-minded people are responsible for such teachings, by virtue of which people of a particular race, color, and language have learnt to consider the rest of the humans, outside the pale of humanity. Then, understanding or granting the rights of the latter is a far cry. They do not consider even crushing their rights a big deal. The Qur'anic use of the term 'mankind' in this relevance is in fact a negation of this very unnatural division of the human race.

The Qur'an, having taught us the greatness of the concept of collective virtue, has pointed the way for the Muslims towards achieving the high aim of serving humanity, which is far removed from any kind of discrimination. It teaches us that for a nation bound by its duty towards humanity; the restrictions of race, color, creed, and nationality are not valid. It teaches us that the artificial geo-political bounds are meaningless, that the span of duty to humanity engulfs the whole world. In its perspective the entire lot of the children of Adam (AS), is one race, it is therefore the duty of every individual and nation, to serve them all. That is to say, prohibit them, the evil and work towards establishment of virtue. Thus having broken the age-old taboo of limited thought opened the vista of universal duty. The Qur'an says,

> "Thus we have appointed you a middle nation that ye may be witnesses against mankind and the messenger may be a witness against you"
>
> (Al-Baqarah: 143)

The concept is further explained as:

> "And strive (do jihad) for Allah with endeavor which is his right. He hath chosen you and hath not laid upon you in religion any hardship; the faith of your father Abraham is (is yours). He hath named you Muslims (Those who surrender) of old time and in this (scripture) that the messenger may be a witness against you, and that ye may be witnesses against mankind. So establish worship, pay the poor-due, and hold fast to Allah. He is your protecting friend. A blessed patron and a blessed helper!" (Al-Hajj: 78)

The above two verses, addressing the Muslims, say here as well, that the reason for their existence, is service of humanity and that Allah has specially entrusted them, endorsing their word and deed, that which is the truth and right, so that they may demonstrate to the world, the true meaning of justice and virtue. Affirming what is right is the purpose of their live, and they have been given the name of Muslims (those who surrender to the will of the Lord). Later it is explained that there is no narrowness in Islam i.e. there is no discrimination in it based on color, caste, language, nationality, or statehood. All those who accept it, whatever caste, race or nationality they may belong to, are equal to other Muslims in matters of religion. Similarly, the service they have been entrusted with extends to the entire humanity, without discrimination. The same concept is stated from a different standpoint as,

> "Those who, if We give power in the land, establish worship and pay the poor-due (zakat) and enjoin kindness and forbid inequity. And Allah is the sequel of all events" (Al-Hajj: 41)

Here, it is explained that the, use to which Muslims are to put their might are, the augmentation of the servitude of Allah, make piety common and to put an end to evil on earth. The choice of the words, "in the land", is by reason of explaining the universal applicability of the concept. Muslims have been instructed hereby to spread the word of God to all corners of the globe, establish virtue, and combat evil, wherever it makes its appearance.

God does not have affiliation with any particular group. He is the Creator of the entire universe and of the entire human race; His relation with all men is that of the Creator. Therefore, He is angered by strife and oppression in all places, and not in any specific place. That is the reason that 'service to mankind' entrusted to Muslims is of general applicability and not restricted by any division.

The Truth about Establishing Virtue and Prohibiting Evil

From the forgoing, it is clear that the reason for Muslims being termed as the best of nations is that they have been created not to serve themselves, but their mission is the service of the entire human race. Let us now consider what establishing virtue and prohibiting evil means, what kind of service is required in its performance and its true meaning. In Arabic, virtue can be loosely translated as 'maroof'. It can also stand for 'that which is a fact', or 'that which is known to be correct, or the truth'. It can be used to denote that which human intelligence acknowledges as correct and what every person will feel as good. Its antonym, vice or evil can be translated into Arabic as 'munkar'. Apart from vice, it can mean 'that which is unknown or unfamiliar'. In usage, it can denote ' action that is disliked by nature, which is considered wrong by human intelligence and which is disliked by normal humans'.

Honesty, truth, piety, diligence, caring for the weak and old, sympathizing with those effected by grief is 'amr bil maroof', translated here as virtue or virtuous acts. As opposed to: undependable, evil, despicable behavior, lying, promoting strife, creating trouble, injustice, crossing one's bounds, depriving others of their rights, aiding the oppressor, suppressing the truth, troubling the weak and the old. These and other suchlike actions against humanity, against the dictates of consideration and against nature, come under the ambit of 'munkar' (evil); avoiding them as well as prohibiting others from indulging in them, is 'nahi an al munkar' (prohibiting evil).

In this commandment, in general, one has to sequentially keep oneself from evil, ensure one's own piety and then to set out to establish piety. This preference in the order of precedence is also confirmed by the fact that the command for establishing virtue and prohibiting evil is preceded by the command to establish prayers (salat) and pay the poor-due (zakat) i.e. paying attention to one's own piety is first. It is but obvious that one has to be pious first before preaching piety.

However, as feeding others is a more pious act than feeding oneself, establishing virtue and prohibiting evil have higher standing than avoiding evil and being pious oneself. Since the former is service to humanity and the latter is service to self, the latter is humanity and the former is a very high degree of humanity. Indeed, no one can claim to achieve a high level of piety unless he ensures piety not only of himself, but makes it a general trend and tries his best to obstruct and contain evil.

It is human nature that when a person dislikes something, he tries to give it up. On further progress, dislike becomes hate; one then does not even want to see or hear of the object of his hate. A degree further is such enmity wherein one wants to totally get rid of that object. When this hate acquires its extreme form, the destruction, and removal of the object of his hate becomes the mission of one's life. Conversely, when a person likes something, he wants to acquire it for himself. If he loves something he feels pleasure in seeing it or hearing of it. On further progress, love becomes a deep desire or longing, he wants that each grain of sand should reflect the image of his loved one. When this love reaches its climax, he dedicates his entire life and offers whatsoever is his, to the service of his love.

'Establishing virtue' or the desire to do so, is the result of a Muslim's deep desire, longing and love for what is pious, true and right. And that is the extent of 'amr bil maroof' that is, commanding and establishing or trying to do what is virtuous, pious, right and true. Conversely, 'nahi an al munkar' that is, prohibiting evil, vice, what is wrong; springs from extreme dislike, hatred, intolerance and enmity of what is evil.

Another emotion that is a deep motivational factor in establishing virtue and prohibiting evil is the love for humanity and the human race. A selfish man enjoys the blessings of God that come his way but is unwilling to share them with others. Likewise, if he is in trouble, he does his best to extract himself out from it, but he is not willing to extend any help to others facing similar trouble. In contrast, the person who has love and empathy for humanity as his quality, includes others in sharing his blessings, when he sees others in trouble, he is disturbed as if he was himself in trouble.

Normally, when we consider the effects of the emotions of empathy and selfishness, the sphere of consideration of their effects is restricted to the material and the emotional. However, in the fields of morality and ethics, these two emotions conflict with each other much more severely. Since material well-being is deeply influenced by a person's moral and ethical well-being, a true human being cannot be truly satisfied being pious himself but would endeavor to set others free of the grip of vice and evil and put them on the path of virtue. His soul is as troubled, seeing others devoid of the apparel of virtue as would a mother's, when she is unable to protect her child from the ravages of a cold.

The truly virtuous person, on seeing the utility and wholesomeness of something, would like that others gain from it. He believes that which is good for him is good for all. That it is his duty that all of Adams children are made aware of it. If something is bad for him in reality, he desires that the rest of humanity be protected from it.

Being satisfied with ones advantages oneself and not caring to share their benefits with others; avoiding the harmful and the evil oneself and not caring to protect others from their ill effects, is indeed, the lowest degree of selfishness and egoism. However, this is not selfishness alone; it is also a form of suicide and self-destruction. Man is a social animal. He cannot survive in isolation. His good and bad are collective in nature. If the congregation he belongs to is evil, he will be unable to avoid its influence on himself. If the entire city is littered with refuse, no matter if, a man himself is very particular about his own cleanliness and personal hygiene; he may not be able to remain safe from an epidemic that strikes the city. Similarly, if the people of the place he dwells in are generally unethical and indulge in evil practices, the scourge that will grip the city, will not be confined to the impious, vicious, and evil people, rather would affect the few good and pious ones equally.

"And guard yourself against a chastisement that cannot fall exclusively on those who are wrongdoers, and know that Allah is severe in punishment" (Al-Anfal: 25)

A saying of the Prophet (SAW), amplifying on the verse, states: "Allah does not send his scourge on a people, until such a time that the good people, on witnessing evil, despite having the ability, do not stop it. When this happens, then Allah will surely send his scourge on the people, the common, and the elevated alike." Thus, 'establishing virtue and prohibiting evil' is not only service to others, but also a service to self. In fact, collective good has the wisdom of seeking well for oneself.

The Status of the Concept of 'Establishing Virtue and Prohibiting Evil' in Collective Life

Establishing virtue and Prohibiting evil is the spirit on which depends the collective well-being and safety of a society. Till such a time, that there is the mutuality of enforcing virtue and prohibiting vice, or in the very least, there is one such organized group of people, which takes upon itself, the performance of this function, a nation can be said to be in fair shape. However, if neither is possible, then gradually, vice starts prevailing and such society falls into the pit of ethical depravity and moral destruction. The Qur'an states of this as follows:

"If only there had been among the generations before you men possessing a remnant of (good sense) to warn (their people) from corruption in the earth, as did a few of those whom we saved from them! The wrongdoers followed that by which they were made sapless, and were guilty. In truth thy lord destroyed not the townships tyrannously while their folk were doing right" (Hud: 116-117)

At another place, stating the reasons for the Children of Israel earning the wrath of Allah, the Qur'an states:

"Say: O people of the scripture! Stress not in your religion other than the truth, and follow the vain desires of folk who erred of old and led many astray, and erred from a plain road. Those of the children of Israel who went astray were cursed by the tongue of David, and of Jesus, son of Mary. That was because they rebelled and used to transgress. They restrained not one another from the wickedness they did. Verily evil was that they used to do!" (Al-Maida: 77-79)

In the explanation of this verse, Abu Daud, Tirmizi, and Ibn Maja who are all Islamic scholars of eminence, quote the saying of the Prophet (SAW), that the shortcoming that had developed in the Children of Israel was the mutual tolerance of evil. This had reached to such a stage that their consciences had become dormant; one would find himself indulging in, what he had considered evil earlier. The hadith states,

"When one of the Bani Israel used to meet another he used to tell the other to give up such and such act, since it is forbidden. However, the next day the former was also seen committing the same act. The same afflicted both ill and their consciences were dead."

When the Prophet (SAW) was related this, he was lying down. He got up in excitement and said, "I swear by Allah, in whose hands is my life, it is incumbent on you that you enforce virtue and prohibit vice and grip the hand of the evil-doer and turn it towards virtue, for if you don't, Allah will let your hearts be affected by that evil and you will also have to bear his scourge, as them (Children of Israel) did."

The example of Children of Israel has universal significance. Just as the welfare and salvation of one nation is dependent on establishing virtue and prohibiting evil, the salvation of the entire humanity also depends on it. This is necessary that there is always a group or organization in the world that would have as its charter, commanding what is virtuous, obstructing what is evil, continuously caring for the human beings, establishing justice, keeping mischief-makers in control and gripping the hand that commits evil, saving God's creation from general and wanton destruction and keeping the earth safe from strife disorder and cruelty. The Qur'an states on the subject,

"And there may spring from you a nation who

invite to goodness, and enjoin the right conduct and
forbid indecency. Such are they who are successful"
(Aale Imran: 104).

It is not enough that we consider 'establishing virtue and
prohibiting evil' a good thing and an emotion of high virtue.
Actually, it is a necessary course of action for the establishment of
universal peace, for making a world of the virtuous, and for the
people of the world to strive to progress from sub-humanity to the
very zenith of humanity. God has entrusted this service to one
international body of human beings and definitely, there is no
better service to humanity than this.

The Difference between Establishing Virtue and Prohibiting Evil

This supreme universal service entrusted to the international
community of Muslims consists of two parts, one is commanding
virtue, and the other is prohibiting vice. Although the objective of
both is common, that is, making men out of humanoids, but there
is a difference in their statuses. There is therefore a difference in
their modus operandi. It is necessary that the difference be clearly
understood.

In the world of ethics, man's duties can be divided into two
types. For the performance of one, he is answerable to someone or
to society; their fulfillment can be demanded from him. The other
types are performed out of freewill; there is no apparent
compulsion on him for their performance.

The minimum that a society demands of an individual is that he
should avoid evil, that he should not usurp other's rights, that he
does not treat others cruelly, that he does not disturb other's peace
and tranquility and that he should not indulge in activity that would
make his person disagreeable and harmful for the society. The
other types of duties are concerned with higher ethical objectives.
By fulfilling these, man achieves respectability and a high status in
society. Examples of these are acknowledging the rights of Allah
and man and acting accordingly, being pious oneself and putting
others on the path of piety, serving one's family, nation, and
humanity in general, defending what is right etc. None can perform
these duties until one is aware of their true nature; the purity of

one's soul compels one on their voluntary performance. Thus, the choice of achieving respectability in society is voluntary. In fact, the ethical makeup of society should be such that the desire to achieve a high status and respectability in it should come as a natural discourse to each of its members.

The difference in the natures of 'establishment of virtue and prohibiting evil,' is much on the same lines of division of duties connected with the performance of each of the two. Salvaging man from the depths of savagery and putting him on the path of humanity, preventing his becoming a problem and a cause of harm for the society is 'prohibiting evil'. Whereas, helping a man progress from humanity to the zenith of humanity, is 'establishing virtue'.

In sequence, 'establishment of virtue', comes ahead, of 'prohibition of evil', but the latter is more important than the former. As a farmer's real motive is to grow food, but before he can sow his seeds, it is necessary that he plough his fields to exterminate the weeds on the land and to make it nice and soft. Similarly, Islam's motive is to make man excel as a member of society, but before sowing the seeds of excellence in him, it is necessary that evil be weeded out from this person.

Islam invites all to the path of excellence and entices man to follow that path by showing him the excellence of virtue, but evil is that obstruction that prevents him from seeing the charms of virtue. It is necessary that this impediment is removed and the full vista of 'excellence' may become apparent to him. When man accepts the invitation of 'excellence', many of its stresses on virtuous conduct, pointed out to him as advantages earlier, do not remain just advantages. They acquire the garb of obligations, for when a man attains the degree of zenith of humanity, excellence of conduct and establishment of virtue do not remain a matter of free will for him but they become his nature. However, if despite being pointed out, the eye remains oblivious to the attraction in the path of excellence and high virtue, Islam satisfies itself in 'prohibiting evil' in respect to that person and leaves the rest to his conscience.

From a different angle, the difference between establishing virtue and prohibiting evil can be explained by equating it with the two aspects of Islam. One aspect of Islam is just inviting people towards piety and faith, the other aspect is leading life in accordance with the dictates of Islamic law. When a person accepts Islam, the two aspects combine to make one whole; the advantages pointed out to him earlier are compulsions now. However, prior to accepting Islam, the clauses of invitation and clauses of subjection to Islamic law remain divorced.

The objectives of invitation to Islam are that man would develop the capability of becoming Allah's Khalifah (vicegerent) on earth, the purpose he was created for. Whereas, the objectives of the Islamic law are that man should at least refrain from spreading strife and bloodshed on earth, if he is the noblest of creations, he should at least not stoop to the level of the basest. If he does not spread the light of piety in the world, he should at least not destroy its peace and tranquility by the darkness of his evil. The former is dependent on man's inner nature and the light of wisdom that has lighted his inner self with; obviously, strictness and punishment cannot inculcate it. However, the latter is concerned with establishing bounds and patrolling them; obviously too, accepting the bounds voluntarily cannot be expected from all, or be enforced by sermons alone. Sometimes the use of force becomes unavoidable.

The Methodology of Prohibiting Evil

Much can be said on the subject. Later it will be clarified further, but let it suffice here, that for impressing on the non-Muslim world, the excellence of virtue, the methodologies of invitation and instruction have been defined as the right way. For the suppression of evil, however, the restrictions of invitation do not apply and different methodologies have been suggested to keep the various forms of evil at bay:

> "Call unto the way of thy lord with wisdom and fair exhortation, and reason with them in the better way" (Al-Nahl: 125)

> "And argue not with the people of the scripture unless it be in (a way) that is better, save with such of them as do wrong" (Al-Ankabut: 46)

> "And speak unto him a gentle word, that per adventure he may heed or fear" (Ta Ha: 4)

For combating evil action, the use of force has been advised. In this connection one of the sayings of the Prophet (SAW), quoted earlier is repeated here,

> "You are obliged to grip the hand of the evildoer and turn it towards virtue"

Apart from this, many other sayings of the Prophet (SAW) can be quoted to bring home the point. One of them is,

> "If any of you see evil, you should change it with your hand, if you are not capable, with your tongue, and if you are incapable of even this, consider it evil in your heart, and this is the weakest degree of faith".(Muslim)

In the saying, the word 'hand' is not the physical hand, but use of force is implied, both to make evil action impossible and to destroy or curtail evil, in order to establish virtue.

Another saying of the Prophet (SAW) states,

> "Allah will not punish you for the evil of others unless your tolerance reaches the stage where you see evil taking place before your eyes and despite possessing the capability, you do not stop it"

Only preaching against evil by word or by the pen is not enough. It is prescribed to use force where it is necessary, to curtail, and to rid the world of evil. If Muslims have the strength and capability to endeavor to stop evil in the entire world, it becomes their duty to continue the struggle until virtue, and justice is established in its place. It is also their duty, to strive to gain sufficient strength for the purpose, if they do not already possess it.

War against Strife and Turmoil

In order to differentiate between this second form of evil and the first, the words 'strife and unrest' have been used. The use of force has been prescribed to combat and eliminate it. The Holy Qur'an states on the subject:

> "Fight against these till strife remains"

> "If God had chosen not the extermination of one people at the hands of another, the world would

have been filled with strife and unrest"

"And strife is worse than killing"

"If anyone murders another, except when that person has killed someone or spread strife in the world, it will be as if he had committed murder of the entire human race"

"They wanted to spread strife"

"Whenever they go back towards strife, they become part of it"

In all these verses, the word evil has been replaced with 'strife and unrest'. These, in fact, cannot be combated and eliminated without the use of the sword.

Investigating Strife (Fitnah)

Usually, strife and unrest are understood to mean a fight between two groups. First, "unpleasantries" are exchanged, and then some stalwarts from each side arm themselves with available weapons, fight, and kill each other untill their anger is spent.

Although, the above is also a form of 'strife and unrest', in the Qur'anic language the meaning is broader. In that, this encompasses other ethical crimes as well. We really do not have to look for explanation of these terms elsewhere, the Qur'an itself tells us what it means by 'strife and unrest'.

Arabic dictionaries describe 'fitn', a grammatical form of 'fitnah' (translated here as strife), as determining the purity of gold through the process of heating it. The dictionaries also state its meaning as casting humans into fire. The Qur'an, in describing the 'day of reckoning' also uses the word in this sense. A derivative of that is the term trial and tribulation or 'that which puts man on trial'. Therefore, man's wealth and family have also been termed as 'fitnah' (trial, strife). Use of the word in Qur'an, in relation to wealth and family as such, is because these things put a man on trial, whether he holds them dearer or the truth. Bliss and tribulations have also been termed as 'fitnah' because in these conditions as well, man is on trial. The revolutions and changing colors of history are similarly termed so, since whole nations are on trial at such times. Putting more loads than a man can bear is also a 'fitnah', since it is a test of his endurance.

The word 'fitnah' has been used in all these senses in the Qur'an. Its meanings manifest trial and test, which may result from plenty or scarcity, desire or fear, pain or fear of it. This trial, if it is from Allah, it is justified, since the Creator has a right to test His creations and the success in the trial can result in elevating one's stature. However, if the same trial is because of a man, then it is cruelty, since the intention can be no other than depriving the other of his freedom of conscience, making him his own dependent and casting him in a pit of ethical and moral depravation.

In usage, the word can be equated with 'persecution', in a limited sense. However, the Arabic equivalent (fitnah) denotes, as explained, several shades of persecution, vice or evil. In the Qur'an, its usage depicts the following conditions:

a) Treating the weak with cruelty, usurping their rights, depriving them of their homes, and subjecting them to hardships.

> "Then lo! Thy Lord -- For those who become fugitives after they had been persecuted, and then fought and were stead fast -- lo! Thy lord afterward is (for them) indeed forgiving, merciful"
>
> (Al-Nahl: 110)

> "They question thee (O Muhammad) with regard to warfare in the sacred month. Say: warfare therein is a great (transgression), but to turn (men) from the way of Allah, and to disbelieve in Him and in the in violable place of worship, and to expel his people thence, is a greater with Allah; for persecution is worse than killing" (Al-Baqarah: 217)

b) Suppressing what is right by force and obstructing acceptance of truth and that, which is right.

> "But none trusted Musa save some scions of his people. (And they were) in fear of Pharaoh and their chiefs, that they would persecute them" (Yunus: 83)

c) Obstructing and preventing people from following the way of Allah.

In Surah Al-Anfal, the crime of the non-believers is initially defined as "debarring men from the path of Allah". Soon after having given them tidings of victory and ordering the Muslims to fight the non-believers, the affairs of the non-believers are mentioned as 'fitnah' and Muslims were encouraged to fight with them.

d) Leading people away from the path of piety and obstructing the right cause, through deception and coercion.

"And they indeed strove hard to beguile thee (Muhammad) away from that wherewith we have inspired thee, that thou shouldst invent other than it against us; and then would they have accepted thee as a friend" (Bani Israel: 73)

"But beware of them lest they seduce thee away from part of what Allah hath revealed unto thee----- ------ is it a judgment of the time of (pagan) ignorance that they are seeking" (Al-Maida: 49-50)

e) Waging war for other than a rightful cause and wrongfully causing bloodshed, lawlessness, and behaving arrogantly.

"If the enemy had entered from all sides and they had been exhorted to treachery, they would have committed it, and would have hesitated thereupon little" (Al-Ahzab: 14)

"Ye will find who desire that they should have security from you, and security from their own folk. So often as they are returned to hostility they are plunged therein" (Al-Nisa: 91)

f) Defeat of the righteous at the hands of the forces of evil.

"If you do not so (protect the believers) there will be confusion (turmoil) in the land and great corruption" (Al-Anfal: 73)

Investigating Turmoil (Fasad)

In English, the Arabic word 'fasad' can be equated to trouble, turmoil, turbulence, uprising, and unrest. Let us see what 'fasad' stands for in the Qur'anic language.

The Arabic dictionary states that fasad is that thing which is beyond the reasonable. Its antonyms are, reason or reasoning. From the standpoint of the dictionary meaning, any unreasonable and unjust act is fasad (turmoil). However, in Qur'an its usage is concerned with collective unethical interaction, a system of civilization and political upheaval. For example, it holds Pharaoh, Aad, and Thamud responsible for turmoil (fasad) and quite often explains the crimes, by virtue of which they have been classified as 'those who create turmoil' or 'troublemakers' (mufsid).

> "Dost not thou consider how thy Lord dealt with (the tribe of) Aad, with many columned Iram, the like of which was not created in the lands; and (the tribe of) Thamud, who clove the rocks in the valley; And with Pharaoh, firm of might, who (all) were rebellious (to Allah), in these lands, and multiplied iniquity therein" (Al-Fajr: 6-12)

At different places, the Qur'an itself states the crimes of the people, because of which they reached the infamy of being termed as 'those that spread trouble and turmoil'.

Of those it says the following:

a) The Qur'an states of Pharaoh that pride was his big failing, he used to create strife and turmoil between his people and on that basis consolidated his rule. Without due cause, he used to have the weak amongst his people, murdered and caused wanton bloodshed.

> "Lo! Pharoah exalted himself in the earth and made people castes. A tribe among them he oppressed, killing their sons and sparing their women. Lo! He was of those who work corruption (turmoil)"
>
> (Al-Qasas: 4)

He used to obstruct the path of acceptance of the right way. Thus when even the magicians who had been casting their magic against Musa (AS), seeing his divine miracle, accepted the call of the faith, Pharaoh declared,

> "(Pharaoh) said: Ye put faith in him before I gave you leave. Lo! He is your chief who taught you magic. Now surely I shall cut off your hands and your feet alternately, and I shall crucify you on the trunks of palm trees, and ye shall know for certain which of us hath sterner and more lasting punishment" (Ta Ha: 71)

On finding it weak, he enslaved the entire nation. Thus, when he was recounting his favors to Musa (AS), he (Musa) replied,

> "And this is the past favor wherewith thou reproachest me: that thou hast enslaved the children of Israel" (Al-Shuara: 22)

Intoxicated with his might, Pharaoh ruled people with brute force, and even laid claims to divinity. Where, as a ruler his duty was to do justice and treat his people with kindness.

> "And Pharaoh said: O chiefs! I know not that ye have a god other than me ----------- And he and his hosts were haughty in the land without right, and deemed that they would never be brought back to Us" (Al-Qasas: 38-39)

He had caused such moral and ethical degradation in the people he ruled, that they willingly accepted his slavery:

> "Thus he persuaded his people to make light (of Musa) and they obeyed him. Lo! They were a wanton folk" (Al-Zukhruf: 54)

His rule was based on laws that do not have the sanction of the Lord and those were wrong,

> "But they did follow the command of Pharaoh, and the command of Pharaoh was no right guide"
>
> (Hud: 97)

b) The crime of the nation of Aad is described as their willing acceptance of the overlordship of cruel and headstrong rulers,

> "And (they) followed the command of every forward potentate" (Hud: 59)

> "And if ye seize by force, seize ye as tyrants"
>
> (Al-Shuara: 130)

In their arrogance, wrongfully, they established overlordship on the weaker nations,

> "As for Aad, they were arrogant in the land without right, and they said: who is mightier than us in power" (As-Sajdah: 15)

c) Thamud's tumultuous behavior and turmoil have been stated in the Qur'an as the willing acceptance of the sovereignty of their rulers who were cruel and headstrong; the Prophet Saleh (AS) chastised them thus,

> "And obey not the command of the prodigal, who spread corruption in the earth"
>
> (Al-Shuara: 151-152)

The nation of Thamud was such haughty people that they were bent on the murder of a righteous person (Prophet Saleh) only because he tried to stop them from committing evil acts and preached righteous behavior. In order to justify their evil designs, they invented the worst kind lies and falsehood.

> "And there were in the city nine persons who made mischief in the land and reformed not. They said: swear one to another by Allah that ye verily will attack him and his household by night, and afterward we will surely say unto his friend: we witnessed not destruction of his household. And lo! We are truth-tellers" (Al-Namal: 48-49).

d) The Qur'an also terms the nation of Luth (Lot) as being those who caused turmoil, by virtue of their evil behavior. Their behavior has been described thus,

> "Lo! Ye commit lewdness such as no creature did before you. For come ye not onto males, and cut ye not the road (for travelers), and commit ye not abomination in your meetings" (Al-Ankabut: 28-29)

This was the condition of these people, which the Lord referred to as turmoil (fasad). Apart from their lewdness, they were also known for highway robberies and their collective ethics had reached such a state that they committed immorality, not in privacy, but even in gatherings. There was no one to stop them.

e) The people of Madian have also been termed as those who cause turmoil. Prophet Shoaib (AS) exhorts them towards righteous conduct by saying,

> "Give full measure and full weight and wrong not mankind in their goods, and work not confusion (turmoil) in the earth after the fair ordering thereof. That will be better for you, if ye are believers. Lurk not on every road to threaten (wayfarers), and to turn away from Allah's way, him who believeth in Him, and to seek to make it crooked"
>
> (Al-Ae'Raf: 85-86)

They replied,

> "But for thy family, we would have stoned thee, for thou art not strong against us" (Hud: 91)

From the foregoing it is apparent that the people of Madian (Jethro), were generally dishonest and their dishonesty had reached the limit in their commerce. Hold-ups were common on trade routes, and honest people were obstructed from following the way of the Lord. They had become so biased against righteous conduct that when one person invited them towards following the honest way of life, he was not tolerated and they even threatened him with stoning to death.

f) Theft has also been termed as turmoil (fasad). That is why, when the brothers of Yusuf (Joseph) (AS) were accused of stealing a glass, they said,

> "By the Lord! You know well that we are not thieves and have not come to spread turmoil in the land" (Yusuf: 73)

g) As a result of conquests, the conquered nation's ethical life is badly affected. This process has also been termed as turmoil.

When Queen Saba (Sheba) received Solomon's (AS) letter, she stated to her courtiers,

> "When kings enter (a conquered territory), turmoil becomes a common affair; the respectable people in

them are treated ungraciously and other such acts
are committed" (Al-Namal: 34)

h) The Qur'an explains fasad (turmoil) as destroying those
relations and connections between men that are actually the
basis of civilization. It states,

"And those who break the covenant of Allah after
ratifying it, and sever that which Allah had
commanded should be joined, and make mischief in
the earth: theirs is the curse and theirs is the ill
abode" (Al-Raad: 25)

Most Qur'anic commentators when commenting on the above
verse have taken the meaning of the words in a rather limited
sense. They have taken it to mean the breaking up of existing close
relations. However, the fact is that these words encompass the
entire spectrum of legal relations that exist in the areas of
civilization and civics, between men and between organizations.
These include relations between spouses, neighbors and friends, as
well as between countries or governments; also included are the
relations of understandings, for pacts or promises of mutual trust
and of business. These are the relations that form the basis of
human civilization and on their good health depends, the peace,
security, and welfare of people. For this reason, the spoiling or
breaking up of these relations has been termed by the Lord as
'fasad' or turmoil, and is condemned in the severest terms.

i) That way of ruling has been classified as turmoil (fasad), in
which instead of being used for good and just purposes, the
state machinery is used in the cause of persecution, cruelty, and
destruction. The Qur'an has expressed Allah's extreme dislike
for its perpetrators,

"And when he turneth away ('from thee', it may
also mean, 'when he gets power') his effort in the
land is to make mischief therein and to destroy
crops and the cattle; and Allah loveth not mischief"
(Al-Baqarah: 205)

j) Obstructing the way of a person following the path of Allah,
which has been explained earlier, has been referred to as
turmoil. The Qur'an states,

"For those who disbelieve and debar (men) from the way of Allah, We add doom to doom because they wrought corruption (turmoil)" (Al-Nahal: 88)

k) God has clearly stated that he does not hold dear, those who spread unrest and turmoil in the world. The Qur'an states that the sins of such people as:

"And thou seest many of them vying one with another in sin and transgression and their devouring of illicit gain. Verily evil is what they do"

(Al-Maidah: 62)

"And we have cast among them enmity and hatred, till the Day of Resurrection. As often as they light a fire for war, Allah extinguisheth it. Their effort is for corruption in the land, and Allah loveth not the corrupters" (Al-Maidah: 64)

It will be clear from the above two verses that the sins that ethically destroy man are those sins that can affect others and are termed as turmoil. Examples of this kind of sin are bribery and usury, by means of which, people are deprived of their wealth in a sinful way. Others of this kind are harboring malice and bitterness towards someone and personal enmity, which leads to war and bloodshed.

The Need for a Government Based on Divine Injunctions to Combat Strife and Turmoil

Having understood the meaning of 'fitnah' (strife) and 'fasad' (turmoil), if we glance through them again, we will notice that these are indeed products of a system of a government, which neither fears God nor gives recognition to individual rights of its people. If it is not directly involved in sponsoring a particular evil, it is definitely responsible for its continued unreformed existence.

Such a government is not a government at all; it is just confusion and turmoil, because it is far removed from the factual purposes of governance. It cannot remain just as one form of evil, but it will soon be a collection of evils or a fountain of evils from which sprout all forms of strife and turmoil. It obstructs the way of the Lord: it is responsible for crushing justice, and it is a fountain of strength for evildoers, oppressors and is responsible for promulgation of laws that destroy the very social fabric of the nation. It causes war and bloodshed and because of all these evils, the nations that tolerate such a government, become fair candidates for the scourge of God.

Islam is the only religion that has given the world a system that provides a methodology of ridding the world of evil and exploitation through organized exertion and direction (jihad). Even if the only means available is war, all such governments should be removed, if it is possible, and should be replaced by such that are based on fear of Allah and on the divine law. In such a system, only those people will be recognized as capable of governing, who are free from personal, community or national biases and whose sole purpose is service to humanity and whose aim is 'amr bil maroof wa nahi an al munkar' (establishment of virtue and prohibition of evil).

The Qur'an is quite emphatic in its instructions against acceptance of sovereignty of cruel oppressors. Man has been warned frequently against the acceptance of the overlordship of the evil and the oppressor on the pain of doom. At several places, the Qur'an has spoken on the subject:

> "And obey not the command of the prodigal, who
> spread corruption in the earth, and reform not"
> (Al-Shu'ara:151-152)

> "And obey not him whose heart We have made
> heedless of our remembrance" (Al-Kahf: 28)

The reason for the doom and destruction of a nation has been attributed to the phenomenon mentioned above,

> "(They) followed the command of every forward
> potentate. And curse was made to follow them in
> the world and on the Day of Resurrection"
> (Hud: 59-60)

At yet another place, it is clearly stated that a people are destroyed only when its wealth and governance goes into the hands of evil people,

> "When We decree that a habitation should be
> destroyed, we give command to its well to do
> people, and they show disobedience; then that

habitation incurs a just torment and We totally exterminate it" (Bani Israel: 16)

Of all the factors that influence civilization, the strongest and the most effective is government. If the system of government is wrong, its reins will go into the hands of people who would use it to serve themselves and the cause of turmoil rather than that of humanity. Under such conditions, the well-being of virtue, of reformative efforts and of spreading ethical excellence, will be in doubt. Since by nature, such a government is the caretaker of evil and mischief, it not only involves itself in evil acts but much of its efforts are expended in cultivating collective evil.

In contrast to the above, if a government is legally and constitutionally based on justice as its strong point, whose aim is the service to humankind and the motivation of those who run it is not service to themselves or their communities will have the effects of its good governance felt on all walks of life. Evil will not be only curtailed but the springs from which it flows will dry down.

In short, the only sure way to combat strife and turmoil universally is to follow the course of action the Qur'an recommends. That is, to eliminate all governments involved in spreading strife and turmoil and in their places establishing such governments, whose principles and actions are both based on virtue and the pursuance of it.

The Commandment for Armed Resistance and Defiance (War)

The two circumstances in which use of the sword has been made allowable are 'self-defense' and for combating evil, strife, and turmoil, wherever their existence is evident. This is, in order to deprive the mischief-makers of the capability of spreading strife and turmoil in the world and for making them subservient to the cause of virtue. Commandments to this effect are emphatic and precise in the Qur'an:

> "Fight against such of those who have been given
> the scripture as believe not in Allah nor the last day,
> and forbid not that which Allah hath forbidden by
> the messenger, and follow not the religion of truth,

until they pay the tribute readily, being brought low" (Al-Taubah: 29)

In this verse, war has been ordered against those who in spite of being the 'people of the book', believe neither in God nor the 'Day of Resurrection'; who do not hold prohibited which God has declared so, and neither do they accept the religion prescribed by Him. The sequence of the stated crimes is not without significance. In fact, on careful consideration, the relevance of this sequence, the reasons and significance of the commandment for war will become apparent.

The verse states that the books have been sent to the people that seek to exhort them towards righteous thought and action and they have been shown the right way by clearly defining the rules, which should govern their lives. Nevertheless, they abandoned these books and established religions based on their own thought and psyche. Such religions as these are, removed from the dictates of righteousness and devoid of the strength of truth.

Because of this alteration of the truth, both their thought and action suffered. They lost faith in the day of reward and punishment by the Lord and in their action could not differentiate between the permitted and the prohibited. They therefore, started spreading strife and turmoil, which God and His Prophets sent to them, had specifically instructed them to avoid. When God reiterated the message, which they had lost, they refused to believe it and remained adamant on their wrong thoughts and deeds. Had they accepted its call, they would have been bound by one law and their thoughts and actions would have undergone a change for the better, and there would have been no strife or turmoil left in the world.

If they refuse to accept the true word, obviously they cannot be forced to do so. However, they cannot be allowed to impose their wrong laws on humanity nor can they be allowed to spread strife and turmoil in the world.

Causes and Objectives of War

The objectives of war are clearly stated in the fore quoted verse, where it says, "Fight----------------- until they pay tribute readily."

(The word used in the Arabic text is 'jaziya', translated here as 'tribute'. Jaziya is the tax levied on conquered non-Muslims who become protégés of the Muslim State, on the termination of hostilities, for the protection and security, granted to them by the state).

Nowhere is it written that men can be forced to accept Islam. The acceptance of payment of jaziya is the last limit to which war can be extended. After that, the forces of Islam are forbidden hostile action against the conquered, rather they become the protégés of the Islamic State, regardless of whether they accept Islam, or they do not.

Islamic jurisprudence states:

> Allah has declared that acceptance of 'jaziya' is the limit to which war can be extended. The payment of 'jaziya' ends the necessity of war. Thereafter, the defense of the lives, property and respect of the other party at war, becomes the responsibility of the Muslims. Their life, property, and dignity are to be protected even if Muslims have to fight and spill blood for this cause.

Ali Ibn Abi Talib states, that the acceptance of 'jaziya' has made the other's blood and life as sacred as that of Muslims' and they (Muslims) become responsible for their protection.

Umar Ibn Khattab states in his last words that sanctity of pledges made on the authority of Allah and his Prophet should be maintained. The pacts and pledges with non-Muslims should not be violated and they should not be made to pay, what they cannot afford.

In this connection the Prophet (SAW) has stated,

> "Anyone who breaks pledges will be denied even the fragrance of heaven, although this can be felt at distance covered by 40 years of traveling."

It is not correct to assume that the respect of life and property of the non-Muslim protégés is based on pledges and pacts made with them. In the event that the non-Muslims surrender unconditionally, their lives and property become equally sacred for the Muslims. Books of Islamic jurisprudence state that if an area is concurred by the Muslims and if there is no agreement made with the conquered non-Muslims, even then they will be declared the protégés of the Muslims and the leader of the Muslims after imposing 'jaziya' on them (the conquered), will take them in the care of Allah and his Messenger. (Bidae wa Sanaya, vol. 7, page: 110, 112)

It is obvious that this command for war is not based on any religious animosity, or it could not be so, that the same people with whom war is mandated, their life and property become sacrosanct for Muslims, immediately as they accept sovereignty of the Muslims. Although, relieving one's emotions of revenge and satisfaction on the conquered would be simple. It is also beyond reason that these wars are for the purpose of collecting 'jaziya'. In consideration of a paltry sum of money, accepting the responsibility for the protection of those who pay 'jaziya' and ensuring it, whatever the cost may be, is not wholly, wise commerce. It will be beyond understanding, that the non-believers, on paying 'jaziya', are free to lead normal lives and enjoy all its blessings, while Muslims, who take their responsibility, are standing ready to protect them, even at the risk of their own lives. Even though, it is possible for them to accept 'jaziya' and then induct them (the conquered) into military service as well (jaziya is the tax in lieu of military service for non-Muslims).

By declaring the end of hostilities on acceptance of 'jaziya' and then taking the responsibilities of the defense and protection of the non-Muslims, proves that the only reason for war is the suppression of strife and turmoil and making the conquered subservient to law and constitution. Jaziya is the tax imposed on them in order that they too participate in their own defense and that they remain constant in accepting sovereign of Muslims.

Facts about 'Jaziya'

Imam Ibn Taimiah, an eminent Islamic scholar, explaining the Qur'anic verse on 'jaziya' (Al-Taubah: 29) writes,

> The clause, "till they pay 'jaziya' readily", in fact is a pact and understanding that exists between all governments and the governed, by virtue of which, all people pay civic taxes, the honest and regular payment of which is taken as fidelity to the state

and its non-payment, as disloyalty. Similarly, regular payment of 'jaziya' would show allegiance to a pact and non-payment will amount to disloyalty and treason. For this reason, 'jaziya' is levied on the mentally and physically soundmen, capable of bearing arms. Women, children, the mentally unsound old people, the blind, and the disabled are exempt from paying it.

'Bidae wa Sanaay' states,

> "God has imposed 'jaziya' only on those who are capable of war. This is a necessary condition. Any who do not possess the capability are exempt." (Bidae wa Sanaya, vol. 7, page 111)

The wording of the Qur'an and books of jurisprudence imply that the payment of 'jaziya' once imposed, should be willing and unforced. If those on whom it is imposed, show reluctance and there is a constant requirement of force for the collection of these taxes, then neither constitution by virtue of which it has become mandatory, is being adhered to, nor do the non-Muslims remain protégés of the Muslims, for which the acceptance of sovereignty and loyalty is a condition.

For the amount payable as 'jaziya', it has been stated that, it should be low enough, paying that will not be too big a burden and even its acquisition should not be devoid of kindness and prudence. Imprisonment, punishment etc. for the purpose is not allowed, as is overburdening. This aspect has been repeatedly stressed on those involved in receiving it.

Once an amount bigger than usual was brought before Umar (RA), the 2nd Caliph of Islam, he stated to the collectors, that he suspected that they had used undue force in obtaining it. They swore by Allah that they had not and only after further questioning, when he was sure of the correction of their statement, he accepted it for the treasury.

Ali (RA), the 4th Caliph, stressed on a freshly appointed administrator, that he should not be so strict in matters of 'jaziya', that those under his authority would be forced into selling off their animals, clothes and other belongings to pay them, but to treat them humanely.

When Hakeem Bin Jazaim (RA), a companion of the Prophet (SAW) saw some people arrogant and strict in collecting 'jaziya', he stopped them and said that he had heard the Prophet (SAW) say that those who put people to hardships in the world, Allah will put them in hardships on The Day of Judgment.

It will be clear from the foregoing that 'jaziya' levied on the non-Muslim, is not a punishment. Its sole purpose is the insurance that they will adhere to peace and the constitution, through their unforced and voluntary adherence to the law of the land and according to their ability, will assist in the functioning of the state. The state, which gives them the opportunity to live in peace, protects them from cruelty, mistreatment, justly distributes their rights, keeps the strong from mistreating the weak, avoids enslavement of the weak by the powerful and which keeps the arrogant within the bounds of humanity and ethics; such state does require the allegiance that is demanded.

The Qur'an itself on many occasions, while stating the valid reasons and utility of war, declares that disabling the non-believers' capacity for imposing their wrong laws on humanity and for spreading strife and turmoil is, in realty, promulgating the laws of the Lord. The ready acceptance and subservience of these laws is in line with avoiding strife and turmoil in the world.

The purpose and utility of war have been stated as the termination of strife and turmoil and the crushing of the ability to spread them, and that it is for establishing the supremacy of the word of Allah. This is the true purpose of war; the establishment of order and peace in the world, the unrestricted moral ethical and material pursuit, the promulgation of divine laws and termination of self-made and altered rules of the non-believers, and the termination of satanic discrimination. The prevalence of discrimination only based on righteousness and piety as opposed to impiety and evil, will definitely follow, and this is the utility of war.

In short, we find that the only objective of the commandment for war is, disabling the perpetrator's ability to spread strife and turmoil, which should establish factual freedom in all walks of life; the freedom that favors humanity, that recognizes the restraints of ethics and morality and is not unnecessarily shackled nor is totally unbridled. The sword is only raised against arrogance, strife, and turmoil, whether the targets of the satanic oppressors are Muslims or non-Muslims, and until they (oppressors) give up the foul use of their might, this conflict will continue. However, the very moment they give it up and accept being subjects of the laws of righteousness and justice, their life becomes sacrosanct and the responsibility for the safety of their material belongings and their honor becomes the responsibility of the Muslim State. Then they have the complete freedom of pursuing their trade, commerce and industry, education and literature, civilization and codes of conduct. There is no hindrance to their progress in any field and they have complete freedom of using their resources to attain the very peak.

The freedom of action that Islam provides to its protégés is unique. This is because there is a basic difference between the laws of Islam and others. Whereas, the others are based on the Caesarian principle, that the conquered are the domain of the conqueror and according to it, they become their property, which can be used as the owner wills. For that reason, magnanimity, and charity of the master's notwithstanding, their interests cannot be identical to those of their master's and the interest of the conquered can always be sacrificed for the betterment of the master.

In modern times, although outwardly democracy gives equal rights to the minorities, the country actually belongs to the majority. The minorities either get eliminated or would absorb themselves beyond recognition in the majority. As against this, in the Islamic System, which is based on the welfare of humanity, the relation between the conquered and the sovereign is that of a servant and his master. The interest of the ruler is actually no more than bettering the righteous interests of his subjects. They are given the right to rule their areas, only for the reason that they may combat evil that affects their moral, ethical, and material life and bring it to the level of humanity. Their Muslim overlord just seeks to bring his subjects within ethical bounds and then leaves them totally free, not allowing his personal, group or class interests to interfere, rather assists them in their endeavors.

Islam and Imperialism

Some of the imperialistic nations have made claims that the actual reasons for their conquests is the progress of humanity and civilization, the reform of the rest of the nations of the world, and establishment of peace and security. In contrast to their verbal claims, what actually happens is that they usurp the freedom of the weaker nations and instead of the progress they claim to have lent, they actually destroy all the good qualities of humanity one by one. The obviousness of the contradiction between the claims of the imperialistic Western nations and actuality can put the Islamic claims as well in doubt; there is even some resemblance in the claims of Islam and the others. Islam claims the responsibility of jihad for universal reform is totally for Muslims, so the imperialists proclaim that the mission for universal cultural reform is theirs alone. Although, a careful study of the previous discussion will leave little room for anyone to entertain such doubts, if some do remain, let us examine the subject further.

It is common knowledge that the basic quality of imperialism is the dominance of one particular nation or country. British imperialism is pertinent to the residents of the British Isles, German imperialism is the domain of no other than the Germans, and Italian imperialism is the Italian only. As if it is out of question that any other nation can be British, German, or Italian, similarly, no other nation can be a part of their imperialism. Wherever the British go, they will take their British nationality with them. If they become rulers of some place they will be British rulers; if they become heads of some political gatherings they will be British heads; if any is leader, he will be British first.

Regardless of how well they adopt the British culture, people of other nationalities will never be allowed to hold a position of any great power or influence in the British Empire. Similar is the situation in the cases of other systems of national imperialism.

(In the time period since the original book was written, the world has witnessed political and military alliances under the names of some socio-political systems. However, the imperialistic color of their assertion and ills associated with it has remained the same; this is the neo-imperialism in which dominant world powers gather together to achieve imperialistic objectives under the camouflage of socio-political reforms)

In the imperialistic situation, the right to rule definitely belongs to the people of one country or race and naturally race and

homeland are not matters of one's own choice, Allah alone makes
the decision. Thus, the doors of imperialism remain closed to
people of other nationalities and for this reason, they can play no
major role in running its affairs. This gives rise to the development
of other faults in the system and characters of the subject nation.
They develops a weakness of character, lose self-esteem and the
sense of righteousness. Even if the ruling nation does not treat the
subjects with outright cruelty and arrogance, their (the subject
nation's) character sinks to such a low ebb of ignobility that they
become quite incapable of striving for attaining and maintaining
self-rule for a very long time. This is a natural result of denial of
self-rule for a long period and is quite detrimental to progress.

In contrast to the above, Islam is not the name of any race,
nationality or country. It is a law of life and a way of life. Its doors
are open to everyone, no matter that he is an Arab, Persian,
Abyssinian, Chinese, Indian, or European. Anyone can accept and
be accepted by Islam. After that, their rights and positions
according to the system are the same as other Muslim's and they
are equal participants in the government. Most governments
require that a man pass the civil services or other such
examinations to establish his eligibility and capability of acquiring
any high administrative post. Similarly, in Islam, the level he
attains in following the Islamic code of life and law will determine
the eligibility as such. By virtue of this alone, one can establish his
eligibility; his caste or color will have no bearing. Islam does not
recognize the principles of rule by a certain class or even self-rule.
It only recognizes the rule of the pious and God-fearing, even if the
pious one is a black slave, it does not disqualify him from the
leadership of the best. The Prophet (SAW) states,

> "Listen and obey your leader, even if he be a
> hairless Abyssinian."

The last call of Islam sprung from Arabia, and Arabs were the
ones to promulgate its teachings, but it never identified governance
with the Arabs. Until they remained pious and God-fearing, they
ruled half the world, but when they lost the capability, the very
same Non-Arabs, who were beaten in battle and conquered,
occupied the throne of the Islamic empire. These Turks were the
deadly enemies of Islam, but when they entered the fold of Islam,
more than half of the Islamic world recognized their leadership and

their administration spread from Chittagong to Carthage. It is a fact that discrimination based on nationhood and color has crept in among the Arabs, to an extent, but this phenomenon has no connection with Islam. Islam has never taught or preached the slightest discrimination on that basis.

The foregoing explains the apparent and obvious difference between Islam and imperialism, but the non-obvious differences are more significant. Imperialism is the name given to a nation's desire for expansionism and procurement of wealth and riches. When the government and the wealth within its country fail to satisfy a nation, it attacks other nations to gain more territory and authority. It makes its people subjects or slaves and expands its trade and industry at their cost.

This has been the modus operandi of the arrogant nations since time immemorial. However, now the Western imperialists have named their looting and plunder 'the spread of civilization and service of humanity'. In their constitution of civilization and culture, 'Might is Right,' is the first clause. The weak have no right to live, is a sub clause. The method they have invented to spread culture and civilization is that they enrich the conquered nation with jewels of illiteracy, poverty, slavish depravity and unconscionability. Their spirit of service to humanity is on display when two or more of these imperialistic powers clash and destroy the peace and tranquility of the rest of humanity. The holy teachings of Islam are far removed from this evil concept. In contrast, it champions the termination of such powers, and in their place establishes a just system of government. It proclaims that the sovereignty belongs to Allah. Man may only serve humanity as His Khalifah (vicegerent) on earth and any power he may attain may be used for the betterment and welfare of others, rather than of self. The very basic requirement for man for achieving eligibility for vice-regency or caliphate is his piety:

> "Allah has promised such of you who believe and do good work that he will surely make them to succeed (the present rulers) in the earth even as He caused those who were before them to succeed (others)" (Al-Noor: 55)

> "And verily we have written in the scriptures, after

the Reminder: My righteous slaves will inherit the
earth: Lo! There is a plain statement for folk who
are devout" (Al-Ambiya: 105-106)

Those who attain sovereignty and vice regency on earth, have
been warned with emphasis that the authority they have been
awarded over God's creation, is Allah's alone; they are just the
keepers and administrators of it; they should not make the mistake
of considering it their personal effects and use it for furthering
their own interests. When Prophet Dawood (AS) was granted
sovereign of his country, he was emphatically advised:

"O David! Lo! We have set thee as viceroy in the
earth; therefore judge aright between mankind and
follow not desire that it beguiles thee from the way
of Allah. Lo! Those who wander from the way of
Allah have an awful doom, for as much as they
forget the Day of Reckoning" (Suad: 26)

When man attains overlordship, the biggest weakness that
develops in him is that he starts considering himself a being of
superior status to his subjects and starts believing that others have
been born just to serve him. Islam prohibits the development of
such a psyche in the strictest terms and declares that the attainment
of salvation depends on avoiding it,

"As for that abode of the hereafter, We assign it
unto those who seek not oppression on earth nor yet
corruption. The sequel is for those who ward off
(evil)" (Al-Qasas: 83)

The basic objective of government is treating people with
justice; justice is not just passing correct judgment between
contesting parties. Real justice is that the ruler, when dealing with
the subjects, keeps truth and righteousness foremost in his
considerations, even if there are chances of injury for his personal
pride or for his office. In spite of possessing the ability to do
otherwise, gives the correct decision, regardless of who suffers,
even if those were he himself or his dear ones. Islam teaches this
very concept of justice:

"O ye who believe! Be staunch in justice, witnesses
for Allah, even though it is against yourself or

(your) parents or (your) kindred, whether (the case is) of a rich man or a poor man, for Allah is nearer unto both (than ye are). So follow not passion lest ye lapse from truth and if ye lapse or fall away, then lo! Allah is ever informed of what ye do"

(Al-Nisa: 135).

The more significant lesson of Islam is that justice is to be dealt out, even to one's enemies,

"And let not hatred of any people seduce you that ye deal not justly. Deal justly, that is nearer to piety. Observe your duty to Allah" (Al-Maidah: 8)

The natural result of acquiring power and ability is the unholy desire for expansion of national frontiers, by usurping others' lands. This in turn leads to arrogance and cruelty. Islam strictly forbids this and not only does it exhort its avoidance, but commands jihad against those who indulge in it. This particular aspect has been discussed earlier while examining strife and turmoil.

A hadith of the Prophet (SAW) states,

"Anyone who acquires even a few inches of land through cruelty and oppression will have to bear the weight of shackles made of seven such pieces of land around his neck on the Day of Reckoning."

Another 'hadith' states,

"Wealth and affluence are indeed delicious morsels for anyone who acquires them righteously and spends them so, they are indeed very wholesome. But, for those, who acquire them through evil means and spend them on evil purposes, they are like food that does not satisfy hunger"

Political ethics are stated in detail and the smallest detail pertaining to it is present in the Qur'an and books of hadith. However, summarily speaking, Islam declares prohibited all luxuries and glamour of kingship and sovereignty, for the satisfaction of the greed for which, man makes all efforts to acquire sovereignty.

The Muslim sovereign is not being superior to the rest of his subjects in anyway. His position does not lend him any supremacy; neither can he expect people to bow down before him nor can he move an inch beyond the rules of righteous conduct; neither can he save any from the rightful demands of the lowliest of his subjects nor can he make the smallest gains wrongfully or can he acquire the smallest piece of land for himself. He always fears that he is answerable for his acts and that he will have to account for the smallest amount of wealth or the smallest piece of land foully acquired, if he is found guilty of the smallest arrogance, cruelty, injustice or egoistic behavior, he will be liable to strict punitive action.

Abu Bakar (RA), the first Caliph of Islam, in his inaugural speech, illustrates the essence of the responsibilities of kingship and sovereignty. He says: "O people, I have been entrusted with governance over you, though I am no better than any of you. The weakest among you is the strongest, until I am able to get him back his rights and the strongest among you is the weakest, until I can get from him what is rightfully due. My status is that of any ordinary man. If you see me following the righteous way, be of my followers, but if you should see my path crooked, straighten me."

Umar (RA), the second Caliph of Islam stated in his address: "my relation with your wealth is the same as that of a guardian's is with an orphan's. If I am well off, I will take nothing from it, but if I am in need, I shall take that which is rightfully my due for services I render. You have some rights over me and you can demand these of me. I consider it my duty that on your possessions, I should not impose any unjust tax and it is your right that whatever I acquire should be spent only on just and righteous causes."

Hence, after removing, the regal splendor, luxury, wealth and all that is for the satisfaction of ego, from the office of the head of an Islamic State, the insipid and unglamorous conditions that come his way are described in the Holy Qur'an as,

> "Those who, if we give them power in the land, establish worship and pay the poor-due (zakat) and enjoin kindness and forbid iniquity" (Al-Hajj: 41)

These are not just the theoretical claims of Islam, but also those which have been practically demonstrated and whose practicality has been demonstrated by the Prophet (SAW) and the first four caliphs of Islam, to the world. The object of this book is neither discourse on law nor the relating of history. However, it is pertinent that some examples are put forward to illustrate what the spirit of Islam really is.

Once, a woman from the tribe of Banu Makhzoom was brought before the Prophet (SAW) with accusation of theft. The people of Quraish fearing that she will suffer the punishment of amputation of her hand, sent Usama bin Zaid (RA), the person the Prophet (SAW) loved much, to intercede with him, on her behalf. The Prophet (SAW) declared to him, that the reason nations had perished earlier, was that they excused the crimes of the influential, and punished the common person for theirs's. And declared with passion, "By the Lord, in whose hands is my life, even if my own daughter had been guilty of theft, I would have had her hand cut off ".

On the culmination of the Battle of Badr, among the people brought prisoners of war to the Prophet (SAW), one was his own son in law, Abul Aas. The Prophet (SAW) advised him to call for his ransom money from his home or remain a prisoner. The Prophet's daughter, Zainab, Abul Aas's wife did not have anything of value at home, except a necklace, her mother Khadijah (RA), the Prophet's wife, had given her in dowry, this she sent as ransom for her husband. The Prophet (SAW) was so deeply moved by the reminder of his wife that he could not control his tears. However, he, on his own, did not excuse the ransom of his son in law. He requested the common Muslims if they would allow that he return the necklace to his daughter and only on general agreement, granting his request, the necklace was returned and Abul Aas was set free. (Abu Daud and Tabard). (Abul Aas, at the time, was a non-believer and remained so, until he accepted Islam in the year 7 A.H.).

At Hudaibiya, a treaty was agreed upon between the Prophet (SAW) and the Quraish (the rulers of Makah). One of the clauses of the treaty was that if any from among the Quraish defected to the Muslims, he would be extradited, but any Muslim who sought refuge with the Quraish would not be extradited. The treaty was being drawn up for finalization, when a Muslim Abu Jandal (RA), an escaped prisoner of the Quraish, sought refuge in the Muslim camp. He was in a pitiable shape from the torture he had received. He appealed to the Muslims to save him from further torture of the Quraish. The Muslims were moved, there were 1400 well-armed Muslims ready for war in the camp, and freeing Abu Jandal (RA) would not have been a problem, but the Prophet (SAW) refused to give him the requested refuge, asking Abu Jandal (RA) to bear the treatment of the Quraish with forbearance and fortitude, since he could not ask the Muslims to go back on their word. (Fatah al Bari vol.5)

On the occasion of Battle of Yarmuk, Rome had gathered a huge force, with the declared intention of driving the Muslims out of Syria and Palestine and breaking the back of their military might. At such a time, obviously the Muslims needed every penny they could muster in order to prepare for war. Instead, they approached the people of Khums, who were Christians and had been paying jaziya. They were advised that their (Muslim's) own survival was at stake, therefore the protection of Khums was not possible for them and hence wanted to return all the money received from the people of Khums, as jaziya. The people of Khums refused the money, stating that they would rather take their chance along with the Muslims rather than go back to the condition they were in under Roman rule previously. (Futuh al Buldan, Balazari)

During the Battle of Siffain, Ali (RA), the fourth Caliph of Islam, lost his armor, later the armor was discovered in the possession of a Jew, in the capital city. Instead of using his authority to re-appropriate the armor, Ali (RA) applied to the local judge for justice. The judge, instead of just passing judgment in favor of Ali (RA), asked him to produce evidence to prove his case. Ali (RA) produced one slave of his and his son as witnesses. The judge disallowed the evidence of Hussain (RA) his son, stating that a son's evidence in his father's case is not admissible. The Jew on witnessing all this proclaimed the 'Kalimah' (proclamation of faith in Islam) aloud and embraced Islam immediately, stating that if such was the justice in it and Islam was a true religion. (Suyuti)

The second Caliph of Islam, Umar (RA), on seeing a vast sum of money brought to the treasury as jaziya from the non-Muslims protégés, expressed his doubts that much money could only have been gathered by the use of force, by the Muslim administrator of the area. Only after much questioning, assurances and oaths to the contrary by those involved, when he was sure, did he accept the jaziya for the treasury. (Fatah Al-Bayan)

Abu Yusuf, in his book, 'Al khizraj', states that when taxes of Iraq were brought to Umar (RA), ten responsible officers from Kufa and ten from Basra accompanied it. They had to solemnly swear that force had not been used in the collection of the taxes either on Muslims or on non-Muslim protégés.

Abu Shahamah, Umar's son was once arrested while drinking. Umar (RA) who was in office awarded him the punishment of lashing. He himself administered 80 lashes on his son, who died as a result. (Ibn Qutaiba 'Story of Umar's Children')

When Amr bin Aas (RA) was the governor of Egypt. His son, Abdullah once beat up a person. The aggrieved person complained of this to Umar (RA), who awarded Abdullah, the punishment of lashing, to be administered by the aggrieved.

Amr Bin Aas (RA) was himself reported to have acquired wealth beyond his means. Umar (RA) asked his explanation. The reply stated that Egypt, for which he was the governor, was a very rich province and he could save that much from his legal earnings. Not satisfied, Umar (RA) sent a plenipotentiary envoy to investigate into the matter. The investigation revealed that the amount Amr Bin Aas (RA) had, was more than what he could have legally saved from his pay. All surplus wealth was confiscated and sent to the central treasury. The extremely powerful governor, whose authority extended to Libya, could but look on while this happened.

It was reported of Mughira bin Shoaba (RA), the governor of Basra, that he had developed illicit relations with a woman. Umar (RA) dispatched a prominent companion of the Prophet (SAW), Musa Ashari (RA) to Basra with orders to investigate the situation there, and dispatch Mughira bin Shuaba (RA) along with relevant witnesses to Madinah for trial of the case. Later, during the hearing of the case, the witnesses were seen to be unsound and their evidence full of contradictions. Mughira (RA) was declared not guilty. Umar (RA) declared that if he had been found guilty, he would surely have been awarded the punishment of being stoned to death. Balazari has quoted this incident (in detail it is present in Tabari and Ibn Athir, also in Balazari with minor differences).

It may be noted that Mughira Bin Shoaba (RA) was one of the highly reputed companions of the Prophet (SAW). He had rendered highly commendable political and military service and was one of the four foremost political figures of Arabia (the others being Amir Muawiya, Amr bin Aas and Ziyad bin Abu Sufyan) His respect, esteem and high rank of governor, nothing was of any avail, he was produced before the Caliph as a common criminal.

In the ephemeral governments of the world, man's indulgence in acts of dishonor, is his personal matter. In fact, illicit relations even between consenting adults are not a crime at all. However, in a system that has as its mission, the establishment of virtue and prohibiting evil, there was no place for a person whose personal life did not conform to the highest principles of virtue.

Once the Muslim army laid siege to town Shahr Yaj in Persia, soon the condition of the besieged city was such, that its fall became imminent. At this time, a Muslim slave wrote on a piece of paper that the people of that city were in his protection, tied it to an arrow, and shot it in the city. The next day when the Muslims launched an offensive against the city, the city elders opened city gates and showed the attackers the letter claiming that they were in the protection of the author. It was confirmed that the slave had indeed written such a letter to them. The case was referred to Caliph Umar (RA), who declared that the word of a Muslim, no matter that he was a slave, had to be upheld. The siege was lifted.

After the death of the Prophet (SAW), Abu Bakar (RA) assumed the leadership of the Muslim State. The day after that he was appointed as the Caliph of Islam, he was seen going to the marketplace, with a bale of cloth on his shoulders. Umar (RA), on learning that he was going to sell the cloth, advised him, that such work did not suit the Caliph of Islam. Whereupon Abu Bakar (RA) surprisingly asked him that if he did not do this, how else could he feed his family. Umar (RA) arranged that one, Abu Ubaida (RA) would take over his (Abu Bakar's) commercial activity and provide the necessities of life for the Caliph; a small stipend, amounting to 500 Dirhams was arranged for him.

On his death, Abu Bakar (RA) made his last wish that whatever was found in his possession, above what he had when he assumed office, should be handed over to his successor in office. When an inventory was taken after his death for the purpose, his total property was found to consist of one slave, one bed sheet and one she camel.

At the time of Umar (RA), Muslims held sway over areas from Iran to North Africa, money received annually as taxes ran into millions. Nevertheless, the condition of the leader of this vast empire was such that with patched-up clothes, old worn out slippers in his feet and an old dilapidated head cloth, he could be seen moving about among his needy subjects. When he was among the ordinary people, it was difficult for an outsider to distinguish him from the others. When he visited Syria, only one slave accompanied him and for those who were to receive him, it became difficult to differentiate between him and the slave.

When he entered Jerusalem as a conqueror, he was afoot and on his body were clothes of such coarse cloth that even the Muslims were embarrassed at what the Christians would think of him. Camels' milk, olive oil, wheat bread, and vinegar were about the best food that was his lot. When he died, there was not enough in his possession to pay off his meager debts, and the house in which he lived, had to be sold off for the purpose.

These are not fairy tales or essays, but real facts of history.

After being shown such caliber of leadership, can anyone point out any one example, where the foundations of constitution and governance were laid on such piety and purity, on such compassion and humility, on such boldness and steadfastness, on such justice and fairness, on such trustworthiness, sense of duty, selflessness, and nondiscrimination? Is this claim false that leadership of the world or rather the service of humanity is deservedly the lot of such people? If these people removed from the thrones, those non-Arabs, who worshiped nothing but luxury; if they (the Muslims) removed from the thrones, the untrustworthy, scheming, and despotic Roman rulers; if they overthrew all the neighboring satanic powers and in their places, established justly ruled principalities, can anyone claim this was cruelty to humanity or was it a service towards it?

When we are in knowledge of such greatness, can we even lend an ear to the lying Western propagandists, who have no concept of piety and abstinence, who have never been exposed to faith and honor, whose ignorance is total where selflessness trust and justice are concerned, who are unaware of any other emotion except for their all-consuming, deep desire, for imperialism and for gaining power. Granted that the rule of Muslims in later years was far removed from the concept and principles followed and exemplified by the early caliphate, but this does not point to any defect in Islam, rather it points to the followers. Islam is but a law in accordance with the Qur'an and the preaching of the Prophet (SAW). Any government that is in accordance with these principles is Islamic Government and any that does not, is not an Islamic government. Our concern is not how kings acted or act now, neither are their actions a beacon that points out the way. Our concern is only the Islamic constitution. If anyone can find fault with that, he may point that out.

The Real Motives behind Islamic Conquests

Before proceeding further, it is necessary that we address one other factor. It has been stated several times in this book that to raise the sword for purposes of expansionism and for extending the domain is absolutely prohibited. Then the question arises, that if this is a prohibition, how can aggression against Syria, Armenia, Egypt, Iran, Iraq and North Africa, be justified? Specially, since it was undertaken by none other than the well-instructed companions of the Prophet (SAW) and on the behest of the first four pious caliphs of Islam. This question is emphatically raised by the retractors of Islam, and has as emphatically been answered several times by Muslims and historians. However, while answering them, none has really taken into consideration the difference in the perspectives of Muslims and non-Muslims. Therefore, those who have made concessions to the non-Muslims point of view in their answers have represented Islam not in an entirely correct light, while those who had utterly disregarded that have only given rise to much misunderstanding.

The fact is that in matters of governance, Islam does not distinguish between the 'national' and the 'foreign', but does very thoroughly discriminate between 'justice 'and 'cruelty'. The sovereign of a local citizen, who is debauch, egoistic and unsympathetic, is as abhorable as a foreign sovereign of the like qualities. As against this, even if a non-Arab ruler of the Arabs deals with justice in all matters of the state, shows devotion and trust in his dealings, is sympathetic in the woes of the luckless, returns the rights to the rightful, is not arrogant or egoistic and works for the betterment of the lot of the general citizenry; is more preferable for the Arabs, than the Arab ruler devoid of these virtues. That a Turkish ruler will not be acceptable to Iraq, only by virtue of his being a non-Arab is a completely false and baseless supposition. Governance in Islam is not viewed from the perspective of race or nationality. A pious and righteous man is definitely more preferable to an impious and unrighteous man, and in considerations of virtues of a man, race, color, or nationality have no place. Piety and justice, being the only criteria for the acceptability of a government, overthrowing or even planning it, is considered sinful and oppressive. However, if the opposite is the case, its removal and replacing it with a just system, is an important religious duty.

In general, however, that foreign rule tends towards oppression. In fact, the reason for foreign occupation is to gain control of the human resource and riches of another country and use them for their own purpose, while intrinsic rule tends more towards reformative action, but this is not true in every case. The possibility exists that the government even in the latter case, is in the hands of arrogant, oppressive, and egocentric individuals. Who, to further their private gains, would prove very harmful for the country. On the other hand, it is also possible that imposition of foreign rule would free the country of the yoke of oppression and cruelty and would open venues for civic, moral, and material reforms.

From the foregoing, it will be a mistake to draw the conclusion that Islam is not in favor of national governments, but in its concept, when degeneration of ethical condition is such that the nation accepts sovereignty of evil and oppressive people, it loses all rights of self-government and other more righteous nations acquire that right. The Qur'an on numerous places has warned the unrighteous and morally degenerated people of this phenomenon:

"And if ye turn away He will exchange you for

some other folk, and they will not be the likes of
you" (Muhammad: 38)

"If ye go not forth He will afflict you with a painful
doom, and will choose instead of you a folk other
than you. Ye cannot harm Him at all"

(Al-Taubah: 39)

"If He will, He can remove you, O people, and
produce others (in your stead)" (Al-Nisa: 133)

Other verses of similar meaning are in plenty in the Qur'an.
They all support the argument that kingships or governments
depend for their continued existence, on competence. When a
nation loses its sagacity and ability to effectively rule, it also loses
its right to the same. Nevertheless, whenever a nation develops this
competence within itself, it also retains the right to government.
This competence should not be taken to mean military competence
alone. It actually refers to the ability to promote virtue and
discourage to a very high degree, vice, the ability to remain
steadfast in accomplishing something virtuous and being fully
aware that they are answerable for their deeds.

"They believe in Allah and the Last Day, and enjoin
right conduct and forbid indecency, and vie one
with another in good works. They are of the
righteous" (Aale Imran: 114)

To have righteous people is not the birthright of any one
nation. They are a requirement and therefore the capital of the
entire humanity and the universe. If they confine their services to
any particular small group, area or if the humanity is not able to
extract the benefit of their services, it would be humanity's loss.
Islam does not specify any geographical or racial bounds for them,
but has made the entire humanity and universe the beneficiary of
their capabilities. The Qur'an states,

"And verily we have written in the scripture, after
the reminder: My righteous will inherit the earth"

(Al-Anbiya: 105)

This is the real spirit of the teachings of Islam on governance
and statehood. After understanding this, the reasons for the
successful warlike steps of the Prophet's companions can be easily

understood. The steps that led them to victory over Persia and Rome, that led to the break-up of the magic and charm attached to each throne.

After accomplishing internal reforms, when the Muslims set their sights outwards, they saw all neighboring countries under the rule of cruel and oppressive despots. The weak, the slaves of the powerful, the poor made the property of the rich and the man declared himself God over other men. Law and justice had lost their meaning on the whims and fancies of the sovereigns and rulers. People's rights were usurped, women dishonored, homes destroyed and the destiny of nations sealed, the hard-earned money of the subjects blown on the satisfaction of the immoral desires of the ruling class. The rulers themselves were symbols of immorality. Therefore the subjects were in all kinds of problems; drinking, having illicit relations with women, and gambling were condoned by law; bribery and untrustworthiness rampant; egoism boundless and the ethical condition of the society in such a state of depravity that behind the curtains of grandeur and glamour of civilization, the condition of humanity would put even animals to shame. [2]

For details of the prevailing conditions mentioned above, it is important to be unbiasedly conversant with these; instead of the books on Islamic History, those written by Western writers are

---

[2] Persia, Egypt, Rome etc. were all at the time in the condition of political, ethical, moral and religious bankruptcy. History is replete with discussions of these. In sexual depravity, man had lost the capacity to distinguish his own daughters and sisters; even religious leaders were not above indulgence in immorality. In Persia, the 'Mazdaki' religion had destroyed all social order of the society. In Rome, the egotism of the chieftains and rulers had taken that nation down the pit of degradation. In Egypt, and North Africa, long drawn slavery of Rome had completely destroyed their value systems and they were transformed into a wholly unethical and immoral congregation. Even in areas adjacent to Arabia, Iraq and Syria, the effects of the empires had their morality and ethics influenced, to the worst extent.

For details of the prevailing conditions-and it is important to be unbiasedly conversant with these; instead of the books on Islamic History, those written by Western writers are recommended. Among these Sir John Milton and Edward Gibbon, both historians of repute, are worthy of special mention. The book, 'History of European Morals' is chiefly recommended, to get a glimpse of the ethical and moral conditions of Rome at the time).

recommended. Among these, Sir John Milton and Edward Gibbon, both historians of repute, are worthy of special mention. The book, 'History of European Morals' is chiefly recommended, to get a glimpse of the ethical and moral conditions of Rome at the time.

Under those conditions, a dedicated and fully devoted band of the pious and virtuous, took it upon itself, the mission of reform of humanity. At first, they adopted the means of preaching through sermons, lectures and invited all to follow the way of righteousness and justice, to give up the evil ways and accept Islam. The invitation was also given to the rulers of Persia, Egypt, and Rome. When they rejected it outrightly, it was demanded that they vacate the thrones, in favor of the more deserving. However, when they even rejected this and the sword was preferred as an answer. Only then did the Muslims enter into war and then, a handful of Muslims took on the mights of the two superpowers of the time, the Persian and Roman empires, both at the same time and overthrew them. From the borders of India to Africa, the oppressed were thus freed of the yoke of oppression. One definitely has all rights to call it, the process of empire building or cruelty, but one cannot deny the fact of history that Islam raised these people from the pit of depravity and placed them close to the zenith of ethical, moral, and even material achievement. Those countries that had become quite barren of culture and civilization, were given such a boost that some of the vitality, the fragrance can be felt even today.

The religion of nationalism may yet pass the verdict, that even if Persia and Rome had perished; Arabs had no right to attack them. However, the religion of truth speaks out, that the Arabs did a great service to humanity. It is unfortunate for the world that a large part of it remained deprived of this service to humanity, by a class that has no peer in matters of piety, uprightness, and steadfastness.

Chapter Four

Sword and the Spread of Islam

Conversion of non-Muslims to Islam is not among the objectives of war as defined by Qur'an, 'hadith' of the Prophet (SAW) and various other authentic books on Islam. In fact, none of them state that the sword may be used to force people even to accept the thought that Islam is the only true religion. However, the amount of misinterpretations and wrong impressions created by some writers, who are not fully conversant with the correct Islamic teachings pollute their patrons to believe in false information. It compels us to clarify the concept.

The verses that explain the orders of war, while describing its objectives, have clearly drawn the boundaries, beyond which war may not be extended. These bounds have been highlighted in numerous verses of the Holy Qur'an. The Holy Qur'an states,

> "And fight them until persecution is no more, and religion is for Allah" (Al Baqarah: 193)

Here the limit prescribed is the end of strife. When this aim is achieved and there is no hindrance in the path of those who follow the path of righteousness, the necessity of war ends. Therefore, later in the verse, it is stated,

> "But if they desist, then let there be no hostility except against wrongdoers" (Al Baqarah: 193)

Later the conditions in which life remains sacred and where it is forfeit are described very emphatically,

> "Whosoever killeth a human being for other than manslaughter or corruption in the earth, it shall be as if he had killed all mankind" (Al Maidah: 32)

We find from the above that only two conditions warrant depriving a man of his life: either that he has taken another's life unjustifiably or that he has been involved in spreading strife and

turmoil on earth. Taking of life for any reason other than the two
mentioned, has been declared such a major sin that it has been
equated to the murder of the entire humanity. In Surah Al-Taubah,
where the paying of 'jaziya' has been specified as the limits of
war, it states:

> "Fight against such of those who have been given
> the scripture as believe not in Allah or the Last Day,
> and forbid not that which Allah hath forbidden by
> his messenger, and follow not the religion of truth,
> until they pay the tribute (jaziya) readily"
>
> (Al Taubah: 29).

This means that if such people agree to pay 'jaziya' and to the
imposition of Islamic law in the land, war cannot be waged on
them. The Qur'an explains that there is no room for war against
those who do not treat others with cruelty, and are not unduly
arrogant,

> "There is no punishment for those who avenge
> cruelty done unto them. Punishment is for only
> those who are cruel unto others and are unduly
> arrogant in the earth. Lo! There is painful
> punishment for such as these" (Shura: 41-42).

Surah Al-Mumtahanah states that Muslims have enmity only
with those non-Muslims, who are enemies of Islam and its
followers. Apart from these, nothing forbids dealing with others
with graciousness, justice, and piety:

> "Allah forbideth you not those who warred not
> against you on account of religion and drove you
> not from your homes, that ye should show them
> kindness and deal justly with them. Lo! Allah
> loveth the just dealers. Allah forbideth you only
> those who warred against you and driven you out
> from your homes and help drive you out, that ye
> make friends of them-- (All) such are wrong-doers"
>
> (Al-Mumtahanah: 8-9).

It is clear from the foregoing that the sole aim of war is
curtailing cruelty, arrogance, and strife. Conversion of people to
the Islamic faith by dint of war is nowhere mentioned or implied.
In fact, those who are not cruel, who are not completely immoral,

who do not suppress or attempt to destroy Islam, who do not seek to destroy the peace and security of the Lord's creations, war is a prohibition against such people and their blood is sacrosanct to the Muslims. No matter whether their religion is based on falsehood, their lives and property is safe from the sword of Islam, but for those who spread strife and turmoil in the world and are bent on destroying Islam and its followers, the sword is ready and their necks are not safe from it.

No Coercion in Religion

The above subheading, a quote from the Holy Qur'an, is in itself sufficient to explain the bounds of war. But the Holy Book has in unmistakable terms teaches that for invitation to Islam, the use of the sword is absolutely not permissible,

> "There is no coercion in religion and he who
> rejecteth false deities and believeth in Allah hath
> grasped a handhold, which will never break. Allah
> is hearer knower" (Al Baqarah: 256).

The wordings of the verse are unambiguous and distinct, but if we study the circumstances in which the verse was revealed, it would further add to its lucidity. In the days before Islam it was a custom among the people of Madinah (Yathrib), that if the children of a woman did not survive after birth, she would take an oath that the first of her children to survive, would be brought up as a Jew. As a result, many of those among the people of Madinah, who accepted Islam, had children who were Jews. In the year 6 A.H., when due to their activities Jews were banished from the city, many mothers who did not want to send their children away pleaded with the Prophet that they would compel their children to become Muslims. The Prophet (SAW) did not allow this, staying, "There is no coercion in religion".

Abu Daud, Nisai, Ibn Abi Hatim, all noted traditionalists, and scholars have reported the incident with minor difference in wordings. Saeed bin Jubair, Mujahid and Hasan Basri are unanimous in stating that this was the incident, for clarification of which the verse was revealed. Ibn Abbas was quoted by Ibn Ishaq, as saying that, 'among the Muslims of Madinah; there was one who has two sons who were Christians'. They were adamant that they would not give up their religion and accept Islam. Their

Muslim father inquired of the Prophet (SAW) whether he could compel them to accept Islam. According to this tradition, this was the occasion when the verse was revealed.

Although the traditions as to the circumstances of the revelation of the verse differ, the gist is similar, i.e., "There is no coercion in faith". Allama Ibn Kathir, a scholar of note writes in his commentary, that the circumstances in which this verse was revealed clearly depicts the Islamic teaching. "Do not force anyone to enter the folds of Islam, since, as it is, the teachings of the faith are so clear that there is no necessity to force any one into joining it. If God has in his wisdom, given a person guidance and has opened his chest for the acceptance of truth, one who has been bestowed with understanding, will accept it on the strength of its clear reasoning. However, if one whose sight and hearing have been sealed, coercing him into accepting it is useless".

Another well-reputed Qur'anic scholar Zamakshari, in his commentary 'Kashaaf', has also expressed similar thoughts on the verse. He states, 'In the matter of faith, Allah has kept aside coercion and use of force and left it to the understanding and freewill'. The same is elucidated by the words, "If your God wished, the population of the entire world would have accepted the faith. Will you then force people to accept it"? If God had so wished that people should be coerced into accepting Islam, He would have Himself made them accept it. However, he refrained from doing it and left it to the freewill of the people.

Imam Razi in his commentary on the Qur'an, while commenting on this verse, writes an extract from Abu Muslim Isphahani and Faqqal: 'This means that Allah has not kept the religion on the bases of force and coercion, but has left it on freewill. When the reasoning of oneness of Allah has been explained, with such lucidity and so emphatically, there is no reason or excuse for non-believers to insist on maintaining their beliefs. If they do not accept the faith even now, they can only be coerced into it. However, in a world of trials and tribulations, like our own, it is prohibited, since use of force and coercion, renders trials and tribulations meaningless. This is clarified when Allah says, "Now whosoever wishes may accept the religion and whosoever wishes to remain a non-believer, may do so," and at a different place states, "If your God so wished, all people in the world would have accepted the faith. Then do you wish to force becoming pious Muslims". In the Surah, 'Al-Shuara' He states, "You may die of sadness that they do not accept the true faith. If we so desired, We would have sent from heaven such an omen that they would have bowed to it. But we do not want that."

Imam Razi also writes in favor of the above, "This belief is further strengthened by the fact that immediately after the verse Allah states, 'Guidance has been shown to be superior to waywardness'. It means that clear reasoning has been put forward and reasoning has been lucid and emphatic now only the way of force and coercion is left and that is not permitted, since it is against the dictates of responsibility and faith."

Much has been said about the verse. Some say that this verse has been abrogated, others say that the verse is only relevant to the 'people of the book', some say that it is in favor of the Muslims of Madigan. Some have even gone so far as to suggest about the words of the Lord that in the matters of faith, no coercion is coercion, meaning thereby, that if anyone accepts Islam, even at the point of the sword, one should not say he was forced to.

Such beliefs and words are confined to books only. In 1400 years of practical life, force has almost never had to be relied on except maybe in a couple of cases, which may be termed as exceptions not the rule. If any of this were true, the Muslims would have at least on some occasion converted people by dint of force. However, this has never taken place, even during the time when Islam was in its full glory during the pious caliphate, nor did the Prophet (SAW) indulge in it. He held the non-believers several times in his power and large groups came under his control, but not once did he force anyone to accept Islam. He only attempted to cleanse their hearts with his teachings and example. In fact, Muslims were emphatically told not to deal harshly with people.

When Maaz bin Jabal (RA) and Abu Musa Ashari (RA), two of the prominent companions of Prophet (SAW) were sent to Yemen, they were specifically instructed not to act with harshness and to cultivate happiness and goodwill, rather than enmity.

When the Prophet (SAW) entered Makkah as a victor, he left free, the non-believers who were his sworn enemies and did not force anyone to accept Islam. Later in the Battle of Hunain, 20,000 of these non-believers fought alongside the Muslims, on their own freewill.

Some groups were sent to the outskirts of Makkah to invite people to Islam. They were instructed strictly not to enter into any fight. Allama Ibn Jarir states: in the tribe of Jazimah, when Khalid bin Walid (RA) reacted aggressively, killing people, the Prophet (SAW) publicly censured him and 'even dogs of the tribe received compensation for this act'. Nevertheless, these are isolated examples, apart from which, there is not a single example where people were made to accept Islam under duress.

According to a hadith related by Imam Ahmed on the authority of Anas (RA), a companion of the Prophet (SAW), reports that the Prophet (SAW) invited one person to accept Islam. The man replied that he felt a hesitation in doing so. The Prophet (SAW) asked him to accept anyway and that Allah will grant him sincerity too. It is surprising, that how this hadith can be used in support of the opinion for the abrogation of the verse "there is no coercion in Islam," the hadith does not contain the word mukrahan rather it has karihan, which is taken as, not fully convinced. How does it prove that the Prophet (SAW) forced the person to accept Islam?

Those who hold the opinion that the verse "there is no compulsion in religion" was abrogated, have no other argument except that it was abrogated by the verse containing commandments for war. Otherwise, there is no tradition or quoted Qur'anic verse that gives the opinion any validity, therefore, we do not need to indulge in the debate, about the type and quality of arguments required to argue that what are the requirement to consider any Qur'anic verse abrogated. It may be mentioned that the objections to the verse are an invention of the post prophethood era. Even the learned and well-instructed companions of the Prophet (SAW) were quite unaware of this annulment. If the companions had been aware of this objection or controversy, the learned and conscientious followers of Islamic jurisprudence would not have made the acceptance of Islam a matter of option or choice.

Ibn Abi Hatim states a tradition in which the Uzbek slave of Umar (RA) states: 'I was the Christian slave of Umar Ibn Khattab. He used to invite me to Islam, but I used to refuse. Thereupon he would state the Qur'anic verse, "There is no compulsion in religion," and he would add that if I had been a Muslim, he would have used my services for the Islamic cause'. There are some minor differences among the Islamic scholars, regarding the tradition, but all draw the same conclusion from it about the validity of the verse, i.e. it is a valid verse. The statement if Imam Ibn Jareer Tabari is bit different from Imam Razi and Ibn Kathie in this regard. After analyzing all relevant traditions and statements of the early generation, he declares about the abrogation of the particular Qur'anic verse as follows:

> "it shows that the meaning of 'no compulsion in religion' is that from whom the jaziya can be collected, after he agrees to pay it and to stay under the rule of Islamic State, such person will be forced to change his believe to Islam. Thus if anyone says that the verse was revoked or superseded by the verse permitting war, his assertion is meaningless. If someone raises the question that, what about the tradition related by Ibn Abbas (RA) that this verse was revealed for the Madinite Muslims (Al Ansar) who wanted to force their children to convert to Islam? We will say to them, that the tradition is worthy of consideration and has we agree with its authenticity, definitely, this verse was revealed to guide the Muslims in a special circumstance, but its application in generalized to other such situations commandment is validated by other verses, similar in matter to circumstances of their revelation. According to Ibn Abbas, the people for whom the verse was revealed, had already accepted the Jewish faith, therefore Allah forbade forcing them to change their religion. But the words indicate that the forbiddance is valid for all faiths, from whose followers 'jaziya' is permitted."

Those who assert that the verse is pertinent only to the 'people of the scripture' also do not quote any hadith or verse of the Qur'an to back their assertion. Every commandment in the Qur'an was revealed to clarify the action to be taken in a particular set of circumstances. However, its pertinence is not confined to that particular situation only, but is generally applicable. So is the case with this verse. If we restrict its application to the particular situation in which it was revealed and take its text to be relevant to one particular incident, we then have to treat all other commandments of Qur'an in similar fashion.

The argument that the verse on 'jaziya' has made limited the applicability of the verse "there is no compulsion in religion." Consider that the scholars and mujtahideen are unanimous in declaring that 'jaziya' is applicable to all non-believers, despite its particularization for 'The people of scripture'. Although, the majority of scholars of Hanafi fiqh regard the ayah of jaziya is not applicable to the idol worshippers of Arabia (whose existence had vanished even before the revelation of the ayah of jaziya). However, Imam Malik, Abu Yousuf, Imam Auzai and others have even included the idol worshippers of Arabia in the fold of the mercy of this ayah. Therefore, from the beginning to the present day, the way of the Muslims has been that they have accepted all non-believers in the protection of the Islamic state, who agreed to pay 'jaziya. Then if the verse on jaziya is of general applicability, it cannot be a basis of another verse being of pertinence to a particular circumstance. Specially, since the wordings of the verse itself do not suggest anything but its general applicability.

The True Concept of Invitation to Islam

The fact is that the verse that contains commandment for war is not affected in the least by the verse, "there is no compulsion in religion," as has been wrongly understood by some. Initially the verse was unconditionally applicable to all and later it was restricted by some conditions. In the beginning, the strength of Muslims was not such that they were in a position to fully accomplish the task that Allah intended for them. They therefore just content themselves with inviting people to Islam and then leaving them to their beliefs and their actions. At that time, the modus operandi of both "Establishing virtue" and "Forbidding evil" was the same. That is to say, like the Prophet (SAW) and his companions restricted themselves to inviting people to believe in oneness of Allah, prophethood of Muhammad (SAW), belief in the Day of Resurrection and to inviting people for prayers. Similarly, they would restrict themselves to condemning and preaching against illicit sex, theft, killing one's own children, arrogance and hindering people following the path of Allah. However, this was done through the word of mouth only.

When Muslims gained sufficient strength and ability to ensure progress of their mission, they remained committed to the principle of freedom of religion and of not coercing people to accept Islam. In addition, it was decided that wherever it was possible, they would stop people from spreading strife, turmoil, and committing sinful and unethical deeds. At the same time, the ways of 'establishing virtue' and 'prohibiting evil' were separated. The scope of activity of 'establishment of virtue' remained limited by the concept; "There is no compulsion in religion".

It has been discussed earlier that Islam has a duality of functions. In the first case, it is a law of the Lord for the world. In the second, it is an invitation to lead a life of piety, goodness and of success in this world and the next. In the first case, the objectives are the establishment of peace in the world, to prevent the destruction of humanity at the hands of the cruel and the arrogant and to ensure that human beings remain within the bounds of humanity and ethics. For the fulfilling of these objectives, the use of force is a necessity. In the second case, the objectives are a little different. Here it seeks to cleanse the heart and control desires, cleanse the spirit and cleanse the person of the carnality-thus making him distinguishable from the beast. For the achievement of these objectives, not the sword but the light of guidance is the requirement; not the binding of hands and feet but the voluntary submission of the spirit is the requirement. If at the point of the sword, one accepts Islam but at heart, one remains idolatrous, His acceptance of Islam is quite meaningless. Islam obviously requires sincerity and total commitment, not hypocrisy, but this is a matter of religion, a matter of establishment of truth and piety. Even in material life, no movement can be successful on account of hypocrites. Expecting success while carrying the burden of such insincere people, is obviously expecting for impossible. Islam does not seek success in its worldly mission only. Its main objective is achieving success in the hereafter. It considers only that action correct, which is based on true belief and that action worthless, which is not based on sincerity and truth.

Islam came into being for the reform of the entire humanity and achieved supreme success in its mission, the success that was not the lot of any other movement. Such success could not have been achieved by dint of the sword alone, since it is not possible that such a signal success could be the lot of those who were not totally sincere or totally committed, but had accepted Islam under duress or were coerced into it. It could not have been achieved by followers in whose heart, instead of the fear of Allah dwelt the fear of the sword and it definitely could not have been the lot of the cowardly and fragile followers, whose hearts are un-encumbered with sincerity and truth and who had accepted the faith only to save their necks.

None can understand the psychological makeup of man better than Allah Himself. He has therefore sought to make man understand the import of the subject in the best possible way, throughout the Qur'an,

> "The good deed and the evil deed are not alike. Repel the evil deed with one, which is better, then lo! He, between whom and thee there was enmity (will become) as though he was a bosom friend"
>
> (Ha Mim Sajdah: 34)

At another place Allah says,

> "It was by the mercy of Allah that thou wast lenient with them, (O Muhammad), for if thou had been stern and fierce of heart, they would have dispersed from round about thee" (Al Imran: 159).

At another place, He explains the way to invite people to Islam,

> "Call unto thy lord with wisdom and fair exhortation, and reason with them in the better way" (Al-Nahal: 125)

The stress on being considerate and soft is such that Muslims have been instructed not to speak ill of even the Gods of the idolaters,

> "Revile not those unto whom they pray besides Allah lest they wrongfully revile Allah through ignorance" (Al-Anam: 108)

The Secret of Guidance and Transgression

The point has been exquisitely explained in the Qur'an several times that if Allah intended, He could have arranged it so that man could not refuse accepting the true faith. He did not need such a faith, which was included in the nature and psyche of a person. Such a creation He already had (in the form of angels). What He intended, was a creation with freewill, who out of their own volition would accept His sovereignty; whose obedience would be of their own freewill and who, while possessing the capability for transgression, would choose to be obedient to Him.

To fulfill this purpose, He created man. Then, for a period, in the light of His own wisdom, left them free, giving them the choice of either accepting faith in Allah or otherwise. Allah sent to man, guidance through his own kind, periodically, that he may be guided to the right path, that he may be shown the merits of following the true path, that he may be free of the malaise of ignorance. Then He made man aware of the Day of Judgment, when blessings would be showered on those who chose the true path of their own accord not on any compulsion and considered obedience to their Lord as their duty. Those who went astray, followed the path of unrighteousness, refused to accept Allah's message, and continued their disobedience to Him despite clear signs of warning in the following ayahs:

> "And if thy lord had willed, he verily would have made mankind one nation, yet they cease not differing. Save him on whom thy lord hath mercy; and for that He did create them. And the word of thy Lord had been fulfilled: verily I shall fill hell with the Jin and mankind together" (Hud: 118-119)

> "And if thy Lord willed all who are in the earth would have believed together" (Yunus: 99)

> "Had Allah willed, they had not been idolatrous"
> (Al-Anaam: 108)

> "It is not for every soul to believe save by the permission of Allah. He hath set uncleanness upon those who have no sense" (Yunus: 100)

"Lo! Thou (O Muhammad) guidest not those whom thou lovest, but Allah guideth whom He will. And He is best aware of those who walk right"

(Al-Qasas: 56)

Thus when Allah Almighty, the Maker Himself wants the subservience of man, of his (man's) freewill and not under duress, then obviously man has no right to compel others to offer to the Lord the insipid offering of faith. For this reason, the Prophet (SAW) was often advised not to use force in matters of faith, but to keep on guiding those who are inclined to accept guidance and that his task was just to convey the commandments of the Lord to man.

"We are best aware of what they say and thou (O Mohammad) art in no wise a compeller over them. But warn by the Qur'an him who feareth my threat"

(Al-Qaaf: 4)

"Remind them, for thou art but a remembrance, thou art not at all a warder over them"

(Al-Ghashia: 21-22)

"Wouldst thou (Muhammad) compel men until they're believers" (Yunus: 99)

"The guiding of them is not thy duty (O Muhammad), but Allah guideth whom He will"

(Al- Baqarah: 272)

Role of the Sword in the Spread of Islam

The fact is that Islam does not want its acknowledgement through coercion, but prefers that man should be guided through reasoning and example, in order that the difference between transgression and guidance should become clearly apparent to all. After man has been made aware of both ways, Allah gives each of them the freewill either to accept the right guidance and achieve the true and eternal well-being or to continue his waywardness until he reaches the pit of doom. However, let it not be understood from the foregoing that Islam is completely pacifist in nature and has no concern with the use of the sword (force), for that is not true.

In the preaching and teaching of Islam, definitely, the use of the sword is out of question. However, apart from preaching, there are some other actions needed for the spread of Islam, which require the support of the sword. It is in the nature of man, that once he starts leading a life free of restrictions and ethical bounds, he gradually starts becoming used to it and starts finding pleasure in this cruel, but apparently pleasurable way of life, and soon becomes so addicted to it, that it becomes impossible to give it up. Sermons, advices and reasoning, no matter how convincing they are, have no effect on him. He is unable to discern between the evil and the pious or between the permissible and the prohibited. Nothing convinces him to change his lifestyle.

The continuous indulgence in his satanic pleasures deprives him of the capacity to listen to good advice. Even if a spark of conscience is perchance present, it is not strong enough to overcome the prodding of his evil nature. As against this, if such advice is backed by the injunctions of law and the situation is intelligently handled, which, while showing man the ill effects of his conduct, possess the capability to incapacitate his further indulgence in it. It is very possible that the effect, that advice and reasoning alone could not achieve, will gradually start making its way into his psyche. That person would gradually learn to distinguish between evil and virtue and accept the bounds of ethics, which he was not ready to do earlier.

Let us envision a society where there is no law in force. Every individual is free of bounds, where he can acquire anything that he desires, if not legally, by stealing, looting, or snatching it. There are no restrictions on him as to the means of fulfilling his desires, where he can settle his enmities by eliminating the enemy, if he can, where he is quite unaware about the permitted and the prohibited. His concepts are unencumbered by the perceptions of rights and duties and his only preoccupation is with his own desires and possible means of fulfilling them.

In these conditions an ethical problem arises, it is necessary that someone educate the society as to the right and wrong of things. He tries to teach the difference between the permitted and prohibited and determines their bounds, to show the society the difference between the aims of righteousness and evil. He tries to dissuade people from theft, unlawfully acquiring wealth, unwarranted bloodshed, illicit sex, and disgraceful exhibitionism; tries to establish the rights and duties of individuals and tries to establish a complete code of ethics in the society. However, if he does not have the potent to back his reforms and the only means available to him are arguments, reasoning and sermonizing, one cannot imagine that the reforms, no matter how attractive they may be, will have any chance to take off from the ground. For the corrupt society of its own volition will not accept the restrictions and bounds sought to be imposed. Neither will the society, impressed by the logic of the arguments, accept willingly, the subservience to law nor will it be so moved by the sermons that it would voluntarily deny itself the pleasures of evil living.

Anyone with the crudest knowledge of human nature will agree that such a reformer will always remain a non-achiever. Such individuals are numbered, who accept goodness for goodness' sake, or who would give up evil, because they have become aware of its nature.

However, if in case the person seeking reforms in the society is not merely a sermonizing theoretician and just a 'nice guy' in general. However, he is in fact the sovereign, who has the capacity to form a government, with the potent to remove all evil from the society then all will have to agree that it is definitely possible to transform that corrupt society into one that is revered and respected by all.

The spread of Islam bears a striking resemblance to the fore going proposition. If Islam had been just a collection of a few principles, if it had consisted of just the acceptance of the singularity of Allah, accepting the prophethood, belief in angels and the day of judgment, and apart from these, it did not demand anything from man, it is possible, that the satanic powers would not have found much to be in conflict with it.

The fact of the matter is that Islam is not only a set of beliefs, but it is also a law, such a law that in fact seeks enforcement of its bounds on practical life and constant of policing them. Therefore, its accomplishments do not depend on sermons, alone. The tip of the tongue has to be complemented by the tip of the sword. The arrogant retractors are not so much against Islamic beliefs as they are against compulsory obedience to its laws. They seek condoning theft, but Islam threatens them with chopping off of their hands. These want illicit sex permitted, but Islam threatens them with lashing. They want usury condoned, but Islam informs them that this is like challenging Allah and the Prophet (SAW). They desire freedom from the bounds of the permitted and prohibited, in order to indulge themselves in the pursuits of their egotism, but Islam does not allow such pursuits out of the bounds of the permitted. Hence, the egocentric finds it undesirable and abhorrent and this abhorrence and the constant indulgence in sin is like rust that forms around the psyche of the individual, shielding the ray of guidance from reaching his inner self.

This obduracy was the very reason that, for thirteen years, the Prophet (SAW), preached Islam to the Arabs, adopted the best possible methods for delivering his sermons, put forward clear arguments and reasoning and tried with excellent logic and address to convince them, showed them the miracles of Allah, showed them with his personal example how to lead a pure and honest life, and in fact, made all efforts to make them see the light. However, despite clear proof and demonstration of righteousness, was unable to convince them to accept the righteous way.

The Arabs had seen the worst of evil ways, had seen their ill effects, righteousness had been well demonstrated to them; they were convinced that the right way was the way of guidance. In spite of this, they persisted in their ways. Their disinclination to follow the right path was for the reason of their disinclination to leave the cherished evil ways of the period of the nonrestrictive idolatry. After failing to raise the Arabs above their level of depravity through sermons and reasoning, the Prophet (SAW) raised the sword and declared, 'Every distinction by virtue of birth, every demand for blood, (for which revenge is sought between families and tribes), all demands for wealth (which are on idolatrous basis), are under these feet (That is they are not allowed to raise their heads now).

All ascendancy based on birthright was ended, all the accepted qualifications passed down from the period of idolatry, for respect of overlordship were suspended, and a principled government was set up in their place in the land. Ethical laws were enforced, and lawlessness and vice, the desire for which was making them senseless, were terminated. Tranquility and peace, the essentials for the ethical, material, and spiritual well-being of man, took their places. Gradually, then, the inclination for evil and mischief started being removed and their nature started the process of rejecting the poison that had for so long kept them from leading virtuous lives. Their eyes, now unveiled, could clearly see the path of righteousness; they could bow their heads in acceptance of the supreme guidance they had so far avoided.

Like the Arabs, the other nations that accepted Islam, in succession, followed the same route. The veil of evil had to be struck down with the point of the sword to make the atmosphere conducive for the acceptance of the knowledge of ethical conduct. Under these circumstances, within a century, a quarter of the entire world had accepted Islam.

Those governments or kingships that were backing evil, were dismissed and the evil that was blocking the way of righteousness was eliminated and in its place was established the code of law that salvaged man's humanity and proved to the world, that for the betterment of man, there was no better way.

In short, it is incorrect to say that Islam used the point of the sword to convert people to the religion. It will also be incorrect to say that the sword had no role in the spread of Islam. The theoretical teaching, the sermons, and the invitation can be equated to the sowing of the seed, while the role of the sword, to the softening of the earth, in which the seed may find it easy to germinate. As the sowing of the seed is an important function in producing a good harvest, so is softening the earth. Both play an equally important part. The case of producing a harvest of righteous and God-fearing human beings is similar in nature. All, who claim knowledge of human nature, must be aware that in the process of spreading righteousness, at times before the mind and the spirit can be addressed, it becomes necessary to address the physical being and the body of a person.

Chapter Five

Islamic Laws of War and Peace

So far, we have studied the effect of Islam on the ethical aspect of war. Let us now examine the effect that Islam had on the practical aspects of warfare.

The virtuosity of an act can be based on two of its aspects. These are its objectives and the methodology of achieving them. If the objectives are good and based on virtue but the methods employed in achieving them are below the level of humanity and piety, the objectives cannot remain unaffected and suffer some loss in their virtuosity. For example, if the aim of a person is to look after the orphans and widows, but in order to generate resources to accomplish this noble task, he steals and commits robberies; he will be as guilty in the eyes of the law as a genuine thief or robber. On the other hand, if the aim of a person is to swindle and con others, in order to first impresses others with his piety. For example if he is often found in the mosque, giving Qur'anic lessons and sermonizing, these very noble acts of his, become soiled by the evil of his aims. In fact, the evil committed is much graver since he has exploited religion to take advantage of others.

War too, can be an undertaking of great virtue or of evil, depending on the objectives and the modus operandi. The aim of a war could be to deprive weaker nations of their independence, looting their wealth and depriving the creatures of Allah of their rights. In such case, regardless if the war is fought in the most disciplined way, no matter if the rights of the non-participants have been given due respect. For example, if the wounded cared for and the casualties treated with honor, no matter that the conventions of war have been adhered to, it will be in any event, a war of aggression and the constraints, adherence and discipline involved will not change its quality. The only difference could be that the perpetrators are guilty of lesser oppression, but guilty they will be.

However, if the objectives of war are noble, for example, the protection of the rights of a people or the termination of strife and mischief, but in the conducting of war, ethics have not been given regard, cruelty is its way, its sole aim is to destroy the enemy or make it suffer grievously and vengeance is the prime emotion involved, then even wars for such noble causes bring themselves to the level of savagery. For war to be termed righteous, in fact, it is necessary that both its objectives and modus operandi should be noble and pure. So far, our discussion has been just to prove the purity and nobility of the objectives. Let us now examine whether Islamic wars, in their execution, have achieved the same ethical excellence.

Now, before going in to the details of Islamic warfare, it seems appropriate, that we see what war was like before Islam, among the old pre-Islamic nations. In this way, we can better appreciate the reforms that Islam brought in the conduct of warfare.

The Pre-Islamic, Arab Methods of Warfare

In Arabia of old, warfare had assumed the status of a national occupation. Limited means of livelihood, scarce resources, coupled with lack of forbearance and discipline could be counted among the reasons for their aggressiveness. Aggression had become so much a part of their character, that murder, bloodshed and looting could be said to have become their attributes. In fact, they were quite proud of these qualities.

In all probability, the cause of such aggressiveness was for the procurement of scarce food and scarcer water, or for procuring grazing rights for their domestic animals; occasionally, vengeance could also have been the cause. Whatever the cause may be, the centuries-old lifestyle had developed in them a taste for such vicious living that bloodshed did not need a cause; it was rather a cause in itself. Along with their cruelty, vengeance, and blind allegiance to family, beastliness and savagery had all become a part of their personality.

Tribal and inter-family rivalries were generations old. In order to quench their fires of revenge, utmost cruelty and all available means were resorted to dishonor the enemy. At other times, just to establish ones bravery and be able to boast of it, bloodshed was resorted to.

The Arabic Concept of War

We have only two sources that educate us on the conditions of the Arabs of old. One is the set of stories by the name, 'Ayyam ul Arab' (Days of the Arab); these were common and told and retold stories among the Arabs. They are a valuable source of information, as their contents vividly describe the ways and events of the time with some accuracy. The other source is the works of poets of the time. These too, depict with some accuracy, the economics, cultural life, affairs, and activities of the society. Arab poetry, unlike its Non-Arab especially Persian counterpart, was not much concerned with emotional delicacies, romance, and romantic misrepresentation. It was just a frank portrayal of events, the scenario, and naked emotions of the time. Hence, Arab poetry, apart from being just that, was also an almost correct diary of events and an accurate picture of national character. We are able to determine from these poets what the Arabs thought of war, their concept of war, their ways of fighting, their behavior towards the enemy, the causes that led to war, and the aims and objectives of their wars.

The poets used analogies, parallels, and similarities to express their thoughts on war to good effect. Some examples of their parallelism and analogies are shown below.

Harb: This in common usage means war, but it can also be used to denote the state of anger.

Tehreeb: Generally means making someone angry, but can also mean sharpening the spearhead.

Harab: means looting someone.

Hareeba: Loot, on which depends a man's livelihood.

Mahroob and Hareeb: A person who has been plundered

Ahrab: Guiding someone for the purpose of plundering one's enemy.

Roo: generally means a fight but can also be used to depict fear. In fact, war has been shown here as analogous of fear.

> "These are those who go forward in steps with the danger of war" (al-roo is used in this verse for war).

Wagah: This also in general usage means war, but its dictionary meanings are noise and disorder. The poet states:

"Known of Banu Marra (a tribe) often with enemy
blood, the thirst of spears they quench, but once at
least in war (wagah) surely their spears they drench'

Shar: It really means, impiousness, but has been used to denote war as well.

"When war (Shar) comes to put them in fear, they
come in groups or singly to meet it when it is near"

Karibah: It is also used to depict war, but its real meaning is hardship and trouble. The poet says:

"They are unflinching in (Karibah) battle; none can
reach them lest he dares to hear the sabers rattle"

Hiyaj: It really means, eye-catching anger, but can also be used to depict war, "going to war (Hiyaj) with ease depends on what you gather in peace."

Mughazaba: This also means eye-catching anger, but can also depict getting ready for war.

"If Zaid for war (Mughazaba) Bani Zabal doth call,
We fight for Bani Zara that is discretion best of all"

War has been equated to the fight of the rams, to crushing of something under the chest of a camel, to deep involvement, to the grindstone and to fire. In fact, all these comparisons, equations, and parallelisms depict that in the eyes of the Arabs, war was a condition that contained the qualities of loot and plunder, noise and disorder, anger and crushing the enemy or burning him to ashes. Completely destroying him and heaping such hardships on him, that he would become silly with fear. In the old literature, the horrors of war and bravery of the participants are well depicted, but there is very little concern with the necessity, honor, and nobility of cause.

Effect of the Frequency of Armed Conflict on the Character of Arabs

War was considered one of the most honorable of pursuits and desirable of things by the Arabs in the time before Islam. They believed that the spirit of the person who died in bed escaped through his nose, while that of the person who died on the battlefield, escaped through his wounds. Death on the battlefield was much more preferable than death in bed. The poets speak with great pride that none of their chiefs died the death of the nose.

Responding to the call for war was, among the Arabs, of the status of following God's commandment and responding without hesitation was a solemn duty. The cause for the war was of no importance. Avoidance of war was cowardice and if restraint was a decision on a national level, its citizen felt ashamed to belong to such a nation. The poet writes proudly of this attitude:

> "Among the Bani Mazan, if for help a brother calls,
> without waiting to know reason or cause they jump
> into the affray one and all"

Another poet writes:

> "But my nation although of numbers strong, does
> not care for war big or small, right or wrong"

> "O! I wish I was to that nation born, that plundered
> on horses and camels borne"

The old Arab literature is full of such works, which depicts that the Arabs thought participation in wars a matter of great honor and in their eyes, causing bloodshed was something creditable.

Causes of War

Love of Booty

Among the factors of motivation for war, the main one was their love for booty. The Arabs considered wealth gathered through commerce or hard work as lowly and the only honorable wealth was that which had been looted. Tribes attacked each other often, that they might gather loot, and slaves, men and girls. One poet writes of this fixation:

> "If I live, to such battles I will go where booty
> aplenty is found or else die in battle as a brave man
> standing his ground"

Another poet in praise of his tribe writes:

"And when of Janab our horses plundered the town
but found no booty of renown,

Then not caring who lives or dies they fell upon the well
mounted of Ahab and Zabba tribes.

Not finding loot or plunder off another, we attack too, even
our brother."

When men went out to fight, their women took a solemn oath
from them that they would not return without great amounts of
booty. A poet narrates of a woman speaking to her departing man:
"and when in battle ye do find, soldiers decorated grand, swoop on
them sword in hand and bring for me slaves in strand."

At another place, the poet writes:

"When they returned, with loot and slaves, girls and
men, we returned home with; hands tied, kings of
men"

The poet describing the victory of Tarfa tribe in the war of
'Tahlaq Al-Lillum' writes:

"With shining swords baring their legs they strode,
and riders gathering droves of camels, away they
rode"

Zubair describing the victory over Aale Rabia writes:

"Of Taghleb we looted every maiden fair, who
sleep till late and their lips give tired brains a care"

The victory of Bani Shaban over the Bani Kalb is described by
a Shabani poet as:

"That night their unity fled and fleeing they kept
and their wealth and tall virgins we kept"

This love of booty enticed the booty seekers to join the tribal
horde going for war. The poet writes:

"For their assistance looters and thieves formed part
of the stock as though chasing prey, stalks a hawk"

Later he writes:

"On Bani Tamim we then sullied and in the

forbidden month their daughters we carried"

Looting and plundering were the prime motives of war for the Arabs. They considered that war a wastage in which they could not get enough war-booty. Akram bin Saifi, a well-loved and respected personality of his nation states that:

> "The best victory is that, which brings many slaves
> and the best booty is that which brings many goats
> and camels"

Pride

Apart from their love for war-booty, another emotion that could compel the Arabs to war was their obsession to establish their bravery, respectability, and supremacy; conceit was one of their major failings. They would accept all dangers and hardships to prove their superiority, strength, greatness, and respectability among their fellowmen.

It was a matter of pride for the powerful that no one else's camels could graze in his pastures, and the spring from which he drew water, would be sacrosanct for him and his alone. The place where he rested during a journey would be out of bounds for all others, the likes of the dress that he wore would not be worn by anyone else. That no one else would be considered his superior and no one else would be praised in his presence, that he could take anyone's life and not be answerable for it, and that no one would hesitate in serving him.

The poetry of Pre-Islamic Arabia is full of depictions of such conceit and egoism. One poet writes of the conceit of his tribe as:

> "All tribes of Moad, since their existence, are aware
> we stop whom we please and stay where we care
>
> Angered, we leave without fear and pleased, we
> take what we care
>
> To our servers, saviors we are and on arrogant war
> we declare
>
> For others it is grime and slime but springs we reach
> first, for us are as crystal clear"

A poet, Qais bin Saalba writes:

> "With scents we use, our hairs are white, our bowls always full for who we invite.
>
> For those we kill, not revenge is dared, just money for blood is their right."

Another poet writes of the pride of Bani Wabar:

> "Of such a nation I am, that if, of another tribe I killed a man unafraid of castigation I stand and not like sheep I scram"

Hajar bin Shalbi, a poet writes of his tribe with pride:

> "For all others our pastures are kept strictly out of bounds, but for us, our spears have opened those, that stalwarts of other tribes guard the grounds"

The poet Ajnas, stating the pride of his nation writes:

> "I see of their nations, for their camels they shorten the strand, but ours are free to roam and graze wherever they stand"

We learn from the collection of stories, 'Ayyam-e-Arab', that most of the conflicts that took place in Pre-Islamic Arabia were mainly the results of Arab conceit. The well-known inter-tribe conflict between Banu Bakar and Banu Taghlib known by the name of, 'Basus Jabani', which lasted for forty years, was started on a minor incident. It was a custom for long times that the animals of one tribe were not allowed to graze on the pastures of another. Nor was it permissible to use each other's hunting grounds or water springs.

> "On one occasion, the chief of the Banu Taghlib tribe, kaulab bin Rabin, spotted one camel belonging to a guest of Banu Bakr tribe, grazing with his camels. He shot an arrow that pierced the she camel's udder. When the owner saw his camel, he cried out, 'oh! What an insult'. This was enough to infuriate the Banu Bakar tribe. One of the tribe went and slew the Taghlib chief. The slain chief's brother stood up to avenge his brother's death and

consequently such a war ensued, that it all but completely destroyed both the tribes." (Ad Al-Fareed vol. 3, page 74-77 and Ibn Aseer vol. 1, page 384-397).

Another war, 'Harb Dahas', started only on account of a horse race, in which one horse was faster than the other. The chief of Bani Dabyan tribe, Qais bin Zubair, owned two horses renowned to be the fleetest in Arabia. The chief of Bani Badr tribe, Huzaifah bin Badr did not like that the horses of a fellow chief would gain such renown. Consequently, he challenged Qais to a horse race. A bet of a hundred camels was laid on the winner. During the race, as expected, Dahas was winning; one of the Bani Badr struck the face of Dahas, turning it away from the race. A quarrel ensued, in which Qais killed Huzaifah's son Madba. Thereupon Huzaifah killed Malik a brother of Qais. The conflict that broke out lasted for nearly half a century and did not end until the horses and camels of both tribes were nearly completely wiped out (Ibn Aseer, page 34-421).

"The conflict between Aus and Khazraj tribes that lasted for a century started for a very minor reason. A member of the Bani Saad tribe was living in the protection of the chief of Bani Khazrej. In a market place, he once declared that his sponsor, Malik Bin Ajlan, was the greatest and noblest of all. A person of the tribe of Aus could not bear this and killed the declarer. The conflict of Aus and Khazraj, that resulted, would have continued, until both tribes completely destroyed each other. Fortunately for them, the advent of Islam came to their rescue."
(Ibn Asher, vol. 1, page, 494-511).

In the fair of Okaz, a man of the Kanana tribe, by the name of Badr bin Masher, sat down with his leg spread before him and declared that he was the most respectable man in all of Arabia and challenged any man who claimed to be more respectable than him could strike his leg with his sword. A young man of Banu Dhaman took up the challenge and struck Badr's leg with his sword. This was enough to spark a conflict between the two tribes. The conflict originally known as 'Harb Fajaar', escalated to a full-scale war, which enveloped even the allies of both tribes. The last confrontation between the two, in the series of 'Harb Fajaar', was said to be the bloodiest ever in Arabia.

It so happened that in the 26th year before Prophethood, the king of Herah, Noman bin Manzar, decided to send a caravan to the Okaz market fair for the purpose of trade. When he inquired of the Arab chiefs as to who would guarantee his caravan safe passage, Baraz bin Quais, the chief of the Kanana tribe, declared that he would guarantee the caravan safety from the Katana. The chief of Hwazin, Arwatul Rehal declared that he would grant the caravan safety in all Arabia. Baraz took this as an insult and when the caravan was on its way, he waylaid it and killed the caravan chief. This resulted in one of the bloodiest of wars in Arabia. There were many fierce battles fought between the Banu Kanana and Banu Hwazin, in which the Quraish sided with Kanana and Banu Saqif tribe sided with the Hwazin.

Vengeance

Vengeance was another emotion for which the history of Arabia has been rendered bloody. The Arabs believed that if a man was murdered, his spirit escaped his body in the form of a bird. The mythical bird given the names of 'Hamah' and 'Sada' roamed desolate mountains and plains and cried out to be returned to the dead body, until his death was avenged. Some believed that until the dead person was revenged, his grave remained dark. Others believed that a murdered person who was avenged remained alive and the unavenged, lay in his grave, lifeless, until he was avenged.

Such beliefs, made the dead man's relatives, tribesmen and even those of the allied tribes, believe that it was their solemn duty to avenge those who had been killed, to satisfy their souls. If the killer was of a lower status than the one who was killed, it was necessary that someone of equal status from the killer's family or tribe be killed to complete the vengeance. The resulting bloodshed and their counteractions lasted for decades. Hesitation in avenging the dead or accepting blood money were considered shameful and cowardly and the respectability of the tribe, guilty of such conduct, lessened in the eyes of all the others.

The poets of the period of idolatry used the theme of vengeance quite often in their poetry. The theme was exploited to fan the flames of war, and often would proudly state that their tribe did not let the blood of any murdered person go waste. Salman bin Adiya writes:

> "None of our chiefs the death of the nose tasted, nor the blood of the killed of our tribe wasted"

Haris bin Hilizzah writes:

> "If from Malha to Saqim all graves ye dig, ye will find some dead (who are not avenged), they are thine some alive (whose death is avenged), these are mine"

Qais bin Asim, coaxing his tribe to seek revenge states:

> "Oh! In what woe the spirit (Sada), cries out in desolation, to avenge the death of Ibn Khalzan, is their none?

> Those are the thirsty spirits, to listen, to their pleas, not a family's, not a tribe's son, to quench their thirst where the streams run"

Sabit Sharra stating his pride writes:

> "They choose death when they have the choice, to seek revenge or take the price"

A poet of Bani Asad, in his last wish to his tribe states:

> "Price for my death from the enemy, I beg, do not take your respect will be left when the money has gone waste"

A poet of Bani Khaza incites his tribe to take revenge, saying:

> "What they offer for blood, do not even consider, for all their friendliness, they bring poison not succor.

> Will ye that blood money retain even seeing on it my bloody stain.

> If ye do, that status ye will gain, that camels of burden do attain.

> Take the money if ye dare but respect, ye will lose and for you none will care"

Kabash bint Madi Karb incites her tribe of Zubaid into avenging her brother's death by saying:

"Abdullah, dying, cried out to his nation take not money for my death, as concession

Take neither money nor camels, big or small and sit lest I lie at Saad, with my grave unlit

Took you the money and unpunished the enemy left like the shameful ostrich will be ye, roaming with his ears cleft

And then, near your women do not come, except during periods when bloody, even their heels become"

Such were the real reasons behind the decades old enmities and conflicts of the Arabs. One fails to detect any high aim or respectable motive or objective among these. They are not far removed from the animal desires of the savage beasts, to tear open and eat whatever accosts them. The more sophisticated of the Arabs too, had these urges for bloodshed and carnage; only their means of satisfying these base desires were far more dangerous, as it involved many more people and sometimes took the shape of unlimited warfare. They were very incognizant of the fact that war could only be justifiable in the pursuance of some higher aim or for the betterment of humanity.

Savagery in the Conduct of Wars

The objectives of war for the Arabs were as impious, degrading, and devoid of chivalry as their concept of war itself. Consequently, their conduct of war was also savagery in its extreme. In their perception, war was the catastrophic manifestation of extreme anger and savagery, of carnage and pillage, of oppression and disorder that burnt to ashes everything in its path or ground it to dust. Consequently, their conduct of war was commensurate with their perception of it. In their view, waging war was for the purpose of completely wiping out the enemy and stripping it of all respect and self-respect, by whatever means possible.

Ethics played no role in their conflict and in these, they were just charged with the emotion of destruction. The means of achieving their aims has been the common theme of poetry of the era.

Oppression of the Non-Combatants

In the view of the pagan Arabs, there was no difference between combatants and non-combatants. Every individual of the enemy nation was considered an enemy and none was exempt from hostile action. Women, children, the aged, the sick, or the wounded, none was exempt from the actions of war. In fact, women were the main targets of the conquering army. Dishonoring them and treating them with disrespect, were a part of the honors of war. Poets describe this with great pride. One of them writes:

> "Women, whose husbands at the slightest slight to
> them rankle, I undid the adornments of their fair
> ankle"

Another poet writes:

> "That time, fair maidens, our attention captures not
> the camels returned from their pasture"

Umro bin Kulsoom writes that the valiance of their fighters was because of the deep apprehension for their women and their deep desire to guard the honor of the women of their tribe:

> "If we lose, we leave behind women fair with hair
> dark as raven, who will satisfy lusts of some and be
> by others craven"

Often in the throes of their anger and emotions they would rent the bellies of the pregnant women open. Aamer bin Tufail, narrating the victory of his tribe at Feef Al-Reeh, writes:

> "In our Anger we unseamed the bellies of the
> pregnant women then to Nahda and Khasham of
> Feef Al-Reeh, on war, we gave a lesson"

Ravages of Fire

There was no limit to the torture, which prisoners of war had to endure. Even torturing them to death and burning them alive was not off limits. A well-known incident of the past is that Zunawas, the king of Yemen, had all those who rejected his religion, caught, and burnt alive. When Manzar bin Munzir Al-Qais defeated the Bani Shehban tribe, in the battle of Awara, he started casting all young girls of the tribe into fire. Only the intercession of one man saved the lives of some. Asaa Isi, a poet relates the incident with pride:

> "He rescued and delivered from the pain, when we
> would their women, by fire have slain"

Umro bin Munzir made a vow that he would burn alive a hundred men of Bani Darim tribe as repentance for some misdeed the tribe had committed. For the purpose, he attacked Bani Darim, but could lay hands on only 99 men. When these were being burnt, a traveler from Barajim tribe, on smelling roasting meat, went into the camp of Umro. Now in order to complete his vow, Umro being one man short, had the traveler cast into the fire, to complete the score. Jamie, a poet, writes of the incident:

> "O! Where are those who in the fire Umro threw?
> And where is Asad who was among you"

Mistreatment of Prisoners of War

Prisoners of war were treated worse than animals. Sometimes the victors, in rage and for vengeance, would severely torture them to death. The story of Ukkal and Urena can be found in books of hadith. Some shepherds of the Prophet (SAW) were captured. These people cut their limbs, blinded them, and left them on the burning sands of the desert, to die of thirst and writhing in pain.

The incident of the battle of Awara is well known. In this, Imrao Al-Qais had all prisoners of war gathered on the summit of Mount Awara with orders to his soldiers to start killing the prisoners and not to stop until their blood reached the base of the mountain. In the end, when their numbers reached hundreds, he had water added to the blood, so that it did reach the base and his vow was fulfilled. (Ibn Aseer vol. 1, page 409)

The father of Imrao Al-Qais, Hajar bin Haris, once attacked the Bani Asad tribe. In the conflict, every prisoner they caught was killed. Hajar's soldiers had orders not to kill them with swords, but to beat them to death with stave. (Ibn Aseer vol. 1, page 276)

Surprise Attack

Attacking the enemy when there was no active hostility between them currently and without declaration of war, was one of the favored war tactics. According to these tactics, maximum surprise was achieved when the attack was mounted in the last quarter of the night. This had become such a common trend that the word 'Tasbih' was accorded the meaning of 'attack at dawn'. Qurra bin Zaid, writes:

> "When Qais Bin Asim descended on them in the Morn, he found none but those, whose chests spears hath torn"

Abbas bin Mirdas writes:

> "No tribe like Shehwar have I seen, but in combat, none like ours has ever been"

For this reason, a common prayer for friends was, 'may you live through the dawn'. Ghutra bin Shadad, prays for his sweetheart:

> "O! House of Abla of Jua, to me, something speak from ravages, for you, protection I seek"

Having opposing chieftains murdered in their sleep was common. The act was called 'Fatak' and those who undertook it were known as 'Fataak'. Haris bin Zalim, Baraz bin Qais Kanani, Sulaik bin Sulka, Tabit bin Sharra, were some of the famous fataak of the time.

Sacrilege of the Dead

Not even the dead escaped vengeance; revenge of the living against the dead was done by lopping off the ears and noses and amputating the limbs. The savagery committed on the dead bodies is truly horrifying. It is a documented fact that in the Battle of Uhad, Quraish women had lopped off the ears and noses of the Muslim martyrs and wore garlands made of them. One woman, Hind the wife of Abu Sufyan, had the liver of Hamza, a stalwart of Islam, taken out of his body and chewed it up.

In the battle of Haymim, when Asba bin Umro of Jadila tribe was killed, a person from the opposing Sumbas tribe cut off his ears and attached them to his shoes. Abu Sarda Sumbasi, a poet writes:

"And with your ears, we patch our shoes"

Another Sumbasi poet writes, addressing the Jadila tribe:

"If you hold a grudge against us, it is well, for we
cleft your ears and noses and captured you to sell"

Sometimes for the satisfaction of the living, the dead were dragged by their feet, a poet writes:

"A second attack they made, dragged them by their
feet and targets of their bodies made"

One of the customs was that in case of extreme enmity, one would swear that he would drink wine from the enemy's skull. In the battle of Uhad, two brothers, Musafa bin Talha and Jalas bin Talha, met their deaths at the hand of Asim bin Sabit, a Muslim fighter. Their mother swore that she would drink wine from the skull of Asim. When Asim was killed in a subsequent battle with the Quraish, a vigorous search for Asim's body was launched so that the finder may attain a price for the skull from the mother of the two fallen brothers. In the war of 'Fasad', which lasted for 25 years, many drank wine from the skulls of each other's enemies. (Tabrezi mentioned this in his work, Hamase). In the battle of Yahmim, similar incidents took place. Abu Sarda Sumbasi narrating these incidents, writes:

"We drink from your skulls wine with distaste"

Leaving the bodies of enemies to be devoured by scavengers was considered a matter of pride. Antara, a poet writes:

"I made their father a morsel for vultures and for
beasts, now if they abuse me that is the least"

Another poet Shureh Absi writes:

"Were he not, I swear, armor clad, as feed for
vultures and beasts, to leave him, I would be glad"

Atika bint Abdul Mutalib of Harb e Fajjar with pride writes:

"Our soldiers left Malik on the ground, to be
ravaged by hyenas from around"

Unreliability

Treaties and agreements were of little value to the pagan Arabs and were virtually ineffective in connection with wars. Even during the period of the Prophet (SAW), incidents of non-compliance with treaties were common. Banu Qainuqa, Banu Nazir and Banu Quraizah had pacts with the Prophet (SAW), which were broken by each. Banu Nazir was involved in the attempted murder of the Prophet (SAW), Banu Quraizah fought openly against the Muslim army at Ahzab. Banu Qainuqa was the first to declare war against the Muslims on the instigation of the Quraish. The Rial and Zakhoon tribes themselves asked for assistance from the Prophet (SAW). When he sent seventy of his companions for their help, they had them all murdered at Bir Manna. Three companions of the Prophet (SAW), Khubaib, Zaid bin Dasra and Abdullah bin Tariq, were granted sanctuary by the Banu Lihan tribe. When they threw down their arms, the tribe had all three tied up, killed one and sold the other two in Makkah. Of such incidents, the Qur'an says, "They do not hold sacred any pact or friendship with Muslims".

This was the methodology of war of the pagan Arabs. A poet gives its gist in his poetry:

> "Not a citizen of respect I be, bear in mind, if at your doors a vicious horde ye do not find.
>
> Seeing it, even the mighty are fearful, and pregnant women, loads in their wombs, can no longer bear.
>
> Young virgins, of fear, old maids soon become, knowing that we have come.
>
> Afraid they scamper around, those that always stood their ground.
>
> Bani Najaar roam here as lions of jungle dense, where lions are silent and only cries of the dying does one sense"

Roman and Persian Methodologies of War

The Arabs of course, were savages, uncivilized, uncultured and ill bred. In them, such beastliness and savagery is understandable. However, let us examine the condition of those nations who are said to have reached the peaks of civilization and culture at the time.

History tells us much about wars and battles of the era. Those who have glanced through it know that at least in this regard, the level of civilization had very little influence. Complete annihilation was the aim of attacks of one nation over the other. Discrimination between combatants and non-combatants was essentially not existent. Every person from the enemy area was an enemy and therefore fair target for actions of war. Age, sex, state of health, station in life, and profession were unimportant considerations.

Destroying crops and orchards, pulling down buildings, burning habitations, or plundering them was a common and accepted practice. That is to say, the city that fell after a stiff resistance had in fact invited its death. When the angered and infuriated victor entered a conquered city, killing was wanton and when even this did not quench his anger, entire cities were set aflame. Even Alexander the Great suffered this weakness. When Tyer fell after defying his siege for six months and Alexander entered the city in a terrible state of mind, he ordered the general slaughter of the inhabitants. Thus, the nation that lay claims to being the most civilized nation in the world caused the death of eight thousand innocent people and sold about twenty thousand of them as slaves. Prisoners of war at the time could look forward only to being killed or enslaved. If the commander or King himself fell into enemy hands, he met a very bitter end after much torture and public humiliation.

Respect of ambassadors and envoys that came to the enemy camp was accepted as a convention. They were to be at least accorded fair, if not honorable treatment, security, and respect. Nevertheless, as often as not, these too suffered humiliation and were not safe from oppressive behavior. Carrying to the enemy camp a message that they (the enemy) might consider offensive was like inviting death. For such envoys to meet with insult, injury, and imprisonment or to be summarily killed was nothing extraordinary.

The religious cadre suffered the most in wars lost if the victor's religion happened to be other than the vanquished nations. His first act used to be to pull down the places of worship, dishonor places of religious importance, and humiliate the religious leaders. The limit was that the victor would force the vanquished nation to accept their religion on pain of death. Rome and Persia were the most civilized of nations in the world. They far exceeded others in matters of learning, culture, civilization and so forth, however, a glance through their history of warfare would make one see them in a different light.

Religious Oppression

Rome and Persia, apart from their political rivalry, were also opposed to each other in matters of religion. Whenever fire-worshiping Persia and Christian Rome confronted each other and advanced in each other's territory, they made the opponent's religion their main target.

During the reign of Qubad (501-531 A.D.), on behest of the Persian Empire, Munzir the king of Herah attacked Syria; he captured 400 clergymen and sacrificed them on the altar of his God, Uzza (History of Persia, Sykes, Vol. 1 page 482).

When Khusro Pervez, the king of Persia declared war on Rome, he razed to the ground all Christian Churches and monasteries in his kingdom, plundered them and forced the worshippers of the cross to worship fire.(Gibbon, Roman Empire, vol.5, para XLVI). In 615 A.D., when he conquered Jerusalem, he captured Pope Zakariya and along with him, the original cross, on which according to Christian belief, Eisa (AS) the Christ was crucified, was taken away. The grand cathedrals of St. Helena and Constantine were set ablaze, relics and valuable offerings gathered for 300 years were plundered, and 90,000 Christians put to death or taken prisoner. In reply, when Hercules the Roman emperor, attacked Persia from the north, he razed the holy places of the fire-worshipers in the town of Urinea and made all efforts to humiliate their religion (E.A. Ford Byzantine Empire, and Gibbon, Roman Empire, vol. 1, chapter XLVI).

The Christians of the Persian Empire had been safe and had not been molested until the Roman Empire accepted Christianity as its state religion. Afterwards, the Persian attitude towards its Christian citizenry changed. In 339 A.D., Shahpoor Zulaktaf had Bishop Marshimun and 105 other clergymen were put to death and many Christian cathedrals and monasteries were looted. After this, for 40 years, Christians remained under oppression (Sykes vol. 1, page 448).

The action that Bahram took to suppress the sect 'Manwiya', were the most horrifying of all. When Mani invented his own religion and people started flocking to it, Bahram used to have them captured and killed. He had Mani captured and skinned. His skin was stuffed with straw and hung over the gate of the city of Jandi Sabur. The gate for a long time was known as Mani gate (Alberuni in his book, Aasar-e-Baqiya has mentioned this incident).

Treatment of Envoys

The concept of treating ambassadors with respect and honor was accepted and political thinkers were in agreement with it. It however was almost never followed. An ambassador from Ardeshir, king of the Persian Empire, arrived at the court of Caesar Alexander. The message he carried stated that Rome should content itself with European territories, leaving Syria and Anatolia for the Persian Empire. This annoyed the Caesar, who had him thrown into prison. (Sykes vol. 1, page 426)

King Nausherwan known for his justice and fair dealing treated envoys no differently. When ambassadors of Wezabil Atrak came to his court with a peace proposal, instead of just agreeing or otherwise, had them poisoned to death (Alberuni, in Aasar-e-Baqiya).

The victorious Persian Emperor, Khusro Pervez, conquered from Rome, its territories in Asia and Africa. After the fall of Syria and Palestine, when Egypt fell, he was at the doors of Constantinople. Hercules of Rome sent envoys to Khosro Pervez and sued for peace. He had the chief of the envoys skinned alive and sent a reply to the Roman message, which started thus:

> "From Khusro God and supreme ruler of the world,
> to the lowly and stupid slave Hercules-------"
> (Byzantine Empire, page 101).

Unreliability

Upholding the sanctity of treaties and agreements were not the characteristics of these respectable and civilized nations. History has scores of examples of incidents when one nation seeing the other in trouble, disregarding all pacts and treaties, declared war on it. Even such respected rulers as Justinian of Rome and Nausherwan of Persia, who are stated to represent the best in sovereignty, appear prominent among the violators of agreements in history. When Nausherwan felt the need for concentrating on the internal reforms of his country, he readily accepted the peace proposal that Justinian had forwarded and signed a treaty with Rome. Nevertheless, when he saw Belisarius of Rome increasing in strength and influence had the king of Herah attack Ghassan, which was under Roman influence and sent troops to his assistance. He expected Rome would enter the field to assist Glasson (Byzantine Empire, page 101). On the other hand, when Elikhan Itrak lost favor with Persia, in 571 A.D. Justinian exploited the situation and in 575 A.D. declared war on the Persian Empire disregarding the peace treaty with it.

Savagery in War

The concept of rights and duties during war was in existence in its crude form since ancient times. Greece had made it a rule that those who died in battle were to be buried, while those of captured cities who took refuge in places of worship were not to be killed. The athletes and keepers of shrines were also not to be molested (Grotte, History of Greece). It may be noted however, that firstly these rules were not valid for international conflicts, but were effective in internal conflicts only. Secondly, neither any independent nation had ever accepted these laws practically, nor these rules had any legal sanction.

The Roman Empire did not even recognize the other empire's existence. Therefore, there was no concept of having treaties or pacts with them. Similar was the thinking of the Persians, who considered all non-Persians as savages, and that their territories were actually a part of the Persian Empire, which had reneged and rebelled. Therefore, there was no ethical compulsion of maintaining peace with them.

The makeup of the Roman and Persian armies was such, that ethical limitations could not be imposed on them. Mostly, their forces were consisted of untrained volunteers. They were not educated in principles of warfare, nor were there any means of keeping military discipline among them.

During war, ordinary warlike citizens joined up in hordes. Their motivation being, the quenching of their thirsts for bloodshed, the desire for plunder, the elimination of a neighboring state, capturing slaves for their service and beautiful women to warm their beds. Even among these cultured and sophisticated nations, there was no high aim of war, just that the enemy should be humiliated or destroyed. For this reason, during their advances into another nation's territory, women, children, the aged, animals, trees, places of worship, nothing in their reach was safe. That which could be looted was taken and that which could not be taken was burnt down.

Rome was always at war with the Goths of Europe and the Vandals of Africa. The barbaric treatment meted out to these nations forms a large part of the area's history. When Caesar Justinian advanced on the Vandals, he exterminated the entire nation. Before the war, the nation had 120,000 able men; in addition to that, there were women, children, and slaves in large numbers. When Rome gained control over them, not a single able person was left. Gibbon states that the whole nation was almost completely eliminated. A foreign traveler, who happened to be there, could spend the day in the city, without laying eyes on a single human being. When he had last visited the city, some twenty years ago, he was surprised at the bustle of commercial activity in the city, its agriculture, and the large populace there. Now after twenty years, the place wore a deserted look. The population of half a million fell victims to Justinian's military action and cruelty (Gibbon vol. V, chapter XL111).

Treatment of the Goths of Europe, at the hands of Romans, was not much different from that of the Vandals. It is said that when the Gothic king Tortilla was wounded and retreated from the battlefield. Romans tracked him down to a far off place, took off his bloodstained clothes, and along with his crown, sent them as a present to Justinian, leaving the Totilla's dead body naked.

"In 70 A.D., after the Roman emperor, Titus', attack on Jerusalem, Tall girls were chosen and kept for the victor. Thousands of men over 18 years of age were captured and sent to work in mines in Egypt. Several thousands of others were sent to amphitheaters in Rome, so that their deaths at the hands of swordsmen, by each other or by wild beasts could provide entertainment to the Roman public. During the war, 97000 men were captured, 11000 died of hunger, since their captors refused to feed them. Apart from these, those killed in the war or subsequently slaughtered totaled 133,749." (Ferrar, Early Days of Christianity).

The conflicts between the Romans and Persians were no less gruesome. These two pillars of civilization and culture displayed the savagery that matched any of the brute nations. When Shapor Alaktaf advanced on Algeria and Almeida (presently, Dayar Bakir) fell after a stiff resistance, the victor entered the city in a horrific state of mind and ordered general slaughter. The town was so destroyed that it could never recover.

In 540 AD., when Naushewan advanced in Syria, its capital was completely destroyed. Men were slaughtered and buildings razed to the ground, and when even that did not satisfy him, he had the city set ablaze. He entered Syria again in 572 A.D. and after plundering and pillaging Fania and Antakia, 296,000 Syrians were captured and sent to Persia as slaves. Many beautiful women were captured and sent to Alykhan Atrak to appease him and to coax him into abandoning his alliance with Justinian.

In 576 A.D., he attacked Armenia and when Theodosopolis resisted his siege and did not fall, he entered Kepadosia and destroyed everything that came in his path and Meltine was burnt to ashes. Towards the end of Khusro Pervez's reign, when he attacked the Roman Empire, what Syria, Palestine, and Asia Minor witnessed, was nothing lesser than hell. The savage brutality that Jerusalem faced has been stated, but the conditions in the other cities were not much different. (All these details are in the books of Gibbon Sykes and Ford). In his conflicts, he was not averse to using the cowardly means of plotting, sneaking, and murder. When Khusro could not defeat Armantan, he had him murdered by one of his officers. Such incidents are not uncommon in the histories of both Rome and Persia.

Conditions of Prisoners of War

Prisoners of war were the most ill-treated among the groups. The ancient Greco-Roman civilization considered all nations other than itself as barbarians. Therefore, prisoners of other nations could not look forward to anything but death or slavery. Even the enlightened philosopher Aristotle, without any consideration of ethics, states, that nature had created barbarians for slavery. (Politics, book 1, chapter 2 and 4). The same at another place states, that acquiring slaves was among legitimate causes for wars, since they had been created for the purpose anyway (Ibid, Book 1, chapter viii).

Such beliefs had made the Romans quite disdainful of the life and property of the non-Roman nations. At the same time, the Roman society had developed such a taste for violence and bloodshed that even their entertainment consisted of seeing blood-curdling violence. In these, they preferred reality to play-acting or representation. They preferred to burn someone's abode to see the effects of fire. Similarly, burning a man alive or having him torn up by lions, was acceptable, rather, spectators could be appeased by nothing lesser. They always were in need of men for these inhuman sports and definitely respectable free Roman citizens could not be used for it, therefore prisoners of wars served the purpose.

Sometimes these sports were of such proportions, that thousands of prisoners became targets of swordsmen. Titus, known as the 'Darling of the Human Race', had several thousand Jews placed in the arena with 50,000 wild beasts to provide sport for Roman spectators. In Trojan sports, 10,000 men were made to confront 14,000 wild beasts. Claudius, in order to depict war had 11,000 men, armed with swords fight each other. Augustus Caesar states in his memoirs that he had witnessed such sports of 8000 swordsmen and 3510 beasts.

All these sports were obviously on account of prisoners of war. But, apart from this, the prisoners of wars had another function; they served free Romans as slaves. As slaves they were accorded the lowest grade of humanity. They had no rights, their lives were not worth anything and their function was to fulfill every one of the master's desires. According to Ferrar, they spent their childhood in degradation, youth in hard labor and old age in cruel neglect. (Ferrar, page 2)

The conditions of prisoners of wars in Persia were not much better. Even Caesar of Rome, Valerian, when he became a prisoner of war, in the reign of Shahpor-1, was paraded through the capital in chains. Later he had to lead a life of slavery. After Valerian's death, Shahpor's vengeance still not satisfied, had his body skinned and the skin filled with straw (Sykes, vol-1). It is well known that Shahpor Zulaktaf, in his vengeance had the Arab prisoners of war from Bahrain drilled through the shoulders and tied together with a rope running through these holes. He is remembered as 'Zulaktaf 'on this account.

These horrors are made more horrible, when one considers that they were not committed for any aim other than gaining popularity with the people and for demonstrating the magnificence and power of the regality. Sometimes just to satisfy some base desire of kings, thousands of men met their death. Even during the time of the Prophet (SAW), before he could affect his reforms, such idiosyncrasies of horror were prevalent. When Khusro Pervez heard of the beauty of the daughter of Nauman bin Manzar, he ordered Nauman to send his daughter forthwith to the royal harem. Nauman's Arabic pride could not tolerate this and he refused. Khusro ordered that Herah, be occupied and Nauman captured. Nauman leaving his family in the care of Bani Shehban tribe proceeded to the court of Khusro to plead with him to change his mind. Khusro, instead, had him killed and sent a force of twenty thousand to capture Nauman's family from the Bani Sehban. A bloody fight ensued between the Arabs and the Persians at Zakhar. Blood flowed in streams and thousands died in the battle. All this bloodshed was just to satisfy the carnal desire of a king for a beautiful woman.

From this brief narration of history, it may be apparent that the aims and conduct of war knew no ethical bounds and that the rights and duties of combatants were not even a minor consideration. In addition, there was no tendency for striking a balance between kindness and wanton destruction. Even highly civilized and cultured nations, where war was concerned, were in the very initial stages of development.

In these times, war was just turbulence and disorder, killing and destruction, trouble and oppression, to be unleashed for the fulfillment of the desires of the mighty. Savagery, barbarism, and ruthlessness had entered the bounds of warfare. War meant wanton killing, destruction, plunder and centuries of neglect had made war synonymous with these terms, none could imagine war without these attributes. In wars, age, sex state of health and station in life were not the considerations for relief from molestation and persecution nor were the places of worship safe and people could be molested just on account of their faith.

Islamic Reforms

This was the state of the world in which Islam raised the standard of reform, a new concept, with which the world was unfamiliar. In this concept, war was an evil, which was to be avoided to the maximum limit. Only if a greater evil afflicted the world, i.e. if strife, turmoil, and oppression had spread and the arrogant had endangered its peace and tranquility, only then, waging war was permissible. In fact, under those conditions war would become a duty and avoiding it, sinful.

The Islamic Concept of War

According to the Islamic concept, the main aim was not the destruction of opposing forces. It was rather, the suppression of evil. Therefore, Islam put forward the principle of 'Economy of Effort '. That is, the use of only that amount of force which is necessary for the suppression of evil. The force may only be applied against the group or class actively involved in spreading the evil or oppression or at the most, against those who are likely to become thus active. Those not actively involved in the oppression or evil should remain safe from the effects of war. Even those materials and objects that do not actively aid the enemy in the pursuance of his aims should remain safe as far as possible.

This concept was materially different from what non-Muslims had become familiar with. Therefore, Islam setting aside the established lexicology and terminology of warfare established a new term, 'Jihad fe sabeel illah' (Effort in the cause of Allah). The term explains the aims and objectives it stands for and divorces itself from the savagery that wars so far had come to exemplify.

The dictionary meaning of 'jihad' is making all efforts to achieve an objective or to complete a task. This word in no way implies the wanton destruction, suppression and oppression of the Arabic term 'harb' (war), neither does it imply the fear and extreme fear, the term 'roo' (war) stood for, nor the evil and mischief of 'shar' (war). It definitely does not imply the trouble and tribulation of 'kariyah' (war). In contrast, it simply means, that the object of those involved in 'jihad', is just the elimination of evil and oppression, with the expense of just that much effort, as is necessary for the purpose.

In usage, the word 'effort' can apply as much to virtue as to vice. Since the word 'jihad' alone could not have been sufficient, the clause, 'fe sabeel illah' (in the cause of Allah) was appended to it. After that, the term 'Jihad fe sabeel illah' could not apply to, satisfaction of the ego, conquest of territory, satisfaction of fancy for a woman, satisfaction of personal enmity or the gaining of wealth, sovereign over-lordship, popularity etc.. Only that effort would fall within its bounds, which is for the sake of Allah, which does not have the slightest link with 'ego' and which is for the achievement of those objectives alone, that please Allah.

Based on these pure concepts mentioned above, Islam lays down the complete code of conduct during war, its ethical bounds, the rights and duties of opposing forces and the difference between combatants and non-combatants. The rights of all concerned with war, including the rights of those under treaty, the rights of envoys and captives of war and the rights of the conquered, were clearly stated. Rules to pursue all orders and instructions were laid down. Apart from these, examples of the conduct of the Prophet (SAW) and the first four pious caliphs have acquired the position of references, to be applied in the changing conditions of war.

Reforms of the Causes of War

Obviously, the Islamic laws regarding warfare, being in fact reforms, needed promulgation, and enforcement, just compiling them was not enough. For the reason, the age-old concepts needed to be erased first. It was difficult for the pagan Arabs to comprehend the reason why people would risk their lives going for wars, whose objects were neither the gains in territory and sovereign popularity nor respect and satisfaction of ego. Therefore, the first task that the Prophet (SAW) undertook was to clarify the actual meaning of 'Jihad fe sabeel illah' (War in the cause of Allah) and to make all understand what the bounds of such wars were, that made them nobler in status to wars for evil causes. There are many sayings of the Prophet (SAW) (hadith), in this regard. A few of these are quoted below.

> "A person said to the Prophet (SAW), that there were those who undertook wars for gathering spoils, some for making gains in respect and power and others to establish their reputation for bravery. After stating this, he inquired of the Prophet (SAW), as to which of these was in the cause of Allah. The Prophet (SAW) replied that, the only war alone was in the cause of Allah, which was to spread His word." (Narrator was Abu Musa Ashari).

Another similar hadith, related by Abu Musa Ashari, states,

> "A person inquired of the Prophet (SAW), what 'Jihad fe sabeel illah' stood for. He further inquired whether that if the person fought when angered or for the supremacy of his nation, whether that could be termed as 'jihad'. The Prophet (SAW) raised his head and replied; only that war was in the way of Allah, which was for the furtherance of His word."

Abu Amama Bahily relates a hadith that states,

> "A man came to the Prophet (SAW) and inquired of him, that if a man fought for wealth and status, what his gain would be. The Prophet (SAW) replied that it would not be worthy of any reward in the eyes of the Lord. The man, not satisfied, came back and repeated his inquiry and was given the same response. The person not yet satisfied asked the question twice more. To satisfy the man, the Prophet (SAW) stated that Allah did not reward any act that was not purely to please Him and to gain His favor."

Ubada bin Samit (RA) relates a hadith, in which the Prophet (SAW) said,

> "If a person proceeds for fighting in the way of Allah and desired even a rope to tie his camel with, only that rope is what he will get, no other reward from Allah for him."

Maaz bin Jabal (RA) relates a hadith, in which the Prophet (SAW) stated,

> "There are two types of conflicts, one that is for seeking the pleasure of Allah. In this, a person leads the fight, spending of his best wealth, avoids strife and turmoil. During such a fight, his being awake and his sleep are both worthy of Allah's reward. The second type is for the purpose of exhibition, and for personal gains in wealth and glory, and the fighter is not obedient to his leader and spreads turmoil in the land. The reward of such a fighter will not even be as if he had gained and lost nothing (meaning he would rather be liable to punishment)."

Abu Huraira (RA) relates that the Prophet (SAW) once stated,

> "On the Day of Resurrection, three types of people will be dealt first. Firstly, the person who fought in the way of Allah and died while fighting. Allah will recount His blessings on the person and ask him what he had done for Allah. The man will reply that he had fought and died for Him. Allah will respond that he (the man) lied. He had only fought to establish his bravery on others. The man will then be dragged by his head into hell."

Abdullah bin Masood (RA) relates that the Prophet (SAW) once said,

> "On the Day of Judgment, one man will come before Allah, holding the hand of another and state that, this man had murdered him. Allah will inquire of the man, as to the reason for his act. The accused will reply that he had killed the man that honor and esteem would be his (Allah's). Allah will state,

indeed honor and esteem are for Me. Another man will come, holding the hand of another and state that, this man had murdered him. Allah will inquire of the accused as to his reasons for doing so. The accused will reply that he had killed that honor will be for such and such. Allah thereupon will reply that honor was not the right of such person, and then the accused will be answerable for his sin."

These teachings of Islam strip warfare of all objectives of material gain, personal fame, esteem, and sovereign. Quests for wealth, satisfaction of personal and national enmity, all are negated as rightful causes. In fact, there are no worldly objectives, for which war has been declared rightful. Thus the only rightful cause that remains is the dry and insipid (in worldly terms) purpose of religion and ethics.

Even if others spread strife, the sword may only be raised when there is no other option available for correcting the situation. The Prophet (SAW), states,

"Do not seek conflict with the enemy rather pray for peace and tranquility. But once conflict erupts, fight hard and know that paradise lies in the shadow of the swords."

Reforms of the Methodology of War

Along with making the cleansing of aims of war, one of the objectives that the Prophet (SAW) undertook was for the reforms in the methodology of achieving these aims. Gradually the savagery that typified conflicts of the pagan times was brought to an end. Rulings that prohibit savagery in all of its forms, individual and collective, are in abundance in the books of Islamic jurisprudence.

Due Consideration of Non-Combatants

Of the nations participating in wars, the citizens have been divided into two categories those were, combatants and non-combatants. Combatants are those who directly or indirectly participate in wars or those who are mentally and physically capable of such participation. While, the non-combatants are those, who do not directly or indirectly participate in warlike activities, or those who in the normal course would not take part in these activities. Such as: the children, the aged, the womenfolk, the wounded, the mentally or physically disabled, the non-residents, the spiritual who normally reside in shrines, those responsible for the care and maintenance of places of worship and all those who may be considered harmless.

In wars, Islam allows the killing of those who fall in the category of combatants and forbids taking the lives of non-combatants. Once the Prophet (SAW) saw the corpse of a woman in a battlefield, in anger, he stated that woman was not a combatant, (why had she been killed?). He then dispatched orders to the commander of the troops Khalid, that women and common laborer were never to be killed. According to another tradition, he forbade the slaughter of women and children after that incident.

A hadith states,

> "Do not take the lives of the aged and weak or that of the women and children and whatever you get in the war in the form of booty be collected at one place. Do not steal from the booty. Deal with all with kindness and beneficence and know that Allah loves the beneficent".

At the conquest of Makkah, the Prophet (SAW) had instructed his troops in advance that they should not attack the wounded and not to pursue those who flee from the fight. If one stayed home with doors locked, he is to be taken into protection (Futuh ul-Baldan, page 47).

Ibn Abbas states a tradition, that, when the Prophet (SAW) sent out his troops, he would give instructions not to kill the harmless keepers of the places of worship and the spiritual, whose abodes are shrines.

In the light of these traditions, the Islamic jurists have enacted the general rule that those who are disabled and those who according to custom avoid conflicts, are exempt from acts of war against them. However, this exemption is conditional to their de facto avoidance of battles. If any of them is involved in warlike activities, such as a sick man is found directing the moves of the enemy from his bed, a woman is involved in espionage, a child is gathering information to be relayed to the enemy or one of the religious cadre is known to incite the enemy to war, then killing those is permissible. They have acquired the status of combatants and have denied themselves the privileges and security of the non-combatants.

The essence of the chapter on Islamic law on warfare is that all eligible combatants, whether they actually participated in a particular battle or stayed away from it, are liable for killing, while non-combatants are only liable to death if their participation is de facto (Hidaya, Kaifiyat al-Qital, Fatah ul Qadeer, vol. 4, page 29-292; Bida us Sana, vol.7, page 101).

Rights of the Combatants

Having stated the rights of the non-combatants, Islam also states that unlimited freedom of action has not been granted against those who actively participate in wars against Muslims. Even against such people, there are bounds that may not be exceeded. These bounds are explained sequentially in detail, below.

1. Avoidance of Surprise Attacks

Traditionally the pagan Arabs used the cover of night to launch attacks on the enemy. Such attacks were usually made in the last quarter of the night. The Prophet (SAW) forbade them and made it a rule that attacks should not be launched before daybreak. Anas bin Malik, relating events of the Battle for Khyber states, that whenever Prophet (SAW) reached an enemy encampment during the night, he would refrain from attacking them until daybreak.

2. Prohibition of Killing by Fire

Arabs and non-Arabs alike, in their quest for vengeance, would burn the enemy alive. The Prophet forbade this savage practice. A tradition states that the Prophet (SAW) once stated,

> "Afflictions of fire, is the right only of the Maker of fire."

Abu Musa Ashari (RA) relates a hadith, in which the Prophet (SAW) once ordered that if they came across such and such, they should burn them. But when the troops were about to depart he called them and stated, that he had ordered such and such to be burnt, but he added afflictions of fire is only Allah's right, therefore if they came across those persons, they were just to kill them.

3. Prohibition of Killing a Tied-up Prisoner

The Prophet (SAW) forbade killing a person after tying him up or torturing him to death. Obaid bin Yala (RA) states about of an incident when he was a part of the force under Abdur Rehman bin Khalid (RA). During the campaign, four people were brought as captives before Abdur Rehman (RA). He ordered them to be tied up and killed them. When Abu Ayub Ansari (RA), a respected companion of the Prophet (SAW) came to know of this, he stated that he had heard the Prophet (SAW) about such killings. Swearing by Allah, he declared that he would not have killed even a chicken in such a way. When Abdur Rehman (RA) heard this, he had four of his slaves released as penance.

4. Prohibition of Plunder

After the battle of Khyber, when truce had been established, some fresh converts lost self-control and started wanton looting and destruction. The chief of the Jews presented himself before the Prophet (SAW) and in an angry tone inquired of him whether it became customary of him to kill their donkeys, eat away their fruit, and beat up their women. The Prophet (SAW) instructed Ibn Auf (RA) to gather the troops. When all had gathered he addressed them and inquired whether they considered only those things prohibited that Qur'an prohibits. He impressed on them that even those things were prohibited that the Prophet (SAW) himself prohibits. Meaning that, the prohibition was of equal and sometimes of more severe nature than the prohibition of the Qur'an. He added that Allah did not permit their entering the houses of the 'People of the Book' without permission or beating up their women or eating their fruit, since they (The Jews) had paid what was due from them.

At one time, when the Muslim army was marching for battle, some of the troops looted some goats and cooked them. When the Prophet (SAW) heard of this, he had the pots overturned, stating that the food so gained was unholy and forbidden (Plunder and loot here refers to those material things, which the army when marching in enemy territory misappropriates from normal civilians. It also refers to the war booty that is appropriated, before formal distribution).

Abduallah bin Yazid (RA) states, that the Prophet (SAW) prohibited loot and plunder. If one comes across a cow, even drinking its milk is forbidden, unless one seeks the owner's permission. If the need is great, it is sufficient that one shouts out for the owner three times and if none comes forward, the required milk may be taken.

5. Prohibition of Wanton Destruction

6. Prohibition of Desecration of Dead Bodies

7. Prohibition of Killing Prisoners of War

8. Prohibition of Killing Envoys

9. Prohibition of Dishonoring Treaties and Pacts

10. Prohibition of Disorder and Mischief

11. Prohibition of Clamor and Pandemonium

12. Prohibition of Savagery in Wars

In the 7th century A.D., the Prophet (SAW) adopted the method of briefing the troops going out to wars, reminding them of the ethics of war, the West was not aware of any such method, until the middle of the 19th century. It was customary for the Prophet (SAW), that when he dispatched troops to wars, he would remind the commander and the troops to remain steadfast in piety and fear Allah. He would then instruct them saying:

"Proceed in the way of Allah and fight in his cause, against those who have transgressed. However, during the war never dishonor your word. Neither misappropriate from the booty nor desecrates human bodies, and do not take the lives of children". After this he would further instructs them to give the enemy three alternatives: to accept Islam, pay 'jaziya' or be ready to do battle. If the enemy accepted Islam, they were not to raise their hand against them. If they agreed to pay 'jaziya', then they were to be granted security of life and property. However, if they agree to neither of the two, seek Allah's help and fight them.

When Abu Bakar, the first Caliph of Islam, dispatched his troops against Syria, He gave them ten broad instructions. All historians and compilers of hadith are in agreement that these instructions were indeed given. These were:

a) Do not kill women children or the aged.

b) Do not desecrate fallen enemies.

c) Do not molest the clergymen and those who have dedicated their lives to piety and do not destroy places of worship.

d) Do not hew down fruit bearing trees nor destroy any field.

e) Do not render any dwelling desolate.

f) Do not kill animals.

g) Always honor your word.

h) The lives and property of those who accept your sovereignty, is to be given the same respect as that of any Muslim.

i) Do not misappropriate of the spoils of war.

j) Do not turn your backs to the enemy, in battle.

Results of the Reforms

From the above it is clear that Islam had cleansed wars of savagery, which had become an inseparable part of the wars of that era. Killing of prisoners of wars and envoys, killing people of treaty nations, killing of those wounded in wars, killing of non-combatants, amputating limbs, desecration of the dead, torture by fire, looting and plunder, discomforting travelers in the line of march, wanton destruction of crops and dwellings, dishonoring one's promises and agreements, turbulence, disorder, as well as the clamor and pandemonium of battles, were all placed beyond the realm of warfare. Wars that remained were an instrument with which the pious and the brave could deny the enemy, the capability of causing strife, without causing undue destruction. The best example of the results that these reforms brought about within a very short period of eight years can be seen from the events that unfolded, subsequent to the Conquest of Makkah.

The conquest of Makkah was the culmination of a long-standing enmity, a major enemy had been defeated, and one of its major cities had fallen. Can you imagine how the victors, no matter whether they were the pagan and savage Arabs or the suave and civilized Romans and Persians, would have behaved under the circumstances? Keeping that in mind, consider that the same Arabs, who, until eight years earlier, were used to paganism and savagery as a way of life, enter the city as victors. The same city had been recaptured from which they had been expelled after undergoing immense difficulty and torture. They had achieved victory against those who had not only rendered them homeless, but had also made every attempt to dislodge them even from the place they had taken refuge in. However, subsequent even to such a victory, there is no manslaughter and plunder, the life, property and honor of none is ravaged and there is no vengeance inflicted on sworn, age-old enemies.

In the fall of this major city, only 24 lives were lost and even these were of those who had themselves initiated hostile action. Consider then, that upon his entry, the chief of this victorious army orders that: not a finger is to be raised against anyone unless that person initiates the hostile act and that anyone who shuts his doors and stays indoors, is to be taken into refuge, anyone who lays down his arms is to consider himself safe, and any who take refuge with Abu Sufyan, is also to be granted asylum.

The chieftains are brought in the presence of the victor, after some order had been established in the fallen city. These are the same enemy chieftains who had caused the victor to suffer atrocities for thirteen long years and forced him to flee the city, later, for whose termination; they had fought the battles of Badr, Uhud, and Ahzab. These sworn enemy chieftains are asked what they expect their treatment should be. They reply that he (the victor) is their beneficent brother and the son of a beneficent brother. He declares them free and tells them that they are not answerable, that day, for any of their past misdeeds. Not only are they set free and given back their property, but also are granted the property they had usurped from the Muslims, eight years previously.

There were among these some extreme enemies of Islam, whose deaths had been ordered, prior to the conquest, but when they found themselves in the power and control of the Muslims, even they were not deprived of the beneficence of the most outstanding and generous of victors.

Hubar bin Asood, who was the murderer of the victor's daughter, Zainab, he accepted Islam with humility, and was pardoned. Wahshi bin Harb, who had killed Hamzah, a loved uncle of the Prophet (SAW), was granted pardon, and Hind who had in vengeance chewed up his (Hamza's) liver, despite her inhumanity and savagery, also benefited from the forgiveness and graciousness of the victor.

Ikramah, the son of the greatest enemy of Islam, Abu Jahal, and himself was a big enemy, was granted pardon after he accepted Islam. He later earned the position of a respected companion of the Prophet (SAW). Apart from these, Abdullah bin Siran, Sarah, and Kaab bin Zubair, who were the sworn enemies of the Prophet (SAW) himself, were pardoned. Only Huwairis bin Nuqaiz, Abdul Aza bin Khutal, and Muqees bin Shababa were killed, and this was not account of enmity, but as punishment for murder.

Thus was reformed the world's most savage nation within only eight years. Even today, all are aware what atrocities are committed, when an enemy town falls. In the present {19th} century, the atrocities committed when enemy towns fell, during the two World Wars, is known to all. There are eyewitnesses living who can relate the horrors committed by those who claimed to be the flag bearers of Western Civilization and culture. Then consider that thirteen {fourteen} centuries ago, when the pinnacles of civilization were Khusro Pervez of Persia and Hercules of Rome. An unlettered and uncivilized nation of Arabia, when it overcame its worst enemy, the restraint and respectability it displayed, must have been a result of some mammoth reforms, some supreme civic teachings, and extremely correct and dedicated training in military discipline and good order.

The Laws of Warfare Based on Principles

So far, we have studied the laws, rather the conventions of warfare, prevalent at the time that Islam came to expunge. Let us now consider the reforms that saw their introduction for the first time in warfare. Since our intention is to study the laws that Islam authored after expunging the evil practices of warfare, it is sufficient that we study the principles that such laws are based on. They form the basis on which Islamic jurists and commanders can make laws to suit prevalent local conditions. We therefore do not have to go into the details available in the books of jurisprudence.

Allegiance to Commanders

In the interest of creating a system out of the disorder and confusion of war, the first step that Islam introduced was the 'Centralization of Command'. Strict discipline and obedience amongst the soldiery followed. Thus, the foremost principle that Islam introduced was that even an insignificantly small military action could not be taken without the prior approval of the principal commander. Although killing an enemy, capturing its wealth, imprisoning someone from the enemy camp, and destroying its war machinery in themselves fall within the bounds of permissibility, undertaking even these actions without the express permission or command of the commander, becomes prohibited and sinful.

In one incident, Abdullah bin Jahash (RA), a companion of the Prophet (SAW), initiated an action against a group of Quraish, and elicited some booty. The Prophet (SAW) was angered by this act of Abdullah and declared that such booty was impermissible. Other companions of the Prophet (SAW) condemned the act, as it had been undertaken without orders.

When Khalid bin Waleed (RA) was sent to the tribe of Jazima to invite them to Islam, on some misunderstanding, he indulged in armed confrontation with the tribe and killed many of them. When the Prophet (SAW) heard of this, he was so angered that he was unable to sit and he stood up, condemning the act. He dispatched Ali bin Abu Talib (RA) forthwith to obliterate that act of paganism. (Fatah ul Bari, vol. 8, page 42)

Islam has equated allegiance to the commander with obedience to the Prophet (SAW) and to God himself. A hadith states:

> "There are two types of conflicts. One is for seeking the pleasure of Allah, in which one is obedient to the commander, spends the best of one's wealth, and avoids strife. In that case his sleep, and his wakefulness during the conflict, is all worthy of

reward. The other type is that, which is for gains in popularity, in which one is disobedient to the commander and spreads strife in the land. Such conflicts would not be even as if he had done neither good nor bad" (he would rather be liable to punishment).

One other hadith states,

"One, who obeys me, is as if he has obeyed Allah and one who disobeys me, is as if he has disobeyed Allah. Then if one obeys the commander, it is as if he has obeyed me and one who disobeys the commander, it is as if he has disobeyed me."

These instructional orders lent a system to warfare. It did not remain a bloody sport anymore, in which every individual was just a cause of death, destruction, and plunder. In paganism, every soldier had the freedom to plunder anyone, to kill anyone, set afire any dwelling or field and in general could take any step to destroy the enemy. Even the army of Alexander the great, renowned for its discipline, when it advanced on Persia, the freedom with which they indulged in death and destruction is well preserved in the books of history. As opposed to this, the rules and regulation imposed by Islam do not allow such freedom of action to any individual. In the perception of Islam, taking the lives of men is such a responsibility that it cannot be entrusted to any or all. If it has to be indulged in, necessarily, it should be under checks and kept to the minimum. Not all have the capability to decide the necessity of such acts or the lack of it and not all can be entrusted in the heat of the battle, to decide how much, enough is. In the Islamic law, one commander has been made responsible, for the overall conduct of war, and compliance of his orders has been made mandatory on the entire force. A soldier, individually, does not have, even the freedom to pluck fruit from a tree in enemy's territory.

Honoring of Oaths and Agreements

Islamic law demands that oaths and agreements be honored in both war and peace. One of the basic principles of Islamic ethics is that even in the severest conditions, all agreements and pacts have to be honored. The biggest advantage of dishonoring a pact or agreement cannot equal the loss that human ethics and spiritualism suffers in doing so. While the gravest disadvantage of honoring pacts or agreements, cannot lessen the spiritual and ethical gains accrued by such acts.

The same principal governs, with equal force, both individual and national interactions. Today the trend is that even those acts that a person in his individual capacity considers shameful are undertaken with impunity at the collective or national level and not considered worth even the slightest embarrassment. National leaders, no matter how strictly they personally conform to the principles of ethics and culture, will stoop to lying, cheating, dishonesty, and dishonoring agreements and promises, where they perceive the slightest advantage for the nation. In relation to performance or non-performance of pacts, oaths, or treaties, Islam does not differentiate between the individual and the congregation, between a person and the nation and between the government and the governed. It has declared dishonoring of agreements, in the interest of advantage, prohibitive, whether the advantage is individual or national. Surah Al-Nahal states:

> "Fulfill the covenant of Allah when ye have covenanted, and break not the oaths after asseveration of them, and you have made Allah surety over you. Lo! Allah knoweth what ye do. And be not like unto her, who unraveleth the thread after she hath made it strong, into thin filaments, making your oaths a deceit between you because of a nation being more numerous than (another) nation. Allah only trieth you thereby, and he verily will explain to you on the day of resurrection that wherein ye differ" (Al-Nahal: 91-92)

There are many verses on the subject in the Qur'an. Some of these are quoted below:

> "Such as keep the pact of Allah, and break not the covenant; such as unite that which Allah hath commanded be joined, their's will be the sequel of (heavenly) Home" (Al-Raad: 21-22)

> "(The chosen of Allah is) he who fufilleth the pledge and wardeth off (evil); for lo! Allah loveth

those who ward off (evil). Lo! Those who purchase a small gain at the cost of Allah's covenant and their oaths, they have no portion in the hereafter"

(Aale Imran: 76-77)

"And those who keep their treaty when they make one, and the patient in tribulation and adversity and time of stress. Such are they who are sincere. Such are the God-fearing" (Al-Baqarah: 177)

"And if you give your word, do justice thereunto, even though it be (against) a kinsman; and fulfil the covenant of Allah. This he commandeth you that haply ye may remember" (Al-Anaam: 152)

"And keep the covenant. Lo! Of the covenant it will be asked" (Bani Israel: 34)

The practical demonstration of this teaching, by the Prophet, in his life, declares the value that Islam attaches to honoring of pacts, agreements, and oaths. At the time of the battle of Badr, Muslims were severely short of manpower, the Quraish were three times their size; at this time, Huzaifah bin Al Yaman (RA) and his father, Husail bin Jabir, set out to join the Muslim Army. The Quraish, who suspected their intention, stopped them on the way. They (Huzaifah and his father) told them that their intent was to proceed to Madinah. The Quraish let them go, after making them take an oath that they would not join the Muslim army in the ensuing battle. When they reached the Prophet (SAW) at Badr, they related the incident to him. The Prophet (SAW) instructed them to proceed to Madinah and fulfill their oath and that they (Muslims) would seek Allah's help.

At Hudaibiya, the terms of a treaty had been agreed upon and the treaty was being drawn up for signing. At this time, Abu Jandal (RA) bin Sohail, an escaped Muslim prisoner, from the Quraish, bearing marks of torture on his body and pain and fear apparent from his face, sought refuge with the Muslims. There were 1400 well-armed Muslims in the camp. All were moved by the condition of Abu Jandal (RA), and awaited for the slightest indication from the Prophet (SAW) that would enable them to free Abu Jandal (RA) from The Quraish. However, one clause of the treaty required that any person from the Quraish seeking refuge with the Muslims would be repatriated to them, while any Muslim seeking refuge with the Quraish did not have to be. The Prophet (SAW) therefore refused to grant him refuge, advising him forbearance and asked him to trust in the Lord, He would find another way of rescuing him.

When he returned to Madinah, another person, Abu Baseer (RA), escaping from the Quraish prison, reached him, seeking asylum. Two persons, sent by the Quraish also arrived and demanded the he be handed over. The Prophet (SAW) well knew the treatment-escaping prisoners could expect from the Quraish if apprehended. However, controlling himself, in the interest of honoring the treaty, he handed Abu Baseer (RA) back to them.

In order to assess the correct import of the incident, we have to keep in view the deep-rooted comradeship and mutual trust that existed among the Muslims. There are many similar incidences recorded from the period of the Prophet (SAW) and of the first four pious caliphs that reinforce the significance attached to honoring of the word. Be it in the form of oaths, pacts, or agreements.

Rights of the Neutral Party

There is no definitive term for neutrality in Islam, but the essentials of the term have been included in the treatise. From the Islamic perspective, non-Muslims fall in two categories. One category is that, with which there is a pact or treaty, while the other is that with which no pact or treaty has been entered into.

The treaty-states will be dealt with, in accordance with the terms of the treaty and transgression will be avoided at all costs-this is indeed the very essence of neutrality. As regards the non-treaty, non-Muslim states, whether they are at war or peace, they will be considered potentially hostile. Islam does not recognize any condition between complete peace and the lack of it.

All dealings with the treaty-states, as stated will be in accordance with the terms of the treaty, Islam, however, has reserved some rights for them:

Until the treaty-states conform to the clauses agreed upon, there would be no transgression from the Muslims.

"Those of the idolaters, with whom ye (Muslims)

have a treaty and who have neither since abated nothing of your right nor have supported anyone against you. (As for these), fulfill their treaty to them till their term. Lo! Allah loveth those who keep their duty (unto him)" (Al-Taubah: 4)

If some group of Muslims settles in a non-Muslim state with which there is a pact or treaty and they are treated with cruelty, the Muslim State does not have the option to physically help them.

"But if they (residents of non-Muslim treaty states) seek help from you in matters of religion, then it is your duty to help (them) except against a folk between whom and you there is a treaty. Allah is seer of what ye do"

During wars, the rights of the treaty-states may not be transgressed in any way. If an enemy flees into their territories, it is impermissible from the Islamic forces to pursue it therein.

"If they turn back to enmity, take them and kill them wherever ye find them, and choose no friend or helper from among them. Except those who seek refuge with a people between whom and you there is a covenant" (Al-Nisa: 89-90)

These are the principals of neutrality. Laws based on these principles may be made, to suit local and prevalent circumstances.

Declaration of War

When a treaty state is seen to be guilty of violation of some of the clauses of the treaty, the relevant Islamic law specifies that it be given a warning to desist from such violations. It is to be given sufficient time to amend its attitude, but if it insists on violation of the treaty, war may be declared against it.

"And if thou feerest treachery from any folk, then throw back to them (their treaty) fairly. Lo! Allah loveth not the treacherous" (Al-Anfal: 58)

"Throw back to them fairly" has been explained by commentators as, warning the treaty-state that it's acts are a violation of the treaty, therefore the treaty between them and the Muslim State stands annulled. After that, some time is to be granted to that state to amend its attitude. If it persists on acts amounting to non-performance of the treaty, war may be declared against it.

Exempted from this principle of commencing hostilities are those states that have defiantly broken the treaty or have indulged in warlike activities against the Muslim State. Pagan Arab actions prior to the Muslim conquest of Makkah provide examples of such non-performance of treaties. In such conditions, declaration of war is not mandatory in order to begin military action. Such action may be commenced forthwith, as was done by the Prophet (SAW) in these particular circumstances.

Allama Ibn Hajar, a prominent Islamic jurist, states in the context,

> "'Throw back to them fairly' means, to throw back the treaty at them in such a way, that the message that the treaty stands annulled, is received by them 'loud and clear'".

Allama Ibn Kaseer states in the connection:

> "'Throw back to them (the treaty) fairly' means, that the non-Muslim signatory to the treaty be advised that they have broken the treaty, so that they are aware that they are now on equal footing; that they are enemies of the Muslim State and the Muslim State is their enemy and that there is no treaty or pact in existence between the two".

Azhari states:

> "When a Muslim State has a treaty or pact, with a non-Muslim state, and it is feared that the non-Muslims will violate it, the Muslims should not directly commence hostilities against them. First, a warning has to be given against the non-performance of the pact or treaty."

Other jurists have stated that the non-Muslims should not only be warned, but have also recommended that they be given enough time to rectify the situation. If they persist in their violations, only then war is to be declared against them. The validity of this contention is borne out by an incident that occurred during the reign of Abdul Malik bin Saleh. In this incident, the people of Cyprus had violated an existing treaty. Abdul Malik consulted the prominent Jurists of the time, to obtain a ruling on the options available to him as per the Islamic jurisprudence. Fortunately, many of the rulings given at the time are preserved today, as references for the future. Some of the replies of these prominent jurists are stated below:

Lais bin Saad wrote:

> "'The Cypriots be given one year to undertake internal consultation. In that period if any Cypriot wishes to seek protection of the Muslim State, he may immigrate to there. Anyone, who wishes to immigrate to Rome, he may do so. War may be waged against those who wished to stay in Cyprus and fight."

Imam Malik stated:

> "In his opinion, undue haste should be avoided in the annulment of treaties. First, there should be consultation between the two treaty-states, to find a solution if possible. Quoting from the Qur'an, he declares that Allah grants the Muslims, permission to attack them, if despite being given latitude and concessions, they do not desist from violations of the treaty."

Musa bin Aain writes:

> "Earlier when such situations have arisen, the non-Muslim states have been given time to reconsider their actions, by the Muslim rulers. It is quite possible that the generality of Cypriots is not in agreement with the actions taken by the ruling class. He ruled that the treaty with Cyprus be kept operative and not annulled, even though some of the Cypriots were adamant on causing strife."

In similar circumstances, Umar (RA) bin Khattab (RA), the second Caliph of Islam, also gave the ruling, that violators of treaties be given time to reconsider. In his caliphate, Umair bin

Saad (RA) wrote to him that in the Islamic territories, there was a place named Urbasoos. The people of Urbasoos, he wrote, were known to pass on Muslim State secrets to the enemy, but failed to supply information of the enemy to the Muslims. The Caliph wrote back, advising Umair (RA), first to go to those people and offer double of what each possessed, for vacating the territory. If they did not agree to the offer they were to be given a period of one year, to vacate the place. When that period elapsed, anyone of them still found in the area be forcibly evicted (Futuh al-Buldan, Balazuri, page 162-163).

Prisoners of Wars

It has been stated earlier, that Islam has prohibited killing prisoners of wars. It does not however stop at that, but recommends a very high degree of kindness in their treatment. The Qur'an commends the acts of feeding, the needy, the orphans and the prisoners, and terms it an act of great piety.

> "And feed with food the needy wretch, the orphan and the prisoner, for love of Him, (saying): We feed you for sake of Allah only. We wish for no reward or thanks from you; Lo! We fear from our Lord a day of frowning and of fate" (Al-Dahar: 8-10)

The Prophet (SAW) always recommended treating prisoners with forbearance and due respect. In the Battle of Badr, Muslims were able to capture some of the Quraish. These were the same people, who had earlier expelled the Muslims from their homeland, after much mistreatment and in some cases physical torture. The Prophet (SAW) instructed his companions to treat them with forbearance and kindness. As a result, they were accorded the comfort and food that the Muslims could ill afford even for themselves. Some of the companions ate dates only, so that their prisoners could be given proper food. When the prisoners did not have proper clothes, the Prophet (SAW) personally made arrangement for their appropriate clothing. Among the prisoners, there was one, Sohail bin Amrao, a very well lettered person, who used to make resounding speeches against the Prophet (SAW). Umar (RA) bin Khattab advised that his teeth be knocked out. The Prophet (SAW) refused, stating that if he incapacitated prisoners, Allah would incapacitate him. Later all prisoners were released after receiving their ransom. Islam specifies that at the end of wars, prisoners of wars should either be released on taking ransom or without it. Until the time they remain prisoners, however, they are to be treated equitably[3].

---

[3] The books of hadith and commentary relate the incident of the POWs of Badr. When they were brought in as captives, the Prophet (SAW) consulted his companions, as to the treatment to be given to them. At this time, the treatment meted out to the Muslims themselves, and expulsion from their homes earlier, by these very prisoners was fresh in their memories. Even this particular battle had been to dislodge them from the place that had given them refuge (Madinah).

The Muslims were pining for revenge; apart from this, the Muslim forces were many times weaker than the forces of the non-believers. At this time releasing them would be adding to their own disadvantage. Further, Muslims at this time were in the grip of extreme want; Days passed when even there was no food for themselves. Under these circumstances, providing for the prisoners untill the end of hostilities was a very difficult task.

Keeping in view the conditions, Umar (RZ) bin Khattab advised that the prisoners be killed; Abdullah bin Arwah (RZ) recommended burning them alive; but Abu Bakar (RZ), the most respected of the companions of the Prophet (SAW), recommended that they be freed. On this the Prophet (RZ) stated that Allah had made some hearts soft of the quality of milk, while some hard as stones. Abu Bakar's was of the Quality of Abraham's and Jesus, while Umar's was of the quality of Noah's. He decided, ultimately, to accept ransom being offered for the prisoners and released them. A well-known tradition states that Allah was angered during the Battle of Badr and the following verse was revealed,

> "It is not for any Prophet to have captives till he hath made slaughter in the land. Ye desire the lure of this world and Allah desireth (for you) the hereafter, and Allah is mighty, wise" (Al-Anfaal: 67-68)

As opposed to this, some scholars are of the opinion that the verse was not revealed in connection with the captives, but as an admonition to Muslims who had indulged in acquiring the spoils of war, before permission for it had been granted by the Lord. Imam Tirmizi in his book, Al-Tafseer; Imam Abu Yusuf, in his book Al-Kheraj; and Imam Ibn Jarir Tibri, in his commentary have stated the following tradition.

"When the Battle of Badr took place, the Muslims, before taking of war booty was made permissible, indulge in looting. On this occasion, the verse Al-Anfal: 67-68 (quoted above), was revealed".

Whatever the circumstances, it is confirmed that the verse was revealed on the occasion of the battle of Badr, it was especially relevant to that occasion and that it was not of general applicability.

Surah Muhammad, (Quoted in the main text above) was for the general

"And when ye meet in battle, it is smiting of the
necks until, when ye have routed them, then making
fast of the bonds; and afterwards either grace or
ransom" (Mohammad: 4)

From the above quoted verse, some scholars have taken the
meaning of grace as the release of prisoners without ransom,
though grace includes treating prisoners fairly, even when they are
not released and remain prisoners.

In accordance with the provisions of the verse, the Prophet
(SAW) very often, released the prisoners out rightly, without
ransom, but also took ransom, sometimes. At Jabal-e-Tamim,
eighty people of Makkah attacked the Muslim force. All were
captured alive but released later without ransom. During the Battle
of Hunayn, 2000 men of the Huwazin tribe were released with due
honor. Similarly, Samama bin Usal, the chief of the Yamama tribe,
was released without ransom after being made captive by the
Muslims.

The Question of Slavery

The nature of permissibility in Islam, of making slaves of
POWs and keeping women of conquered nations, has been oft
questioned. If this permissibility is indeed a fact, the question is,
whether it conforms to the spirit of the Qur'anic injunctions of
"treating the prisoners with grace or releasing them on payment of
ransom." The spirit in which objectors have raised their objections
to the institution of slavery in Islam and the way advocates of
Islam have answered the objections, clearly indicate that neither is
fully aware of the true nature of slavery in Islam.

It is a fact that Islam has permitted taking slaves in wars. It is
also a fact that conjugal rights have been permitted with female
slaves thus taken. However, to understand the nature and factual
position of this permissibility, it is necessary that one understand
the logic behind it.

Firstly, in the era, exchange of prisoners was not in vogue.

---

application. The conduct of the Prophet (SAW), in subsequent wars and
battles was in conformity with the teachings of the later verse. If the previous
verse (Al-Anfal: 67-68) had remained valid, no prisoner would have been
ever taken by the Muslims.

When Muslims became prisoners of wars, they were enslaved by other nations. Therefore, the Muslims had no alternative, but to keep their prisoners. However, whenever there was an opportunity, Muslims did try to negotiate an exchange of POWs. In his book, Fatah Ul Bari, Allama Hajar writes, that if there were Muslim prisoners with the non-Muslims and Muslims had their prisoners, an exchange of prisoners was negotiated. (Fatah ul Bari, vol.6, page 101)

Imam Abu Hanifah, Imam Abu Yusuf, Imam Muhammad, Imam Malik, Imam Shafaee, Muslim, Abu Dawood and Tirmizi, the foremost jurists and scholars of Islam, quote the tradition, that the Prophet (SAW) arranged the release of two Muslims in exchange for one non-believer.

Secondly, it is also a fact that during wars, most men of a dwelling were killed. Sometimes the entire lot of men capable of bearing arms was lost. In these conditions, there was no alternative for the victors but to take over the responsibility of the orphans and widows of the conquered nations. When this was to be the responsibility of the victors, the only way to ensure the safety of the womenfolk and that they had a position in society, was that each be made the responsibility of a particular person and be permitted to have conjugal relations with that man[4]. In this way,

---

[4] Of women who came in possession of the Muslim army, The Islamic Law rules that:

a) Till the Muslim Government, decides whether these women are to be released on receiving their ransom or exchanged for own POWs or whether they are to be distributed as slaves among the Muslim army, the female prisoners are to be kept as prisoners. During this period, anyone who has sexual relations with any of these women will be liable to the punishment prescribed for illicit sex.

b) If the state decides that female prisoners are to be kept as slaves, they will be distributed among the Muslims; in a way, that one woman will be given in the ownership of only one man.

c) When the women have been distributed, the owner of each may not establish conjugal relations with her, till one menstrual period has passed. If the woman is pregnant, it is necessary that she first be allowed to deliver the child she is carrying.

d) Only the man, who has been allotted a woman, may have conjugal relations with her. Any other man indulging in sex with her will be guilty of illicit sex and be liable to punitive action prescribed the severity of they became members of the Muslim society. Thus, the possibility of their exploitation and corruption was avoided, which would have been the natural result of thousands of women left without husbands[5].

Thirdly, Islam has just permitted not ordered making slaves of POWs, no. To take advantage of this permissibility or not, is left to the discretion of Muslims. In fact, from the conduct of the first four pious Caliphs, it has been demonstrated that not taking advantage of this permissibility is worthy of greater nobility and honor.

Huge areas of Egypt, Syria, Iraq, Africa, Armenia and Persia came under Muslim Rule, as a result of wars and many people there, were made captives of the Muslim Army. However, apart from a limited number, there were not many enslaved. At times, it so happened, that the local commander of the Muslim forces enslaved some of the enemy, but when the Caliph came to know of this, he ordered their release.

Balazuri writes that some of the areas of Egypt fell to the Muslim army after much resistance. The local commander enslaved some of the people of the area and dispatched them to Umar (RA), at Madinah. Umar (RA) ordered their release and dispatched them back to their homeland, decreeing that they be allowed to remain subjects of the Islamic State as others of the area. From this, it is Obvious that neither enslavement was necessary nor worth any great honor.

Fourthly, Islam has per force allowed enslavement and then only of those made captives in war. Capturing ordinary people and selling them as slaves is strictly prohibited. The Prophet (SAW)

---

which, all are well aware.

e) Any soldier guilty of indulgence in sex in the area of conflict, in other than under the conditions outlined above, will be guilty, and be liable to be punished.

Obviously, this respectable and pure system is above comparison with the systems that condones the behavior of the conquering forces of today; who on entering conquered areas, indulge in all forms of illicit and forced sex, the lewdness and disgraceful nature of which is beyond description.

[5] (Detailed analysis of the question of concubine is beyond the scope of this book. The author has gone more deeply into the subject, in his books, 'Tafheemat' volume 2, 'Rasael-o-Masael.' and 'Tafheem ul Qur'an'.).

once stated that there would be three people against whom he would personally bear witness; one who made a pledge in his name and did not fulfill it; one who sold a free human being and ate the money, and one who did not pay the laborer fully for his labor. (Bukhari, Kitab ul Bayan)

From the foregoing, it is obvious that Islam permitted slavery of the POWs only as a necessity, though it was possible that slavery could have been made general. Then, however, it would have attained the proportion and quality of slavery, in the times of paganism in Arabia or of the Roman or Persian empires. Then probably a class of low (sic) human beings would have developed as Shudars, in the Hindu society.

The way of Islam is that if reform of an ill is near impossible, it tolerates it temporarily, but does not maintain it for long, at least not in its original form, but brings about changes in that system or concept in such a way that it becomes devoid of its major ills. The same modus operandi was followed regarding slavery. It was not possible to eliminate slavery all together in one sweep; therefore, the institution remained in place, but with such reforms that instead of remaining a social irritant it became an example of supreme humanity.

For the purpose, Islam adopted many means. The three most important of these are discussed below.

Freeing slaves or aiding in their achievement of freedom has been declared a major act of piety and has been encouraged. The Qur'an says,

> "Ah! What will convey to thee what ascent is-- (it
> is) to free a slave and to feed in the day of hunger,
> an orphan near kin, or some wretch in misery"
> (Al-Balad: 12-16)

The Prophet (SAW) adopted many means of instilling in the Muslims, the supremacy of this teaching of Islam. For this reason, freeing of slaves began to be considered an act of honor and of much appreciation in the Muslim society. Once an Arab asked the Prophet (SAW), one way in which he could ensure his place in heaven. The Prophet (SAW) replied that way was to free slaves and to help them gain their freedom.

A hadith states,

> "Any that grants a Muslim slave his freedom will
> have limb for limb of the freed slave, saved from
> hell. Freeing a human from bondage is like paying
> ransom for entry into heaven."

Imam Zain ul Aabideen, heard the Prophet (SAW) say, 'Anyone who frees a slave, will have each of his limb forgiven for each limb of the freed slave'. Directly, the Imam called the slave whom he had bought for 10,000 Dirhams and freed him.

To further this inclination in Muslims, to free slaves, he stated the concept: "The dearer the slave who was freed, the greater will be the reward." Once Abu Dhar Ghiffari (RA), inquired of the Prophet (SAW), freeing of which type of slave was worthy of the greatest reward. He replied the greater the value of the slave freed and the dearer the slave, the greater would be the reward. Similarly, freeing a female slave of bondage and marrying her after training her well, have been declared acts of great piety. The hadith states,

> "The one who trains and educates a female slave
> and then marries her, will be deserving of double
> the reward of freeing a slave"

For the atonement of sins too, the freeing of a slave has been declared the best penance. Similarly, freeing of slaves at the time of solar eclipses has been stated as a means of escaping ill omens. In fact, all means and methods have been exploited to rid the society of the curse of slavery.

The second method adopted was to stress upon the Muslims, to treat their slaves with tenderness, love, and forbearance. The Prophet (SAW) in his parting words, advised the Muslims, firstly to ensure regularity in their prayers and to treat their slaves graciously. Out of the influence of paganism, they had just shed; some of Arabs would occasionally mistreat their slaves. On this, the Prophet (SAW) would scold even the most honored of his companions.

Maroor bin Suwed (RA), once saw Abu Dhar Ghiffari (RA), a very dear companion of the Prophet (SAW), clothed exactly as his slave and remarked on it. Abu Dhar (RA) stated that once he had abused his slave. When the Prophet (SAW) heard of it, he scolded him (Abu Dhar), saying that the effects of paganism appear to be still present in him. Then he stated about slaves,

> "These are your brothers, your servants. Allah has placed them in your care. You should therefore treat your slaves, just as you would treat your brother, who was in your service. Give them the food you eat and clothes, as you wear. Do not task them beyond their capacity, but if it is necessary to do so, join them in their labor."

Abu Masood Ansari (RA) was once beating his slave. He heard a voice chastening him, to restrain himself and reminding him that Allah had more power over him than he had over the slave. When he turned around, he saw that it was the Prophet (SAW), addressing him. He immediately granted the slave his freedom. Whereupon the Prophet (SAW) remarked that, he had thus saved himself from the fires of hell.

Once a man asked the Prophet (SAW), as to how many times one was to excuse the mistakes of one's slave. The Prophet (SAW) replied that if the slave committed seventy mistakes a day, he should be forgiven seventy times, each day.

Suwaid bin Muqaram (RA) states that between him and his six brothers, they shared one slave. Once, the youngest of the brothers slapped the slave. When the Prophet (SAW) heard of this, he ordered them to release the slave. Muawiya (RA), son of the same Suwaid (RA) relates an incident, in which he (Muawiya) had slapped a slave. When Suwaid (RA) learnt of this, he called us and told the slave to punish him. (Kitab Al-Adab, chapter 'Fe Haq e Mamluk')

It was a custom among the Arabs, to address their slaves as 'My slave' and were used to being addressed as, 'My lord'. The Prophet (SAW) forbade it and advised that the slaves be addressed as 'My boy' or 'My girl' and that the masters should be addressed as, 'Sir' or 'Master'.

The Arabs disdained even being seated close to a slave. The Prophet (SAW) advised that the slave should eat at the same place, along with the master. If that was not possible, they should at least have a few morsels from what the master ate. Thus, we learn that the slaves should be kept with respect and in comfort and are to be treated as members of the family.

The third method adopted by Islam, to lend propriety to slavery or to rid the society of it, was to grant legal rights and privileges to slaves that would bring them almost at par with free men. Criminal law provides them the same rights to life and property, as to free men. Theft of their property, their murder, violation of their women, damaging of their person or property are all punishable to the same extent as such crimes committed against the free. Civil law, similarly, grants them the rights of ownership of property and their utilizing it for their use is permissible to a great degree.

The law does not permit the slave owner to spend of that, which is owned by his slave, or to cause any bodily harm or injury to the slave or to dishonor his women. It may be noted, that this was the same era, during which in Rome, any slave girl getting married had to spend her first nuptial night with the owner; even Christian bishops did not refrain from taking advantage of this permissibility. (Amir Ali, 'The Spirit of Islam')

More than the law, the Islamic society, gave slaves equality. Their life in general, was not to any great degree, inferior to that of the free people. In all walks of life, including education, politics, religion and economics, they were free to progress to any level. Being slaves was not an obstacle in their path either in the social or professional field. The Prophet (SAW) himself, got his cousin, Zainab (RA), (who he later married himself) married to his freed slave Zaid bin Haris (RA). Imam Husain (RA) married an Iranian princess who had been taken captive in one of the battles and was then a slave. Imam Zain ul Abedeen (RA) was born of this wedlock. The latter's progeny still occupies a much respected place in the Muslim society. Salim bin Abdullah (RA) and Qasim bin Kahanal bin Abi Bakar, the much respected sons of the Prophets companions, were children of slave women. Imam Hasan Basri, a respected scholar and the forerunner of a popular school of thought in Islam, was the son of a slave. Imam Abu Hanifah, the renowned scholar of Islam; whose school of religious thought is followed by billions of Muslims the world over and who is known as' Imam -e-Azam', is said to have been a slave in the ownership of one of the tribe of Bani Taim. One of the foremost compilers of hadith, Muhammad bin Sireen, was the son of slaves, both his mother and father were slaves. However, his mother held the degree of respect that three of the Prophet's wives prepared her for her wedding. The respected companion of the Prophet (SAW) Ubey bin Kaab (RA) performed her wedding rites. The teacher of Imam Malik, by the name of Naafe (RA), was a slave owned by Abdullah bin Umar (RA). Abu Abdur Rehman Abdullah bin Mubarik, a respected scholar of Islamic jurisprudence, was the son of a slave named Mubarik. Ikrimah whose commentaries on the Qur'an, is a reference, was himself a slave. Muhammad bin Ishaq, whose books on the life of the Prophet (SAW) are also a reference for scholars, was a grandson of a POW of the battle of Yemen. Al-Tamar the compiler of the sayings of the Prophet (SAW), Imam Ata bin Ribah of Makkah, Imam Taoos Bin Kisan of Yemen, Imam Yazid bin Habib of Egypt, Imam Mahkul of Syria, Imam Mamoon bin Mehran of Algeria, Imam Zahak of Khorasan and Imam Ibrahim Ghani of Kufa, were all very learned and highly respected scholars of Islam; they were all slaves.

Salman Farsi, a companion of the Prophet (SAW), of whom Ali bin Abu Talib (RA), the fourth Caliph of Islam and the son-in-law of the Prophet (SAW) states, "We regarded him as one of the family of the Prophet (SAW)", was a slave. Of Bilal, an Ethiopian slave of the Prophet (SAW), Umar (RA) bin Khattab, the second Caliph of Islam, says, "He is the slave of our master and master of all of us. " Suhaib (RA) was a Roman slave, whom Umar (RA) nominated for leading the Muslims in Prayers, in his own place. Salim was the slave of Abu Huzaifah (RA), of him Umar (RA) stated that if he had been alive, he (Umar (RA) would have nominated him (Salim) for caliphate of Islam as his successor.

Usama bin Zaid (RA) was the son of a slave, whom the Prophet (SAW) towards the end of his life had nominated to command the army of Islam. In this army, the foremost companions of the Prophet (SAW), including Abu Bakar (RA), who was later to become the first Caliph of Islam, were under his command. Umar (RA) bin Khattab, said to his son Abdullah (RA), that Usama's father was more cherished by the Prophet (SAW) than his father (meaning Umar (RA) himself and that Usama was more cherished than him (meaning Abdullah).

These are tales of the forebears of Islam, but even when the spirit had weakened somewhat, slaves like Qutub ud din Aibak, shams ud din Altutmash and Ghayas ud din Balban have actually ruled the Indian sub-continent. Mehmud Ghaznawi, who is considered the greatest conqueror of his time, was from the family of Turkish slaves. Egypt was under the kingship of Mamluks for centuries. As the name itself suggests, they were a dynasty of slaves, the dynasty, which descended from a lowly slave and reached the very peak.

Who can term these people as slaves? Were there any that had more opportunity to achieve progress, respect and sovereignty than these slaves had? Did slavery prove any obstacle in their achieving the high status they achieved? If this indeed is slavery, none should object to changing the name of 'freedom' to 'slavery'.

This was the methodology adopted by Islam to gradually wipe out the old concept of slavery until hardly any difference remained between slavery and freedom. The nomenclature, slavery, persisted, but in truth became something else.

The Question of the Spoils of War

The position of spoils of war in Islamic warfare has been a subject of much undue criticism by detractors of Islam and even weak and faulty advocacy has only served to make it a cause of disrepute to the institution. The intensity that the desire for spoils of war had reached among the Arabs has been discussed in preceding chapters. Spoils of war were the main factor motivating Arabs to battle others. Even the risk of grave injury or death could not hold them back. It can be said that in cases, the desire for plunder had attained the position of the primary cause of warfare. The concept of 'harb' (war) was incomplete, unless loot and plunder complemented it.

When Islam arrived, most people entered its folds with their pre-conceived ideas. It was no easy task to approach the subject, negating influences passed down through centuries and generations. The mentality of those, who were to be the subject of the reforms, was such that they were subconsciously drawn towards plunder and at times were unable to control themselves.

Just before Badr, the Prophet (SAW) dispatched a party under Abdullah bin Jahash (RA) to Baan-e-Nakhal to keep an eye on the movement of the enemy and report on it. On route, they came across a caravan of Quraish traders. Seeing the booty, they lost all self-control and attacked the caravan. They killed the traders and looted the goods. Some historians state, that this was the immediate cause of the Battle of Badr. (Tabari, Tab-e-Misr, vol. 2, page 267)

During the Battle of Badr itself, one trade caravan was reported to be approaching from Syria, while the Quraish army was approaching from Makkah. Although, the priority at this time was for the Muslims to consolidate their position against the enemy, the desire of most of the Muslim army was to go for the trade caravan. The Qur'an states:

> "And when Allah promised you one of the two
> bands (of the enemy) that it should be yours, and ye
> longed that other than the armed one might be
> yours. And Allah willed that he should cause the
> Truth to triumph by his words, and cut the roots of
> the disbelievers" (Al-Anfal: 7)

When the fighting ensued, it became impossible, for the companions to hold themselves. Without waiting for permission to take the booty, they commenced their plunder. The following Qur'anic verse was revealed at the time,

> "Had it not been for an ordinance of Allah which
> had gone before, an awful doom had come upon
> you on account of what you took" (Al-Anfal: 28)

In the Battle of Uhud, it was this same desire for spoils of war, that changed an almost certain victory into defeat. No sooner, the Quraish were routed and started retreating than the Muslims, lured by the chance of taking spoils, went off in their pursuit. The lure for booty was such that even the archers positioned at strategic locations, abandoned their positions, and joined in the pursuit. Resultantly, the Muslim army soon lay scattered. Seeing their advantage, the Quraish launched a counter offensive. The intensity of the counter attack was such that they were able to overcome the Muslim Army. In the attack, the Prophet (SAW) got injured as well.

There was a repeat of the same undisciplined conduct, at the battle of Hunayn. The Bani Huwazin were unable to bear the brunt of the first attack and seeing them, near defeat, the fresh Muslim converts, lost self control and started looting and plundering. The Bani Huwazin, seeing the disorder, attacked with their archers. Even the bravest of fighters could not withstand this attack.

Here the object is not to discredit any of the companions of the Prophet (SAW) or to criticize their conduct, but just to depict the intensity that their desire for spoils of war, they had acquired, having been passed down to them through generations. The intensity was such that it had by this time seeped down into their psyche. Even the respected companions of the Prophet (SAW), who had lost all desires for worldly gains, could not resist the temptation for spoils. It was impossible to eradicate completely, this desire, directly. Under the conditions, for a religion, the aim of which was not conflict with human nature, but its reform through controlling it, there was no better way than to temporarily make the taking of spoils of war, permissible. Gradually, the desire for such worldly gains was to be reduced and conditions created, wherein the taking of spoils of war would not remain such an act of honor.

The reasons for making plunder and taking spoils of war permissible have been depicted in a hadith related by Imam Abu Yusuf, on the authority of Abu Hurairah (RA). It reports the Prophet (SAW) addressed the Muslims at Badr, saying, "Before you, for no headless nation, has war booty been made permissible. A fire would descend from the Heaven and consume the booty."

(Here the reference is to an earlier incident related by Abu Hurairah (RA) in a separate hadith. Please refer to Bokhari's 'Kitab Al-Jihad-Khalat Nabi Ahlat Al-Ghanaim')

From this hadith it is apparent that taking spoils was not originally permitted, but ceding to the incorrigibility of human nature, it was made temporarily permissible. However, this permissibility was neither without restrictions nor permanent in nature. Many methods and means were adopted to curb this tendency. Thus this desire, this weakness for plunder, was gradually curbed to great extent. Restrictions and limitations on spoil themselves and limiting its scope aided the process. Three of the methods adopted, are given below:

Firstly, the value placed on the spoils was so reduced that among the pious, interest in gathering it, waned. Initially it was stated that any that undertook military campaigns, for spoils, would not be granted the reward for 'Jihad'. That reward of Allah was the lot of only those who banished from their hearts, all worldly desires for gains and fight only for gaining Allah's approval. It was later stated that the one who fought and achieved the worldly gains he desired, will have a reduced share of reward on his account on the day of Resurrection. The one who fought and neither did not desire or achieved mundane gains would be eligible for the full reward for his effort from Allah.

> "The Army which fought in the way of Allah and acquired spoils of war, has already achieved two third of his reward in this world; only a third is left of his reward. The one, whom did not take any spoils, will be deserving of the full reward." (Muslim, Kitab Al-Jihad; Nisai, Bab Al-Seriat Al-Lati Taqafuf)

The result of this teaching was that among the Muslims, the desire for God's approval gained supremacy over their desire for spoils of war. Their concepts changed. To the extent that when spoils were offered to them, they refused to accept them.

In the later part of the Prophet's life, a call was given, for the Battle of Tabuk. People were being gathered, when a person by the name of Silah bin Anqa (RA), announced that he would give half his share of spoils to the person who took him to the battle. An Ansar chief accepted the offer and took him to the battle. As his share of the spoils, he was awarded three very high quality camels. He took the camels to the chief of Ansar and offered them as fulfillment of his promise. The Ansari refused, saying that he did not join the battle for spoils but for the approval of Allah. (Abu Dawood)

Once a Bedouin was fighting a battle alongside the Prophet (SAW). During the battle, some spoils were captured. These were being distributed among the fighters. When the Bedouin was offered his share, he refused stating that he had not joined the ranks of the Muslims for spoils and that his cherished desire was, that in the battle he would be shot with an arrow through his neck and gain martyrdom. (Nisai)

The second step towards reducing the desire for plunder was

that one-fifth part of all spoils was allotted to the central treasury, for looking after the needy, and others who were granted stipends by the state. The Qur'an states:

> "And know that whatever you take as spoils of war, Lo! A fifth thereof is for Allah and for the messenger[6] and for the kinsmen (who hath need) and orphans and the needy and the wayfarer, if ye believe in Allah and what we revealed"
>
> (Al-Anfal: 41)

In this way, the share of spoils for the fighters was reduced and allotted to the state for undertaking works of welfare.

The third step was that only that was declared as spoils of war that the army took from the enemy, during battle or as a result of it, from the field. Previously, 'spoils of war' denoted that which was taken from the enemy land, regardless of the means adopted. In this way, after the declaration, material looted from civilians, who did not take actual part in the war was declared out of the bounds of 'spoils of war' (Nisai). Even those materials were excluded from its definition that came into the ownership of the Muslims as result of treaties for peace, without actually fighting a battle, included in it were the material goods captured by the army, after the end of formal battle.

In short, anything that was acquired by the Muslims, as a result of war, from the enemy's ownership, fell out of the bounds of the description of 'spoils of war'. This other type of material goods was termed as 'state property' and was not to be distributed among the soldiers, The Qur'an states:

> "And that which Allah give as spoil unto his messenger from them, ye urged not any horse or riding-camel for the sake thereof, but Allah giveth his messenger lordship over whom He will. Allah is able to do all things. That which He giveth as spoils unto his messenger from the people of the townships, it is for Allah and his messenger (for the state) and for the near of kin and the orphans and the needy and the wayfarer, that it become not a

---

[6] For the state, to use for the welfare of common

commodity for the rich among you. And whatsoever
the messenger giveth you take it, and whatsoever he
forbideth, (abstain from it). And keep your duty to
Allah. Lo! Allah is stern in reprisal"

(Al-Hashar: 6-7)

The verses declare, only that material can be termed as spoils
of war that the army acquires in the battlefield as a result of armed
conflict with the enemy. The rest of the material goods, property,
and land acquired without the direct involvement of the sword,
come under the description of 'state property' of the Muslim State.
This state property may only be spent on projects that have the
sanction of the Lord and his Prophet (SAW).

Some companions of the Prophet (SAW) understood it to mean
that the Prophet (SAW) alone has the right to the lands and
property mentioned above. After more careful study, it was clear
that there were other heads of expenditure mentioned. These are:
Allah, the Prophet (SAW), the Prophet's kinsfolk of the Banu
Hashim and the Banu Muttalib tribes, the orphans, the needy and
the travelers. After the Prophet (SAW), there still remained five
heads of expenditure that the state treasury had to bear. Apart from
all else, the wisdom of the distribution, as stated in the Qur'an is,
that the wealth should not be allowed to gather in a few hands,
making the rich richer.

The factors that necessitated the distribution still exist.
Therefore, the Islamic law states, that the property and lands
gained by the Islamic State, in the ways mentioned, are to be
reserved in the name of Allah and the Prophet (SAW) and be used
for the welfare of the general public. (When the army demanded
the distribution of the land and property gained in Iraq, Caliph
Umar (RA) refused, quoting this same verse (i.e. Al-Hashar: 6-7).
The army had to settle for what they acquired from the enemy in
the battlefield.

In connection with the distribution of the spoils of war, Umar's
(RA) letter to Saad bin Abi Waqas (RA) clarifies the Islamic law to
a great extent. Balazari has copied the letter in its own words. It
states,

"Received your letter, you write that the people are
demanding whatever property and land, Allah has

given them as spoils, be distributed. So what you should do after receiving this letter, is that after taking out a fifth of all material wealth, property and animals you have plundered by riding of horses and camels (whatever gained in fighting), distribute it among the soldiers. Leave the lands and canals with the cultivators, to enable giving the salaries of the soldiers. If you distribute these too, there will be nothing left for the Muslims who come after these." (Futuh al-Buldan, Page 374 and Abu Yusuf, Kitab Al-khiraj, page 13-14)

When Abu Ubaidah (RA) conquered Syria, the problem of distribution of conquered lands raised its head again. The Muslim Army demanded that all the conquered territories be termed as spoils of war and distributed among them. Abu Ubaidah (RA) referred the matter to the Caliph Umar (RA), requesting for instructions. Umar (RA) wrote him a lengthy reply, referring the Qur'anic verses quoted in the foregoing paragraph (Al-Hashar: 6-7). He stated that, the land, Allah had awarded him as result of wars and treaties, should remain the property of the original owners and only tax in accordance with the production capacity, be levied on them.

In this fashion, Islam reduced the longing among its followers for spoils of war, which in fact, had become the prime reason for the plunder, loot and destruction that had become synonymous with wars. On the other hand, such rules were legislated that the scope of spoils of war was reduced. Then only that material could be termed as spoils that were taken from the enemy, through military action. Even from the spoils so gathered, a fifth had to be surrendered to the state for its welfare activities.

Here, it is necessary to understand, that whatever the soldier can lay his hands on, does not become his personal property; materials so acquired, will be illegal plunder, which is not permissible in Islam. The righteous way is that each soldier surrenders what he has taken from the enemy, the local commander submits one fifth of the spoils so gathered, to the state treasury and the rest is distributed equitably among the soldiers, who took part in the action. Exempt from this provision are food items, which may be consumed as necessary.

In Islamic terminology, 'spoils of war' has the same definition as in Western Law, and is regarded as the natural right of the conquering nation. The only difference is that the Western Law regards the entire lot of spoils of war as state property, whereas the Islamic law requires that 4/5 of it be distributed among the combatants, while only 1/5 becomes state property, to be utilized for its welfare activities.

Since, according to Western Law, all spoils of war are state property, soldiers are incited to theft and misappropriation, whereas the Islamic laws do not deprive the soldiers of their rights. It rather inculcates in them an honor system. They have to first submit the entire loot, and then the entire loot is distributed as stated earlier.

Truce and Asylum

In Islam, the main object of war is peace. Muslims should be ever ready for peace. Islam does not believe in war for the sake of war, rather treats it as an instrument of diplomacy to bring about reforms and peace. If bilateral talks have a chance of achieving the same ends, they should be given the priority. For the same reason, the limit of conflict defined by Islam is the non-existence of the cause of conflict.

The Qur'an instructs us that if the enemy sues for peace, we should accept the opportunity with an open heart,

> "And if they incline to peace, incline thou also to it,
> and trust in Allah. Lo! He is the hearer, the knower.
> And if they deceive thee, then lo! Allah is sufficient
> for thee. He it is, who supporteth thee with help and
> with the believers" (Al-Anfal: 61-62)

It is also stated that if the enemy surrenders and asks for protection, then the Muslims do not have the right to raise their hand against him:

> "(Do not harm) those who seek refuge with a people
> between whom and you there is a covenant, or
> (those who) come unto you because their hearts
> forbid them to make war on you or make war on
> their own folk. Had Allah willed, he could have
> given them power over you, so that assuredly they

would have fought you. So if they hold aloof from you and wage not war against you and offer you peace, Allah alloweth you no way against them"

(Al-Nisaa: 90)

Similarly, if a few individuals seek your protection, they should not be killed, but allowed to live in your protection. When they wish to return to their homeland, they should be safely escorted back to their country,

> "And if anyone of the idolaters seeketh thy protection (O Muhammad), then protect him, so that he may hear the word of Allah, and convey him back to his place of safety. That is because they are a folk who know not" (Al-Taubah: 6)

Originally, the object of this verse was the spread of Islam. Ibn Jareer and Ibn Kaseer state that the verse meant that they be taken into the protection of Islam and exposed to it through sermons and preaching, so that they may accept the truth. However, if they do not, they should not be killed or harassed, but escorted back in safety to their lands. The words however are of a general nature and not specifically addressed. Most scholars have therefore taken it to mean that if anyone of a nation in conflict with the Islamic State wishes to enter the Islamic territories, with the intent of tourism, trade or education, they should be so permitted and be granted permission for free movement. Their stay however is conditional to their being granted asylum. Otherwise, if they may be suspected of spying, the punishment for spies in the Islamic law, as in other laws, is death.

Imam Abu Hanifa, the foremost jurist of Islam, states that after a period of one year, the asylum seeker be given a notice, either to seek nationality of the Islamic State or go back to his country.(Kitab Al-Khiraj, page 117, and Hidaya, Kitab as Sayyir, chap. Al-Mustamin). Some jurists, however, are of the opinion that after the lapse of a year of asylum, the asylum seeker automatically gains the nationality of the Islamic State.

The difference between the rights of the persons granted asylum and a non-Muslim subject is very little. They have certain privileges, though payment of jaziya' tax will not be the liability of asylum seekers nor would they be liable to cancellation of their asylum, even if they commit any major crime in the host country. For example, if they commit robbery, theft, murder of a Muslim or indulge in crimes of sex, even with a Muslim woman, they would be liable for punishment to the extent a normal citizen would be. Their status would however remain unchanged, i.e. they would not be deported etc. To the extent that even if they are involved in espionage, they will not be deprived of their asylum, they would only suffer punitive action for their crime. (Rad Al-Mohtar, vol.2, page 273)

The only disadvantage he suffers is that if a Muslim or non-Muslim commits his murder, he (the citizen) would not have to undergo the prescribed punishment but would only be liable to pay the adjudged blood money (penalty) to the relatives of the murdered. The reason for this discrimination is that the jurisprudence wishes to maintain some difference between the citizen of the Muslim State and strangers, especially those strangers who may belong to a country with which the Muslim State is not bound by any treaty and it may even be on hostile terms with the Muslims.

Treatment of the Vanquished

Now that the act of war has been discussed, let us consider the actions related to warfare. Treating the enemy with kindness, when it still has some strength and when the flames of vengeance are alive in him, may be influenced by, even if too a very minute degree, the element of fear. However, those who have lost all desire and capability for resistance and laid down at the mercy of the conqueror, treating a fallen enemy with kindness, justice, and piety, proclaim the graciousness of the conquering nation. Basically, his treatment by the conqueror is directly relative to the cause of the war the conqueror set out with.

If the cause was religious intolerance then intolerance, discrimination, and ill treatment on that account will be the lot of the fallen nation. If the cause was the gathering of wealth, forced exploitation will be his lot. If however, the cause of the conqueror was conquest itself and establishing his supremacy on a people, then the consequent rule will be based on establishing his over-lordship and the subservience of the vanquished. Crudity and cruelty of treatment would of course be the tools of such establishment.

As against the above, if the aim of the conquering a nation is reform of that society and nothing else, the victor will neither usurp the vanquished nation's wealth, nor will it subject it to religious intolerance and discrimination, stripping it of its self-respect, or make the vanquished its slave. Its governance will be based on justice, tolerance, and good grace. Its politics will be based on principles and while keeping the vanquished nation from strife, turbulence and arrogance will provide it with enough opportunity to progress in both the material and moral fields.

In view of the criteria, let us study how Islam interacts with the vanquished nations, what position its laws accord to them, what rights its jurisprudence gives them and whether the Islamic Government treats them with justice or lets loose strife and turmoil in the conquered territories.

The Status of Conquered Nations

Islamic law divides the conquered nations into two categories. One category is of those states, which accept the sovereignty of the Muslim State by virtue of treaties before or during war. The other category is of those who fought out the war and having lost it, come under its sovereign. There are some, if only minor differences, in instructions regarding the treatment of the two. Let us therefore study these separately.

Treaty States

The instructions regarding those nations, who before or during war, sue for peace and agree to the conditions laid down by the Islamic State are that their interaction will be in accordance with the clauses of the treaties mutually agreed upon by both parties to the conflict.

A common practice of today, even among the respectable nations, is ensuring subservience of the enemy by virtue of a treaty, and then when these nations are in control, not behaving with them in accordance with the terms of the treaty. Islam terms such lack of faith to be totally impermissible and criminal. It countenances strict compliance of the terms, whether they are to the liking of any one of the signatories. The changing conditions of strength and position will have no effect on treaties to any extent.

A hadith states,

> "If you are in a fight with a nation and gain the upper hand; if the enemy, in order to save its lives and the lives of its children, sues for peace, (another hadith states, if you agree to a treaty), on condition of payment of some ransom, extracting one bit more than the amount agreed to, is incorrect for you."
> (Abu Dawood, Kitab Al-Jihad)

The Prophet (SAW) states in another hadith,

> "Beware, any who treats cruelly, a person of the state with which there is a treaty, who usurps his rights, who places a greater burden on him than he can bear, who takes from him anything, without his approval. Against him, I will personally be the accuser on the Day of Resurrection."
> (Abu Dawood, kitab Al-Jihad)

From these two hadith, it is clear that when there is a treaty between a Muslim and a non-Muslim state, it is not allowable that the clauses of the treaty be altered unilaterally in any way, while its term runs. Neither their tax (jaziya) can be increased, nor either their lands or buildings can be confiscated; they cannot be subjected to any new and strict civil laws; their religion cannot be interfered with nor can their honor be violated. There may not be such action that may be termed as cruelty, trouble, or that which will injure their self-respect.

Because of the preciseness of the divine rules, the Islamic Jurists did not find it necessary to make any particular rules on the subject but were satisfied in stating the rule that all interaction with other treaty states must follow exactly the clauses of the treaty.

Imam Abu Yusuf states,

> "Only that will be appropriated from them which have been agreed to, in the peace-treaty; they will be treated in accordance with the terms of the treaty and nothing more severe will be imposed on them."

Obviously, no rules can predetermine treaties. The existing circumstances can only determine the terms of a particular treaty. However, the treaties entered into by the Prophet (SAW) and the first four pious caliphs can provide a rough guidance for the future. With the intent of highlighting this guidance, the gist of some of the treaties is narrated below.

When the people of Najran sued for peace, the Prophet (SAW), after determining the amount of tax to be levied on them, wrote:

> "The Christians of Najran and those living with them are granted the peace of the Lord, the responsibility of which is the responsibility of Muhammad, Prophet of Allah, for the lives, the religion, the property, of those present and those who are not present; for their camels, for their messengers, their religious relics (meaning crosses, paintings, etc., that are commonly kept in the church). They will remain in the condition they are presently in. There will be no change in their rights and marking. No pontiff will be removed from his pontificate, no other clergyman will be removed from his position and none serving the church, will be removed from his service, whether that which is under his authority is big or small. They will not be answerable for any life lost on their account or oath unfulfilled, during the period of paganism. They will not be forced into military service. No band of troops will be allowed to destroy their crops or damage their fields. (Neither Islamic troops nor foreign enemy troops).If any lays a claim against them, the case will be dealt with justice."

People of Najran will neither be allowed to treat others with cruelty nor will any other be allowed to treat them cruelly. Apart from any, which has indulged in usury, none will be held answerable for any past sin or crime" (by the '------practice of usury-------', here indicates that any claims of interest due on money lent on interest, will not be the responsibility of the Islamic State.).

During the Caliphate of Abu Bakar (RA), Khalid bin Waleed

(RA), when enacting a treaty with the people of Khira, set 20000 Dirhams on the total population of Khira as tax, which comes to around ten Dirhams a head per year, excluding the needy and the disabled. (This is about the equivalent of about 10 cents a year) In return, the Muslim State was to fulfill the following conditions:

> "No Church or other place of worship will be damaged, none of the castles used by Khira for defense against enemies, will be razed. Neither will they be disallowed ringing their bells nor sounding horns for the performance of their religious ceremonies nor obstructed in their religious marches carrying crosses. (Abu Yusuf states that Abu Bakar (RA) ratified the treaty". Kitab Al-Khiraj, page 84)

The treaty document written by Umar (RA) bin Khattab for the people of Jerusalem states:

> 'Peace and protection is hereby granted to the people for their lives and belongings, for their churches and crosses, for their healthy and their sick. This peace and protection extends to the people of Jerusalem. It is undertaken on oath that the Muslims will not use their churches as barracks. They (churches) will neither be damaged nor their boundaries nor buildings be reduced in size, nor will their crosses and other materials be damaged. There will be no interference in their religious ceremonies nor will these be exposed to and damaging influence.'

The truce drawn up for the people of Damascus, by Umar (RA) bin Khattab, states:

> "Peace and protection is hereby granted (to the people of Damascus), for their lives and property, for their churches and for the parapets of their cities. Their houses will not be forcibly entered into nor destroyed nor will they be used as abodes for the Muslims. This is undertaken in the name of the Allah, on the responsibility of the Prophet. -------- They will be treated with piety alone, till such time as they continue to pay their taxes."

The treaty document drawn up for the people of A'anaat by Khalid bin Waled (RA) states:

> "None of their places of worship will be razed. Night or day, whenever they wish, they may sound their bells and other musical instruments, but they must keep in consideration, the times of Muslim prayers. They will have the right to parade with their crosses on ceremonial occasions."

The treaty drawn up for the people of Balbek, by Abu Ubaida (RA) states:

> "This treaty is between the ruler of Balbek and its people whether they be Romans, Persians, or Arabs. Peace and protection is for their lives and properties, their churches and their buildings, whether in the city or outside. Peace and protection is for their grind mills--------Any, who embrace Islam, will have the same rights and duties as any of us. They will have the freedom of movement and trade with any of the Muslim states, with which the Muslim State has pacts or accords. Any of the people who wish to maintain their religion, may do so, but he will have to pay the tax (Khiraj) determined."

The treaty drawn up by Habib bin Musailamah (RA) for the people of Dabil states:

> "This document is from Habib bin Musailamah for the people of Dabil, whether they be Christians, Jews, or Magians; whether they be present or absent. I hereby grant you protection and peace, for your lives and properties, your churches and places of worship and for the parapets of your cities. You are under our peace and protection, till you continue paying your tax (khiraj), it is our duty to remain faithful to this treaty."

The treaty drawn up by Huzaifah bin Aliman (RA), for the people of Azerbaijan, states:

"Peace and protection is for the lives and property
of the people and their religions."

The same Huzaifah (RA) states in the peace treaty drawn up
for the people of Jurjan:

"Their lives, properties, and religions are granted
peace and protection. There will be no corrective
measures in respect of any of them."

In the peace treaty of Mah Dinar (RA), he wrote:

"They will not be forced to change their religion
and there will be no interference in their religious
affairs."

These documents of truce have been copied in such detail so as
to enable the reader to understand the conceptual position of
establishment of peace with the conquered nations. It is possible
that after going through a couple of these documents, it occurs to
some that some of the clauses have had to be included per force of
circumstances, by the Prophet (SAW) and his companions. It is
worth considering here that the documents copied are the treaties
between Muslims on one side and on different occasions, Arabs,
Syrians, Algerians, and Persians, and so forth, on the other side;
scores of other such documents may be found in books of history
and they all depict the same spirit of graciousness of the Muslim
contestants. Only those documents have found their place in this
book, the terms of which have been put into effect, after total
control had been established on the enemy.

The people of Najran had sent on their own, their leaders and
envoys to sue for peace with the Muslims. This was the time when
the supremacy of Islam had been established throughout Arabia.
The people of Herah sued for peace, when their neighboring states
had succumbed to the indomitable sword of Khalid bin Waled
(RA) and they saw their wellbeing only in living in peace with the
Muslims.

Jerusalem and Damascus had almost been conquered fully, and
if they really desired so, bringing these areas under the Muslim
sway by the dint of the sword, it was not a difficult proposition at
all.

Under the circumstances, making truce with them and on the

terms shown could not have been the undertaking of a nation that had set out to totally eliminate other religions or a nation or that had raised its sword for the cause of gaining over-lordship of lands or wealth.

The Non-Treaty States

The second category of the conquered are those nations who fought till the end and did not lay down their arms till the Muslim might had broken their ability and will to fight and they had entered their dwellings, as victors. As regards to such vanquished nations, Islam recognizes the right of the victor to put to death all males capable of bearing arms, enslaving its women and children, and capturing its assets. However, the more desirable way depicted is that the people of such nations be made subjects of the Muslim State and be allowed to live and prosper as before.

We know that the prevailing customs of warfare were that the vanquished were enslaved, their assets appropriated, their towns looted and then general slaughter of the masses carried out. Their military capability was thus destroyed. For Islam, it was difficult to change this trend completely in one sweep, directly. Yet, continuing warfare with the prevailing spirit, under its stated concepts of reforms, was not possible. Therefore, it chose to maintain the prevailing ways in name only, in order to satisfy the age-old biases in the direction. On the other hand, under the influence of the teaching and guidance of the Prophet (SAW) and his companions, there developed such large heartedness and graciousness among Muslims that they voluntarily declined taking advantage of the permissibility. Thus, another trend developed that factually overtook the previous concepts. History can bear witness to the fact that hundreds of cities and countries fell to the Muslim sword, but not in one single instance was general slaughter permitted, neither the people of the conquered nation enslaved nor was the confiscation of their property made general.

In the period of the Prophet (SAW), Khyber was conquered and the Prophet (SAW) made the people subjects of the Muslim State. The Muslims conquered Makkah. However, neither was its land distributed among the soldiers nor was anyone enslaved. At Hunain, the Huwaizin tribe was defeated but was granted amnesty by the Prophet (SAW). At the rein of Umar (RA) bin Khattab, the second Caliph, when Syria and Iraq were conquered for the first time, the desire arose among the Muslim army to take advantage of the rights of the conquerors. They demanded that the conquered land be distributed among the soldiers and they be allowed to enslave the enemy. They therefore put forward their demand to the Caliph. Umar's reasoning and advice had the effect of subduing their desires that were the relics of the past. Imam Abu Yusuf has copied the entire discussion on the topic: in the council of the companions of the Prophet (SAW), Bilal (RA) and Abd ur Rahman bin Auf (RA) were in favor of distributing the land among the soldiery and making slaves of the vanquished, while Usman (RA), Ali (RA), Talha (RA), Abdullah bin Umar (RA), and all chiefs of the Ansar, were of the opinion against the motion. They all believed that such a policy would not be viable. Umar (RA) bin Khattab himself was opposed to the proposition.

Umar (RA) stated in his address that the land be left with the owners, after imposing a tax on their lands (khiraj) and on their lives (jaziya). In such a way, the land could pay for the Muslim soldiers and their dependents. That would be the purpose for which it could be utilized, after it became state property. He enquired of the council how they thought after the landed properties of the provinces of Syria, Algeria, Kufa, and Egypt were distributed among the soldiery, the state was to pay the fixed honorariums and for its welfare activities of looking after the needy and the disabled. On this, the council unanimously agreed to Umar's suggestion and the people of Iraq were made the subjects of the state.

The same problem arose after the conquest of Syria. (Kitab Al-Khiraj pages 13-15) At the time, Zubair bin Al-Awam (RA) was the leader of those demanding the distribution of land. The farsightedness of Umar (RA) gave the same decision, as was given in the case of Iraq. After this incident, the problem never resurfaced. The Muslims captured land from India to Spain, in Asia, Africa, and Europe, but not in one place was this permissibility taken advantage of.

When nations are made subjects, they are granted certain rights. These are discussed in detail in the books of jurisprudence, but their basic brief outline is given below:

1) When the head of a Muslim State accepts a tax on their lives

(jaziya), he becomes responsible for them. The defense of their lives and property becomes the responsibility of the Muslims. (Bidae-us-Sanae, vol. 7 page 111). After this, the Muslims do not have the right to their property or to enslave them. Umar (RA) bin Khattab gave clear instructions on this to Abu Ubaidah (RA) (Kitab Al-Khiraj, page 86).

2) When people of a conquered nation are accepted as subjects, they remain owners of their lands. They have rights of inheritance of their landed properties, of selling them, leasing them, or keeping them as surety against loans etc. The Islamic State will have no rights to these lands whatsoever. (Fatah Al-Qadeer, vol. 4, page 359)

3) Jaziya will be levied in accordance with the monetary status of each subject. The rich will pay more, the middle class a little lesser, and the poor very little; the needy and the disabled, who depend on the others for their sustenance, will be exempt from payment of Jaziya. There was no amount fixed for appropriation as Jaziya, but due consideration had to be given to the fact that the payment of jaziya would not be allowed to become an unbearable burden for the subjects. The rates of jaziya fixed by Umar (RA) bin Khattab were: one Dinar per month for the rich, half a dinar for the middle class, and a quarter for the poor and laborer. (Kitab Al-khiraj, page 36)

4) Jaziya is to be levied on the able bodied, capable of bearing arms only. The non-combatants, including women and children, the mentally unsound, the blind the disabled, the aged, beggars, hermits, and those who look after the places of worship are exempt from payment of jaziya. (Bidae-us-Sanae, vol. 7, page 111-112; Fatah ul qadeer, vol. 4, page 372-373; Kitab Al-khiraj)

5) It is permitted to appropriate places of worship of the conquered areas, foregoing this privilege has been declared more pious. Leaving them intact is considered an act of piety. At the time of Umar (RA), many cities fell to the Muslims, but in none of these, was any place of worship razed or trespassed. 'They were allowed to remain functional', states Abu Yusuf, and were neither razed nor treated with indignity. (Kitab Al-Khiraj, page 86)

Destroying old places of worship is for sure not permitted by God (Bada-us- Sanae, vol. 7, page 114).

Rights of Subjects of the Islamic State

Let us now discuss the rights and privileges granted to the subjects of the Islamic State protectorates in general, whether they are conquered or have come in the protectorship, by virtue of treaties.

1) The lives of subjects of the Islamic State will be worthy of the same sanctity as that of a Muslim. If a Muslim murders a non-Muslim subject, he will be liable to the same punishment, as if he had committed the murder of a Muslim.

At the time of the Prophet, a Muslim murdered a non-Muslim subject. The Prophet (SAW) awarded him the sentence of death. Stating that, he (the Prophet) was the most responsible for the protection of the residents of Muslim protectorates. (Inayah Shari Hidaya, vol.8, page 256; Darkhtani has quoted a hadith relating the same incident.)

During the caliphate of Umar (RA), bin Khattab. A person from the tribe of Bakar Bin Wail murdered a subject, from the protectorate of Herah. Umar (RA) ordered that the murderer be handed over to the family of the murdered. The family put the Muslim to death (Burhan, Sharah-e-Muwahib-ur-Rehman, vol. 3, page 287).

During the caliphate of Usman (RA), the death sentence was pronounced against Ubaidullh bin Umar (RA), the son of the previous Caliph, for the murder of Harmuzan, the daughter of Abu Lulu, Umar's murderer. Ubaidullah (RA) had suspected that Harmuzan had been involved in his father's murder.

During the caliphate of Ali (RA) bin Abu Talib, a Muslim was accused of the murder of a non-Muslim subject. The Muslim was awarded the death sentence. The brother of the murdered man approached Ali (RA) and declared that he forgave the murderer. Ali (RA) was not satisfied and said that he suspected that coercion was used for the declaration by the murderer's relatives. The brother pleaded that he had received the blood money and stated that the death of the murderer would not bring his brother to life. Only then, did Ali (RA) pardon the murderer, stating that the life of a non-Muslim subject is of the same value as a Muslim's life and the fine and punishment for the murder of both are the same (Burhan, vol.2, page 287, referring to the hand written copy present in Madrasa Aminia, Delhi). Based on this incident, jurists have enacted the law that the fine for the murder of a non-Muslim subject will be the same as for a Muslim (Dur ul Mukhtar, vol. 3, page 273).

2) The Criminal law holds that the Muslim and a non-Muslim subject of a protectorate are equal. The one who commits a crime, he be a Muslim or a non-Muslim, will be liable to the same punishment. Whether the non-Muslim subject steals from the property of a Muslim or a Muslim steals from that of the non-Muslim subject, the punishment prescribed is the same. Whether the non-Muslim commits the crime of sex with a Muslim woman or a Muslim commits the same with a non-Muslim woman subject, the punishment prescribed for both is the same (Kitab Al-Khiraj, page 108-109).

3) In civil law, the non-Muslim subjects and Muslims are on the same footing. Ali (RA) bin Abu Talib states that the property of a non-Muslim subject should be safeguarded as that of a Muslim. The rights of a non-Muslim subject are held sacred, that even if their wine or pigs are destroyed/damaged by a Muslim, he (the Muslim) is liable to punitive action. If he has done so, he has to pay the price for the pigs or wine (Dur ul Mukhtar, vol. 3, page 213).

4) Harming a non-Muslim subject, physically or by word of mouth, i.e. beating him up or causing injury to his person or backbiting against him, is as impermissible as in the case of a Muslim (Dur ul Mukhtar, vol. 3, page 273-274).

5) When a Muslim makes a pact with a non-Muslim subject, he does not have the right even to alter it, while its term runs, whereas, the non-Muslim is under no compulsion to follow it to its limit, in time (Bidae-us-Sanae, vol. 7, page 112).

6) Regardless of the gravity of the crimes committed, a non-Muslim subject of a protectorate does not cease to benefit from the protection of the Muslim State. To the extent that even he stops payment of 'jaziya', murders a Muslim, is disrespectful to the Prophet (SAW), or dishonors a Muslim woman, he cannot be

denied the protection granted to him by the Muslim State. Only on two conditions does he cease to be the responsibility of the Muslims; one, when he emigrates from the Muslim territories and joins the enemies of the state and secondly, when he openly revolts against the Muslim State (Bidae, vol. 7, page 113; Fath Al-Qadeer, vol. 4, Page 381-382).

7) Personal matters of the non-Muslim subjects will be dealt with, in accordance with their personal law. In this case, Islamic Law will not be followed. Indulgence in those actions forbidden by both their law and the Islamic Law, will render him liable. However, if some actions are permitted by their personal law, but prohibited by the Islamic Law, they will have the option to act according to their law in their dwellings, but the extent of this permissibility in Muslim localities will be decided by the Muslim Government, at its discretion. (By Muslim areas are meant those areas of the Muslim State, where Muslim Law and Islamic teachings are followed). Bidae-us-Sanae states:

> "In those dwellings and areas, in which the Islamic way is not in practice, the non-Muslim subjects will not be stopped from drinking, selling pigs, taking out processions, holding crosses or sounding musical instruments in the performance of their religious rites, regardless of the number of Muslims living there. However, in areas specified, where Muslims perform their religious services, like the places specified for the Juma or Eid congregations, the non-Muslims must act with constraint......where impious actions are concerned, whose impiety is recognized by Islam as well as by the religion of the non-Muslim subjects, e.g. crimes of sex and other acts of indecency, they will obviously be stopped from indulging in these, whether in their own dwellings or in that of the Muslims.'"

(Bidae-us-Sanae, vol.7, page 113).

Even in the Muslim areas, the non-Muslims have been only prohibited, crosses and statue bearing processions and sounding their musical instruments in the areas where Muslims dwell and perform their religious rites, like prayers etc. The non-Muslims are free to indulge even in such practices in the areas of their traditional places of worship. The Islamic Government has no authority to interfere there (the object of such restrictions is, the avoidance of conflicts between Muslims and non-Muslims).

8) In Muslim areas, the non-Muslims' places of worship, will not be damaged, destroyed or interfered with. If such a place is damaged, it may be repaired or reconstructed at its previous location. However, no new construction of such places will be allowed. (Bidae, vol. 7, page 114)

9) In those areas, which are not purely Muslim dwellings, the non-Muslim subjects have the right to construction of new places of worship and indulgence in the practices of their religion, without restrictions. Therefore, in such areas, places of previously specified for the Muslim rites, like Friday and Eid prayers etc., have been abandoned by the orders of the chief executives of the Muslim State; the non-Muslims may build their places of worship, even there. (Bidae, vol. 7, page 114)

Ibn Abbas has given the ruling that,

> "In the cities, that Muslims inhabit, the non-Muslim subjects are not permitted fresh construction of churches and other places of worship; sound the bell, horns, etc., in the performance of their religious services; indulge in drinking, or raising pigs. While in those non-Arab areas that have fallen to Muslim advances by the grace of Allah, the non-Muslim subjects have the rights as specified by the treaty documents. Muslims have a duty to fulfill their terms." (Kitab ul Hiraj, page 88).

10) In appropriating taxes (jaziya and khiraj), from the non-Muslim subjects, use of force is not permitted. Treating them with kindness and piety has been recommended. It is also impermissible that they be over-burdened. Even in deciding the amount of 'jaziya' or khiraj to be taken, due kindness and consideration has to be kept sight of. (Kitab ul Hiraj, page 81-82). For the appropriation of taxes, it is not permissible that their assets be auctioned. Ali (RA) bin Abu Talib had disallowed, that for appropriating the tax from them, they be inconvenienced to the extent that they have to sell off their livestock or clothes (Fatah ul Bayan, vol. 4, page 93).

On another occasion, Ali (RA) instructed his tax collectors, thus:

> "Be sure that their winter and summer clothing, their food stuff and their beasts of burden are not sold off to pay their taxes. If they are unable to pay their taxes, it is not permitted that you lash them or that they be kept standing in the sun, as punishment. If you disregard my instructions, you alone will be punished by Allah, but if I learn that you have acted otherwise than instructed, you will be suspended from your position." (Kitab Al-Khiraj, page 89).

Umar (RA) bin Khattab, instructed his governor, Abu Obaidah (RA), in Syria, stating:

> "Do not allow Muslims to treat them cruelly, or put them in hardships and forbid them from extracting anything from them illegally."
>
> (Kitab Al-Khiraj, page 82).

During his visit to Syria, Umar (RA) bin Khattab, saw his tax collectors punishing the non-Muslim subjects in order to collect taxes due from them. He advised them, not to trouble them too much. "If you torture them, Allah will put you to torture on the day of Resurrection." (Kitab Al-Khiraj, page 71).

Hisham bin Hakam saw a government official had made a Coptic subject stand in the sun. He stopped him, stating that he had heard the Prophet (SAW) state that Allah will put to torture him who tortures others on earth (Abu Dawood Kitab Al-Khiraj Wal Fay Wal Imarah).

Islamic jurists have only allowed that those who do not pay their taxes be awarded simple imprisonment (without labor). Abu Yusuf has stated the same in his 'Kitab Al-Khiraj'.

11) The non-Muslim subject of a Muslim protectorate, who becomes bankrupt or otherwise, needy, will not only be exempted from paying 'jaziya', but will be provided relief in the form of a stipend from the state treasury.

One of the clauses of the peace treaty drawn up by Khaled bin Waleed (RA), for the people of Kheera, states:

"Anyone who is disabled by virtue of his old age or if some catastrophe befalls on him or he becomes a pauper from a rich man, to the degree that his co-religionists give him alms for his upkeep, he will be exempt from paying 'jaziya' and he will be provided a stipend from the state treasury to enable him to look after his family."

(Kitab Al-khiraj, page 85).

Once Umar (RA) saw an old non-Muslim subject, begging in the street, he enquired of the old man, his reason for the base conduct. He replied that he was collecting alms in order to enable him to pay his 'jaziya'. Umar excused his 'jaziya' and granted him a stipend. He wrote to the treasurer,

"By Allah this is not justice that we benefit from him in his youth and in his old age treat him in such a shameful manner." (Kitab Al-Khiraj, page 72).

On his tour of Damascus, Umar (RA) granted stipends for the disabled non-Muslim subjects of that protectorate (Futuh al-Buldan, Published Europe, page 129).

12) If a non-Muslim subject dies while an amount was due from him as 'jaziya', the remaining part of the 'jaziya' will not be appropriated from what he leaves behind nor would his heirs be burdened by such payment. Abu Yusuf a scholar of note, of the Islamic jurisprudence has clarified this in his book 'Kitab Al-Khiraj, page 70'.

13) Like Muslims, the non-Muslims were also required to pay tax on their trade goods, when their trade goods were of the value of 200 Dirhams, or they owned 20 'Misfals' of gold. (Kitab ul Hiraj, page 70). It is a fact that jurists of the time had imposed a tax of 5% on the non-Muslim subjects, while the Muslims were required to pay only 2-½ %. This imposition of tax, however, was not based on any injunction of the Qur'an or on any hadith. It was rather decided on the basis of prevailing circumstances. The conditions were such that the Muslims were involved in fighting or were ready for defense of the vast frontiers or the Muslim Empire. All the commercial activity therefore, was in the hands of the non-Muslim subjects. This incentive was given in order to encourage Muslims also to take part in commerce, thus providing some

security to that activity as well.

14) The non-Muslim subjects of the Islamic protectorates are exempt from military service. The defense of the territories of Islam, including its protectorates, has been declared the responsibility of the Muslims alone. The 'jaziya' that non-Muslims pay, is for the provision of this defense. Therefore, Islam does not consider it rightful to burden them with this problem as well. Neither does it consider rightful to collect 'jaziya' from the non-Muslims, if it cannot provide them the required security.

For the Battle of Yarmuk, the Romans had gathered a huge force against the Muslims. The Muslims therefore had to be vacated from Syria, in order that a viable force may be gathered to oppose them (the Romans). Abu Ubaidah, the governor of Syria, wrote to all his administrators to return whatever 'khiraj' and 'jaziya' (taxes), they had gathered from the non-Muslim subjects. They were to be informed that since the Muslims were not able to provide them the required security, at that time, they were being returned their taxes (Kitab Al-khiraj, page 111). Following this decree, Muslims returned all collected taxes to the Syrians. According to Balazuri, when the people of Khums were being returned their money, they said that they preferred the just rule of the Muslims to the cruelty and exploitation of their former rulers. They declared that they would not let the Romans enter the city, lest they were beaten in battle by the Romans and were forced to accept them (Futuh al-Buldan, Published in Europe, page 137).

These brief instructions regarding dealings with non-Muslim subjects have been depicted here, to highlight the Muslim attitude. Nowhere in earlier history and to a great extent, in the later and contemporary history, the interaction between the victor and vanquished exhibited such justice, equality and consideration as, displayed by the Muslims, in their dealings with the vanquished.

These instructions regarding the dealings with the non-Muslims are not just worth the paper they were written on, but those were actually followed in letter and spirit; history is witness to the fact. Therefore, to elaborate each facet of it, the relevant hadith and authentic historical references have been stated. On studying these, the reader will become aware, that how meticulously, the Prophet (SAW) himself and the companions followed their injunctions. Whenever some arrogant Muslim administrators have transgressed, they have either been stopped or made to rescind the effects of such transgressions.

A well-known historical event is the forceful confiscation of the church of Jhama in Damascus and the inclusion of a part of its area in that of a mosque by Walid bin Yazid Umuwi. When the Caliph Umar (RA) bin Abdul Aziz ascended the Caliphate, the Christians complained to him of the injustice. He ordered his executive to raze that portion of the mosque, which had previously been part of the church and to return it to the Christians (Futuh al-Buldan, page 122).

Walid bin Yazid, afraid of a Roman attack, had the non-Muslim subjects of the Cyprus protectorate, expatriated to Syria. The scholars and the general public alike condemned the act and were extremely angry. When Walid succumbed to their demands and had all the non-Muslims repatriated to Cyprus, all appreciated his move and said that it was according to the dictates of justice and fairness.

Baluzari states that in one incident, the residents of the Mount of Lebanon revolted against the state. Saleh bin Ali bin Abdullah, sent troops to crush the revolt. The troops overcame them. All men capable of bearing arms were killed. Of the rest, he banished a group from Lebanon and allowed one group to stay behind. Imam Ozai was alive at the time. He wrote a long letter to Saleh, condemning this cruel act of his. A part of the letter stated:

> "You are aware of the exodus, of the people of the protectorate of the Mount of Lebanon. Among the displaced were some that had no part in the uprising. Yet you had some killed and some banished from their dwellings. It is not understood how the generality can be punished for the crime of a few and how their homes and lands can be confiscated. Allah instructs all against such actions. The best advice for you is that you remember the saying of the Prophet (SAW), stating that he would be the accuser against those who would treat the people of treaty nations cruelly and overburden them." (Futuh al-Buldan, page 169). This and many

such examples from history depict that the scholars and religionists were always opposed to the ill-treatment of the non-Muslim subjects, and if on occasion, leaders and kings went against its tenets, Islam cannot be held responsible for their actions."

The Question of Dress for the Non-Muslims

There is another event that has provided the opportunity for detractors of Islam, to raise their objection. That is the regulation of dress for the non-Muslims. They claim that the non-Muslims were told to dress in a particular fashion, to frustrate them and deprive them of their dignity.

There are without doubt some clauses in the peace treaties from the time of the first two caliphs, which disallow the non-Muslims from wearing a particular dress and to make them resemble the Muslims. For example, the treaty with Khera, states that they may wear any dress, except that which the Islamic soldiery wear and to avoid making themselves resemble the Muslims (Kitab Al-Khiraj, page 85).

Among the clauses of the treaty of Damascus, there are certain words that state the Christians will not dress as the Muslims did; their headgear and shoes would be of a different type and they would not part their hair as Muslims did.

(Ibn Kaseer, vol. 4, page 475).

The books of Islamic jurisprudence contain similar instructions for the non-Muslims.

Bidae-us-Sanae (vol. 7, page 113) states:

"They will have to wear such markings, as would indicate that they are the non-Muslim subjects and they would not be allowed to make themselves resemble the Muslims."

Imam Abu Yusuf, in his book, Al-Khiraj, states similarly (pages 72-73).

All these are without doubt correctly stated facts, but their reasons are not the belittling the non-Muslims, but to distinguish each people from the other. Unfortunately, some jurists have also taken the reason of this distinction, as the belittling of non-

Muslims and have written so in their books. The protagonist of this law, Umar (RA) bin Khattab however, does not say so, but is quiet on the subject. To be noted is the fact, that as non-Muslims been disallowed to make themselves resemble the Muslims, so have Muslims been instructed against making themselves resemble the non-Muslims.

Islam is not unaware of the element of strife, this distinction in dress can harbor. (The writer has written a separate booklet on the subject, titled, The Question of Dress 'Libas ka Masla'). In particular, among the conquered nations, this fault develops, that they start spurning their own culture and dress, considering them ignoble and believe, that in copying the ruler nation, they somehow elevate themselves above their own countrymen. This slavish mentality is detectable even today, in most vanquished nations. In India itself, we see that many Indians take pride in dressing as the English do, considering that they have joined the ranks of the national elite and are some kind of high achievers. Though, British disdain wearing the Indian dress and if at all they do, sometimes, it is partly in jest and not with any pride[7].

The Muslim scholars and leaders understood this aspect of the human psychology. For that reason, they discouraged the people of other nations from copying the lifestyle of the victors, the Muslims. Rather than cause the reduction in their dignity, the Islamic injunctions have caused them to maintain their national dignity and character. It is possible that some would consider this a maneuver, to diminish the dignity of the vanquished. We do not think so. In fact, we would have been much happier, if the British had, by law disallowed us the aping of the European dress and life style.

The misunderstanding arose out of the instructions that the non-Muslim subjects were to wear a 'zunnar', wear shoes with two

---

[7] These words were written when the Indian sub-continent was undivided. But even now, when the British have left and though it is realized that there is no particular distinction in dressing as they do and nothing shameful in dressing and living in their intrinsic Indo/Pak life-style, yet copying their's, is in fashion. It is funny that even in these changed circumstances, when the British come here, in the pursuance of their duty or business, they do not feel any distinction in dressing as the locals do. The effect of long slavery has left its mark on the Indian psyche.(Urdu Publisher's comment)

laces, and a cap with a high crown and that the reins of their horses should have a wooden piece in front. The people understood that these were to be the permanent imperatives of the non-Muslim style of dressing.

These were, however, not the principle orders, but advisory in nature. The actual orders were that the non-Muslim subjects wear their own national dresses and do not make themselves resemble the Muslims. From this, the jurists drew the usage that, the dress and style, commonly adopted by Non-Arabs and Christians of Syria, was to be ordained as the style of dressing, to be adopted by the non-Muslims. This has never been the intention of the instructions, that at every place and in every period of history, they would compulsorily adopt that particular mode of dressing. These orders were only for that period. The actual aim was that the non-Muslims could be differentiated from the Muslims and the Muslims differentiated from the non-Muslims.

Some Exceptions

The rules and regulation that have been discussed in the foregoing pages, regarding wars and acts related with wars, in the time of the Prophet (SAW) and during the pious caliphate. However, certain events took place, which apparently, did not seem to conform to the matter of these instructions. These can raise doubts in the uninstructed minds that the real teachings of Islam are different from those stated or that there is some contradiction in these or that the actions of the Prophet (SAW) and his companions did not conform to the laws and the laid down rules. Therefore, it is necessary that we should examine these exceptions to the rule before ending this chapter.

The Exodus of Banu Nazir

Banu Nazir was a tribe of Jews, living in Yathrib (presently known as Madinah) for centuries. After the Prophet (SAW) migrated to Madinah, he made a treaty with them. However, after the Battle of Badr, they were exiled from Madinah. The event is taken by the detractors to show that the Prophet (SAW) (may God forbid) deceived the tribe. That is to say that when the Muslims were weak, he entered into a treaty with them and when they gained in strength, he broke the truce and expelled them from their homeland. However, that is oversimplification of the truth. A little more detailed study of these events will show that the facts were quite the opposite of what is projected. It will become clear that, not the Prophet (SAW) but the Banu Nazir themselves were guilty of breaking the treaty and their banishment from Madinah was not a cruelty, but a righteous act.

It so happened, that when the Prophet (SAW) migrated to Madinah, as with all other Jewish tribes of Madinah, he had a pact with the Banu Nazir, that they would not act against each other's interest and that they would not aid each other's enemies. Hafiz Ibn Hajjar writes that the terms of the treaty stipulated that they (Banu Nazir) would neither fight the Muslims nor would they aid the enemies of Islam. However, the Banu Nazir was all the time busy in clandestine activities against the Muslims. They Maintained contacts with the Quraish and would pass on secret information of the Muslims to them. Musa bin Uqba in his book, 'Mughazi', writes that the Banu Nazir would plot against the Muslims and incite the Quraish to war with the Muslims. (Fath al-Bari, vol. 7, page 131)

They were not content with this, but attempted several times to murder the Prophet (SAW). On one occasion, they invited the Prophet (SAW) to come to a place where they would send three of their scholars to learn of the religion of Islam. If the Prophet (SAW) was able to prove the righteousness of his religion, they said, they would accept Islam. The Prophet (SAW) accepted the invitation. When he was about to proceed to the pre-determined place, a woman from Banu Nazir whose brother had become a Muslim, sent a message to the Prophet (SAW), warning him that her tribe planned to murder him. Whereupon, the Prophet (SAW) abandoned his plans to go (This incident has been related by Abu Dawood in his book, in chapter, Fi Khabar an Nazi, and is also related in the book Fath al-Bari, vol. 7, page 233).

On another occasion, the Prophet (SAW) went to Banu Nazir to settle the blood money of two people. The Banu Nazir appeared to be cooperative, and promised all help they could give. Secretly, however, they hurriedly prepared plans to murder him right there. One person by the name of Amrao bin Jahash bin Kaab would go to the roof and cast a heavy stone on the Prophet (SAW). The Prophet (SAW) learnt of the plan in the nick of time and left the place (Tabari, pub. in Egypt, vol. 3, page 37; Fath al-Bari, vol. 7, page 232; Futuh al-Buldan page 24).

Such incidents were trying the patience of the Muslims. They were afraid they were harboring their own enemy, who would gladly join up with the overt enemy, in case of conflict. The Muslims were even afraid that the Prophet (SAW) might be martyred at their hands. The extent of fear was such that when a Muslim was about to die, he made a will that the Prophet (SAW) would not be informed of his death after nightfall. It may happen that the Prophet (SAW) would decide to join the funeral, providing the Banu Nazir with an opportunity for his murder (Asad al-Ghaba, vol. 3, page 57).

Under these circumstances, it was not possible to keep ignoring the threat. The Prophet (SAW) sent Banu Nazir an ultimatum, stating that they had behaved mutinously with him; therefore, they were given ten days to leave Madinah or to be ready to fight. Meanwhile, Abdullah bin Ubey, the leader of the hypocrites, assured Banu Nazir of his help, against the Muslims. Therefore, Banu Nazir replied to the ultimatum, stating that they would not leave Madinah and that the Muslims were free to do what they felt like.

None can hold the Prophet (SAW) blameworthy of unjustly waging a war against Banu Nazir. They had been treated with forbearance and kindness but their aggressive intent and mutinous activity continued to show. As a last option, the Prophet (SAW) resorted to war to solve the problem. He besieged the dwelling of Banu Nazir, but before any bloodshed took place, Banu Nazir sued for peace. They stated that they would leave Madinah on the condition that they be allowed to carry as much of their belonging as their camels could carry; that which their camels could not carry, would be left behind for the Muslims. They would go towards Syria. (Tabari vol. 3, page 38; Fath-al-Bari., vol. 7, page 233; Futuh al-Buldan, page 24)

Tabari writes, "They agreed to leave the city of the Prophet (SAW), on the condition, that they be allowed to carry whatever their camels could carry on their backs and leave the rest." (Tabari, vol. 3, page 38).

About this agreement, Balazuri states, "they agreed with the Prophet (SAW) on the condition that they will leave the city, leaving their arms and armor, whatever else they can load on their camels is theirs." (Futuh al-Buldan page 24)

Hafiz Ibn Hajjar writes, "they then requested that should be allowed to vacate the land, stating, whatever their camels could carry, would be theirs. Thus an accord was reached." (Fath al-Bari, vol. 7, page 232).

When the enemy was under the power of the Muslims and they had ample opportunity to avenge themselves on them (Banu Nazir), to allow them, not only to leave the country, but also to carry with them their belongings, cannot be termed as cruelty. It was rather a gesture of tolerance and peacefulness. The result of this gesture, however, was that the Banu Nazir set up a conspiratorial net all over Arabia and within a period of two years, gathered a force of ten to twelve thousand, and attacked Madinah.

If the enemy had been crushed when they were under siege, this later act of aggression could not have come to pass. However, the Prophet (SAW) the mercy to mankind, ceded to their appeal for peace, although he was fully aware of the nature and capability of the enemy.

The Exodus of Banu Quraizah

The killings of the people of the Banu Quraizah tribe, has been another subject of propaganda against Islam. They too were Jewish and when the Prophet (SAW) migrated to Madinah, as with all other Jewish tribes, established relations with them on the basis of peace accords. After the conflict with Banu Nazir, the Prophet (SAW) invited Banu Quraizah to renew their accord (Abu Dawood, Kitab Al-Khiraj Wal Fil Imarah, chap. Khabar al-Nazir).

Later however, the Banu Quraizah openly supported the enemy against the Muslims in the Battle of Ahzab. Because of this treacherous conduct, when the Muslims were free from the engagement of the Battle of Ahzab, they attacked Banu Quraizah. Having overcome them, had their men folk killed, their women and children enslaved and their property distributed among Muslims. On the Basis of this incident, the Prophet (SAW) has been accused of violation of pledges and of cruelty.

Again, if one looks more deeply into the matter, we will find the truth is quite the opposite of what the detractors claim it to be. It has been stated that there were two accords with the Banu Quraizah. The first, a general one, as with all Jews of Madinahh and a second one, was the accord reconfirming or re-pledging peace, after the conflict with Banu Nazir.

According to these accords, the signatories were to avoid taking part in hostile activities against each other. It is obvious that the Banu Quraizah would be guilty of violations of the accord, if they had in any way assisted the enemies of Islam. When in the Battle of Ahzab, the powerful tribes on the incitement of Banu Nazir joined up to put an end to Islam, they (Banu Quraizah) too, joined them. First, they incited one, Akhtab Nazri, against Muslims.

When the Prophet (SAW), through his messengers, Saad bin Maaz (RA) and Saad bin Ubada, warned them (RA), to remain faithful to the treaty, Banu Quraizah retorted by saying that they had no accord with the Muslims (Ibn Aseer, pub. in Egypt, vol. 2, page 67; Fath al-Bari, vol.7, page 28).

This defection, at such a critical juncture, in effect had the Muslims trapped in a pincer movement. On one side were the Quraish and Atafan and other tribes, while on the other side was the Banu Quraizah. The main danger was that the fort, in which the Muslims had sent their women and children for safety, was well within the range of Banu Quraizah, who threatened to lay siege to the fort. The Muslims were so perturbed by the situation that the Prophet (SAW) had decided to sue for peace, surrendering one third of the produce of Madinah to the enemy. (Ibn Asser, vol. 2, page 68; Fath al-Bari, vol. 7, page 281) (Sahih Muslim, Kitab al-Jihad, chap. 'Qatal min Aqz al-Ahad': Futuh al-Buldan, page 29) .

The Qur'an, relating the deep concern of the Muslims at the time, states:

> "When they came upon you from above you and from below you and when eyes grew wild and hearts reached to the throats and ye were imagining vain thoughts concerning Allah." Explaining the verse, Huzaifah (RA) states, "That night our anxiety was boundless. On one side Abu Sufyan was

advancing with a huge force and on the other side Banu Quraizah and the attack of the later endangered our women and children also." (Fath al-Bari, vol. 7, page 281; Ibn Katheer, vol. 8, page. 52).

After this great defection, any leniency with Banu Quraizah would have been tantamount to suicide. Therefore, when the external threat had been dealt with, the Prophet (SAW) immediately laid siege to the fort, which the Banu Quraizah were occupying. The siege lasted for 15 or 25 days. Realizing that they could not hold out much longer, they expressed their willingness to surrender, stating that whatever Saad Bin Maaz (RA) decided would be acceptable to them. (In his days of ignorance, Saad's tribe was deeply allied to the Banu Quraizah tribe). Some commentators state that they left the decision to the Prophet (SAW), who appointed Saad (RA) as a mediator, since he belonged to a tribe, strongly allied to the Banu Quraizah and for the reason it was unlikely that he could be accused of partisanship with the Muslims alone. In any event, Saad (RA) was appointed to decide the case. He decided that all mature males of the Banu Quraizah should be put to the sword, all women and children be enslaved and their property distributed among the Muslims. The decision was put into effect.

The charges of violation of the accord are thus allayed. However, the charges of over reaction in vengeance still need to be studied, in this regard. Before any opinion is formed, following points have to be understood clearly:

1) In view of the demonstrated unfaithfulness of the Banu Nazir and Banu Quraizah, it was not possible that new accords be made with them and to expect that they would keep faith. It was conversely more probable that at some critical juncture, the two would break their accords and pledges and endanger the Muslims.

2) Their forts were adjacent to Madinah and with their help; the enemy could gain access to the heart of the city. In their prevailing treacherous frame of mind, it was probable that the access would be available to the enemy, with the blessing of the Banu Quraizah.

3) They could not be banished from Madinah. Earlier their kin

had been so banished and staying in the remoteness of Madinah had been able to gather a huge force and were able to attack the city.

4) In spite of the above, the Prophet (SAW) did not punish the Banu Quraizah for their actions directly, but appointed a person with their consent, for deciding their case, who hailed from a tribe, which had been for centuries, deeply allied to them.

5) It is a universally accepted norm that if an empowered negotiator, Mediator or Go-Between is appointed with the tacit approval of both parties to the conflict, the decision taken by such person, is binding on both parties.

6) The decision taken by Maaz (RA) was based on the teachings of the Torah itself; therefore, no Jew could raise his voice against it[8].

7) Only mature males were killed, since only they presented the danger of war or treachery. The women and children were left without the support of their men, who were killed, therefore the only decent thing to do, was to take over their responsibility.

Keeping all the above considerations in view, one must come to the consideration that the actions taken against the Banu Quraizah were according to the demands of justice and that there was no other option open for the Muslims.

The Murder of Kaab bin Ashraf

Another incident from the period of the Prophet (SAW), which comes under great criticism, is that the Prophet (SAW) himself caused the clandestine murder of one of his enemies. This they say is the 'fatak' of the period of paganism, which is against the norms of warfare and an extremely cowardly act. However, even as regards this incident, critics have ignored the facts.

---

[8] The Torah states: "When you reach up to attack a city, make its people an offer of peace. If they accept and open their gates, all the people in it will be subject to forced labor and shall work for you. If they refuse to make peace and they engage you in battle, lay siege to the city. When the Lord, your God delivers it into your hand, put to the sword all men in it. As for the women, the livestock and everything else in the city, you may take as plunder for yourself" (Istasnan (Deuteronomy), chap. 20, verse 10-14)

Kaab bin Ashraf, was a Jew of the Banu Nazir tribe. He had been present when the treaty between his tribe and the Muslims was signed. However, he harbored a grudge against the Muslims, especially against the Prophet (SAW). He was known to recite impolite and slighting poetry about him (Prophet) and immoral and indecent ones on the Muslim women (Ibn Aseer, vol. 2, page 53; Fath al-Bari, vol. 7, page 236).

When the Prophet (SAW) was victorious at Badr, Kaab was deeply grieved and shouted in disgust,

> "By God, if Mohammad was victorious at Badr, the
> bowel of the earth is better for us than his bowel."

Then he proceeded to Makkah, where he incited the Quraish chiefs to revenge, singing tearful ballads of the sorrowful deaths of those killed by the Muslims. All these acts were, as can be judged, against the provisions of the peace accords between the Jews and Muslims (Abu Dawood, Kitab al-Jihad, Chap 'Kaif Kana Akhraj Al-Yahud').

All this could have been condoned but his arrogance reached the stage, that he planned the murder of the Prophet (SAW). He planned with a group to call the Prophet (SAW) to his home and to quietly murder him. A Qur'anic verse revealed on the subject states,

> "O ye, who believe, remember Allah's favor unto
> you, how a people were minded to stretch out their
> hands against you, but He withheld their hands from
> you" (Al-Maidah: 11)

Ibn Hajjar has mentioned the incident in his book Fatah al-Bari and Yaqoobi a well-known historian writes, "He planned to kill the Prophet (SAW) treacherously. This planning crowned the list of crimes and his enmity was confirmed." When a person breaks his national accord and plans to kill the leader of the nation with which the accord is, deserves nothing but the punishment of death. It was not correct that, on the strength, of the vile behavior of an individual, war could be declared against the entire nation. Neither could it be expected that his nation would keep him from his vileness, since the entire nation's attitude was similarly inclined.

Since Kaab had not until that time come out in open confrontation with the Muslims nor was he expected to, in the future. There was nothing else to do than to kill him with stealth. Reluctantly the Prophet (SAW) ordered his death and appointed Mohammad bin Musailamah (RA) for the task.

It is not correct to conclude from the incident that clandestine murder is an accepted norm of warfare. If it were so, the first persons to be removed in this way, would have been Abu Jahl and Abu Sufyan. Among the Muslims, there was no dearth of those dedicated, who could have murdered most of the enemies of Islam, in this fashion. However, in the entire history there is no mention of such killing except Kaab and one other Abu Rafae[9], although other than these two, there were many more enemies of the Prophet (SAW) and of Islam.

The obvious conclusion from this is that clandestine killing is not a permanent policy of Islamic warfare. Permission may extraordinarily be given for such undertakings in special circumstances only. Such as, a particular enemy is known to plan covertly to harm Islam consistently, and would not expose himself and avoided open confrontation.

The Exodus of the Jews of Khyber

After the period of Prophethood, the objections have been raised against the banishment of the Jews of Khyber. The objectors state that after a settlement had been reached, that the Jews would pay 50 % of their agricultural produce, they had become the permanent subjects of the Islamic State. The Muslims had no right

---

[9] Muslim states, of Abu Rafae, that he made all efforts to harm the Prophet (SAW) and would aid and encourage his (Prophet's) enemies against him. (Kitab al-Ghazi, chap. 'Qatal Abi Rafae'). But, Ibn Aayad has written, that he provided huge amounts as monetary aid to Ghatafan and other Arab hypocrites, in their war efforts against the Prophet (SAW). (Fatah al-Bari, vol.7, page 24).Tabari has added that he had gathered forces against the Prophet (SAW), in the Battle of Ahzab. (Tabari, vol. 3, page 7), Ibn Saad in his book, 'Tabqaat' writes, that he had brought together a large force of Ghatafan and other hypocrites of Arabia to fight against the Prophet (SAW). (vol. 2 page 66). Ibn Asher writes, that he used to aid Kaab bin Ashraf against the Prophet (SAW) (vol. 2, page 112, Taba Europe). All these references prove that, like Kaab bin Ashraf, he never entered into open conflict with the Muslims, but always aided the enemies covertly.

to break the truce and their banishment order by Umar (RA) bin Khattab was illegal.

On the surface, the objections appear legitimate enough, but the circumstances that justified their expulsion are available for all to see. A look at these will be enough to dispel all doubts of the matter.

During the period of Prophet (SAW), When Khyber was first conquered, the initial terms of the treaty stated that the Jews would vacate the area in return for the grant of their lives. (Futuh al-Buldan, pages 29-37 and Ibn Hisham, page 779). The Jews approached the Prophet (SAW), with the proposal that since they were the most experienced in cultivation in the oases, they may be allowed to stay in Khyber. The terms, under which this concession was to be granted, may be negotiated. The Prophet (SAW) ceded to the request, but when the treaty was being drawn up. He clearly stated that they would be allowed to stay there until it was Allah's will (Fatah al-Bari, vol. 5, page 207).

Abu Dawood has clarified the statement stating, "the Prophet (SAW) concluded with them (Jews), on the condition that when the Muslims so desired, they would be expelled from the territory." (Abu Dawood, chap. 'Maja fi Hukm Art Khyber).

The discussion clarifies the fact that on the basis of the words of the treaty there was no infringement of the treaty with the Jews of Khyber, by the Muslims. What remains to be considered are the circumstances that prompted the cancellation of the terms that allowed the Jews to stay in Khyber. The incidents surrounding the expulsion are stated below.

Just a few days had passed, since the signing of the treaty, when a Jewish woman invited the Prophet (SAW) for food. She had the food poisoned. On investigation, the woman confessed her crime. Some other names were revealed in the connection, in the ensuing investigation. (Bukhari relates the incident several times in his narration of the Battle of Khyber, and the Kitab al-Tib describes the incident in detail.)

At the time of the Prophet (SAW), the Jews murdered Abdullah bin Suhail bin Zaid Ansari (RA) and cast his body on the banks of a canal (Usd al-Ghaba, vol. 3, page 179).

During the Caliphate of Umar (RA) Bin Khattab, they once got hold of his son, Abdullah bin Umar (RA), and threw him from the rooftop. The fall resulted in the breaking of both his hands (Futuh al-Buldan, page 31 and Ibn Hisham, page 780).

In the earlier incidents, the involvement of only a person or an isolated group could be determined. However, in the last incident, the responsibility was of a general nature and the aggressiveness of the entire nation appeared defacto. Umar (RA) put up the incident for the consideration of the council of the Prophet's companion.

He stated in his address that the Prophet (SAW) had an agreement with the Jews that they would be allowed to remain there, until it was the will of Allah. Now, when Abdullah had gone there to his estates, he was attacked at night and his hands and feet were broken. At that time, he stated that there were no enemies of Islam remaining in Arabia, except these (Jews of Khyber); he recommended that they be banished from the Islamic territories. The council voted in favor of Umar's recommendation and the banishment orders were issued. The banishment was not however carried out, as was the norm of the day, with only the clothes they wore. They were fully paid for whatever they left behind, from the treasury and the camels etc. to carry them away, were provided by the state (Bukhari, Kitab al-Shurut).

Without doubt, in the same book, the reason given for the expulsion of the Jews was different. It states that when Umar (RA) learnt of the hadith that stated, that two religions should not be allowed to exist together in Arabia, he investigated the authenticity of the hadith and therefore decided on the expulsion of the Jews. Balazuri has copied this explanation from the works of Ibn Shahab, Imam Zuhri, and Abdullah bin Utbah (Futuh al-Buldan, page 37 and Fatah al-Bari, vol. 5, page 207). It was however not the intention of the hadith that all non-Muslims, without any fault be expelled from Arabia.

Imam Zuhri in his commentary has explained, that when the truth of this hadith was established, Umar (RA) had it announced that if there was any document of truce, in the possession of any Christian or Jew, it should be produced before him, so that it could be implemented. Obviously, if the aim of the hadith was that non-Muslims of all creeds should be expelled from Arabia, Umar (RA) would not have called for pacts or treaties, but would have banished them all, directly. Umar's actions indicate that the hadith was not for implementation without consideration, but, that a general policy had been laid down, for implementation, after due consideration being given to all aspects of the question. There is no basis for believing that a subject nation would have been expelled from Arabia, just because having people of more than one creed was considered undesirable. The more likely explanation is that when the mischief of the Jews of Khyber became unbearable and Umar (RA) had decided on their expulsion, he was looking for traditions and hadith that may perhaps render his decision illegal and void. At that time, when this hadith came to light after confirming its authenticity, he implemented his decision, only after his complete satisfaction. The later commentators have colored the hadith in different hues, depending on their own frame of mind and have combined the events into one, confusing the issue.

The Exodus of the People of Najran

An incident of the time of the pious caliphate, that has been a cause of greater censure than even the expulsion of the Jews of Khyber, is the banishment of the Christians of Najran. The Jews of Khyber had in fact been conquered in battle. The subsequent peace that ensued was conditional to their exodus from the area. In the case of the people of Najran however, they of their own accord had a formal treaty with the Prophet (SAW) and had accepted the sovereignty of the Muslims. Under these conditions, the objector's claim that their expulsion by Umar (RA) bin Khattab is direct contravention of the treaty and put more emphasis that it exemplifies unfaithfulness to pledges, by the Muslims. However, careful examination of the facts of the case will prove the falsehood of these detractions.

The Christians of Najran had a peace treaty with the Muslims, on the condition that they would remain loyal to the Islamic State and would continue paying their dues. Their being taken in the peace and protection of Allah, under the surety of the Prophet (SAW), was conditional. Imam Abu Yusuf has copied the words of the treaty. They state:

> "For whatever is in the treaty, is in the peace of
> Allah and everlasting security of the Prophet

(SAW). Until it is so ordained by Allah, until they remain faithful and until they continue to pay all that is due from them (Kitab Al-Khiraj, page 41 and Futuh al-Buldan page 76).

When Abu Bakar (RA) assumed the caliphate, he reconfirmed the treaty, stating clearly:

> "It will be binding on them, to remain faithful and continue paying whatever is due from them."

All the above, clearly show, that as the Islamic Government had pledged to provide security to the lives and property of the people of Najran, they had also been pledged the faithfulness of the people and continued payment of the settled dues. Such mutual undertakings are universal among all governments and the governed. The extent, to which the people of Najran fulfilled their part, remains to be seen.

It was reported to the Caliph that the people of Najran had started gathering horses and war materials, that act could be interpreted as nothing more than a preparation of an insurgency. Imam Abu Yusuf states, "Umar (RA) expelled them from their lands, as he feared that they would revolt against the Muslims since they had gathered arms and horses, in quantity in their areas."

A look at the map of Arabia and its surrounding regions would put one in the correct perspective of the nature of the danger such warlike preparations could signify. In the north of Najran is the sensitive, center of the Islamic Republic, Hijaz (areas including Makkah and Madinah) and in the south across the Red Sea, is Christian Ethiopia. If the people of Najran had been allowed to complete their preparations, an attack on Hijaz would have resulted, with Ethiopia being called in for their aid. The aborted designs of Abraha, of the past, would have been resurrected. It is not too difficult to fathom the problems, the Islamic State and Muslims would have had to face in that event.

Ibn Aseer writes:

> "Peace and tranquility made their (Najranians') numbers grow, till at that time, it peaked 40,000. Excess of wealth had caused gradual decadence in

the society, until continual involvement in internal conflict ensued. Periodically, a party would approach Umar (RA), complaining of another and every such party suggesting the expulsion of another from Najran. At first, Umar (RA) ignored their conflicts, as too petty for the state to interfere in. However, as their strength continued to grow. Until at one time, it grew too big, to be ignored and it began to be perceived as a threat to the Muslims. Umar (RA) took the opportunity and ordered their expulsion." (Futuh al-Buldan, page 73. Ibn Aseer vol. 2, page 112).

In any case, despite the fact, that ample evidence was available of the possibility of an insurrection, by the people of Najran, they were not banished from the Muslim Empire, but only from Arabia. They continued to be the subjects of the State and were accorded the necessary security. They were only displaced from the strategic position between Ethiopia and the heart of the Muslim Empire and relocated in Iraq. Their journey to their destination was made convenient as much as was possible; the executive officers of Iraq were instructed to aid them in all their difficulties and they were exempted from paying 'jaziya' for two years. Imam Abu Yusuf has copied the declaration providing the people of Najran, the amenities. A small portion of the declaration reads:

"The responsible officers of Syria and Iraq, whom these people approach, are directed to provide them cultivable land. The land they choose to cultivate is to be given to them in the name of Allah, since it is in return for their property appropriated from them. In this land, there will be no interference or arrogance in dealing with them. --------------If someone treats them with cruelty, it is the duty of every Muslim present there to come to their aid, since they are of a nation that is under our protection. They are exempted from paying 'jaziya' for 24 months.' (Ibn Aseer, vol. 7, page 112)

Those who object have only taken into consideration that there was a pact with the people of Najran, which the Caliph Umar (RA) broke and banished them from their area. However, in view of the stated circumstances, even in the present century, if any people conduct themselves as the Christians did, and their area was in an equally strategic location, no state holding its security concerns paramount, would act otherwise than as the Muslim State did.

Establishment of the Modern Laws of Warfare

Going through this chapter, one comes to the conclusion that the Islamic Jurisprudence has established a legal framework governing all aspects of war and activities pertaining to warfare. It abolished the savagery from warfare that was prevalent at the time, promulgated new respectable laws of warfare and acts concerned with warfare. Validity of certain ways was maintained, in an altered shape that promised viability in changing circumstances. Similarly, some new reforms were introduced, which would enable extraction of rules and laws to cater for changing conditions of the world. Along with, the Prophet (SAW) his companions, have exemplified all angles of Islamic Jurisprudence and have left us an inheritance of exemplary conduct, which would provide us a guidance as to the posture to be adopted to face the changing requirements of the time. The codes of law, based on these basic percepts by jurists of the earliest period, maintained viability and relevance through centuries of implementation in Islamic sultanates and have served them well.

There are however, many rules and laws propounded earlier, which do not hold their validity today. This is because of the changing demands of time, prompted by newer modes of warfare and the changing demands of civilization. Obviously, laws relevant to these will not be found in the books of ancient jurists. Therefore, to come to correct conclusions, and to make laws not contradictory to Islam, we have to place our reliance on the original data presented by the Qur'an and hadith. Laws based on the laid down principles need to be codified that they may remain applicable to the present needs. The codes should be such that those laws, whose authenticity and required details could be gleaned from the Qur'an and hadith, should be left as they are. Where principles are given, relevant laws in the light of jurisprudence, commentaries, and present day requirements need to be made. Where the jurisprudence allows the option of either maintaining or abandoning certain laws, out of these, those laws that the world does not follow anymore, should be abandoned (not declared prohibitive).

In this connection, total dependence should not be placed on the works of ancient jurists nor should they be totally ignored. Such works, the products of immense effort are neither so vain that they could be discarded as waste nor are they as rigid as the principles of jurisprudence, that they cannot be molded to suit circumstances. There is a medial way that needs to be adopted. That is, the part that is in consonance with the spirit of the modern ways, in accordance with the consensus of the leaders and the scholars, ought to be maintained, and that which has lost its relevance, should be abandoned, and regarding these matters, new laws based on Islamic Jurisprudence be promulgated.

An example of the above is that only principles have been stated in the Qur'an regarding treatment of prisoners of war, the battle wounded and the non-combatants and on other similar matters. The jurisprudence satisfies itself on stating these principles only, means, that permission has been granted to Muslims of different periods to make their own rules in accordance with necessities of the time. It is therefore not necessary that we consult books of jurists of the fifth or the 6th century and implement whatever details are available in them in toto. Our purpose should be to promulgate laws that are based on Qur'an and jurisprudence, which are in consonance with the demands of the time, and whatever agreements and international organizations exist, we should also join them; surely, keeping in view the dictates of Islamic Law.

Keeping the above in consideration, the principles of warfare have been put forward, these are based on the principles extracted from the Qur'an and Islamic Jurisprudence and the relevant hadith. Wherever the commentaries of scholars of hadith and 'fiqh' have been found in consonance with the spirit of modernity, these too have been taken into consideration. Apart from these, such exceptional events have also been stated and explained that on the surface appear to be in contradiction to the laws. Now keeping all these facts in view, it is the job of the jurists to write afresh, on the jurisprudential aspects of JIHAD, for posterity.

Chapter Six

The Status of War in Other Religions

When we seek to determine the desirability of a certain mater related to human life, the first to be determined is the nature of the matter, then the status that human understanding gives to that matter in comparison with other matters of similar nature. Only then is it awarded the position of desirability.

As regards to human conflict, we have gone rather deeply in determining its nature and conceptual position in Islam. As a second step, we have to compare this Islamic concept with the conceptual position in other religions. For that purpose, we would have to go briefly into the field of comparative study of religions and then examine how in modern times, these methodologies compare with the methods of Islam; whether the aims and means in Islamic warfare are superior or inferior to others. If however, some religion holds war as totally impermissible, we have to examine whether the concept is in accordance with human nature.

Comparisons of religions, is indeed a very difficult task. When a person holds a certain set of beliefs, it is not possible that he can do full justice to the beliefs and opinions of others. This is the general failing of human nature, but it acquires its worst form where religion is concerned. When adherents of one religion criticize another, they see only its darker side. The brighter aspects either totally escape their perception or, if it does not, they try to suppress its expression. Their critical analysis is not aimed at searching for the truth, rather to prove the correctness of their premeditated concepts and opinions.

In such comparisons or criticism, other religions suffer. At the same time, no real advantage accrues to the religion of the critic, on account of the methods adopted to prove their point. If the only aim of comparison is to determine the truth and there is no other ulterior motive, even then it is not correct to be pre-opinionated at the outset. Study of other religions only with the intent of highlighting, what in one's opinion or looking for its weak points in order to prove the supremacy of one's own religion, is also not correct. This kind of dishonesty can neither yield any advantage to one's own religion nor can such methods be a source of pride for any true religion. If any person is led into belief through such methods, his belief cannot be worth much, since the very foundation of his religion is based on fraud and dishonesty.

Keeping the foregoing in view, if comparison of religions is to bear any fruit, certain ground rules are to be adopted and followed religiously. In our opinion, the rules and principles that should be so adopted are annotated below:

1) In order to prove the righteousness of one religion; it is not necessary that the teachings of other religions be proven totally wrong. If truth is the hallmark of one faith, its total absence from others is not a requisite. Righteousness is the quality of any true faith, which is not bounded by time and space. Manifestations of truth under all conditions definitely remain the part of one, single, whole entity. If the righteousness found in our religion is also observable in another, it is not a discredit to either religion. It rather proves that both religions spring from the same fountain of truth and righteousness. The fact is that wherever truth and righteousness are found, in whatever quantity, that particular faith has the right to them and should be given respect on account of them, rather than disfiguring the truth in order to discredit that religion.

2) Any person who claims that righteousness and truth are the qualities of his religion alone, that discredits not only his religion, but also righteousness and truth as well. Per fact, truth and righteousness, are present everywhere, in varying degrees. However, when scholars of comparative religion give preference to one religion over others, they mean that in their opinion, only one religion is the epitome of reality.

It is therefore necessary that no scholar of comparative religion should decide beforehand, that apart from his favorite religion, all others are devoid of righteousness. He should rather understand that before him is a confusion of truths, half-truths, and utter falsehood. It should be his duty, to sort out the wheat from the chaff and as far as it is possible, using his understanding and discretion avoid each from confusing or overshadowing the other.

3) While indulging in religious research, it should be ensured that the works of the highly biased or prejudiced be avoided. One should be more particular about this in the initial stages of research, because, one would not be able to reach the correct conclusions having become biased in one direction, and all his following research will be affected by his biases. If one has to reach the right conclusion, one must study the original books, as far as possible, and based on this study, form his own opinion. When one has reached a conclusion, only then one may consult the works of others on the subject, since at that time one would be better armed to discern between truth and falsehood.

In the following dissertation, the teachings regarding war have been examined. The three pre-requisites of such comparisons have been adhered to and a non-partisan examination of the facts to determine the truth and falsehood of the proposition has been attempted.

The Four Major Religions of the World

It is not possible to analyze the teachings of all the religions of the world, regarding war. Such comparative analysis is neither easy nor required. Ordinarily comparative study is limited to such religions that; owing to the large following, the immensity of the effects, their past and present glory, has come to be counted as the major religions of the world. Accordingly, the comparative analysis is herein limited to Hinduism, Buddhism, Judaism, and Christianity.

For the purpose of comparative analysis, regarding concepts of war, these four major religions can be divided into two groups. One of these groups holds war permissible, it comprises of Hinduism and Judaism. The other group, comprising of Buddhism and Christianity, considers war impermissible. We will study these religions individually.

1) Hinduism

The biggest problem faced while discussing Hinduism is in defining what indeed should be termed as Hinduism. The Hindu religion does not satisfy the sense that the word 'religion' is generally used for. Religion requires a central belief, which forms its foundation. However, in Hinduism, one cannot discern any such basic and central belief. Different groups and ranks within the religion have sets of beliefs, principles, prayers and religious books, quite different from the others, yet they all call themselves Hindus. Consequently, when we wish to get a ruling regarding some controversy, we find it difficult to determine as to which particular brand of the Hindu religion should be consulted.

The difficulty has been to an extent overcome lately. Though the class system and sectarianism still exists, the current trend and inclination among Hindus has been to consolidate their theology and centralize it in three books. These are, The Four Vedas, Geeta, and Manu Samirti. Whatever is stated about Hinduism, herein, is based on these three books[10]. (*Because, the doctrine of non-violence was personified in Mahatma Gandhi from the times of the independence movement from the British Rule in India, Hinduism in most of the period since Gandhi is depicted as a non-violent religion and its followers were in general regarded as such. However, lately the violent tendencies associated with Hindu revivalism have overwhelmingly surfaced in the otherwise regarded as the secular republic of India. In this context, the following analysis of the teachings of Hinduism, although performed by Sayyid Maududi much earlier, has certainly become more relevant in this day in age.*)

The Three Epochs of Hinduism

The books mentioned in the foregoing section are actually from three different periods and as regards to warfare, depict three different aspects of Hindu thought.

---

[10] Defining Hindu religion is not easy. Some say it comprises of acts performed by Hindus (Guru Parsad Sen, "Introduction to the Study of Hinduism"). Others define it as a combination of those customs, beliefs, religious practices and traditions, which have been in vogue, by order of the Brahman class and have the authority of their holy books, and have been spread by Brahaminic teachings (Lyall, Religious Systems of the World). Yet others say that those belonging to India, who are not Muslims, Jains, Buddhists, Christians, Zoroastrians or Jews, and those who belong to no other religion are all encompassed by Hinduism. These may range from those who believe in the singularity of God to Idol worshipers. Their religious books however, must be in Sanskrit, (Census report, Baroda, 1901, page 120)

Vedas have their connection to that period of history when Aryans exuded from Central Asia and Invaded India. Here they had to wage wars against a civilization that by virtue of color, creed and race were completely different from them. The poetry in the Vedas describes the Aryan emotions during these confrontations, their attitude towards the locals, their aims, and objectives in these wars and the treatment meted out to the locals.

Geeta is the book from the era in which all northern India had come under the sway of the Aryans and there was a contest between two influential and powerful Aryan families for the establishment of superiority over each other. This book provides us data concerning the Hindu philosophy of warfare, through the words of the eminent Hindu religious scholar and leader, Krishan Ji.

The Manu Samitri is the collection of politico-religious and cultural laws from the era, when the entire Indian subcontinent was under the sovereignty of the Aryans and the non-Aryan entity had been almost totally annihilated. Many details regarding rules of warfare, treatment of the vanquished and their duties are available to us through this book.

The Vedic Teachings of Warfare

'Vedas' is the name given to four books which are individually known by different names. The most ancient of these is the 'Rig Veda'. The others are 'Yajur Veda', the 'Saam Veda', and the 'Athar Veda'.

It is difficult to arrange the divisions of Vedas according to subjects, since in each chapter many varied subjects have been discussed. Therefore, in the interest of simplification only those parts have been segregated and copied in this book, that are concerned with warfare or acts related to warfare.

Note: The writer states that regarding Vedas, he has consulted translations of Griffith and Max Moller. He regrets not knowing Sanskrit; he has had to place his dependence on European translators. He states that the study of erroneous translations of the Holy Qur'an makes him doubt the dependability of the translations of the Vedas too, on account of the European attitude. He requests the scholars who read this book, to notify him of any mistakes these translations may have led him into and any wrong conclusions he may have drawn on account of them. ***The translator also extends the same request for feedback from the scholars of the subject.***

Rig-Veda

The portions of the Rig-Veda, in which the mention of war or conflict is found, are given below:

> "O Inder! Bring that wealth that would give happiness, the wealth that is the total victory of the victors that would help us destroy the enemy in combat" (1:8:1-2)

> "O Brilliant Fire, you on whom holy oil is sprinkled, burn to ashes our enemies, who are protected by unholy spirits" (1:12:5)

> "Inder and Verona! Grant us the victory that will bring us great wealth, which will make our treasure chests overflow with it; O Inder and Verona; I call you for wealth, in a number of ways, keep us victorious always" (1:17: 6-7)

> "Kill all that speak evil and destroy the one who seeks to harm us through sorcery.O Inder! Give us beautiful horses and cows, in thousands. O, Wealthy one!" (1:29:7)

> "Differentiate between Aryans and the non-believing Dasis (Non-Aryans). Punish them, and cast them in the hay kept for the offerings of Gods"
> (1:15:8)

> "Please accept our offerings and may you feel content with the brilliant fire and drops of "Som Rus"; end our poverty of cows and horses. O Inder! Scatter the Dasus (Non- Aryans) and save us from their hatred, and allow us to gather food in plenty. O Inder! Allow us to gather wealth and food in quantity---------.Grant us the strength of the braves, which is a necessity for gathering horses and cattle"
> (1: 53: 4-5)

"O Inder! Grant us increasing honor and grant us the terror and strength, which will overcome nations. And keep safe our wealthy chieftains and protect our kings and guard our wealth and food and pious children" (1:54:11)

"O Agni! (God of fire) May your wealthy worshipers gain food and our chieftains, long life. May we gain war booties in fights with our enemies, and give the gods their share. O Agni! May we, with your help, conquer horses and by horses, men, and by men other braves" (1:74:5-9)

Note: Fair Colored, here, refers to the fair colored Aryans that came from Central Asia and invaded India. They were at war here with the locals of India who were dark colored and are referred here as Dasis or Dasus.

"Mighty Inder Raja, along with his fair colored friends conquered land and sunlight and water. O Inder! Be our guardian and allow us to gather loot without fear" (1:100:18-19)

"O Inder! You have for "Poro" and for your slave Devdas, and for your worshippers destroyed 90 castles. The powerful one has for "Athithgo," brought down "Sambar" from the mountains and with his might have great treasures distributed. Inder helped his worshippers in war. The one who won hundreds of victories in wars" (1: 13: 7-8)

"O Inder! May we with your help, find victory against those who oppose us, and may we vanquish those who oppose us. This day grant holiness to those, who pour Som Rus over your sacrificial fire. Give us strength, in return of our sacrifice, that we may fight and gain and distribute spoils of war"

(1: 132: 8)

"With a good battle plan, when the brave people make the army advance, they gain victory, regularly. And to find fame, they keep advancing and crushing enemies" (1: 132: 5)

"O Inder! You are always the guardian of our men. O Pious Heart, O Giver of victory over our enemies, grant us food that gives us strength, in plenty"

(1: 174: 10)

"O Brave One! Looter of spoils! Lend speed to the carriage of men and like the ship burn to ashes the Non-believing Dasis" (1: 175: 3)

"O Maghoon! O Inder! With your help may we overcome the enemy, who consider themselves strong, be our guardian, and make us advance, make us strong, and help us gain food in quantity"

(1: 175: 5)

"Grant us wealth, and with your help and guidance, and the strength of the Aryans, may we overpower all our enemy Dasis" (2:11: 19)

"O Brave One! Join our war-crazed braves, and show such feats of valor, that you alone can accomplish. The enemy"s pride is in their strength. Kill them and bring us their wealth" (2: 3: 10)

"O Inder! You have fought wars to gain cattle. Many are those who pray to you and sing your praises" (5: 33: 4)

"Inder has control of the sun and horses and the cow that satisfies many a hungry one. He has captured treasures of gold and overwhelming the Dasus and kept the Aryans safe" (3: 34: 39)

"O God of Fire! Any who seeks to attack us in stealth and any neighbor who seeks to harm us, burn him, with the strength of Mitra, burn him with the eternal flame. ----------- Help us fulfil our wish for great wealth, which we will take with our braves"

(6: 5: 4 -7)

"O Inder! Grant us the qualities of bravery, the bravery that gains spoils of war. May we defeat our enemies in the battlefield, whether they be our own, or others. May we be victors in all battles. O Brave

One! May we vanquish both kinds of enemies and prosper with immense wealth" (6: 1: 8-13)

"You have destroyed the seven castles of the Dasus, which were their summer retreat. You have put them under the sword and helped Pur Dakna"

(6: 20: 10)

"O Inder! Give us the wealth, that will help us vanquish the enemy, like the sky spreads over the earth; wealth, that brings prosperity; wealth that conquers the fertile agricultural lands; the wealth that defeats enemies" (6: 20: 1)

"O lord! We have arrived in such a country, which is devoid of pastures, which although is very vast, cannot sustain us. Help us in wars, to gain cattle. O Inder! Make a way for the singer of this hymn. Each day these black- faced creations are being made to flee the areas of the Aryans, by you. The brave one has killed this lowly class where the rivers meet"

(6: 47: 20-21)

"O Inder! When the battle has warmed up, slay those who oppose us. Keep us safe from the prayers of the enemies against us and grant us fame and wealth. Make our enemies easy prey for us. O Brave One! Give us victories and spoils of war and give us valuables to satisfy us. May we gain your supreme favor and may our braves have brave children" (7: 25: 2-3, 5-6.)

"Maghoon! Make our enemies flee, and make easy, victories for us through whom we may gain wealth. Help us in wars for spoils and be our savior"

(7: 32: 25)

"O Brave One! May we in your friendship combat enemies, who are angered to the extreme, and may we remain steadfast in battle against the enemy that has many cattle" (8: 21: 11)

"Destroy the rotting tree; destroy the might of the Dasus. May we with the help of Inder, distribute

amongst us the treasures gathered by the Dasus"
(8: 40: 6)

"O Agni! O God! To gain strength and power, people sing your hymns. Vex the enemy by putting fear in their hearts. O Agni! Won't you help us in gaining cattle and in winning wealth?" (8:64:10-11)

"May we become so in war, that your guidance and help will be assured. We make these holy offerings that we gain spoils of war" (Dal Khela 5 - 7)

"O treasurer of treasures! In our desire for treasures, we hold on to your right hand, since we know you, O Brave One! Grant us excellent fair-faced cattle"
(10: 47: 1, 3, 4)

"We are faced with Dasus, who have no religion, are devoid of intelligence, are outcasts of humanity and are followers of strange laws" (10: 22: 8)

"O Lord! Slayer of enemies, slayer of Dasus; bring us great wealth and treasures" (10: 83: 8)

"Slay our enemies, grant us their lands and property, show the miracles of your strength, and scatter those who hate us. O Manu! Overpower those who fight us; keep breaking and slaying them and treading over them" (10: 84: 2 - 3)

"Fight O True One! Strengthened with truth. Fight and grant us the wealth that has not yet been taken"
(10: 112: 10)

"O Inder! Fight with the Surya and overpower the Dasus" (10: 112: 10)

"Make me the like an ox among my likes and make me the conqueror of enemies. Make me the slayer of my enemies, powerful ruler, and owner of many cattle" (10: 165: 1)

Yajur Ved

In Yajur Veda, we find the mention of war and acts connected with war, in the 'Mantars' (prayers), mentioned below:

"Agni! Grant us huge homes and pleasure, and destroy our enemies and make them flee; she fights to gain spoils in every war, beating the enemy, in its victorious march" (8:44)

"O Agni! Destroy those whom oppose us. Make our enemy flea. O Ajeet! Slay the enemies, who do not believe in our gods, and grant us greatness and fame" (19: 75)

"O Great destroyer of Dasus! You have achieved brilliance from Pathia, you have gained spoils in every war" (11: 43)

"Burn him to ashes, the one who wishes to harm us, the one who sees us with hatred and the one who slanders us and troubles us" (11: 80)

"O Fire! The flames of which are growing as you precede us in battle and burn our enemies. O Great Fire! May the one who has done us evil, burn like dry wood. O Agni! Rise and make them flea who fight us. Show your heavenly strength" (13: 12: 13)

"Wild beasts are its weapons; monsters have been its weapons! Our good wishes to these beasts, may they guard us and have pity on us. May we make the enemy their Morsels; the enemy whom we hate and who hates us" (15: 15)

"O Inder! You are famous for your strength, you are strong, powerful dangerous and a great fighter. You are the victor and you can overpower anyone. You are the son of success and victory; the looter of cows and wealth. You mount the carriage of victory leaving men trailing behind. Opener of stables, and looter of cows, you are the owner of weapons that destroy entire armies. Brothers follow him (Inder) and like yourselves, let the braves go free, and like Inder, show your courage and bravery that would leave your enemies senseless Appu! Capture the enemies and take them away. Attack them and cast their hearts in fire. Burn them, so that our enemies are always in darkness" (17: 37: 38, 44)

Note: Appu is the Hindu Goddess of pestilence. Here Appu signifies the disease and pestilence that spreads in battlefields.

Sam Ved

The 'Mantars' (prayers) of Saam Ved, in which there is a mention of war, are given below,

> "Inder! Grant us the wealth that would enable us to rule over the talented and clever men. And give us the sovereign of wealth and power. May we call Inder and Poshan for friendship and prosperity and for looting spoils of war" (Part 1, 3: 1: 9-61)

> "We the poets call you O Inder! So that we may achieve wealth and overlordship. O Inder! O Chief of Braves, people call you in wars, they call you in horse races; man will achieve spoils of war, only with his true partner, Porandhi" (3: 1: 5: 2 - 6)

> "When we extract our juices, we sing our prayers to you, O Brave One! We do so even when we loot the spoils. Grant us prosperity. With great cleverness, may we in your special protection, gain victories. O Inder! We hold your right hand. You are the real owner of wealth; we seek treasures by your blessing, because we consider you, The Brave One, the owner of cattle; grant us splendid treasures. O Hero of wars! O splendorous and Respected One! Grant us a part of the hordes of cattle"
> (4: 1: 4-5, and 6)

> "Sing with alms and offerings, the praises that make him happy, who with "Rahbovan"Made the Black Hordes flee" (4: 2: 4:11)

Note: By black hordes is implied the dark colored local Non-Aryans, who at other places, have been referred to as Dasus or Dasis.

> "O Brave One! In our fight with the owners of vast herds of cattle, be our friend and help us in our fight with the one who flares at us in anger" (5: 2: 5)

"O Terrible, O Brilliant one! Without tiring make the darkness flee before you, and proceed like the bull. O 'Som Rus'! You make easy prey of the enemy and proceed as if boiling. O Giver of intelligence and happiness! Make those who do not believe in Gods, flee" (6: 1: 1: 5-6)

"Ahead of carriages the brave commander proceeds searching for spoils. And his army rejoices"
(6: 1: 5: 1)

"When we loot the spoils, let the rivers of treasures, that hundreds of others desire, flow upon us"
(6: 2: 1:5)

"May we gain victory and with it all the enemy's wealth and achieve man's greatest splendor and high respect" (Part 2, 1: 1: 8: 3)

"We pray for spoils from the One who has food aplenty and who is the owner of cows in thousands"
(1: 1: 13: 2)

"O Beloved of Gods! Boil out with your satisfying juices and kill the sinners and the enemy along with their hatreds and thus gaining strength boil out more! You are indeed procurer of horses and cows"
(2: 1: 15: 1-2)

"Eternal are the favors of Inder! And never ending his sponsorship and protection, ever he grants his worshipers spoils consisting of cows aplenty"
(2: 1: 3)

"O Magus, O Thundering One! Out of your graciousness take us to some corral that is full of cows" (2: 2: 11: 2)

"O Ever-Vigilant One, join the sons of 'Kanwa' and without hesitating, gain spoils of war in their thousands. O Busy Maghoon! With great desire in our hearts, in our prayers, we wish for gold and cows in plenty" (2: 2: 12: 3)

"O True Lord! May we gain food aplenty and a

place to live, out of your graciousness. O 'Mitro'!
May we become your own. O Mitro! Protect us and
with your protection save us. O desirable protector!
May we overpower the Dasus" (3: 2: 8: 2: 3)

"O Brave One! O looter of spoils! Let the carriage
of man roll fast. O Conqueror! Like a volatile ship,
burn unreligious Dasus" (6: 3: 20: 3)

"O Beautiful One! When you hear our song, do not
keep the wealth of your cows away from us.
Wherever the Slayer of Dasus goes, he opens the
corral of cows, for whomever it belongs to"
(8: 2: 4: 2: 3)

"O Inder and Agni! With outstanding tactics, you
have conquered 90 castles belonging to the Dasus"
(8; 12: 17: 3)

Ather Ved

In this book, the topic of warfare has come under discussion
quite often. Some of the 'Mantars' (prayer) are copied here:

"O Agni! Bring the evil spirits[11] bound, here, and
with your thunder crush their heads" (1:7:7)

"O drinker of 'Som Rus'! Bring the Dasus along
with their offsprings and slay them, or take out the
eyes of these confessed sinners"

"O Mino![12] Come hither stronger than ever, and
with your terror destroy our enemies. O Slayer of
our enemies and Dasus, bring us all kinds of
treasures" (4: 32: 1: 3)

"O king who grants true strength! Burn, who would
give us sorrow and pain; who would behave with us
like an enemy; who without having experienced

---

[11]The word used here is "Dhaan". The same word is used sometimes to depict
"evil spirits" and sometimes to depict Non-Aryan enemies. As Dr. Bredel
Keith states, it is difficult to determine, which particular meaning is intended,
at a particular place. Sometimes however, one may understand its meaning in
reference to the context or through its usage.

[12] Mino is the Hindu God of terror.

pain at our hands or otherwise, seeks to trouble us. May I inflict on him the dual pain of fire"

(4: 32: 1: 2)

"May I with my strength overcome the "Peshachu"[13] and deprive them of their wealth. Whoever causes pain, may I slay him. Enable me to implement my decisions" (4: 32: 4)

"May Roara break your neck O Peshachu! And grind your ribs to splinters and may we live here in splendor.O Mitra Veroana! Beat the sinners and make them flee. May they find no shelter or solace and may they all die" (6: 32: 2)

"May our enemies be deprived of their hands; may we make their lazy hands useless. In this way O Inder, may we distribute their wealth among ourselves" (6: 66: 3)

"Sew them up in rawhide, and make them cowardly like the deer, and then may we capture their cattle"

(6: 67; 3)

"With the help of Inder, may we capture and distribute all the treasures our enemies have gathered. And like the law of Veroana may I humble the arrogant and the mischievous" (7: 90: 2)

"O God of Fire! Enter their skins and burn them with your fire; crush their joints, so that the Eaters of Raw Flesh may find them and kill them" (8: 3: 4)

"O King of Fire wherever you see the enemy, standing or walking or flying, in your anger make holes in his skin, with your arrows" (8: 3: 5)

"Either Pierce the hearts of the enemies with your arrows, or break the arms that are raised against you. Rise in flames in front of the devils, O Agni! Kill them with your leaping flames and may the spotted dead-meat eating donkeys eat them. Seek

---

[13] Peshachu generally is the name given to raw meat eating devils, but here it clearly used for non-human enemies of human beings.

out this unholy and unclean enemy, like a man-eater does and break his upper body parts and with your flames, crush their ribs, O Agni! Make three parts of his lower body" (8: 3: 6, 7, and 10)

"O Inder and Soma! Burn the unholy enemy and destroy him. O God! Come and humiliate those who heap sorrow upon sorrow on us, annihilate the fools, and make pieces of these devils in human form" (3: 4: I Rig Veda, 10: 87: 5: 10)

"Conqueror of forts! Master of Wealth, Inder, Has destroyed the enemy and like the peel of lightning, has overcome the Dasus. With his might, and his bravery, that none can withstand, and with his excellent ability, has overcome the Dasus, of evil spirit and gained treasures of gold. He has completely destroyed the Dasus and made the Aryans safe" (20: 11: 1, 6, and 9)

An Overview of the Vedic Teachings of War

We have copied the Vedic Mantars (prayers) that deal with the subject of war, from the four Vedas, and in the interest of demonstrating the real spirit of the teachings, more than one Mantar dealing with the same topic have been included. Following are the highlights of a careful study of these Mantars:

1. The Aryans were at war with a nation that differed from them in color, race, and creed who belonged to a different country. Aryans wanted to take over their lands and to make their own settlements on these occupied lands.

2. The Aryans regarded their enemies as devils in the shape of men and evil spirits. These locals were known and addressed by the Aryans by the degrading titles of Dassi, Dasu, Rakshas, Yatu, Dhan, Peshach etc. They were considered exempt of humanity, deprived of intelligence and understanding, and of a lower status of humans compared to the Aryans; they refused to give them a status equal to their own.

3. In their view, war did not hold any elevated ethical purpose. The Aryans were in pursuit of treasures, abundance of cattle, horses, other domestic animals, fertile lands, and comfortable

homes. Maintaining ample stores of food was a fixation with them. Establishing their supremacy over other nations and being well regarded among their own people for their bravery and courage were their ideals. In the four Vedas, nowhere a more superior motive for war is perceivable.

4. In their wars with Aryan nations, there was no option for settlement through negotiations. The only end to such wars was perceived that one of the two parties to the conflict would either be completely annihilated, or overpowered.

The main reason for the Aryan wars was that the other nation was not Aryan and did not hold their gods and religion sacred. It was not possible under these conditions that there could be any peace through negotiations, since a man cannot change his race and the Vedas do not prescribe spreading the religion through religious instructions. Nowhere is it mentioned in the Vedas that other nations were invited to their religion or that others had been included in their society, conditional to accepting certain laid down norms. On the contrary, there is ample evidence that the Aryans considered the Non-Aryans a lower category of human beings, of evil spirit and not worthy of being included in their worship or even of touching their religious books. This was the reason that wars with the locals continued, until these locals accepted life as untouchables or condescended to living in jungles and on mountains.

5. In the Vedas, it is not discernible, exactly, what treatment was meted out to the locals, but it is clear that they wanted to punish them terribly. Among the favored punishments desired for the enemies from their Gods were skinning men alive, cutting off flesh from their live bodies, burning men, cutting off their limbs, having them torn up by beasts and even having the children of the enemies slaughtered. If these were their desires, one can imagine what their actions could have been.

Geeta's Philosophy of War[14]

The position that Geeta occupies in the Hindu religion is

---

[14] Two reliable sources have been consulted regarding the teachings of Geeta. One is the well-known works Mr., Bal Ganga Dhar Tilak, translated by Mr. Shanty Narayn Lahori. The other is the book titled, "Sacred Books of the East" by Mr. T Thaling, published by Oxford Press.

mainly due to the fact that it is attributed to the great Hindu leader, Krishan. The clarity with which the Hindu religious philosophy has been put forward in Geeta is not discernible in the entire rest of the Sanskrit literature. Although it deals to a great extent with Hindu Sufism, but the main stress of the book is on war. It has been written to incite a person of low morale into war and to excite a heart disgusted by bloodshed, to war again.

A well-known incident of the period in which the Hindu culture was at its peak, is that the desire for wealth and authority caused a rift in the royal family of Santapour. The family was divided into sub clans of Korus and Pandus, both in conflict with each other. All the rich and powerful noblemen were forced to take sides. Initially, a negotiated settlement was attempted, but when negotiations failed, war was resorted too. In this war, Krishan sided with the Pandus, since the chief of the Pandus was his disciple. In order to ensure success for the Pandus in the war, he assumed the reins of the command himself.

When the opposing forces confronted each other in the battlefield, Arjun lamented, seeing his friends, relatives, and brothers, pining for each other's blood. He was deeply affected by the situation and decided to quit the confrontation. On this, Krishan gave him a long lecture covering the various aspects of the philosophy of war. This very same philosophical lecture is Bhagwat Geeta.[15]

Translator's note:

"From this it is apparent that Krishanjee's lecture has not reached us as delivered in the Pandu camp to Arjun, but as reported by an author from the opposing camp, which he states,

---

[15] Krishan's lecture was actually delivered verbally. However, the writer of Mahabharat has clarified that the reason the lecture could be obtained in writing was, that when the Koru elder, Dharat Rashter, felt disinclined to personally see the decimation of his family, Dayas ji, appointed one, Sanjay, a scribe, to report the conditions of the war to Dharat Rashter. In reporting there happenings of the war, Dharat Rashter, Sanjay also reported the conversation between Krishan and Arjun in the Pandu camp. Later these same reported reservations of Arjun and his disinclination for war and the subsequent lecture by Krishan, to boost up the Morale of Arjun, was included in the part of Maha Bharat, Known as "Bhesham Parab" and was named as Bhagwat Geeta. (Please see for details, Thaling's. Commentary on Bhagwat Geeta, page 3 and Tilak's relation of Geeta, part 4, page 1)

was delivered by Krishan. (This Koru author's source or how he
reached the Pandu camp is neither known nor understandable.)"

The declamation commences when Arjun seeing his relatives
and friends in conflict with each other, gets disenchanted with the
war and declares his sorrow to Krishanjee, stating:

> "Hail Krishan! Seeing my relatives here, desiring
> battle with each other, my limbs go numb, my
> mouth feels dry, and I cannot control the shivering
> of my body with sorrow. I feel powerless to even
> hold my bow. O Kesu! I feel all things going upside
> down. In laying my own relatives, I do not see
> myself achieving any good. O Krishan! I do not
> desire victory or sovereignty or even satisfaction. O
> Govind Raj! What is the worth of this life and
> sovereign, these pleasures of kingship and
> satisfaction, when these people, have given up the
> very same luxuries, and have gathered here to do
> battle with each other.
>
> Even if the kingship of three such nations was at
> stake and they desired my death, I cannot find in me
> the inclination to slay them. O Madhu Sodan what
> indeed is the worth of achievements in this world? -
> -------------------- Killing one's own relatives can in
> any way be justifiable. How, O Madhu Sodan, can
> we remain happy in the knowledge that we have
> killed our own? --------------- We can clearly
> perceive the disadvantages of being anchorless,
> without the family support, then why should we
> strive for the destruction of our families. Why
> indeed should we not feel the inclination for
> avoiding this sin? ----------.The destruction of
> families mean the destruction of values and faith
> and with the destruction of values, vagrancy sets in.
> It is said that those who lose family values are
> indeed a condemned lot. See! We stand here, to
> actually kill our own relatives for the sake of the
> luxuries of kingship. This indeed, is a great sin we
> have undertaken. It will be much better that I do not
> put up any resistance and lay down my arms and

then some well armed Koru should come and kill me" (Adyal: 1, Ashlok: 28-46)

Hearing these pure and tender words of Arjun, Krishanjee taken by surprise, states to him:

"O Arjun! Whence have these vagrant thoughts entered your heart! No noble person has ever entertained such thoughts. These can only lead a man to depravity and infamy. O Path! Do not act in such an unmanly fashion; this attitude does not become your splendid stature. Ascend from this weakness of heart and stand! (2: 2-3)

Arjun replies:

"Rather than killing the Korus, it is better that I spend the rest of my life as a beggar. Even if I kill my elders from the Korus, for their wealth, I would have to use their blood stained material wealth in this world. ---------- How can we bear to live this life, having slain these elders? These very same people are arrayed against us" (2: 5-6)

From the words of Arjun, it is clear that the Korus and Pandus were the sub-groups of the same family, who, for the purpose of gaining sovereignty, were bent on destroying each other. Arjun could not bear the thought of the ensuing avaricious fratricide. The kind hearted, noble soldier, affected by the pricking of his conscience, became disenchanted by the prospect. However, Krishanjee negated his thoughts and put forward a new philosophy, which in the words of Geeta, is stated below:

"The thoughts and doubts that should be far from you, at this time, you are speaking of them now! And all this talk about understanding! Men of understanding do not put much value on life. One should not feel sorrow at any ones death. As a man achieves his childhood, youth, and old age in the same body, similarly a man achieves another body on death. The real occupier of the body is the eternal spirit, and it is beyond comprehension. The bodies given to the spirit alone are mortal. So, O

Arjun! Fight on the one who thinks the spirit kills or is killed, do not possess true understanding. The spirit is neither ever born or dies and it is not that once it comes into being, will never attain this status. It is eternal and continual. Therefore with the death of the body, the spirit does not die.

O Mortal! How can one who understands, that the spirit is immortal non-aging and indestructible, ever kill a person. The way a man takes off his clothes and puts on new ones, so, the master of the body, the spirit, castes his old body off and assumes a new one. No weapon cuts this spirit, no water draws it, no air dries it up, -----------. Therefore, considering the spirit, of that nature, does not do you credit"

(2: 18-25)

"If you consider that the spirit is born with the man and dies with him, even then, O Mahabahu, grieving for it is not right for you, because anyone that is born has to die one day, and the one who dies has to be born again. Therefore, grieving for this pre-destiny does not become you" (2: 30)

Later, Krishan Ji stated another philosophy, which is in his own words given below:

"Even if you are the greatest of sinners, this boat of understanding will enable your crossing the sea of sins. Like the lighted flame burns all its fuel to ashes, similarly O Arjun, this fire of understanding, will burn free your acts of the bounds of vice and virtue" (4: 36-37)

"O Dhanjai! The understanding spirit cannot remain bounded by vice. He who has the support of his understanding, and who made distant all doubts through his understanding, is able to rise above the discrimination of right and wrong. Therefore, cut asunder the doubts that have risen in your heart with the sword of understanding and with the strength of belief set up for war" (4: 41-42)

"One who cleanses his heart and keeps his senses in control and the spirits of all animals becomes his spirit; he can do anything without getting the effect of the reward or punishment for his crimes." (5:7)

"Who does his deeds is absolved from any crimes. He is not affected by the sin like the water does not stay on the lily pad. "(5:10)

A Brief Review of the Philosophy of Geeta

The Crux of the teachings of Krishan Jee in plain words is as under:

Based on the belief in reincarnation, a man after his death is reborn. Therefore, killing him is not a sin or crime. He will become alive again after his death anyway and his immortal spirit will not have any effect by his murder.

The body is for the spirit as the garment for the body. Therefore, cutting someone's link between his body and his spirit is like tearing apart a piece of cloth. Regarding such acts as murder and its results as death and afterwards considering it as a sin or a crime and mourning it, is complete ignorance. In the light of true knowledge and enlightenment, a person who apparently kills someone but in reality he did not. Rather he only removes the covering of the body from the spirit and this is something to neither be sad about nor mourn. It would have been a sad story if the spirit would have also faced the death.

The thing that is an accident is bound to vanish. Therefore, a human who is bound to die, what is the problem in killing him? That which is bound to happen, whether it happens with our hand or through nature, tomorrow the nature is going to bring death to him anyway, then if we kill him today, what is the difference?

The one who found the transcendental connection (Giyan), for him there is no restriction of good or bad. For him all the deeds are permissible. The distinction of good and bad is only for those people who do not have this "Giyani" or connection. So just achieve this connection (Giyan), then even the worst of the worst deed is not a sin for you.

The logical end result of such philosophies is that human life would become valueless. Whoever so desired would destroy his brother's body, considering it an old garment and when questioned, he could put forward this philosophy of immortality of the body and evanescence of the body, and thus claim exemption from punishment for the crime of murder. Then when a person lays claims to deep understanding (Giyan), for him murder does not remain murder, no crime remains a crime and no sin, a sin. He would remain innocent whatever the crime he commits.

The teachings of Geeta nearly coax a man to war, but nowhere in it, is discernible the cause and aim for the achievement of which war is so liberally espoused. Nowhere in its pages is the reason presented which could justify the breaking up of the relation between the spirit and the body (shedding of human blood), stated, or amplified. The basic consideration that could elevate war above the level of meaningless fracas and bloodshed is the aim or cause of the war. Only if the cause to be achieved is pure and morally sound can it lend piety to the undertaking. Conversely, no matter how gallant and principled the conduct of war, it would yet remain prohibitive and from the ethical viewpoint, would remain barbaric and inhuman, if the cause is deprived of piety and purity.

Geeta has totally ignored this basic aspect of war and in this connection shows no inclination for the guidance of man. The style and delivery of some of its teachings however, do give an idea as to what probably is Geeta's standpoint on the subject. At one point, Krishanjee states,

> "O Arjun, this war is the door for deliverance, which has opened up for you. Such chances come the way of very lucky Kashatris (Hindu caste of soldiers). Therefore, if you refrain from this war, you would damage your own faith and your fame and increase your sins instead. People will eternally sing songs of your infamy. This infamy and censure are worse than death for a man" (2: 32-34)

> "All will believe that you fled the battlefield out of fear. Those who respect you today will consider you unworthy of it, your ill-wishers, and enemies will speak such words censuring your might and bravery that should not be uttered. What can be more painful Translator's note than that? On the other

hand, if you die fighting, you will achieve heaven and if you are victorious, you will achieve over-lordship of the world. Rise! Therefore and resolutely do battle" (2: 35-37)

"All aside, if you consider your faith alone, losing heart at this time, does not do you credit at all, since, for a Kashatri, nothing in the world is worth more honor than to fight for a just cause" (2: 31)[16]

"O Arjun, I am the scourge, that has come to slay men. I have come to destroy them. Even if you do desist from the fight, all these soldiers arraigned for war will be slain. Therefore live! And gain your battle fame. Overpower the enemy and enjoy the fruits of victory and supremacy over large territories. I have already slain the enemy" (11: 32)

The words are no different from those spoken to fighters before battle to raise their morale and fighting spirit. The stated causes are also not much elevated from those that have often resulted in unwanted bloodshed. The same greed, the same craving for fame and glory, the same thirst for power and throne, the same fear of the despair of defeat, the same fear of the ignominy and censure are all in evidence here; the very same that induce worldly men to turmoil and conflict. There is no elevated ethical teaching in this, nor any supremacy of cause introduced. Man has not been instructed or guided beyond the satisfaction of his animal desires and emotions.

Manu's Instructions on War [17]

The holy books of Manu are the best on Hindu religious

---

[16] This is the only place in Geeta that has the mention of "just cause". Unfortunately, nowhere has it been amplified. When two branches of a royal family lay claims to the throne, only one is the legal heir, and if that branch rises and indulges in fratricide to establish its right, the term loses its ethical virtue. Such wars of succession are not uncommon, but no reasonable person has ever termed this fratricide and bloodshed for the selfish motive of gaining the throne, a very elevated, noble, or pious cause.

[17] For reference, the writer states that he has used the English translations by two scholars. One was by Sir William Jones, written and published in 1794, from Fort William College, Calcutta and the other by Dr. Burnal, edited and

instruction and have been in vogue for about 1400 years among Hindu states and nations as an instrument for the conduct of affairs of state. The personality of the author has been lost in ambiguity, and neither has the period of its first publication been established[18]. It is an established fact, however, that it is from that period when the Aryan society had progressed much and there was a need to codify and regulate the conduct of the affairs of the state. For the purpose, other books have been written in that period, but among all these, the status of Manu is unique. Other works are either criticism of Manu or almost a verbatim agreement of the original book; the Hindu scholars have rejected them. The current trend is to put full dependence on Manu and not on other books. We have in fact, no better reference material than Manu.

Manu's writings are of the period when the Aryan kingdoms were established and there was much progress in the cultural and social life. It became necessary that the conduct of the affairs of the state be codified and adhered to. For that reason, the book provides us ample material regarding conduct of wars and related affairs and the laws governing them.

Causes of Wars

The first aspect that begs attention, when studying wars, is its causes. Manu has not gone into any details regarding this aspect. However, the causes that he considers legitimate can be gleaned from the extracts given below:

> "Those rajahs (rulers), who on the face of the earth, either for the purpose of killing others or for defaming them, wage wars against them and do not turn back, will go straight to heaven, when they die"
>
> (7: 89)

---

published by Professor Hopkins, in 1884. The earlier of the two, is considered the more authentic and dependable.

[18] Sir William is of the opinion that the period of the writing is 1250-500 B.C.; Professor Monier dates it at 500 B.C.; Johanathan, the German scholar of Hindu Mythology, believes that the correct period is about 350 B.C.Shlegal dates it at 100 B.C.Professor Crook, however states that the writing is no older than 200 A.D.But Dr, Burnals research dates the book between 100 and 500 A.D.(End of notes)

"The world respects him whose forces are always on the alert and ready for war. It is incumbent on such rajahs to establish, with the help of his forces, his over-lordship over all creatures of the world"
(7: 103)

"After readying for victory, rajahs should ensure that his opponents either accept his sovereign or he should use other means. These include but are not limited to, bribing, and appeasement of the influential in the enemy camp, clandestinely breaking up alignments and alliances and warfare"
(7: 107)

"The most important obligation of a rajah, after performance of his religious duties, is the establishment of his sovereign, over areas that have so far not been subjected and to adequately secure them" (9: 251)

"The Rajah, who acts according to his faith, has as his primary duty, the conquering of other countries, and never avoiding war" (10: 119)

From the above extracts, it is evident that Manu's flight of imagination was not of any greater elevation than Krishan's. His imagination too could not take him beyond the worldly pursuits of extension of empire, conquests of other kingdoms or the belittling of other rajahs. It could not elevate him beyond these goals towards some grand ethical pursuits. Like any normal being, he too considered kingship and sovereignty the peak of achievements of the powerful and advises them to always use their might in such pursuits.

Such limited concepts can never be the epitome of some elevated thinking or high and pure ideals. The desire and pursuit for empires can never in themselves be the aim of ethics. The high aim of ethics and virtue are the wellbeing and welfare of humanity. From this standpoint, human blood, a nation's freedom, and the state of peace in a country are definitely more valuable. Ethics stands for the peace and progress of humanity; it deems the horrors of war, permissible, only in the event that there is no other option left, to rid humanity of the material, moral and spiritual usurpation, by some greed-crazed usurper. However, apparently Manu or any other Hindu philosopher never achieved that height of understanding. Some, who did choose to rise higher, crossed all bounds and arrived at the outskirts of "Ahinsa," which is no less harmful for humanity, than the unrestricted permissibility of bloodshed. In fact, the ends of both philosophies are the same, i.e. the total destruction of a nation at the hands of mischief and troublemakers.

Ethical Bounds of War

The code of conduct of war according to Manu is quite enlightened. In fact, its bounds are not very unlike the bounds imposed by Islam. His instructions are copied below for the benefit of the reader:

> "No participant in a battle shall use hidden weapons, or those dipped in poison multi-edged arrows, or spearheads heated in fire, for the purpose of killing the enemy" (7: 9)

> "Nor can a horse or carriage mounted soldier kill a foot soldier. Nor can one kill the one who begs for his life, nor the one whose hair have gone frenzied and open, nor the one who declares that he is one's prisoner, nor the one who is asleep, nor the one who is armor-less, nor the one who is naked, nor the one who is unarmed, nor the one who is not a participant in the battle, nor the one who is at the time, in combat with another" (7: 91-92)

> "Remembering the virtues of a nobleman, he should not kill a man whose weapon has broken, or one who is in extreme sorrow, or one who is grievously wounded, or one who is in a terrorized state, or the one who turns his back" (7: 93)

> "Carriage, horse, elephant, Umbrella, apparel (except the jewels that may be sewn in them), grains, domestic animals, women, all kinds of precious and solid materials (except gold and silver), are the property of the one who wins them in war" (7: 96)

"Of the things looted in war, a part of them is to be offered to the rajah, and those things not personally looted, are to be distributed among the rajah's army" (7: 97)

"When he lays a siege on an enemy and is encamped, He should burn the country to ashes and destroy the opposing rajah's logistic support (Animal feed, food storage etc.) and his water resources" (7: 195)

"All wells and trenches that are the need of the enemy should all be destroyed. He should aim to put the enemy in fear, night and day" (7: 195)

"When the enemy has been conquered, one should offer prayers to their god, their idols[19], and to their pious Brahmans. He should extend his appreciation to those of the enemy, who deserves it and declare general amnesty" (7: 106)

"After carefully taking note of their (conquered enemy's) reactions and plans, one should appoint a person from their royal family as the ruler, who should be under one's instruction" (7: 202)[20]

---

[19] Manu's writings indicate that by "their gods", he could have meant the gods of the conquered nations, but the addition of the clause, containing the words, "their pious Brahmans," negates the likelihood that Manu intended that the gods of the Non-Aryans should also be prayed to.

[20] This order is specific for warfare between kingships that are both Aryans and more specifically Hindu Aryans. Clause 202 is not of independent applicability but is a part of the clauses 26-203. The same idea has been confirmed by other sources as well.

Professor Hopkins states:

"It will be interesting to note that Manu and Vishnu, both state that when a raja conquers another kingdom, he should a point a prince of that foreign nation as the king (not of his own nation) he should not destroy the enemy's royal family, unless that royal family is of a lower caste to one's own" (Cambridge History of India, vol., 1, page 290)

"Fights between various Aryan clans and with non-Aryans (Wohosh, Dasi and Dasus), were frequent. It was an established tradition that such wars should not be for the extension of one

> "And he should declare the laws as enacted by them
> (enemy), still operable and valid and attempt to gain
> the gratitude of the new raja as well as the chieftains
> with gifts of gold and precious stones" (7: 203)

It is not possible to adhere to some of these instructions in actual combat. For example, the instruction that a mounted soldier should not slay an enemy on foot, or that the one whose hair opened up and were in disarray or the one who was armor-less, should not be slain, or the one involved in combat with another, should not be attacked.

In such laws and instructions, the attempted reform has been overshadowed by exhibitionistic ethics, resulting in the necessities of war and the bounds of ethics not remaining in balance. Naturally, a soldier cannot, in the heat of battle, always keep such dictates of ethics foremost in his consideration, and if he does, cannot fight. Conversely, at places, Manu has sacrificed the ethical considerations totally to the necessities of combat. In the conduct of war, completely burning and destroying the total logistics of a nation thereby forcing them to death by hunger, cannot be in consonance with the dictates of ethical sensibilities.

Overall, however, the instructions of Manu are very refined and moralistic. In them, the enlightened thinking is evident, that even in enmity, there are some rights that a man has on others. In this regards, Manu's thinking are very close in nature to the Islamic rules of war, though they are not so moderate and modern.

Treatment of the Fallen Enemy

It has been stated earlier that Manu's laws came into effect when the non-Aryan might had been crushed and there was not a single such kingdom left that could challenge the Aryans in all India. Therefore, it is quite fruitless to search in his laws for those that are specific for conflicts with the non-Aryan entity. In this era, all non-Aryans, who in Vedic terms are known as Dasi, Dasu, and

---

raja's rule and the defeated raja should not be made to quit the
throne, but that the conquered should make him, his vicegerent.
This consideration of tribal sensitivity prevented the Aryan
customs from facing any upheaval. (History for Aryan Rule in
India, page 33-34)

Rakhshas etc., had either left the habitations, and took refuge in the mountains or having accepted defeat, had become a part of the Aryan society. They were allotted the lowest of human castes and being given the name of "Shudars." We can only find from Manu's laws of warfare, how in inter Hindu-Aryan warfare, a Hindu-Aryan conqueror can treat another Hindu-Aryan conquered enemy. They do not show us what treatment a non-Hindu vanquished should get. For this purpose, we would have to examine Manu's rules for the treatment of Shudars. Extracts from these are given below.

1. Manu considers the Shudars of a lower status. He, on account of their birth, not their actions, considers them creatures below the level of humanity.

> "Brahma gave birth to Brahmans from his mouth, Kashatris from his hands, the Vesh from his calves, and Shudars from his feet." The same is stated in Rig Ved (19:9:12) and in Bhagwat Pran (2:5:37)

> "The first part of a Brahman's name should be indicative of respect and holiness; the Kashatri's, of strength; the Vesh's, of wealth and the Shudar's, of lowliness"(6: 13)"The second part of a Brahman's name should indicate well-being, the Kashatri's, security, The Vesh's, wealth and the Shudar's, slavery and servitude" (2: 32)

> "Only three castes are worthy of respect, the Brahman, the Kashatri and the Vesh. The fourth has but one life" (4:10)

> "Elephants, horses, Shudars, the detestable "Milch" people, tigers, cheetahs, and pigs are those creatures who have been created from the darkness" (12: 43)

2. Manu considers Shudars, low, dirty, impure, and despicable. He advises the "Dawaij" (respectable Aryans) to avoid all contact with them.

> "By allowing a Shudar girl to sit on his bed, a Brahman goes to hell" (3: 17)

> "He may not even stand in the shade of the same tree as a person expelled from his family or a

"Chindal" (A person born of a Brahman mother and Shudar father)" (4: 79)

"He, who teaches religion and the conduct of religious rites, will go to the hell called Ism warath" (4:81)

"He should not recite the Veda in the presence of a Shudar" (4: 99)[21]

"He should not eat the food of the Shudars"

(4:112)[22]

"The food of a Shudar terminates the aura of spirituality of a person" (4: 218)

If a Brahman eats the food of a Shudar, by mistake, he should fast for three days and if he does so, on purpose, the punishment prescribed is the same, as for a person who consumes the menstrual fluids of a woman, or urine or excretion. (4: 322)

If while he is eating his food, a Shudar touches him, a Brahman should leave his food. (Apstambh 1:5)

"The one, who touches a Chindal, can only attain purity by bathing" (5: 85)

"The funerals of Shudars should be taken out in the Southern direction, out of a town and a child's in the North-western or Eastern directions" (5: 92)

"If a dead Brahman does not have a person of his own caste present, his coffin should not be allowed to be touched by a Shudar, since any part of it touched by a Shudar will not go to heaven" (5: 104)

---

[21] If some Shudar intentionally listens to the words of the Ved, molten lacquer should be poured in his ears. If he reads any part of the Ved, his tongue should be cut out and if he commits any part of it to memory, his body should be cut into two pieces. (Gotam 12:4-6)

[22] Eating the food prepared by a Shudar, even if his hand did not touch it, is impermissible. (Apstambh, 1:5: 12-22) If some Brahman dies while the food of the Shudar is still in his body, he will in his next life be born a pig of the village (Wushanth, 6:27). If a Shudar touches the food of a Brahman, he should leave the food (Alpastambh, 1:65:17}.

"Children, born of a Brahman, Kashatri or a Vesh mother, from Shudar father, is of an outcast class and is known as "Chindals", "Kushtars" and "Aewgo" respectively, and these are the lowliest of creatures" (10: 12)

"The dwellings of the Chindals and Swopas people should be outside the villages and townships. Their property should consist only of dogs and donkeys; they should wear the clothes of the dead; their eating utensils should be partly broken and their jewelry should be of iron. They should always live as nomads. He one, who is careful of fulfilling his worldly and religious duties, should keep no contact with them. All their relations should be among their likes and marriages should also be between the people of the same status"

"They should be given food in pieces of broken pottery, but the giver should avoid contact with them. They should not roam about in the dwellings at nights. If they come to the dwellings during the daytime, the particular mark or sign, allotted to them by the rajas should be prominently visible on their bodies. They should perform the task of carrying away unclaimed bodies. The Chindals should act as executioners of those who have been awarded the death sentence; they have the right to the clothes and jewelry of the person so executed"

(10: 51-52)

"The Brahman should never take alms from a Shudar. If one does, and offers no sacrifice, he will be born a Chindal in his next life" (11: 24)

"If a Brahman drinks water that has partly been drunk by a Shudar, will have to drink water boiled on grass and nothing else from dawn to dusk, for three days" (11: 44)

"If a Brahman eats food partly eaten by a Shudar first, will have to consume Aashh Ju only, for seven days" (11: 153)

3. Manu insists that Shudars should be the slaves of the Dawaij (respected Aryan class). He states that the Shudars have been created only for the purpose of slavery of the Dawaij and that is their only purpose in life. He states:

> "The only duty, that the all powerful has ordained for the Shudar is that he should, without complaint, serve the three. (Brahman, Kashatri, and the Vesh)"
>
> (11:91)

> "To continue to serve the Brahman is the best service that a Shudar can perform. Apart from this, whatever service he will perform, will not avail him at all" (10: 123)

> "The rajah should order every Shudar into the service of the Dawaij" (8: 48)

> "Whether the Shudar has been bought or not, the Brahman can insist on service from him, since slavery of the Brahman has been pre-ordained for the Shudar class" (8: 413)

> "Even if a Shudar is set free by his master, he cannot be a free man, since slavery is the condition pre-ordained for the Shudar" (8: 417)

4. Manu does not recognize the Shudars right to own property. He states:

> "A Brahman can without hesitation, take over the property of his Shudar slave. He (Shudar) is such an entity, whose property can be legally appropriated by his master" (8: 417)

> "Even if a Shudar possess the ability to gather wealth, he should be prevented from doing so, since the wealthy Shudar is a cause of discomfort and pain for the Brahman" (10: 129)

5. In the law of inheritance, the Shudar class is discriminated against. In some instances the Shudar class is totally disqualified from inheriting anything and in some cases, their rights of inheritance are limited as compared to those of the Dawaij.

"If a Brahman has four wives, one from each of the four castes and if all of his wives give birth to sons; his property will be inherited by his sons in accordance with the caste of the mother of each. The Brahman woman's son will receive as his inheritance, all the cultivators, the servants, bulls, the riding horses, carriages, jewelry and the house. Of the remaining part of the property, even, the Brahman will receive the greater share"

"The Brahman woman's child will receive a third part of the remaining inheritance, the Kashatr's son, 2 parts, the Vesh woman's child 1.5 parts and the Shudar woman's son, 1 part"

"Alternately, a man of law may divide the total property of the deceased Brahman and divide it among the inheritors, in such a way that the Brahman woman's son gets 4 parts, the Kashatri woman's, 3 parts, the Vesh woman's 2 parts and the Shudar woman's, only one part. Even if the Dawaij women have no sons, the inheritance of the Shudar woman's son will be limited to the same 1/10 of the total"

"A Shudar woman's son is not eligible to any inheritance from a Brahman, Kashatri, or Vesh father's property, except that which the father gives him in his lifetime"

(This part of the law of inheritance differs from the above. The difference did not escape Manu, who amplifies it, by saying in his other works, "Kaloka" and "Madhu Tethi," only that child of a Dawaij is eligible to inheritance who is pious and whose mother was his father's formal wife.)

"The children of the Dawaij father from Women of the Dawaij classes will inherit their father's property in accordance with their mother's castes"
(9: 149-156)

6. In the civil law, Manu has treated the Shudar class most harshly. He gives them hardly any rights to life and self-respect.

Comparatively, he has granted such protection to the rights of the Dawaij that the rights of the Shudars are literally, almost non-existent.

> "If a Shudar is disrespectful to a Dawaij, his tongue may be cut out" (8: 270)

> "If a Shudar insults a Dawaij, by name or by caste, an iron rod of 10 fingers length, heated in fire may be shoved down his throat" (8: 271)

> "If he arrogantly instructs the Brahman on his duties, the Raja may order burning hot oil be poured down his mouth and ears" (8: 272)

> "If the person of the lowest caste (Shudar) ventures to sit alongside a person of the highest caste (Brahman), the rajah should punish the Shudar, by having him branded on his back, or have him expelled from the country, or have his hips cut off" (Sureen)

> "If out of arrogance, he (Shudar) spits on a Brahman, the rajah should have his lips cut off; if he urinates on the Brahman, he should have his phallus severed; if he throws his excreta on the Brahman, his anus should be cut off"
> (Goz sadu) (8: 282)

> "If a Shudar snatches at Brahman's hair, feet, beard or throat, the rajah should forthwith order his hands cut off" (8: 283)

> "If a Shudar rapes a Dawaij woman, the Shudar will have those parts of the body, with which he committed the rape, cut off and all his property confiscated. If the woman is married, the Shudar will have to forgo all that is his, even his life.

If a Vesh man rapes a Brahman, his punishment will be confiscation of his property and one year's imprisonment. If a kashatri man commits this crime, his punishment will be a fine of 1000 Upans. (Denomination of currency), or he will have his beard and moustaches shaved off with the urine of a donkey. If a Brahman man commits the same crime, if it is without the consent of the woman he will have to pay a fine of 1000 Upans and if it is with the consent of the woman, the fine will be 500 Upans." (8: 374- 378)

"A Raja should never have a Brahman put to death. He may without depriving him of his caste or property, order his banishment from the country. There is no greater sin on the face of the earth than shedding the blood of a Brahman. Therefore the rajah should not even think of this." (8: 380- 381)

(Apastambh Dharam Shastar, states that the severest punishment that can be given to a Brahman, for the major crimes of Theft, robbery, or murder, is that he may be blinded "2:17" but if a Shudar commits the same crime, his penalty will be death. "2:2. 27")

On their own, these orders are an explanation of loathsomeness with which the Hindu law treats the vanquished; these laws amply illustrate the low stature accorded to them. In comparison, if we examine the rights of the non-Muslim subjects in Islamic law, we will find a mammoth difference.

Racial Discrimination

In modern times, some Hindu writers, under the pressures of modern thinking, have declared that the division of castes is not by virtue of birth or race but on professional grounds and by virtue of the nature of the job performed. Indeed, it is a pleasurable thought, but one not supported by the original books on Hindu law and constitution. From those, what is apparent is that the Hindu religion has the least concern with professions and qualities, while stratifying society.

Initially, the local people were known by the degrading titles of Das and Dasiu and later came to be called Shudars, not on account of their professions or actions but only because they were non-Aryans. A glance at the criminal and economic laws and the laws dealing with inheritance will make this fact obvious. We can observe that the most pious and righteous of Shudars do not possess the rights that a Brahman, who conducts himself most disgracefully, does. The Brahman's son, born of a Shudar woman, regardless of his abilities and righteousness of character and actions does not have rights equal to his brother, born of his father's Brahman wife. A Brahman mother's child born of a Shudar father, on the other hand, will be termed a Chindal just on account of his birth and would have to go through life in the disgraceful conditions reserved for the Chindals, according to Manu. Why should this be so? Does being born a Shudar's son, naturally make a person guilty of moral turpitude and being born of a Brahman just naturally righteous? This in fact is not discrimination on account of character, conduct, or profession. It is outright racial discrimination at its worst. The righteousness or immorality of a person and his status in life has been pre-determined on account of his progeny, not his conduct.

In this regards Manu himself has been quite lucid and states:

> "A person born of a righteous man and a disgraceful woman has a chance of becoming righteous by his conduct. However, a person born of a disgraceful father and a respectable woman will always remain disgraceful. (10: 67), although he cannot attain the full status of respectability, equal to the person having born of parents of respectable lineage" (Manu, 9: 149-156 and 11: 127)

> "Like the growth of a tree of high quality is dependent on the quality of the seed and the land it is planted on, only the man born of a respectable father and respectable mother, can attain the status of a full-fledged Dawaij"

> "Brahma has himself judged that the Shudars, who act righteously, as the Dawaij should, and the Dawaij who act in the lowly fashion of the Shudar are neither comparable, nor incomparable. That is, neither does the degree of respectability of their action changes their status, nor is the actions of both are such that they cannot be compared"

Note: Incomparability of status here denotes that the status of the Shudar and the Dawaij, in society, will remain the same as pre-ordained. The righteous actions of a Shudar are no doubt more respectable than the unrighteous action of a Dawaij; "the degree of respectability of the actions are comparable, not the respectability of the person who undertakes them."

After consideration of the above, none can deny that the stratification of humanity, in accordance with Hindu religion, is based on racism and not on anything else.

Modern consenters do not even attempt to deny that the Shudars are the local inhabitants of India and that they did not belong to any low caste of the Aryans. Unfortunately, even after clear proof, this fact remains unacceptable. No doubt, the Shudar caste includes some of the Aryans who have been expelled from their caste and society for gross violation of religious edicts (Vedic Index of Names and Subjects, vol.: 2, page 265 and 393). However, also without doubt is the fact that the title Shudar is reserved in general for those of the local inhabitants, who chose not to seek refuge in the mountains and accepted the subservience of the conqueror, the Aryan nation.

Historical and linguistic research, has in fact, established that "Shudar" was the name of the first Indian tribe who the Aryans overpowered, in the valley of Attock, in the Northwest of India. After that, whichever tribe in India accepted their subservience, were included in the nomenclature. Those who put up resistance were known as Dasius or Milch. (Wilson, Indian Castes, vol. 1, page iii).

One of the basic Brahmanic teachings is,

> "Brahman is a caste born of gods, while Shudars are
> born of the evil spirits"
>
> (Muir, Sanskrit Texts, page 14)

This saying removes all doubts that the Hindus consider Shudars a progeny of evil spirits. Scholars of ancient Indian history are in agreement that it is so. Some of the references are copied here.

Raguzan writes:

> "This is to differentiate between the Aryans and
> Non-Aryans; we are aware of the former, of the
> later we have reached the conclusion that they were

the local Non-Aryan inhabitants and none else. These were the people that the Aryan immigrants found, when they came to India. These were the people brought down after extended warfare, to a very ignoble condition. There is very little doubt that it is here that the caste formation initially started. The present day division of Hindus into Dawaij and Shudras bears a striking resemblance to the original differentiation.

Apart from all else, the word "waran" has been used in the context of racism, in the Sanskrit language. Later on, we will see that this differentiation or discrimination, based on color, of the fair-skinned Aryans and dark skinned Shudars, has been oft repeated in the Vedic poems.

The word Dasiu, with the many changes it has undergone, tells us a tale in itself. This is an ancient Aryan word, which the Persians used in its original meaning, to depict race or nationality. In India, it took over the meaning of enemy (in the Arabic language too, the usage of the word "nation", without qualification, often depicts enemy nation). Then the word easily assumed the meaning of evil spirits or ghosts in the Vedic discourses of the super natural, and generally, it began denoting the evil forces of darkness and those that cause famine.

Inder was always ready to combat these evil forces with the powers of light. This adoption of the meaning by the word 'Dasiu', though natural and logical, creates some difference in understanding the Veds. Wherever, in Vedic words, Inder is requested to rid the Aryans of the Dasius, and to kill them or where it is stated that, "Inder put an end to the Dasius," it is often difficult to determine whether the real or the imagined enemy is indicated.

In the last adoption of meaning, the word just indicated a servant or slave. With a little alteration of the word itself, it became "Das". In this way, the process of changes in the word indicates to us the Aryan journey to victory over the Locals. The word itself continued its progress, until it reached close in meaning to the word Shudar. Accordingly, the correct sequence of the social division follows the following pattern:

Aryans ---- Dasius

Dawaij ---- Shudars

If further evidence is required to confirm that the Shudar race was made a caste of servants through conquest, we should refer to the collection of laws of Manu. In Manu's laws, it is declared that a Dawaij under no condition should accept the servitude of a Shudar, though the Shudar be a raja. In this, the Shudar raja can be no other than of local origin.

Although the words, Aryan-Dasiu or Day, follow a correct pattern, it is incorrect to assume that Shudars or Dasius were any particular race. The usage follows the same pattern, under which all races that were not Roman or Greek were termed as Barbarians." (Vedic India page 282 - 285).

Professor Rapsin writes:

> "The authors of Rig Ved were not aware of any finer meanings of race and nationality. They only knew that there were different castes of humans. The religious caste known as "Brahmans", the ruling and fighting caste known as Kashtris, the tillers of land, known as Vesh and the servant class known as Shudars. There was a huge gap between the first and the last class. The highest class is of Brahmans and the lowest that of the Shudars. The difference between these is in color (Waran). Generally the Aryans were fair-colored and the Dasius dark-colored."
>
> (Cambridge; History of India, vol. I, page 54).

Dr. Bradel writes:

> "The big difference between the Aryans and the Dasius was in color. One of the main factors behind the Hindu caste system is the "Arya Waran" and the dark color. The overpowering of the dark-skinned and forcing them into subservience, was one of the most important undertakings of the Hindus. Although the Veds mention wars and advances against the Dasius and the capturing of new lands, but it is confirmed that the total eradication of the locals, was not attempted. Some of the local

inhabitants fled into the mountains of the Northwest, and took refuge there, but others (who remained there) were enslaved."

(Cambridge, History of India, vol. 1, page 84-86)

Professor Hopkins writes:

"The Shudar slaves had been accepted as a part of the total social structure. The name itself indicates that they were a part of a conquered nation. Just as the word "Karian", came to mean slave, in ancient Athens, similarly the word Shudar assumed the meaning of slave. The Shudars however were not exempt from the class of human beings. They came to be included in the domestic affairs of the home and were also included in certain domestic functions."

(Cambridge, History of India, vol. 1, page 234).

The same writer later writes:

"If we compare Gotham's ruling (12: 22) on the case, where an Aryan woman has an illicit relation with a Shudar man, with the ruling of Apsthum Dharamshastar,

(2: 26, 20, 27, and 9), we find ample proof of the belief that the Aryans were a superior race to the dark-colored people. Mr. Cataher has been a little irresponsible in his book, "The history of Divisions in India," where he states 'There appears to, be no difference between the Aryans and Dravidians.' It is true that those people, who were expelled from their castes and their society, were thereafter not called Aryans. Conversely, no Shudar has ever become an Aryan. The Aryan race, has since the period of Rig Ved till much later, been the proponents of this racial discrimination".
(Cambridge, History of India page 246)

From studying these pieces of evidence, it becomes amply clear that, in the Hindu religion, those who have been termed as Shudars are actually the vanquished non-Aryan nations. Therefore, the laws prescribed for them in the books of Hindu religious code and the attitude of the Hindu religion in their connection is the attitude of the conqueror in relation to the vanquished.

2) Judaism

A distinct advantage of examining the laws dealing with warfare in Judaism is that unlike in Hinduism, we have to consult just one book, the Torah, to get the required information and to see the true nature of the religion.

(At the time when the original book was written, Judaism had not attained the status of the religion of any state worldwide for many centuries. However, after the creation of the Jewish State of Israel, much of what Sayyid Maududi has analyzed in the following sections with regards to Judaism have become much more relevant, more so in view of the continued aggressive military assertion of Isreal since its formation.)

Many books have been written by Jewish scholars in the compilation of their jurisprudence. Among those, renowned ones are: Aqeeba Bin Yusuf's "Mishna" and "Midrash" of the 2nd century A.D.; "Talmud", which is a combination of "Mishna" and "Gumara", of the 6th century A.D.; Isaac Al-Fasih's "Halakhos", which was written in the 11th century A.D., and is considered the best book on Talmudic law; Musa Memuni's "Mishna Torah", which was written towards the end of the 12th century A.D.; Yaqoob Bin Asher's "Tur" of the 14th century A.D. and Yusuf Qaro's "Sholkhan Arooq", written in the 16th century A.D., in which all laws and benedictions have been compiled in accordance with the old traditions.

Nevertheless, the critical analysis of the material in these books is not of much benefit, since none of these is acceptable to all sects of Jews and none, which may be considered the foundation of Judaism. In fact, the Jews themselves have expressed their dissatisfaction with them and except for Torah itself; the generality of Jews do not accept all the books. In July 1906, the Central Committee of American Jewish Rabis, in its congregation in Indianapolis, openly expressed their resentment and protested against following the varied doctrines of their religion. Therefore, to avoid ambiguity, ignoring all these books, we will place our dependence regarding the Jewish concepts of war, on the Torah itself[23].

---

[23] It is necessary to mention the statement of the fact that, whatever we state

Causes of War

Mention of war is plenty in the Torah and war has been ordered quite frequently. However, apart from the one cause espoused by the Torah in Deuteronomy chapter 2 and the Book of Numbers chapter 33, none other can be detected.

On the plains of Moab by Jordan across from Jericho, the Lord

---

herein, will not be in reference to the Torah that was revealed to Musa. Rather, it will be in reference to the Torah, which is also known to the world, by the name of "Old Testament". Our research shows that the "Pentateuch" of the Old Testament is not the original Torah. The real and original Torah is not in existence in the world. This assumption is borne out by the Old Testament itself. According to which, in his last days, Musa compiled the entire Torah, with the help of Joshua and placed it in a box. (Deuteronomy, 31: 24-28)

After his death in the 6th century BC, when Bakht Nasar set Bait Al-Muqaddas (modern Jerusalem) aflame, the box containing the Torah and all other books compiled till then, on the religion of Musa (AS), were destroyed. Later, after about 200 years Uzair (AS), according to Bible, with the help of divine revelation, recompiled the Torah. (Ezard Rasin, vol.2, chap. 4). But even this compilation could not escape the ravages of time. The flood of conquests of Alexander the great, not only spread the sovereignty of the Greek, but also its education, literature and culture, throughout the Asia Minor. In 280 B.C., all books of Torah were translated into the Greek language. After gradual discard, only the Greek translations remained as the official version.

The official Greek version is what we today know as Torah and which none can claim to be the original Torah of Musa (AS). This however does not mean that the Torah of today does not contain anything of the original. Rather, along with the pieces of the original, much else has been added and it is quite possible, that much of the original has been left out.

Anyone who studies the Torah analytically, cannot fail to notice, that along with their divine revelations, the book contains much other material, including the commentary of Jewish scholars, the national history of the Bani Israel (Israelites), the legal deliberations of the Jewish scholars of jurisprudence and some other material. All these have become so amalgamated, that it is quite impossible to extract the true word of God from these.

We wish to clarify that the religion of Torah was no different from the one, the Qur'an invites man to and, that Musa (AS) is as much a Prophet of Islam as Mohammad (SAW). The Bani Israel (Israelites) were originally followers of the same Islam. They later modified the religion, according to their own fancies and propounded a new religion, by the name of Jewism. Our discussion of Jewism, therefore, would be based on this form of Judaism, not the Judaism of Musa (AS).

said to Musa:

> "Speak to the Israelites and say to them: when you cross the Jordan into Canaan, Drive out all the inhabitants of the land before you. Destroy all their carved images and their cast idols, and demolish all their high places. Take possession of the land and settle in it, for I have given you the land to possess" (Book of Numbers, 33: 50-54)

The book Istisnah (Deuteronomy) further states:

> "Set out now and cross the Arnon Gorge. See I have given in your hands, Mori Sihon, the Amorite king of Heshbon and his country. Begin to take possession of it and engage in battle" (Deuteronomy, 2: 24)

> "But Sihon king of Heshbon refused to let us pass through. For the Lord Your God had made his spirit stubborn and his heart obstinate in order to give him into your hands, as he has now done. The Lord said to me, "See I have begun to deliver Sihon and his country over to you. Now begin to conquer and possess his land." When Sihon and all his army came out to meet us in battle at Jahaz, the lord our God delivered him over to us and we struck him down, together with his sons and his whole army. At that time, we took all his towns and destroyed them completely -- men, women, and children. We left no survivors. But the livestock and the plunder from the towns we had captured we carried off for ourselves" (Deuteronomy 2: 30-35)

> "Next we turned and went up along the road toward Bashan, and Og King of Bashan with his whole army marched out to meet us in battle at Edrei. The Lord said to me, 'Do not be afraid of him, for I have handed him over to you with his whole army and his land. Do to him what you did to Sihon king of the Amorites, who reigned in Heshbon." So the Lord our God also gave into our hands Og, King of Bashan and all his army. We struck them down,

leaving no survivors. At that time we took all his cities -------We destroyed them completely, as we had done with Sihon, king of Heshbon, destroying every city - men, women, and children. But all the livestock and the plunder from their cities we carried off for ourselves" (Deuteronomy, 3: 1-7)

From these it is apparent that the cause espoused and made permissible by Torah is the gaining of sovereignty over lands, overpowering its inhabitants, by dint of the sword and based on "the right, is of the more powerful," taking over and establishing their rights over the belongings, property and even the lives of the less powerful. In its sight, this very same terrorism and subjugation forms the basis of the inheritance of God's earth, promised to the Bani Israel (Israelites).

In contrast to this the Qur'an states,

"My righteous slaves shall inherit the earth"

(21: 105)

At another place it states,

"The earth is Allah's. He giveth it for an inheritance to whom He wills. And Lo! The sequel is for those who keep their duty (unto Him)" (7: 128)

This concept of inheritance is primarily different from the concept put forward by the Torah. Whereas the Torah declares the Israelites alone are the inheritors of the earth, the Qur'an does not make it the heritage of any particular people but declares that it is reserved for the righteous only.

Whereas, the Torah's concept of inheritance of land comprises the conquest of a nation, usurping its lands, property, lives, and respect of its people and after destroying it, becoming the masters of the lands themselves. The Qur'anic concept is different. According to it, a particular group will be chosen for the vicegerency of the world, because of the righteousness of its conduct. Such a nation would rid the world of cruelty and strife and in its place, establish a system of law and justice. As stated, according to Torah, the inheritance of the earth comprises of the subjugation conquest of other nations, which translates into expansionism alone. The true cause for war outlined in the Torah, conceptually, therefore, in contrast to the Islamic "Jihad fe sabeel illah", is the acquisition of wealth and the establishment of the superiority of one particular nation over others.

Limitations of War

We do not find much detail regarding the limitations and rules of warfare in the Torah, but we do find the treatment the Jewish religion recommends for the enemies. On the subject, the book of "Deuteronomy" states:

> "When you march up to attack a city, make its people an offer of peace. If they accept and open their gates, all the people in it shall be subject to forced labor and shall work for you. If they refuse to make peace and they engage you in battle, lay siege to that city. When the lord your God delivers it into your hand, put to sword all men in it. As for the women, the children, the livestock and everything else in the city, you may take these as plunder for yourselves. And you may use the plunder the Lord your God gives you from the enemies" (Deuteronomy, 20: 10-141)

> "However, in the cities of the nations, the Lord your God is giving you as an inheritance, do not leave alive anything that breathes, completely destroy them" (20:16-17)

> "When you lay siege to a city for a long time, fighting against it to capture it, do not destroy its trees by putting an axe on them, because you can eat their fruit" (20: 19)

> "And when the Lord your God has delivered them over to you and you have defeated them, then you must destroy them totally. Make no treaty with them, and show them no mercy" (7: 2)

> "Break down their altars, smash their sacred stones, cut down their Asherah poles and burn their idols in the fire" (7: 5)

"These are the decrees and laws you must be careful to follow in the land that the Lord your God of your fathers, has given you to possess-- as long as you live in the land. Destroy completely all the places on the high mountains and on the hills and under every spreading tree where the nations you are dispossessing worship their gods. Break down their altars, smash their sacred stones and burn the Asherah poles in the fire; cut down the idols of their gods and wipe out their names from those places"

(12: 2-3)

The book Khurooj (Exodus) states:

"Obey what I command you today. I will drive out before you the Emeritus, Canaanites, Hittites, Perizzites, Hivites and Jebusites. Be careful not to make a treaty with those who live in the land where you are going or that will be a snare among you. Break down their altars, smash their sacred stone and cut down their Asherah poles" (34: 11-13)

The book Adaad (Book of Numbers) states:

"The Lord said to Moses, 'Take vengeance on Midianites for the Isaerlites. After that, you will be gathered to your people' So Moses said to the people, 'Arm some of your men to go to war against the Midianites and to carry out the Lord's vengeance on them. Send into battle a thousand men from each of the tribes of Israel. So twelve thousand men armed for battle, a thousand from each tribe were supplied from the clans of Israel. --- -----------.

They fought against Midian, as the Lord commanded Moses, and killed every man----- The Israelites captured the Midianites women and children and took all the Midianites herds, flocks, and goods as plunder. They burned all the towns where the Midianites had settled, as well as all their camps. They took all the plunder and spoils, including the people and animals, and brought the

captives, spoils and plunder to Moses and Eleazar
the priest and the Israelites assembly at their camp
on the plains of Moab, by the Jordan across from
Jericho ------- Moses was angry with the officers of
the army - the commanders of thousands and the
commanders of hundreds -- who returned from the
battle. 'Have you allowed all the women to live?' he
asked them ------------- 'Now kill all the boys and
kill every women who has slept with a man, but
save for yourselves every girl who has not slept
with a man" (31:1-18)

The book "Joshua" states:

"They devoted to the Lord and destroyed with the
sword every living thing in it-- men and women,
young and old, cattle sheep and donkeys ----------
then they burned the whole city and everything in it,
but they put the silver and gold and the articles of
bronze and iron into the treasury of the Lord's
house" (Joshua, 2: 21-25)

"But they took the king of Ai alive and brought him
to Joshua. When Israel had stopped killing all the
men of Ai, in the fields and in the desert, where
they had chased them, and when every one of them
had been put to the sword, all the Israelites returned
to Ai and killing those who were in it. Twelve
thousand men and women fell that day -- all the
people of Ai. For Joshua did not draw back the hand
that held out his javelin until he had destroyed all
who lived in Ai. But Israel did carry off for
themselves the livestock and plunder of this city, as
the Lord had instructed Joshua" (8: 23-27)

From the foregoing, it is apparent that the Jewish religion
divides its enemies into two kinds. One, who have not been placed
in the Jewish heritage; the others are those who have been placed
in their rightful heritage. The dealings with both these types of
enemies follow different patterns.

Regarding the first kind, there is the provision that, before
inflicting war on them, they will be given the option to either sue

for peace or fight. If they sue for peace and hand over their country to the Israelites, they will be awarded the responsibility of serving them (the Israelites). However, if they opt for war, after victory has been achieved, all male members of the enemy should be put to death; all their women and children enslaved and all their property confiscated. Cutting down or otherwise harming trees and crops is however forbidden, not in the interest of avoidance of strife, but, for they would be of use to the victors later.

The laws regarding the second type of enemy are such that they deprive them of all human rights and afford them very few privileges. Regarding them Torah's Law is, that war should be declared against them outrightly and no truce should be entered into with them. Their buildings and places of worship should be razed; their women, children, and even their domestic animals should be put to the sword. Such destruction should be unleashed on the enemy, that the civilization is totally exterminated. The justification given is, that the Torah requires, the nations in their heritage, should be completely destroyed and they should not be offered any conditions, accepting which, may enable them to live.

These teachings are self-explanatory. Moreover, the manifest demonstration of the philosophy and the actions of Israel, vis-à-vis Palestine, even in the 21st century are distinct examples of the same.

3) Buddhism

We have so far studied the concepts of warfare, in religions, where it is held permissible. The differences that Islam has with these, are not because of the permissibility factor, but are purely of the ethical and practical nature. The other type of religions comprise of those, which consider war totally impermissible. Islam has been censured by these religions, for permitting it. In the historical order, Buddhism comes first in the list.

The Basics of Buddhism

Before proceeding into the discussion of the ways of Buddhism, we must understand that we have no way of finding out, what actually were the teachings of Buddha or whatever we acknowledge today as Buddhism, is really based on his teachings, as Buddha did not reduce his sayings into writing. He neither wrote a book in his lifetime nor had left the beliefs and rules regarding his religion in written form, so that his followers could learn his religion, in his own words. History tells us that even after Buddha, none of his disciples attempted to write down his sayings. Some traditions however reveal that in his Mourning kingdom, a huge meeting was held, in which one or two of his specially favored disciples delivered lectures on his teachings. However, for one, it cannot be historically proven that such a meeting did actually take place, and even if it did, the lectures in this meeting were not recorded for the progeny. The best available source that describes the events that took place in Buddha's lifetime and a little later is the "Mahapar Nayyaban Suttar". This is also silent about the" Grand Council" (Buddha Suttra page X1 - X111).

The present books of the Buddhist religion were all authored long after Buddha. A century after he died, a council of scholars and religious leaders was held in Vesali and after great discussion, the rules, principles, and laws of Buddhism were enacted or an attempt was made to compile them. However, regarding these, the writer of "Deep O Masse" states, that the Buddhist priests (Bhikshus) changed the real principles of the religion. Some changes were made even in Buddha's sayings and some new sayings were introduced. (Max Muller, Sacred Books of the Buddhists, Preface)

This is the period when Buddhist teachings started being reduced to writing. The process continued until 1 B.C. i.e. for about 400 years. Again, it had to face a revision, to the extent that even the basics of the religion underwent changes.

In the primary concept of Buddhism, there was no mention of God. Now an everlasting entity was introduced, whose physical manifestation was Buddha. In the initial concept, there was no concept of heaven and hell but it was now introduced; good deeds would take a person to heaven and evil deeds to hell. Initially the rules for leading a pious life were very stringent, but now they were softened in consideration of necessities. This last change occurred in the period of Kanishka, which was around 1 A.D.

History tells us that a council was held on the behest of Kanishka in Kashmir. In that council, with alterations and changes, new laws of Buddhism were enacted (Hackman, Buddhism as a religion: page 51-55.).

A small group rejected the modern laws; however, the majority of the Buddhists accepted them. Those who accepted the revision formed a sect of Buddhism, which came to be known as 'Mahayana'.

It is apparent from the above, that what in the real sense can be termed as the "religious book" of Buddhists, is in all probability, missing from Buddhism. We cannot, for certain satisfy ourselves, as to what the teachings of Buddha really were. At the maximum, we can place our reliance on the books that escaped Kanishka's revisionism and reached us. These are three in number:

1. 'Vinai Petakk', which is a collection of laws and rules, following which, a man can attain piety. These were compiled between 350 B.C. and 250 B.C. during different periods. However, the author or authors of these cannot be identified.

2. 'Sutt Petakk', which is a collection of the sayings of Buddha, that lay down the means of achieving salvation, i.e. they deal with the ethical philosophy of Buddhism. Unfortunately, even in this case, history does not convey to us the identity of the author.

3. 'Abhi Dum Petakk', this too deals mostly with the philosophy of Buddhism. The only thing known about this book is that it was in existence prior to the end of 3 B.C. (For further details consult Professor Hess David's "Holy Books of the East," vol. 11).

Whatever is written in the following pages is based on the teachings of Buddhism, conveyed to us through these books and not on his real teachings, which we have no means of knowing.

The Teachings of Ahinsa

Buddhism is a religion that follows the dictates of 'Ahinsa'. In this, every living thing has been considered innocent and for the human being, the smallest insect has been considered worthy of respect. No living thing may be aggressed on under any circumstance.

The first of the Ten Commandments of Buddha is, "Do not kill any thing," the person who does so is guilty of an unforgivable sin (Vinaya texts, volume 1, page 46). The limit is that for three months of the rainy season, a person is forbidden to step out of his home, since if he does so, he might kill some minute insect (Vinaya texts, vol. 1, page 298- 301).

Under the influence of these strict rules of Ahinsa, let alone permitting war, even thinking of it appears criminal. Where the respect for life is so heightened, the religion must be inclined towards treating such acts with disgust, that involve killing, not of insects but of thousands or tens of thousands of men. For that reason, Buddha does not permit a Buddhist to witness the bloodshed of battles, even as a spectator. Paktia Dharma Clause 48 states,

> "The follower who without due cause, goes to witness an army readied for war has sinned"

Clauses 49 and 50 state:

> "The follower, who has a reason, to go where an army is ready for war, may stay there for a maximum of 3 - 4 days"

> "And if he stays there two or three nights and witnesses soldiers in the battlefield, or the roll call of the soldiers, or arraigning of soldiers in battle order or the inspection of troops, He will be guilty of sin" (Vinaya texts vol. 1 page 43)

The Philosophy of Buddha

From these orders, Buddha's point of view regarding war is obvious. However, to fully judge the concept, only knowing about these orders is not enough, it is necessary that we understand the philosophy in its entirety of which, Ahinsa is just a part. Ahinsa, in fact, is just one of the many means that Buddha has chosen to mold humanity in accordance with his wishes.

The means are useful in leading men in the direction he has chosen, we need therefore to examine, the countenance of; what Buddha wishes humanity to acquire, the way he wishes men to follow, the end to which he wishes to lead men, his aim and the means he wishes to utilize for the attainment of this aim. Without understanding all these factors, grasping the real meaning of

Ahinsa and its deep effect on humanity would be difficult.

Buddha's perspective of life is far removed from that of other scholars and intellectuals. He has not concerned himself with the cause and reason for man's being on earth and his purpose of life. It makes sense therefore, that he has not addressed the question of the right way for man, towards his and his progeny's true well-being; he has concentrated entirely on trying to understand the oppression and revolutions that effect man's life. The factors of oppression which are operative in the many changes like childhood, youth, ageing, good health, sickness, birth, death, sorrow, happiness, content and frustration, and the ways to overcome the oppressiveness of each change and tumult. He considers that these are the only questions worthy of attention and has totally ignored all other temporal and religious affairs of man's life.

After much contemplation, Buddha reached the conclusion that life itself is a sufferance that man is subject to, from his birth to death. His existence is totally purposeless and if at all there is a purpose, it is his tolerance of suffering and pain. The world is no place for man to live in. Here, behind every satisfaction, there is a frustration, behind every happiness, there is a sadness, and behind every birth, there is a death. All this tumult dislocation and oppression is under the influence of a universal plan, which in itself is oppression.

Buddha states that the reason for man being subject to this oppression is his own desire, consciousness, and cognizance. These forces of ego, establish a man's link with the material world and this same link brings man repeatedly back in this world. In every reincarnation, he gets a new body to live in and every time he has to live a different emotional and intellectual life and until he remains under the yoke of his desires, he has to undergo the torments of birth, life, and death repeatedly.

Buddha states that the only way of avoidance of this suffering is through "Nirvana" (a state of rest and freedom from desire). He explains that when life is oppression and the cause of this suffering is human desire, then pure contentment is only in his complete freedom from desire and in the end of this worldly life, leading to oneness with the spirit of the universe. This state can only be achieved through severance of all relations with the material world, self-denial of all longings, feelings, and pleasures. Man should reach a frame of mind, in which he has no attraction for anything material. He is cleansed of all emotions, feelings, and desires, in such a way that he does not acknowledge any connection with the world, which would have been the cause of his reincarnation in this world. In the way he would free himself form the bonds of his "being," thus achieving freedom from temporal existence and complete freedom from desire. This is "Nirvana"[24] and according to Buddha, is or should be the ultimate aim of man.

Finally, the question is, how can a man achieve this state of Nirvana[25]?

At this point Buddhism acquires a practical aspect and outlines eight aims of life, for the achievement of Nirvana.

1. Correctness of belief, i.e. understanding fully, the four basic truths.

2. Correctness of aims in life, i.e. making firm resolutions to give up all pleasures of life and total avoidance of hurting or harming other people and creatures.

3. Correctness of speech, i.e. avoidance of speaking or listening to rash speech, falsehood, and discussions of others ills.

4. Correctness of behavior, i.e. avoidance of depravity, murder, and misappropriation.

5. Correctness of economy, i.e. earning one's livelihood through fair and permissible means.

6. Correctness of effort, i.e. striving honestly towards following the dictates of belief.

---

[24] Scholars differ in their interpretation of the word 'Nirvana'. Henson Oldenberg, Hess Davids etc. take it to mean, a condition of ego, in which it is free of all desire and sin and being free of the concerns of this world, is in a state of complete contentment. Max Moller, Schmidth, San Heller and Hardy, opines that it means a man's complete freedom from his state of "being" or existence.

[25] The four questions examined in Buddhism dealt with; Oppression, causes of this oppression, means of elimination of this oppression and the methodology of elimination of this oppression, are the basic factors of life. (Vinaya Texts page 94 - 97)

7. Correctness of remembrance, i.e. remembering one's past actions.

8. Correctness of thought i.e. without the consideration of pleasures of life and personal satisfaction, striving towards achievement of Nirvana.

For the achievement of these eight aims, Buddha has outlined ten means. Of these ten means (commandments), five are mandatory in nature, while five are de-rigueur. These are given below.

1. Do not kill.

2. Do not steal.

3. Do not indulge in illicit sex.

4. Do not lie.

5. Do not consume alcohol or other intoxicants.

6. Do not eat except at the appointed time.

7. Avoid Music and other pleasurable activities like games, plays, etc.

8. Avoid use of perfumes and other scented stuff.

9. Avoid sleeping on soft beds.

10. Avoid being in possession of gold or silver.

These eight aims and ten means or commandments, form the ethical foundation of Buddhism. The ethical corner stone of all instructions given by Buddha is self-denial and forsaking the world, his ultimate aim, being the achievement of Nirvana, which is not possible without sacrificing the ego. Therefore, for erasing the ego factor from human consideration, he has prescribed many stringent exercises. Some of these are: plucking out all the hair from one's beard, moustaches and head, so that the conceit of beauty is erased; always being in the standing position; lying down on beds of thorns or nails; always maintaining the same posture during sleep; rubbing dust on one's body, and other such painful exercises that seek to make man accustomed to self- denial.

Apart from the above, Buddha has instructed with equal severity on the conduct of daily routine affairs. It is not possible to go into details of all the instructions here, since it would require several volumes. A few however are mentioned here for the benefit of the reader[26].

The four things for which man has been advised strict avoidance are:

a) Sex[27]

b) Theft, even of a single blade of grass

c) Killing on purpose, even the smallest insect

d) Affecting apparel etc. to indicate one's superiority over others[28]

After a person adopts a religious life, he may not wear new clothes. He may only wear clothes made of discarded cloth gathered from refuse bins or from coffin cloth in which a dead person has been buried. Even such clothes, in his possession, should not exceed three in number.

He should be mostly unemployed, roaming from place to place, begging for his food. Such livelihood from beggary is the purest of all[29].

He should not make or own a house but should live in the jungles, in the shelter of trees. If he falls ill, he should use no medicine; Auto urine therapy is the best medication for him. (Vinaya Texts, Part 1, page 173-174)

He should not attempt to keep himself clean. He is permitted to

---

[26] Buddha has suggested many such exercises, which are given in details in the book, "Dialogues of Buddha", page 226-232.

[27] In Buddhist commandments about sex, there is no distinction between permissible and illicit sex. It is stated in Vinaya Petakk, that when one person, after becoming the disciple of Buddha wanted to continue conjugal relations with his wife, he was prohibited from doing so. (Vinaya Texts page 236-268)

[28] According to a well-known tradition, when the daughter of chief of the Urvila tribe died, she was buried in a close by graveyard. One day Buddha dug up the grave, took off the coffin cloth and after washing it in a pond, sewed himself a shirt of the material.(Saint Hillary, 'Buddha and his Religion'. page 50)

[29] Buddha himself used to beg for his food; he called his followers "Bhikshus" (beggars) and himself "Maha Bhikshu" (the Big Beggar). (Saint Hillary, Buddha and his religion, page 101)

have a bath, once in two weeks at the most. (Vinaya Texts, part 1, page 44)

He should not have any money in his possession. He should avoid trade, business etc., which involve transactions of gold or silver. (Vinaya Texts, part 1, page 26-27)

He should not even own a comfortable bed, a coarse and old blanket should be good enough for him and should last him a minimum of six years. (Vinaya Texts, Part 1, P 24-25)

The True Weakness of Buddhism

In the foregoing, we have stated the ethics of Buddhism. 'Ahinsa' is just a part of these. In this philosophy, without doubt there are some excellent ethical instructions. It would be an injustice, if we proceed without praising the piety and abstinence that Buddhism preaches and which Buddha practiced in his venerable life. However, despite its many good qualities, in principle, the entire system is wrong and so is the way it prescribes for reaching its goals. After seeing the changes in life, its revolutions and turmoil, Buddha appears to be stunned by them, both at individual and collective levels, He has failed to understand the cause of all these and does not go much into their depth to uncover the actual truth. He does not prescribe that man bravely endeavor to combat them and strive towards the final goal. Instead, he summarily glances through them and reaches the conclusion that there is absolutely no reason for man's existence, that all affairs of the world are meaningless, that there is no cause and reason for the collective and individual changes in the world and that they are purely for the purpose of causing pain and agony to man. Human intelligence, feelings, understanding, awareness, emotions, physical prowess and whatever else has been gifted to man, have no better purpose than to cause trouble, discomfort and pain.

He states that world's wealth, culture, society, politics, governance, trade and in fact, all its activities have no purpose but to establish man's links with the material world. This in turn becomes the reason for his reincarnations in the world, repeatedly. Man should have no other aim and objective in life, but to remain cut off from all relations of the world, except with his own self and even regarding his own self, he should keep away from all pleasures, being in a continual state of endurance, hardship and pain. To the extent that he frees himself from the bondage of "being," ego and desire, thereby reaching the state of "not being," total death and absorption in the spirit of the universe.

Obviously, the person who, being afraid of the turmoil of life, abandons the world, severs all collective and individual ties with it, concerning himself only with his own deliverance and even for the purpose chooses the route, that takes him not through the world but from outside of it, such a person cannot be expected to strive, fearlessly for his country and nation, family and progeny. He cannot be expected to utilize his emotional, physical, and intellectual capabilities to exploit his possessions and wealth, for the betterment of the society. He cannot be capable of ridding the society of cruelty, enmity, strife, turmoil, arrogance, and evil and establishing in its stead, law, and justice and raising the banner of truth. He cannot be expected to combat with bravery the difficulties that attend naturally, each of man's undertakings.[30]

The striving, the heat of activity, the bravery and manliness, the sinister problems of the battlefield, the hurts and injuries of the sword, the politics and governance, the burden of responsibilities etc., can only be borne by the person who considers that he has come into the world for a purpose, who has high aspirations, who considers that he fulfills an important role in the world and that he is answerable to a Supreme Being. Only he, who has firm belief that whatever he does in this life will bear fruit in the eternal life, can bear all this, Not the wretched person, frustrated by life, dissatisfied with the results of his life work, sad at all that is happening around him, fearful of accidents of the world, cowed down by every problem, afraid of all revolutions, hiding in the lap of death and praying for his eternal termination. How can the poor wretch be expected to bear the burden of responsibilities? It cannot be expected that he would unnecessarily commit himself to the hardships of "jihad" and war of politics and kingship. That person has already forsaken the world and its turmoil and made the attainment of death and eternal death his aim in life. Why would such a person, enter the arena of the world ready for action and

---

[30] We will not discuss here the teachings of Buddhism, of "abandonment of the world", since it will come under discussion later, when we are discussing Christianity.

waste his time in its administration, whose life he consider a meaningless waste of time?[31]

Buddhism's 'Ahinsa', is not fulfilling worldly responsibilities and then declaring war as unnecessary. It is, in fact forsaking the world totally. It therefore, naturally has no concern with war and no concern with the sword, since it cannot aid its follower in attaining his aims. These are a Buddhist mystic's limit of foresight.

The Effects of Ahinsa on the Followers of Buddhism

The teachings of Buddha have never acquired a position of strength or a separate culture. It has never been able to overcome a culture and establish its own. Whatever country it reached, it was only able to leave a negative effect on the ethics of its society and has never been able to affect its system of politics or culture and establish a better one. There was not even an attempt in the direction.

Without doubt its teachings reached far and wide, The East, Middle East and the Far East, all benefited from it. The acceptance and popularity it achieved is unmatched. Today its number of followers is greater than all other religions. There are however, no examples in history of any revolutionary changes it brought about in a nation or that it became a reason for any outstanding achievement. Conversely, whenever it was pitted against a different power or culture, it failed.

India, which is the birthplace of the Buddhist religion, was almost totally Buddhist in the 1st century A.D., in 3 A.D. 3/4 of the population still followed Buddhism. However, after 4 A.D., when the Brahmanic religion started its influence, within three centuries, it succumbed to it. Today, out of a population of 3.5 billion, there are hardly 300,000 to 400,000, Buddhists there (at the time this book was originally written).

In Afghanistan, similarly, Buddhism gained much popularity under the auspices of Ashoka and spread far and wide. In 2 A.D.,

---

[31] Rheis Davids, in his book, 'Buddhist India', discussing the downfall of the religion, has tried to prove that Buddhism's downfall was not the result of the strength of the sword. If we accept the analysis, it strongly favors our contention. To succumb to the strength of the sword, only results from a material weakness. But to succumb to a peaceful opposition, shows the weakness of its reasoning against that of Brahmanism.

the king of Kabul, Minander (or Malinda), himself converted to Buddhism. However, when Buddhism came in opposition to the power and culture of Islam, it could not withstand the impact, even for a little while. (Smith, Early History of India)

In China, whatever stability was the lot of Buddhism was because of its alignment with Taoism. Else, the religion of Confucius had almost brought an end to the Buddhist religion there.

In Japan, it had to compromise much, to reach an understanding with Shintoism. It even had to compromise on its principal beliefs in the contest (Hackman, Buddhism as a Religion, page 90 - 91).

In the rest of the countries, like Ceylon (Sri Lanka of today), Burma (Myanmar of Today) and Tibet, there was no influence or power, it had to contest against and therefore it was easy for Buddhism to spread there. However, it is evident from history that it could never influence their cultural life in any way. They remained as lifeless and ineffectual as they were before.

Above all else, it is an uncontroversial fact that Buddhism never attempted to stand up against any government or dared to reform any society. It does not play even a minor role in the politics of any nation. It has never attempted to participate in a government or to change it. Instead, it has espoused acceptance of all governments whether they are cruel and oppressive, or just (Vinaya Texts, Part 1, page 301).

Buddhism has even gone to the length of responding to the satanic powers with humility and to cruelty with acceptance. Its teachings have instilled in its followers a tolerance, similar to that of a lover, that they cannot even utter a cry in the face of extremes of cruelty. It is their firm belief that the debacles of life are a direct result of a person's sins, which he may have committed in his past incarnation. For the reason, if a person faces cruelty and hardships, he should not consider the perpetrator responsible, but himself. That he is receiving the treatment because of sins, he may have committed in his earlier life. This religious belief, serves to calm down the emotions of vengefulness and self-esteem and in their stead, infuse a willing tolerance of insult and injury.

Obviously, for any despotic government, nothing can be more

desirable than a nation of men, of the qualities that Buddha prescribes. Such people, instead of being a source of danger to the government, seek to lend it stability. They can be subjected to all kinds of cruel laws, heavy taxation, unfair appropriation of wealth; their life property and honor can easily be usurped, and they can be used in all ways to satisfy the satanic idiosyncrasies of the rulers. This is the reason that Buddhism did not face any conflict with any ruler or government. In fact, many countries, instead of opposing it, bestowed upon it their favor.

As soon as Buddha started preaching, the Raja of Bim Basara gave him succor and promulgated a declaration in favor of his preaching (Vinaya Texts, part 1, page 136-197). Later, his son, Ajat Sutro, also remained a follower of Buddhism and its firm supporter.

Kosala's Raja Pasnadi (Agni Dutt), invited Buddha to his kingdom, accepted his religion and in order to further ties with him, married a girl from the Ishaka family. (Buddhist India, page 10-11). Apart from these, we find that Raja Avanti pat, of Sura Sanyas and Raja Ilayya became disciples of Buddha.

After this period, we find that in 3 B.C., Ashoka sponsored Buddhism and using all his regal means, caused the religion to spread not only in India and its neighbors but also to the far off countries (Buddhist India, page 16). In the 1st century B.C. Kanishka, was a wholehearted supporter of Buddhism. Vikramajit-1, though himself a follower of the Brahmanic religion, supported and strengthened Buddhism. Then in 7 A.D. when Raja Haresh Singh came to power, he supported Buddhism with such fervor that Brahmanic stalwarts started plotting his murder (Smith, Early History of India, page 349).

Outside India, in Tibet and Mongolia, Kublai khan found it politically sound to spread Buddhism and made all efforts to do so (Buddhism as a religion, page 73-74). In China, King Min Ti, Invited Buddhist preachers and welcomed their religion most fervently. This support and sponsorship continued until much later.

Buddhism continued to spread and survived centuries of turmoil in many countries. This was not because of its inherent strength or its capability of survival, rather because it bowed to every cruel leadership, never dared to oppose cruelty and never even attempted to free humanity of the arrogance and despotism of any rule. For that reason, all rulers found it politic to favor and support it.

. From this brief analysis of Buddhism, the difference in the perspectives of war in it and in Islam will be amply clear. Islam believes that man has come into this world for a specific purpose. His deliverance is dependent on his good conduct in the world. For that reason, it prescribes actions, which are beneficial for his and his posterity's material and ethical wellbeing, the actions necessary to promote order in his worldly life. On the other hand, Buddhism describes life as meaningless and states that the man's salvation is in the severance of all worldly ties, to the extent of ignoring his own self. For that purpose it does not permit him any act or striving, in the direction, that would lead him towards establishing links or relations with anything worldly.

It is now, for one to decide whether the Jihad of Islam or Ahinsa of Buddhism is more beneficial for humanity.

4) Christianity

The other religion that has fundamental difference with Islam on the question of war is Christianity. Like in the case of Judaism, we need only to consult one book to get all the information we require for our purpose. That book is the Bible, the fundamental book of the Christian religion[32].

Before addressing the question at hand and referring to Bible, to seek its guidance, it is necessary to understand that the condition Bible is in today can only reveal to us the beliefs of the Christians of today. We cannot judge from present day Bible as to what the original teachings of Eisa (AS) were. To understand the later arguments in this chapter, it is necessary that we keep in consideration, this factor of authenticity. The examination of the

---

[32] Christianity, is actually not the religion that Eisa (AS) preached, but that which is attributed to him. We have ample evidence that Eisa (AS), did not preach what we term as Christianity today. In fact, Eisa (AS) preached the same Islam, that all Prophets before him, brought to the world and which was later preached by the Muhammad (SAW). Later we will discuss some of the arguments in this context. Here we would like to stress the fact, that whatever is discussed herein does not refer to the religion of Eisa (AS) but to what has been misconstrued in his name.

authenticity of the Biblical presentations before proceeding further, therefore, is in order.

Investigation of the Biblical Books

Today the collection that we know as Bible consists of four books, Matthew, Mark, Luke, and John. However, none of these is of Eisa (AS). Unlike the Qur'an, each verse and each word of which is revealed to the Prophet Muhammad (SAW), we do not find that which was revealed to Eisa (AS), consolidated at any one place. Then again, we do not find even the revelations of God to Eisa (AS) and his sermons, in his own words. These books are neither the word of God nor that of Eisa (AS). They are in fact, the books written by the disciples or the students of disciples of Eisa (AS), who according to their own knowledge and understanding compiled them. The four books are so far removed from the original (Majhul ul Asal), that much dependence cannot be placed on their authenticity.

The first book Mathew is attributed to Matthew, a disciple of the Prophet Eisa (AS). His actual book known as "Loggia" is not traceable. The book attributed to him, was actually written by some unknown author, who consulted Loggia along with other books for the purpose. Matthew has been (grammatically) referred to in the third person and not in the first person, in his book[33].

After reading Matthew, it appears that it has been mostly adapted from the Bible of Mark. If Matthew had himself been its author, there was no necessity for him to consult the book of the author who neither had been the disciple of nor ever met Eisa (AS). Some Christian scholars believe that the book was written in 70 A.D., others believe it was written in 90 A.D.

The second book is attributed to Mark. It is generally believed that Mark was in fact, the author of the book. Nevertheless, it is proven that Mark never met Eisa (AS) and that he was never his disciple. Some say that he was present at the Crucifixion of Jesus (Eisa AS), but even this is not proven. He was in fact the disciple of St. Peter. Whatever he heard from St. Peter, he wrote it down in

---

[33] Matthew Chapter 9, verse 9 states: "As Jesus went from there, he saw a man named Matthew sitting at the tax-collector's booth" Obviously, the writer will not refer to himself grammatically, in the third person.

Greek. For that reason, Christian writers refer to him as St. Peter's scribe. Mark's Bible is believed to have been written between 63 A.D. and 70 A.D.

The third book is ascribed to Luke. It is established that Luke never met Eisa (AS), and that he never benefited from his teachings, in the first hand. He was a disciple of St. Paul and was constantly in his company. His bible consists of what he (St. Paul) quotes from the sayings of Eisa (AS). For that reason, St. Paul refers to Luke's Bible as his own. It however is an established fact that St. Paul himself was never in the company of Eisa (AS). He, according to Christian traditions entered the folds of Christianity, six years after the crucifixion of Eisa (AS). Therefore, one link between Luke and Eisa (AS) is missing. Even the date of the authorship of St. Luke's Bible is unconfirmed. Some say that it was written in 57 A.D., while others claim that it was written in 74 A.D., Hornik, McGriffith and Plummer are of the opinion that it could not have been written before 80 A.D.

The fourth book is John. Modern investigations prove, that he was not the disciple John who wrote it, but it was some other person whose name also happened to be John. The book was written much after Eisa (AS), in 90 A.D., Hornik dates it to 110 A.D., obviously, none of these books can be linked to Eisa (AS) and their authenticity cannot be proved. [34]

On closer examination, the questionability of their authenticity increases. Firstly, all the four bibles differ from each other, to the extent that the "Sermon of the Mount" which is the basis of all Christian teachings, is stated differently and contradictorily in three of the Bibles, i.e. Matthew, Mark and John.

Secondly, the thinking of their authors is clearly evident. The addressees of Matthew appear to be Jews. Matthew appears to be speaking to them argumentatively. The addressees of Luke appear to be Romans whom he wishes to educate about the Israelites. Additionally, Luke advocates the cause of St. Paul and wishes to prove him of a higher stature than the other disciples of Eisa (AS). John appears to be influenced by the philosophies and mysticism

---

[34] The fact is that the authenticity of these books cannot be compared even with that of the weakest Islamic tradition (Hadith). At the maximum, their stature is comparable to the Mauluds (Hymns) in Islam.

that had spread amongst the Christians towards the end of the 1st century A.D. With all that, the difference in concept appears to have surpassed in importance, the difference in wordings.

Thirdly, all these bibles have been written in the Greek language, although the language of all the disciples and of Eisa (AS) himself was Hebrew (Suryani). With the change in language, the depicted thought pattern also has chances of undergoing change.

Fourthly, it was only in the 2nd century A.D., that attempts were made to reduce Bible into writing. Until 150 A.D., it was thought that verbal traditions were better than writings. Towards the end of 2nd century A.D., it was decided to write down the Bible. The bibles of that era, however, are not thought to be authentic. The authentic version of the New Testament was accepted by the Carthaginian Council, which met in 397 A.D.

Fifthly, the oldest Bible in existence in the world today dates to 4 A.D. The second oldest is from 5 A.D. Another one of the old bibles, which has some mistakes, is in the library of the Pope of Rome and is not older than 4 A.D. It is therefore difficult to determine how much the Bible of today resembles the bibles in circulation in the first three centuries A.D.

Sixthly, it was never attempted to memorize Bible as is done in the case of Qur'an. Its circulation initially depended on transmission by word of mouth. In such a case, the possibility of the original text being affected by the personal thought of the one who passed on a tradition cannot be overlooked. After the period, when the Bible started being published, it was at the mercy of the copier. It was easy for the copier to edit the Bible according to his beliefs; whatever he considered in controversy to the beliefs he held, could be eliminated and whatever he considered lacking, he could add.[35]

These are the reasons based on which we cannot say with certainty, that the contents of the four books of Bible are indeed

---

[35] Note: The entire discussion has been adapted from the following books:

1. Dimboola, Commentary on the Holy Bible
2. Y.K. Cheyne, Encyclopedia Biblica
3. Millman, History of Christianity

the teachings of Eisa (AS). Therefore, whatever is written in the following pages, will not be based on the Christianity preached by the Prophet Eisa (AS) but the Christianity practiced by the Christians of the world of today.

The Teachings of 'Love' in Christianity

A study of the Bible reveals that Christianity was severely opposed to the concept of war, regardless of whether war is for a rightful cause or for a wrong cause. The paramount teaching of Eisa (AS) is that after love for God, one should have love for one's neighbor (Matthew, 22:39). Along with this love, it is necessary that one must not be angry with one's brother. "But I tell you that anyone who is angry with his brother, will be subject to judgment" (Matthew 5:22)

This however, is not all. The Bible does not stop at this; Matthew categorically directs that a believing Christian must show tolerance of oppression and mischief, let alone protecting others, one must not even fight for one's own rights. The most important teachings of Eisa (AS) can be found in his "Sermon of the Mount." It forms the basis for Christian ethical values. In this Eisa (AS) states:

> "You have heard that it was said, 'Eye for eye and tooth for tooth' But I tell you, do not resist an evil person. If someone strikes you on the right cheek, turn to him the other also. And if someone wants to take your tunic, let him have your cloak as well. If someone forces you to go one mile go with him two miles. ---------- You have heard it was said, love your neighbor and hate your enemies. But I tell you: Love your enemies, bless those who curse you and pray for those who persecute you"
>
> (Matthew 5: 38 - 44)

> "But I tell you, who hear me: Love your enemies, do good to those who hate you, bless those who curse you, pray for those who mistreat you, if someone strikes you on one cheek, turn to him the other also. If someone takes your cloak, do not stop him from taking your tunic. ---------- Do to others, as you would have them do to you. If you love those

who love you, what credit is that to you? Even sinners love those who love them" (Luke 27-33)

The above are the very basics of the teachings of Christianity. Its meanings are manifest in its wording itself. It clearly means that if a true Christian wishes to be perfect like his 'Father in Heaven' and whose high aim is to achieve high reward and be the 'Sons of the Most High' (God), (Luke 6:35), he should not in any case, confront cruelty and oppression with force but should himself forgo his own rights in oppressor's favor.

The Philosophy of Ethics in Christianity

The teachings of ethical philosophy cannot be fully understood, until we understand the very spirit of Christianity.

Christianity as we know today is a religion of mysticism, monasticism and of complete abstinence. It does not lay down a plan for man's socio-cultural life. A code of conduct, spiritual guidance or a set of rules to be followed to lead life accordingly is not detectable in it. It does not instruct man about his duties towards himself, his family, his nation, his posterity and towards God, nor does it advise him the best way of fulfilling them. It neither instructs man as to the reasons for which the Almighty blessed him with his material wealth and his mental and physical prowess nor does it instruct them on the best way of using them. In fact, it shows a total unconcern for the problems of life.

All the stress of Christianity appears to be on the question of attainment of entry into the 'Kingdom of Heavens'. This question forms the core around which the entire Christian ethical philosophy is woven and is the sum total of Christ's teachings.

The 'Kingdom of Heavens', however, is not a reward for man's good conduct on earth. Christianity does not accept the relation between action and reward. Actually it considers that the two are in contradiction to each other. It considers the Kingdom of Heavens and the kingdom of the world, two distinctly different things. The natural result of this thinking is that it prescribes different routes for attaining the two. Everything that forms a part of the kingdom of the world, is not only absent from the Kingdom of Heavens, but also hinders the path of achieving the latter. For that reason, Christianity instructs man, that if he desires to attain the ultimate objective, he must crush his desires for the material things of the kingdom of the world and if he cannot, he should forsake the desire for the Kingdom of Heavens. For the purpose, it preaches a form of mysticism and divorcing oneself from the socio-cultural activities of the material world. For clarification of the concept, some of the quotations attributed to Eisa (AS) are copied below:

> "If anyone comes to me and does not hate his father and mother, his wife and children, his brothers and sisters - yes, even his own life - he cannot be my disciple" (Luke 14: 26)

> "Do you think I came to bring peace on earth! No, I tell you, but division. From now on there will be five in one family divided against each other, three against two and two against three. They will be divided, father against son and son against father, mother against daughter and daughter against mother, mother-in-law against daughter-in-law and daughter-in-law against mother-in-law"
>
> (Luke, 12: 51-53)

> "Freely you have received, freely give. Do not take along any gold or silver or copper in your belts; take no bag for the journey, or extra tunic, or sandals or a staff; for the worker is worth his keep"
>
> (Matthew, 10: 8 -10)

> "Do not be afraid, little flock, for your Father has been pleased to give you the Kingdom. Sell your possessions and give to the poor. Provide purses for yourselves that will not wear out, a treasure in heaven that will not be exhausted"
>
> (Luke, 12: 32 - 33)

> "If you want to be perfect, go, sell your possessions and give to the poor, then come follow me, you will have treasure in heaven" (Matthew, 19: 21)[36]

---

[36] These instructions were given to a person, who abstained from forbidden sex, theft and lies. Who served his parents well, who loved his neighbors as he loved himself. Eisa (AS) tells him that he could attain salvation only if he sold all his belongings and distributed the proceeds as alms. Matthew, Mark and Luke are all in agreement on this.

"For, if you forgive men when they sin against you, your heavenly Father will also forgive you. But if you do not forgive men their sins, your Father will not forgive your sins" (Matthew, 6: 14 - 15)

"Therefore I tell you, do not worry about your life, what you will eat or drink; or about your body, what you will wear. Is not life more important than food, and the body more important than clothes? Look at the birds of the air; they do not sow or reap or store away in barns, and yet your heavenly Father feeds them. Are you not much more valuable than they? Who of you by worrying can add a single hour to his life? And why do you worry about clothes? See how the lilies of the field grow. They do not labor or spin. Yet I tell you that not even Solomon in all his splendor was dressed like one of these. If that is how God clothes the grass of the field, which is here today and tomorrow is thrown into the fire, will he not much clothe you, O you of little faith! So do not worry, saying what shall we eat? Or what shall we drink? Or what shall we wear?"

(Matthew, 6: 25-31)

From these sayings of the Eisa (AS), it is obvious that the object of the teachings of Christianity is the complete severance of ties with the socio-cultural world. We are well aware of the fact that familial relations form the foundation of society, relations of man within the society are initially dependent on the family and that their inter-actions, become the reason and cause for the life of humanity in general.

The relations and this family life, in fact, are also the basic and the best schools for primary ethical training. However, very first victim of Eisa (AS) is family. He cuts down the first link of the chain that ties man to the society. That, which compels man's participation in the affairs of the world is his need to feed and clothe himself, but Eisa (AS) chooses to overlook this primary cause and espouses, for man, a life of the quality of that of the 'birds of the air' and of the 'wild trees of the jungle'.

For man's satisfaction and well-being and for his collective and individual welfare, some wealth is necessary. In consideration of Jesus (Eisa AS) however, for the sake of spiritual well-being and for the attainment of the Kingdom of Heavens, it is necessary that one should give it up. In the world's system of justice and peace, the peace is dependent on politics and justice, on laws of punishment and the satisfaction of the aggrieved. However, Eisa (AS) states that the "Father in Heavens", Will not forgive us for our sins, unless we fully abandon this system, based on reaction.

In short, in the consideration of Eisa (AS), being religious, in fact, is the forsaking of the world. For the one, who does not relinquish the material world, does not sever his worldly relations, does not give up the business of the world and does not take up a life of abandonment and non-concern with worldly affairs, there is no place for him in the Kingdom of Heavens. Man cannot at one time attain both the Kingdom of Heavens and the world. Attainment of both is impossible for him. Eisa (AS) states, "You cannot serve God and worldly wealth at the same time." These two are opposite in nature to each other. If a man desires one, he will have to give up the other.

The way this teaching of Eisa (AS) is regarded by scholars of Christianity, can be judged from the following:

Reverend Dimboola in his Commentary of the Bible, states in the chapter dealing with the teachings of Jesus (Eisa AS), "Christ has chosen that way of life for man which is to a great extent, different from the way preferred by the world. Instead of self-esteem and uprightness, humility; Instead of fighting for one's rights, bowing down to evil; instead of seeking advancement, being content with one's lot, being happy and satisfied in piety, being humble and tolerant in difficulties are the gifts of Christianity to the world. The comprehensive description of the character of a true Christian, most probably is, that he cannot have one foot in the world and one in the church. He cannot serve God and materialism of the world at the same time. -------- In the sight of Christ, the most compelling cause, that leads man to serve himself, is worldly wealth. Therefore, for becoming a true Christian, the first condition is that he should become unconcerned with wealth" (Commentary on the Holy Bible, Dumellow, page LXXX).

The Weakness of the Ethics of Christianity

It is clear that in Christianity, the teachings of love, forgiveness, tolerance, and humility are the ingredients of an ethical system that forms the basis of mysticism. Since it has chosen a route for the final deliverance, that is different from that of worldly well-being, it leaves the worldly matters to worldly people and takes its religionists, separates them from the others, freeing them for striving to attain the "Kingdom of Heaven."

In such a religion, the fact that there is no war does not mean that it accepts the responsibility of the affairs of the world, but in their fulfillment does not consider use of force necessary. In fact, it means that since it has no concern with the affairs of the world, it finds unnecessary the effort involved in waging wars and shedding blood. It does not say that for the termination of strife, the sword is not necessary, but holds the termination of strife itself, unnecessary. It does not say that mischief can be eliminated without the use of force, but holds the elimination of mischief itself, unnecessary. It states that instead of combating mischief, one should bow one's head down in acceptance and tolerance of it. It does not say that the defense of truth and fairness against cruelty and oppression is possible without bloodshed, but that such defense itself is unnecessary; if cruelty and oppression choose to usurp one's rights, they should be allowed to do so. It does not say that criminals can be punished without violence and the aggrieved can be compensated likewise, but says, that the very system of punishment and compensation should be given up. If someone "commits a crime, not seven, but seventy times, he should be forgiven each time"

In short, establishment of peace in the world, cleansing it of evil and mischief, establishing law and order and protecting humanity from cruelty, strife, and oppression, are out of the scope of activity of Christianity. For itself, it has chosen the life of the oppressed, the overpowered, and the downtrodden. Then, it being against war, it does not matter that it is for a right or a wrong cause, it is understandable. For the lifestyle of this choice, this is the right attitude.

The question then is, whether ethical teachings of humility and tolerance can form a part of a permanent, universal law? The answer to this can be found in the teachings of Christianity itself. It has been proved that its instructions of total avoidance of war are not by themselves, permanent and isolated, but form a part of its whole mystical and esoteric philosophy, which includes, as one of its basic ingredients, the relinquishment of the material world. Therefore, the principal of avoidance of war can only come into force when the clause of relinquishing the world is fully implemented.

Christianity itself does not prescribe for its followers that they should take over the administration of the world, yet stay away from war. According to its teachings, man can accept the way of humility and tolerant inaction only when he fully renounces the world and gives up its various socio-cultural responsibilities.

It follows that this relinquishment, this mystical life, in fact this true Christian philosophy, is neither practically possible nor perhaps what Eisa (AS) prescribed for humanity.

If Christian ethical laws were to be declared universally applicable, all humanity would have to forgo all its socio-cultural activities. If attainment of the "Kingdom of Heaven" is to be man's ultimate objective in life and we accept that activities pertaining to this material world are indeed a hindrance in its path, it follows that the entire humanity, in its attempt to reach this "Kingdom of Heaven", would avoid this obstacle. It would accept a mystical life-style and concentrate fully on subduing its ego and on prayers. Obviously this is not possible, the business of the entire world could close down, the people would quit striving for their livelihood and live like the "birds of the air" or the jungle trees. It cannot relinquish its trade, industry, agriculture and all other activities and accept a life of inaction. It cannot give up the affairs of the world and take up a monastic life. In the unlikely event, however, that all this happens, man cannot still lay claims to the respect and superiority over all creatures that God has bestowed on him. The truth is that he would cease to exist. This condition of life is possible in fertile imaginations only and not outside of them, but God forbid, if it somehow becomes a reality, it would not be the society that any sane person would idealize, aimed for, or desired of. It is therefore ridiculous and farcical to say that the laws of ethics of Christianity are viable or of universal applicability. Only that law can be said to be viable and applicable to the entire humanity, which can be followed by the entire humanity, in all events.

The Christian laws seem ludicrous, not only in their universal applicability, rather are impossible even for a single nation to follow as a whole. Supposing a nation or a state opts for it and starts following all its laws, in order to enter the "Kingdom of Heaven". It would first have to abandon its system of government, disband all its army and its police force, leave guarding its frontiers and looking after its fortresses. Then the neighboring countries, seeing no resistance, would attack it. Following the Christian teachings, this pious and God-fearing nation would not resist the mischief monger and would offer it the other cheek and along with the tunic, offer the enemy its cloak too. Moreover, it would give up all its wealth, business, houses, its shops and even articles of the households, since, the rich cannot enter the 'Kingdom of Heaven' and Eisa (AS) teaching is that, 'one should sell off one's belongings and give the proceeds to the poor as alms'. Then it would not labor for its livelihood, factories would close down, trade would be relinquished, industry, services, and all its businesspersons would take refuge in monasteries. All this because the Christian teaching is that 'You cannot serve God and wealth at the same time' and Eisa (AS) states 'Do not worry about your life'. Then there is only one option of earning a livelihood open for him and that is agriculture; that he should till the soil and grow his food. However, in order to enter the 'Kingdom of Heaven', he would have to give that up too, because Eisa (AS) said, "look at the birds of the air, they do not sow nor reap, even then your Father in Heaven feeds them."

The entire nation would, in this way give up all that it owns to the attackers and become their slaves. Then the enemy would take it for forced labor and when the enemy takes it 'one mile' for forced labor, it would 'go two miles'. If the enemy treats the truly Christian nation cruelly, it would pray for it, if the enemy spurns them, they would ask for Gods beneficence for them, when the enemy tries to usurp its honor and respect, it would offer only tolerance and acceptance in response. From Christianity's perspective, this is the ultimate in ethics. After this, nothing can stop it from attaining the "Kingdom of Heaven". From any other intelligent man's perspective, it can be nothing but a limit of degeneracy. Striving for such an end can be nothing more than committing suicide -- beyond comprehension too, is the nature of this 'Kingdom in Heaven', which seeks such useless and degenerated people -- However, as far as this world is concerned, no nation can make this Christian Law of ethics as its law of life, because it would be compelled to violate each of its clauses, in order that it may protect and provide for itself. In practice, after violating its clauses with frequency and finding it necessary to do so, it would become quite impossible for a nation to maintain its belief in it.

Another possibility is that Christianity is not meant for general applicability and is not even applicable for a single nation in its entirety, but it is meant to be followed by a group in a society, as the explanation of Eisa (AS) sayings suggests. In this form, it is definitely practicable. If different groups of the society continue to function, in order to fulfill the various needs of the society, i.e. different groups look after its trade, industry, agriculture and politics etc., then it is possible, that the society can tolerate a small select group, living like the "birds of the air" or the "wild trees of the jungle", in a state of wasteful inaction. Then only, this select group can concentrate on reaching the ultimate goal of Christianity, based on the relinquishment of the world, breaking all ties with the society and living a life of humility, tolerance, self-sacrifice and of subduing the ego.

However, accepting the fact that it may be applicable for a select few and yet considering it the only way of achieving final deliverance, is accepting that only mystics and monastics have a monopoly on the 'Kingdom of Heaven'. We would have to accept that the majority of Humanity would have to remain deprived of a place in it. Those who are keeping the system of civilization in good order, those who are involved in providing the needs for the defense of a nation and its other necessities of life have no place, have no hope of reaching the "Kingdom". They are the victims of Christianity's primary belief that man cannot enter at the same time in "Kingdom of Heaven" and in the kingdom of earth. For achieving the Kingdom of Heaven, they would have to follow the way that Eisa (AS) suggests. In the list of those who would not enter the Kingdom, are even those who abstain from forbidden sex, theft and lies and those who respect their parents, love their neighbors as they would love themselves, but do not "sell off their belongings, giving away the proceeds as alms".

If we accept this belief to be true, we go back to the first possibility. However, if we accept that the only means of reaching the Kingdom is by following the Christian code of ethics and since the entire humanity cannot follow this code as explained earlier, it follows that we will have to accept that Christianity is not meant to be of universal applicability, since the final deliverance is the objective of the entire human race.

If we hold that it is the only means of achieving deliverance for the entire humanity and as has been proven, it is practically illogical and impossible for the entire human race to tread the path espoused by Christianity, which proves that it is not the route for the final deliverance of the entire humanity. Thus, we come to the conclusion that Christianity was neither meant to be followed by the entire humanity nor is it the only means of deliverance.

Only that code can be termed as the everlasting and only means of deliverance, for the entire humanity, in which a king remains a king, a trader remains a trader, a farmer remains a farmer, and every person while fulfilling his own function, can yet remain steadfastly the follower of that code of ethics and law. That code would not be such, that in following it, man is confronted with insurmountable difficulties, unbearable hardships and unbearable dangers, trouble and pain. The code or law, which is inconsiderate of these is neither a straight and true path, nor the only route of deliverance, nor yet a true code of nature, i.e. It is unnatural.

We however, cannot stop, satisfied at this. We have to go a step further and say that Christianity in its present form is entirely against human nature. It is in fact a misconception of ethical supremacy, in which some virtues have been stressed beyond moderation, while others have been unnecessarily ignored, thus rendering humanity disabled or at least severely restricted[37].

---

[37] These problems and non-possibilities have been felt by the Christians themselves. Therefore, it has been stated that it is not conditional for the achievement of the "Kingdom", that the laws of Christianity be followed fully. Eisa (AS) having been crucified has undergone penance for the sins of the entire lot of believers. Thus, all who believe in him are granted deliverance. If we accept this, there really is no need for the laws of ethics at

The virtues on whose acquisition Christianity stresses, are definitely unquestionable. It cannot be denied that mercy, forgiveness, softness, and tolerance are outstanding virtues. However, to construct the structure of humanity on these high qualities alone is not correct.

Only in the event that the world is cleansed of all evil and mischief, angels inhabit the earth instead of men and the devil finds some other universe to fulfill its purpose, then it can be possible that man, without applying his prowess, can defend his rights, his honor, and his self. However, where there is evil along with piety and human nature is not completely cleansed of its satanic urging, which are always ready to lead man astray, piety cannot be left unguarded. Doing so and refraining from utilizing the God-given prowess is not only suicide, but is also amounts to directly aiding the evil. For surely it is not piety to provide opportunity for the cruel to commit his cruelty and for those who spread strife, to do their job. We can call such inaction cowardice and lack of determination. It cannot be likened to peacefulness, piety, and forgiveness.

Piety in fact is another name for correction. It is the mixing of love with anger in moderation. If evil can be reformed with patience, tolerance, and kindness, these attributes should be utilized. However, in the event that these forces of love and kindness do not succeed, the forces of politics, penal law, redress, and revenge have to be utilized. One must not hesitate to do so, for correction and reform are the duties of man. He must utilize all beneficial and available means for achieving these ends. To unduly discriminate between the means and insist on a particular one, to the extent that it itself becomes a cause of strife, is neither very intelligent nor any great piety.

---

all and man in spite of committing murders, rape and theft, and in spite of troubling his neighbors and hoarding ill begotten wealth, can still achieve the "Kingdom of the Heavens", the only condition being that he believes in Christ. If this were so, all the lessons given by Eisa (AS), via his sermons, would stand negated, so would the saying of Eisa (AS) that no one with crimes mentioned above would enter the "Kingdom of Heavens". But, if we were to consider his sermons and lessons as true, then the belief of penance by Eisa (AS) would stand negated. Both beliefs, in any event cannot be operative at the same time and logically, without some major misinterpretation, both cannot be the part of the same belief or religion.

The Christian perspective, that the main purpose of life is love and apart from this, all other emotions and ethics of man are untrue, and subduing them alone can help achieve deviousness, has its basis on a faulty thought process. The authors of this philosophy failed to comprehend that nothing in the world has been created without a purpose. They reached the conclusion that man's emotions of anger, desire, ego-satisfaction, etc. are purposeless and that there is no place for bravery, courage, fearlessness, firmness, politics, law, justice, and so forth. This is untrue, all prowess of qualities, strengths, abilities and emotions, that man has been gifted with are for a purpose. Like every part of man's body, even his hair have a function, none of man's physical and mental facilities, his apparent and hidden qualities and no emotion is purposeless. The wrong use of these qualities and prowess in no way indicates that they are evil in themselves but that man has not understood their purpose and that his intellect and understanding have not reached the stage where he can guide them for a useful purpose. For example, his "desire" is such an emotion, under the influence of which, man has committed more sins than on the prompting of any other emotion. However, on that basis it cannot be decided that the emotion be subdued or eliminated, for on its basis the well-being of humanity is dependent. Although, craving can make a man slave to his wants and propel him towards the worst of his sins, its total elimination cannot be decided because this emotion can be the reason for actions. Fury or anger has been the cause for numerous fights and cruelty, but from that, we cannot draw the conclusion that it is completely evil, that there is no use of it and that it is the main enemy of peace in the world, for in itself, it also is the main cause of peace being maintained in the world.

Similar to the basic ones examined above is the case of the finer and nobler emotions. While they possess many virtues, their straying out of their bounds can take them to the limits of foolishness and over indulgence. 'Caution', for example, can acquire the shape of cowardice and unmanliness. If 'mercy' is not kept within bounds, it becomes a cause for crime and lawlessness. If generosity crosses its limits, it leads to thriftless behavior and waste. If thrift on the other hand is beyond its bounds, it is miserliness. If love is not subject to moderation, it causes man to become blind to all else. If consideration and tolerance are not within bounds, mischief will be on the rise. If softness and tenderness is out of place, it gives rise to arrogance. If humility is misplaced, the ego and self-esteem are its victims. All emotions of man have the potential for vice or virtue. On the basis of just one of its aspects, their rightfulness or otherwise cannot be decided.

It cannot be said that hands, feet, heart, and mind are the only requirements of the body and we do not really need our lungs, kidneys, and so forth. It cannot be said of our senses, that the senses of hearing and sight are enough and we do not really need the sense of touch and taste. It cannot be said that only awareness and understanding produce feelings and that, for the purpose, memory, and discrimination are not really required. Similarly, we cannot say that love, kindness, forgiveness, and humility are the only required emotions and that we can do without hatred, anger, courage, daring, self-esteem etc.

Just as the functions of the kidneys cannot be fulfilled by the liver and the heart cannot perform the functions of the mind, the functions of the emotions of anger and vengeance cannot be fulfilled by love and kindness and the place of law and politics cannot be taken by forgiveness. Like the good health of the body is dependent on its parts being moderately functional and intelligence is dependent on the functionality of our five senses, ethical excellence can also be established in the event of moderation of desires and emotions; bringing into play all the forces of the ego at the right time and place and utilizing all natural prowess within bounds.

Any religion that is not unnatural, guides man towards this very same moderation and bounds, not combating immoderation with another immoderation and one extravagance with another. Christianity has failed to understand this fact of nature. For that reason, it prescribes the relinquishment of the world for man and advises inaction as the way of life. However, this neither is a step towards the achievement of ethical excellence nor is it any service to humanity. Rather, it is a major disservice towards it. Those who choose to follow its prescribed way of life, on one hand deprive themselves of the pleasures of life that God created for them, while on the other hand, make themselves useless, depriving humanity of their services.

Christianity has separated the Kingdom of Heaven from the

kingdom of the earth. It orders the true follower to give up his wealth and, having forsaken the kingdom of the earth, fully commit himself to the 'Kingdom of Heaven'. The natural conclusion from this is that all pious, brave, decent, tender-hearted, honest and truthful people should give up the world and leave the business of running it to the lowest category of beings in the society, who are deprived of the virtues of kindness and honesty. Then the honest people would have to bear half the guilt for having failed to recognize their responsibility and having vacated the field of activities in favor of the crooked elements.

The Truth about the Invitation to Christianity

From the above discussion, it becomes obvious that the absence of war in Christianity is not an evidence of supremacy, rather of a weakness in the system. Christianity as we know it today has so many contradictions and weaknesses, that it is impossible for any nation to follow its prescribed path.

A little more detailed study reveals another fact. We find that in its teachings, there is nothing more than a statement of some basic beliefs and principles of ethics. It neither contains detailed instructions for the conduct of religious affairs nor is it a viable code of ethics and there is no mention of rights and duties. All this, to the extent, that there exist no instructions even for the conduct of prayers. Obviously, such a system cannot be termed as viable.

After knowing some basic principles of belief and ethics the followers still require guidance to deal with problems of the various spheres of life. The religion that is incapable of providing such guidance does not possess the potential of becoming a complete, distinct, and absolute religious system. The logical question that arises after this is, whether Eisa (AS) intended to pass on such an incomplete system of beliefs and religion as a permanent and viable one for his followers. Was he not aware that such a religion could not provide the required guidance to be followed by the whole human race or even by a nation?

When we study the history of Christianity, the conditions it was born in and the reasons for its being, we have to find answers to the questions in the foregoing discussion. The fact is that Christianity was never intended to be a separate and viable religion. It was in fact the culmination of the Mosaic religion and a completion of instructions to the Israelites.

When the Mosaic religion was revealed, it was the period of Israelite's intellectual infancy. At the time, they were quite incapable of accepting any complicated ethical instructions. Therefore, Musa (AS) gave them a simple set of beliefs and teachings of some basic principles of ethics. Obviously, these were not complete in regards to the finer points, ethical dealings, spiritual cleansing, and religious spirit.

For some centuries, the Israelites continued to follow this system of beliefs, but when they were accosted with more and more complicated affairs, the shortcomings of the system started showing their effects[38].

Gradually, the ethical conditions of the Israelites started deteriorating, until the condition reached the lowest point. Firstly, the communal system started to break down, and then conflicts between the various sections arose, which finally ended in their enslavement. This brought them to a very base level.

After that, they remained in the slavery of the Babylonians. Again in 573 B.C., the Iranians came and extended their mastery (Sabras). After that, Alexander the Great gained mastery over them. Their condition remained so between 334 B.C. and 323 B.C. After the death of Alexander, the Ptolemies of Egypt gained control over them. Again, a Greek family Sloucedea was their masters in 198 B.C. and forced them into idol worshiping.

Around the middle of the second century, the Jews had the urge for freedom. They revolted and in 141 B.C. managed to establish their own government and state. This state existed for 80 years; due to their ethical conditions, they were not able to continue for very long in that condition. Internal conflicts arose and finally they themselves invited the Romans to their land. Sixty years before Jesus (Eisa AS), Romans attacked Palestine and by the time Eisa (AS) was born, the entire nation was under Roman domination. In

[38] Here again the readers are reminded of the fact, that the discussions herein are based on the present Torah, Bible, Christian literature and the modern study. The Qur'an describes the situation differently. Since this is no place to state what it says, those interested in knowing that, are advised to go through the writer's tafseer of Qur'an "Tafheem ul-Qur'an" (English translation available).

this way for seven to eight centuries, the Jews had to undergo the oppression of slavery of the Assyrian (Ashur) and Babylonian star-worshipers, the Iranian fire-worshipers and the Greek and Roman idol-worshipers.

The natural consequence of this long slavery and subservience was that the Jews became devoid of all ethics, decency, religiousness, and humanity. In the Bible itself, we can find much evidence of this degenerated condition of the Jews. In 7 B.C., the evil ways that were being patronized and encouraged by Manasseh, the kings of Jerusalem, exemplify the degeneration that had set in among the Jews.

> "He rebuilt the high places his father Hekiekiah had destroyed; he also erected altars to 'Ball' and made an Asherah pole, as Ahab, king of Israel had done. He bowed down to the entire starry host and worshiped them. He built altars in the Temple of the Lord, of which the Lord had said, 'In Jerusalem I will put my name'. In both courts of the temple of the Lord built altars to the entire starry host. He sacrificed his own son in the fire, practiced sorcery and divination, consulted mediums and spirits. He did much evil in the eyes of the Lord, provoking him to anger.

> He took the carved Asherah pole he had made and put it in the temple, of which the Lord had said to David and to his son Solomon, 'This temple and Jerusalem, which I have chosen out of all the tribes of Israel, I will put my name forever'"
>
> (Kings, 2: 21).

In the Bible, Hosea, the Prophet (284-147 B.C.), states of the ethical condition of the Jews of the era:

> "Hear the word of the lord, you Israelites, because the lord had a charge to bring against you who live in the land: There is no faithfulness, no love, on acknowledgment of God in the land. There is only cursing, lying and murder, stealing and adultery; they break all bounds, and bloodshed follows bloodshed" (Hosea, 4: 13).

The Prophet Isaiah (740-701 B.C.), describing the conditions of the Jews states:

> "Why should you be beaten anymore? Why do you persist in rebellion? Your whole head is injured, your whole heart afflicted. From the sole of you, foot to the top of your head there is no soundness-- only wounds and welts and open sores, neither cleansed or bandaged nor soothed with oil.
>
> (Isaiah, 1: 5-7)

> "Your country is desolate, your cities burned with fire; your fields are being stripped by foreigners right before you, laid waste as when overthrown by strangers" (Isaiah, 1:70).

> "See how the faithful city has become a harlot! She once was full of justice; righteousness used to dwell in her-- but now murderers! Your silver has become dross; your choice wine is diluted with water"
>
> (Isaiah, 1: 21-22)

> "They have harps and Lyres at their banquets, tambourines and flutes and wine, but they have no regard for the deeds of the Lord, no respect for the work of his hand.
>
> Therefore, my people will go into exile for lack of understanding; their men of rank will die of hunger and their masses will be parched with thirst. Therefore the grave enlarges its appetite and opens its mouth without limit; into it will descend the nobles and masses with all their brawlers and their revelers" (Isaiah, 5: 12-14).

> "Woe to those who are heroes at drinking wine and champions at mixing drinks, who acquit the guilty for a bribe but deny justice to the innocent. Therefore, as tongues of fire lick up straw and as dry grass sinks down in the plains, so their roots will decay and their flowers blow away like dust; for they have rejected the law of the Lord Almighty and spurned the word of the holy one of Israel
>
> (Isaiah, 5: 22-24).

Another Prophet Micah states:

> "You leaders of Jacob, you rulers of the house of Israel, should you not know justice, you who hate good and love evil; who tear the skin from my people and the flesh from their bones, who eat my people's flesh, strip off their skin and break their bones in pieces; who chop them up like meat for the pan, like flesh for the pot." (Micah, 3: 2-3)

> "You, who despise justice and distort all that, is right; who build Zion with bloodshed and Jerusalem with wickedness. Her leaders, judge for a bribe, her priests teach for a price and her Prophets tell fortunes for money.

> Yet they lean upon the lord and say, 'is not the Lord among us? No disaster will come upon us,'"
> (Micah, 3: 9-11)

It becomes apparent from the sayings of the Prophets of the Israelites that in that era the religious system of the Jews had become devoid of the real spirit. The strengths of belief, truth, honesty, law, justice, and ethical purity were missing. Making wealth impiously and illegally, greed, immodesty and cruelty and ribaldry had engulfed the nation. Their rulers were brutal and the citizenry generally undependable. Their chiefs had become untrustworthy and their followers extremely materialistic. They had started believing religion was restricted to ceremonies; poetry and the wordings of the scriptures were the real religion and they had started ignoring its real spirit, which actually is the very reason for religion.

Seeing the rampant degeneration, the Prophets of the Israelites, long before Christ, had been attempting some kind of reform in their society. With their sermons and advice, they had been attempting to remind them of the long forgotten truth, that ceremonial sacrifice and prayers alone are not enough to satisfy God and that he is truly happy with uprightness and the fair conduct of affairs. To gain his favor, forgiveness, love and sacrifice are the requirements.

Advice in this context are aplenty in the Bible:

> "The multitude of your sacrifices -- what are they to me says the Lord, 'I have more than enough of burnt offerings of rams and the fat of fattened animals; I have no pleasure in the blood of bulls and lambs and goats ---- Stop bringing meaningless offerings! Your incense is detestable to me. New homes, Sabbaths and convocations - I cannot bear your evil assemblies. Your new moon festivals and your appointed feasts, my soul hates. They have become a burden to me; I am weary of bearing them. When you spread out your hands in prayer, I will hide my eyes from you even if you offer many prayers, I will not listen. Your hands are full of blood; wash and make yourselves clean. Take your evil deeds out of my sight! Stop doing wrong, learn to do right! Seek justice, encourage the oppressed, defend the cause of the fatherless, plead the case of the widow.'

> 'Come now; let us reason together' says the Lord. 'Though your sins are like scarlet, they shall be as white as snow; though they are red as crimson, they shall be like wool. If you are willing and obedient, you will eat the best from the land; but if you resist and rebel, you will be devoured by the sword.'"
>
> (Isaiah 1:11-20)

At another place Prophet Isaiah, preaching of the truthfulness of prayers and actions and the piety of high ethical values, says:

> "Your fasting ends in quarreling and strife, and in striking each other with wicked fists. You cannot fast as you do today and expect your voice to be heard on high. Is this the kind of fast I have chosen, only a day for a man to humble himself? Is it only for bowing one's head like a reed and for lying on sackcloth and ashes? Is that what you call a fast? A day acceptable to the Lord is not this the kind of fasting I have chosen: to loosen the chains of injustice and untie the chords of the yoke, to set the

oppressed free and break every yoke? Is it not to share your food with the hungry and to provide the poor wanderer with shelter - when you see the naked, to clothe him, and not to turn away from your own flesh and blood --- then your light will break forth like the dawn, and your healing will quickly appear; then your righteousness will go before you, and the glory of the Lord will be your rear guard" (Isaiah, 58: 4-8).

At another place, Micah gives the same message, saying:

"With what shall I come before the Lord and bow down before the exalted God? Shall I come before him with burnt offerings, with calves a year old? Will the Lord be pleased with thousands of rams, with ten thousand rivers of oil? Shall I offer my first born for my transgression, the fruit of my body for the sin of my soul?" (Micah, 6: 6-8)

These teachings fell on deaf ears and for seven centuries, the deteriorating conditions did not show any improvement. The ethical bankruptcy that had set in among the Israelites needed stronger medicine. Eisa (AS) appeared as a light from the heavens in the situation. He chose to further the teachings of Isaiah and Micah, with a new fervor and spirit. Like the teachings of the Prophets of the past, his teachings were also based on the Mosaic religion. Its purpose was not to supersede Judaism and introduce a new religion. Rather, its sole purpose was to fill in the gaps left in the teachings of Musa (AS) and to instill among the Jews, an ethical spirit, the lack of which they showed. At this time, the ethics of the Jews were seriously short of sincerity, tenderness, forgiveness, piety, and satisfaction with their lot, pity, kindness and the sense of sacrifice. Their exhibitionism, love of the world, greed, and selfishness knew no bounds. The spirit of religiousness, which is a necessity for humanity, was totally missing from their society. Their foe Eisa (AS) mainly concentrated on correcting these faults. He maintained the Mosaic religion and only made those additions that were the requirements of the time[39].

---

[39] This is now *(referring to the time of original writing)* accepted by the Christian scholars. A few years back, a famous Christian Scholar Deen

In fact, the religion of Christ (Eisa AS) was not a new one, but a continuation of the religion of Musa (AS).

The same is stated in the Bible, in the words of Eisa (AS):

> "Do not think that I have come to abolish the law or the Prophets; I have not come to abolish them but to fulfill them. I tell you the truth, until heaven and earth disappear, not the smallest letter, the least stroke of the pen; will by any means disappear from the law until everything is accomplished. Anyone who breaks the least of these commandments and teaches others to do the same will be called least in the Kingdom of Heaven, but whoever practices these commands will be called great in the Kingdom of Heaven. For I tell you that, unless your righteousness surpasses that of the Pharisees and the teachers of law, you will certainly not enter the Kingdom of Heaven" (Luke, 16:17)

> "The teachers of the law and the Pharisees sit in Moses seat. So you must obey them and do everything they tell you. But do not do what they do, for they do not practice what they preach. They tie up heavy loads and put them on men's shoulders, but they themselves are not willing to lift a finger to move them" (Mathew, 23: 1-4)

The Bible of John explains further,

> "The law was given through Moses; grace and truth came through Jesus." (John, 1: 17).

From the quotations, it is obvious that all the teachings of Musa (AS) form a part of Christianity. Only their truth and sanctity have been further established.

Anjay, who was the top most authority in St. Paul Church, while speaking at Gritten College, Cambradge, accepted this fact that Isa (AS) never discarded the teachings of Musa (AS), neither introduce new teachings nor enacted any new religion in conflict with that of Musa (AS). He desired freedom in spiritual affairs, but accepted the norms of that time and place. For this reason, there was a need of separating from Mosaic teaching, but for Christians, he did not introduce a new law.

The Reasons of Absence of War from the Teachings of Christianity

After the foregoing discussion, it is not necessary that in Christianity all instructions regarding war, treaties, conflicts, government, politics and so forth, given in the Torah have been kept intact, without a word being changed. This was so because at the time of the birth of the religion, there was no occasion for referring to them or for implementing them.

It has been stated earlier, that by the time of Christianity, the Jews had suffered slavery for some seven to eight hundred years. Twenty years before the birth of Eisa (AS), Rome had attacked Palestine and Roman troops had conquered all its territories. When Eisa (AS) was born, the entire nation of Jews was under the yoke of Roman slavery. Their particular homeland, Yahudia, came under Roman control in 2 A.D. and was administered by a Roman administrator, whom they called a "procurator." At the advent of the prophethood of Eisa (AS), Jerusalem was under a very unjust and unconscionable procurator named Pontius Pilate.

The slavery of these sacrilegious and unconscionable rulers had brought the moral and ethical conditions of the Jews to a very low ebb. In the very sight of Eisa (AS), a noble of Galilee, Heroes, had, just to please a dancing girl, put Yahya (AS) (John the Baptist) to death. The esteem they attached even to Eisa's (AS) life is apparent from the fact that they had considered of more value the life of a robber, Barnabas, to his.

Under the circumstances, it was not possible for Eisa (AS) to rise with the flag of war and establish an independent Christian state. He had seen that the spirit had left the Jewish nation, they had no strength of character left, and neither was there any strength left in their nationalism.

> The first and foremost task for him was to extract his race from the pit of ethical depravity it had fallen into and imbue it with the spirit of ethical uprightness, without which, no nation can be capable of casting off the chains of slavery and to maintain its independence. He therefore, in the beginning, concentrated on the character building of the Jews. However, in his continual efforts in this

direction, he also had to ensure that he did not enter into conflict with the Romans. For if there had been a conflict, there were chances that he would neither have succeeded in the contest nor he would have been able to accomplish his mission. He therefore made all efforts to avoid conflict. When the Jewish scholars, attempting to have him involved, pleadingly asked his advice, on whether they should pay taxes to the Caesar of Rome, he replied with a reply that can be interpreted in two ways, that they should pay Caesar his due and God his.

(Luke, 20: 22)

He advised his followers not to rise against mischief makers and pray for the well-being of those who treated them cruel; if someone caught them for forced labor, that they should "go the extra mile" with them; if someone snatched their tunic, they should give him their tunic as too; if someone struck them on one cheek, they should offer him the other cheek as well.

Initially, the objective of these instructions was that there should be no conflict with the emperors and that the Jewish people would get used to tolerating hardships. Later, he gradually started instilling in his nation steadfastness, tolerance, composure, and courage. In order to make them fit to face hardships, he tried to remove from their psyches the fear of death and of the ruler's cruelty and power. He stated,

> "When you are brought before governors and kings,
> and made to suffer torture, remain steadfast"

(Mark, 13)

In order to remove from their hearts the love for life and instead, to imbue them with the readiness to die, he stated,

> "Whoever wants to save his life will lose it, but
> whoever loses his life for me will save it"

(Luke, 9: 24)

He taught them not to depend on the favors of the rulers but be satisfied with the gifts of God, since such favors are the very factor by virtue of which the rulers enchant slave nations. He stated:

> "If you then, though you are evil, know how to give
> good gifts to your children, how much more will

your father give the holy Spirit to those who ask
him" (Luke, 11: 13)

"I tell you my friends, do not be afraid of those who
kill the body and after that can do no more. But I
will show you whom you should fear; fear him who,
after the killing of the body, has power to throw you
in hell. Yes, I tell you, fear him" (Luke, 12: 4-5)

All that he preached was necessary so that the nation, which
had suffered centuries of slavery, gradually be prepared to fight for
its freedom. Initially his teachings were limited to this aspect only.
Later he was proceeding towards the aspect of war and at times
expressed his preference for killing the enemy. He stated on one
occasion that he desired that he (Eisa (AS) should be their king; he
wanted them to be brought before him and killed. He even
instructed his followers to carry swords. Luke states,

"He said to them, 'but now if you have a purse, take
it, and also a bag; and if you don't have a sword,
sell your cloak and buy one. ------.' The disciples
said, 'see, lord, here are two swords'. 'That is
enough,' he replied" (Luke, 22: 36-38)

However, after this progress in attitude, the two to three years
he lived was insufficient time for him to prepare a nation for war in
the cause of God. In that period, neither the number of his
followers was sufficient to take on the might of the Roman Empire
nor was the ethical teaching so complete that, like the companions
of Prophet Muhammad (SAW), they may be ready to face bravely
all the hardships and dangers of leaving their sanctuary and facing
the strongest in battle. Their beliefs by the time were not so firm
that they would openly declare themselves for the righteous cause.
Even the well beloved of the followers of Christ, Peter, was in the
condition that when he was arrested and questioned, whether he
was the follower of Eisa (AS):

"Before the rooster could crow twice, he disowned
Christ, three times" (Mark, 14: 30)

One other of his followers, Judas Iscariot, had him
captured, only for 30 pieces of silver

(Matthew, 26: 14)

> When Jesus was captured, all his disciples deserted
> him (Matthew, 26: 56)

Obviously, when this was the condition of his specially favored followers and trusted disciples, he could not have gone to war with a force of more of such undependable followers. If however, like the Prophet of Arabia, Eisa (AS) had sufficient time, he could possibly also have been able to instill in his followers the spirit of fighting and the willingness to give their lives for a just cause. However, the nation of Eisa (AS) did not give him even three full years to complete his mission, depriving him of the opportunity to do something big for the well-being and glory of the Jews. In that short period of time, only that could be achieved which was actually achieved by Eisa (AS). If we go through the life of Prophet Muhammad (SAW), we will not find in the initial three years of his life in Makkah, any trace of war or battle. In that period, we will detect even there, the teachings of steadfastness, strength of belief and conviction, contentment with one's lot, self-control, and ethical improvement, as we see in the short period of the prophethood of Eisa (AS).

The Relation between Judaism and Christianity

If the teachings of Eisa (AS) are considered in the light of the foregoing and of understanding, we find them having two aspects. One is that in which Eisa (AS) has attempted to bring to a conclusion the teachings of Musa (AS) and where necessary has made required additions.

In the Mosaic, religion there was a lack of graciousness, beneficence, selflessness, and love. Eisa (AS) made an addition of these to it. Where the teachings of Musa (AS) were unbending and the concept of humanity was very hazy, Eisa (AS) made the necessary improvements. He instructed the Israelites on love of humanity, as a whole. Whereas Judaism stressed mainly on the duties of man and subjects, love, kindness and ethical supremacy were not discussed much, thud Eisa (AS) stressed mainly on these aspects, with special reference to alms, open-heartedness, kindness, sacrifice, graciousness and so forth. This part of the teachings of Eisa (AS) was not by itself a separate and viable religion. It was in fact a continuation and a necessary edition of the Mosaic religion.

The second aspect of the teachings of Eisa (AS) is that in which Eisa (AS), keeping in view the particular condition of ethics, politics and collective living of the Israelites, had attempted their reform. For example, among the Jews, the greed for wealth and love of life had gained extraordinary significance; Eisa (AS) tried to overcome these by his teachings of satisfaction with one's lot and preaching that there were other things more important than just existence in the world. Among the Jews, hard-heartedness, cruelty and unkindness were high; Eisa (AS) tried to combat these with his teachings of the excellence of forgiveness, kindness and so forth. Among the Jews, miserliness had peaked; Eisa (AS) in reply preached graciousness and beneficence. The Jewish chiefs and scholars were serious victims of egocentricity; self-love, pride, and arrogance; in order to bring them into moderation Eisa (AS), instructed them in humility, piety, and religiousness. The Jews within the Roman Empire were slaves, weak and unable to help themselves; Eisa (AS) stressed on tolerance of cruelty and stopped them from fighting for their rights. He taught them, that the real strength was in tolerance, steadfastness, patience, and courage.

This second aspect of the teachings of Eisa (AS) was specially addressed to the situation the Israelites were in at that time. It was not his intention to make it a permanent universal code. Specially, the teachings of tolerant inaction, offering the other cheek, going the extra mile, or offering the cloak to the one who snatched one's tunic, were applicable to a particularly slavish mentality that had developed as a result of ages of slavery. Prescribing it as a policy for the politics of an independent nation was neither intended nor was correct.

The Separation of Christian Dogma and Denomination

Only a few years after the crucifixion (according to the Christian belief) of Eisa (AS), all the principles, and rules on which he had laid the foundation of his reforms were broken. His teachings were changed to the extent that the true and the actual ones vanished from the earth. The person responsible for these drastic changes was St. Paul. Nothing can be said of his motives for his actions. It is possible that after remaining strictly opposed to the message of Eisa (AS) throughout the latter's life and till two years after it, he actually sincerely converted to Christianity. It is, however, also a fact that he did not have the benefit of the company of Eisa (AS), thus did not have an opportunity to understand fully the true spirit of the religion. As compared to those followers of Eisa (AS), who had the advantage of the constant companionship of the Prophet Eisa (AS), he could not have the true and in-depth perception of Christianity.

It can be said therefore, that when he re-founded the religion anew, against the advice of such of the companions of Eisa (AS) as St. Peter, his actions, though they may not have been based on unholy intentions, they definitely had their basis on lack of knowledge[40].

The first such alteration was that St. Paul declared that the message of Eisa (AS) addressed the entire humanity, although in fact the real addressees of the message were the Israelites only.

When Eisa (AS) sent his disciples to invite people to his religion, he specifically instructed them, saying:

> "These twelve, Jesus sent out with the following instructions, 'do not go among the gentile, or enter any town of the Samaritans. Go rather to the lost sheep of Israel'" (Matthew, 10: 5-6)

Eisa (AS) himself in his entire life did not invite any non-Israelite nation to Christianity, nor did he accept any such person into the religion. Before the rise of St. Paul, the disciples of Jesus too invited only the Israelites. Until that time, the message of Eisa (AS) was an instruction of reforms for the Jews only (Milkman, History of Christianity, vol. 1, page 337).

In the year 49 A.D., in the Conference of Christian followers, a large group was still in favor of the contention that the teachings of Eisa (AS) were meant for the followers of the Mosaic religion. (Millman, History of the Christianity, vol. 1, page 393, and Du mellow, Commentary on the holy Bible, page LXXX1X).

---

[40] The book, "Acts", by Luke, a disciple of St. Paul, adequately proves that the latter could not benefit from the coaching of Jesus. When he started making the changes in the religion of the Eisa (AS), the disciples adamantly opposed him. It can be said on the authority of Biblical references themselves, that the principles invented by St. Paul, were not only against the spirit of Christian religion, but also against the clear instructions of Eisa (AS).

However, St. Paul, ignoring the truth of the preaching of Eisa (AS), his explanations and the knowledge and belief of the disciples, declared that the teachings were of universal applicability. To uphold his contention St. Paul declared that at his crucifixion and after he had passed away, Eisa (AS) had come to his disciples and told them to "spread the word to the whole world" (Mathews, 28: 19).

It was difficult however, to make the non-Israelite nations subservient to the Mosaic rules, since its many ceremonies and ways were disliked by them. Therefore, the question arose, whether on inviting other nations to Christianity, following the Mosaic system could be made obligatory? In this connection, Eisa (AS) had been specific that "The earth and sky can change, but not a word of the Torah," that "He had come not to cancel the teachings of Torah but to complete them" and that "only he could enter the Kingdom of Heaven, who followed the instructions of Torah". (Millman, History of Christianity, page 392). After these explanations, it was not possible for any true Christian to divorce the Mosaic religion from Christianity. The non-Israelite, non-believers, who partially or wholly denied the Mosaic teachings, could not have entered the folds of Christianity.

St. Paul, however, unilaterally declared that any non-Israelite, whether or not he followed the percepts of Judaism could enter Christianity. These changes and alterations, angered the Christians in general (Acts, chapter 21) and the influential of Christianity protested against it. But St. Paul declared such respected disciples as St. Peter and Barnabas being misled or telling the untruth, started preaching against the teachings of Moses (Galatians, 2: 13). He writes in a letter addressed to the Galatians:

> "Know that a man is not justified by observing the law, but by faith in Jesus Christ. ------- if righteousness could be gained through the law, Christ died for nothing!" (2: 16-21)

> "All who rely on observing the law are under a curse, for it is written: 'cursed is everyone who does not continue to do everything written in the book of the law. Clearly no one is justified before God by the law, because, the righteous will live by faith.

The law is not based on faith; Christ redeemed us
from the curse of the law" (3: 10-13)

"So the law was put in charge to lead us to Christ
that we might be justified by faith. Now that faith
has come, we are no longer under the supervision of
the law" (3: 24- 25)

"It is for freedom that Christ has set us free. Stand
firm then, and do not let yourself be burdened again
by a yoke of slavery (of the law) ----- You who are
trying to be justified by law, have been alienated
from Christ; you have fallen away from grace. But
by faith we eagerly await through the spirit the
righteousness for which we hope" (5: 1-5)

In this way, Christianity separated from the Mosaic dogma.
Therefore, the religious teachings that were really a part of and an
edition of the religion of Musa (AS) were made a permanent and
independent universal religion.

The Effects of the Separation on the Character of Christianity

St. Paul's followers took over the task of spreading this
incomplete religion, which was not in fact the original Christianity,
but which may be termed as Pauliney (in reference to St. Paul),
leaving out the Israelites. They chose for their preaching, the
independent nations of Greece and Rome. However, without an
elaborate system and without a system of law, a set of exclusively
ethical instructions, which were in fact intended for a nation long
enslaved and oppressed, was quite meaningless for free and
politically independent nations.

This version of Christianity (if we like to call it), that contained
no complete canonical instructions which would prove beneficial
in the varying situations that an ordinary congregation of humans
faces in its life. It was just a collection of some pieces of ethical
advice, which tended towards extremism. Obviously being
dedicated to these instructions, only in the absence of an elaborate
superstructure of beliefs and laws, would have spelt the death of a
nation.

Resultant to following this creed, the Christians had to suffer subjection to all kinds of hardships and cruelty. However, they suffered, almost readily, for tolerance was the objective of the teachings given to them and post that no path was outlined for them to follow.

Later, not owing to any planning or effort on their part, but by chance when they gained power and independence, they found it impossible to lead the lives of constraint, prescribed by Paulistic Christianity. They broke all bounds and were close to the limits of cruelty, murder, and destruction.

The effects of the initial teachings of Christianity of offering the other cheek and not fighting mischief, as so strong that even when their numbers grew and their sphere of influence considerably increased, the spirit for fighting for their rights remained absent from their psyches. In 64 A.D. when the numbers of Christians in Rome, Greece, Syria and Palestine, were in thousands, Nero had them falsely accused of enmity of Rome. By his orders, anyone who proclaimed being a Christian was arrested. Some were crucified, some burnt alive, and some were put before dogs, to be torn up. Hundreds of Christian women became the targets of wild animals or of gladiators in the Roman arenas. In 70 A.D., when Titus attacked Jerusalem, 97,000 men and women were enslaved, 11,000 of these died of hunger and thousands were sent to the Roman amphitheaters, to provide their much relished, cruel spectator sport. (Gibbon, vol.2, chapter 16, Early Days of Christianity, page 488-489).

After Nero, Marcus Aerillius, Septimus, Decius and Valerian, tried their hands at eliminating Christianity and Christians, but later, Diocletian surpassed them all in cruelty. He passed an order that all churches and monasteries be razed, all the Bibles that they could lay their hands on be burnt, and everything of value in the churches be confiscated. In 303 A.D. the emperor, himself burned down the Central Monastery of Niko Media and threw the holy books into the fire. In 304 A.D., he passed the general order that any who insisted on Christianity be put to death. Later the persecution reached the extent that anyone who did not agree to change his religion, his body was slashed and vinegar and salt poured on his wounds. Then, piece-by-piece their flesh was torn off their bodies. Sometimes they were locked up in monasteries and then the monasteries were put on fire. For more pleasure, the

Christians were caught and laid on burning coals or their bodies pierced by metallic spikes.

This was the time when the Christians occupied the empire offices in large numbers, holding both high and low appointments. In the emperor's palace, itself a large number of Christians were in employment. (Rev. Cutts, Constantine The Great, page 55-60). However, the Christians had been convinced, however great their numbers may be, however powerful they might become, the instructions regarding tolerance and offering the other cheek and not rising up against oppression, held their validity. For this reason, nowhere in the world, whether it be Rome, Italy, Sicily, Spain, Gaul, Elyria, or Asia Minor, any resistance was put up against the oppressors and the entire nation underwent the cruelty with suicidal inaction.

In contrast, if we look at the Islamic History, the followers of Muhammad (SAW), who had been instructed on the sanctity of fighting for a rightful cause, even when their numbers were as little 300, were ready to take on all of Arabia. They proved to the world that a nation imbued with the spirit of fighting for the right cause, despite the shortage of fighting forces and despite being most poorly equipped, cannot remain subservient to any power. These were the times of weakness and oppression for Christianity. Later, when the emperor Constantine The Great accepted the Christian faith and it became the de facto state religion, this weakness of tolerance, reached in one leap the very limits of excessive behavior.

The reason for the earlier weakness was that Christianity kept itself divorced from politics and the business of civilization and its followers had accepted following the dictates of their religion, that is, they accepted following a life of tolerance. Now when by chance, the responsibilities of governance were thrust on them, another graver weakness took root. Since their religion had not provided them the guidelines for rulership, they, in the absence of dictates of God on the subject, began to rely on the dictates of the ego.

Governance includes politics as well as penalties, war as well as peace, and vengeance as well as tolerance and forgiveness. However, the separation from the Mosaic religion, denied it any rules and guidance in respect of state functions. Except for instructing its followers that they should not oppose the oppressor, that they should offer their cloaks to the one who snatched their tunics, had not provided them any guidance that would help them run the affairs of the state. However, remaining within the bounds of these instructions, it was not possible for them to run the state. Therefore, they were forced to break free of the bounds and found themselves free to follow the dictates of their ego. As a result, the strife, turmoil, arrogance, and turbulence unleashed by the Christians were such that the effects can be felt until today.

During the time of Constantine, more than half the population of the kingdom were idol-worshipers, therefore he could not dare to treat them cruelly. He had to satisfy himself with destroying the gates and roofs of their places of worship, confiscating the valuables, clothes, and jewelry that adorned the idols, and removing the idols themselves from the buildings they were housed in. (Rev. Cutts, Constantine the Great, page 278)

Some years later, when the church gained supremacy in the state affairs, the ardent followers of Christianity, dedicated themselves to crushing the other non-Christian religions and adopted the following principles, which encompassed many others:

1. The sins that the magistrate did not forbid or did not punish those indulging in it would be considered to some extent a participant in them.

2. The Worship of false gods and idols is in fact showing disrespect of the God Almighty and is a detestable crime.

In order to put these principles into force, the Roman senate enacted the law that "the religion of Rome was not the worship of Jupiter but the worship of Jesus" After this idol-worship, religious offerings to the idols and religious sacrifices were all forbidden by law. Severe punishment was prescribed for any found indulging in these crimes. Emperor Theodosius ruled all un-Christian worship, whether open or in private, an offence punishable by death. Along with this, he passed general orders for destroying all temples, confiscating their lands, and destroying generally, all materials of idol-worship.

Initially, the center was cleared of such worship and then it was the turn of the provinces. In Gaul, the bishop took an army of padres and had all temples, other places of worship, idols and even the trees held sacred, destroyed. In Syria, the religious head, Marcellus, who was the Diocese of Apamea, had the magnificent temple of Jupiter razed. He gathered a strong force with the help of which he undertook the destruction of all temples he came across or heard of in his area of influence. In Alexandria, the archbishop of Egypt, Theophilus, had the temple of Serpias, an extraordinary example of Greek architecture, destroyed and had its library, an extraordinary collection of knowledge, burnt down[41]. The statue of Serpias was broken into many pieces and its arms dragged through the streets of Alexandria as an insult to those who worshiped Serpias. Later in the view of thousands, its pieces were burned. Thus without formal sanction in other provinces too, an army of zealots went about wantonly attacking peaceful citizens and destroying historical, architecturally superb constructions, in their religious fervor[42].

The result of this cruelty was that the idolatrous citizenry adopted the religion, in fear of the sword that they really did not accept from their hearts. The Christian monasteries were thus filled with disheartened and unbelieving followers. Just 38 years later, the magnificent Roman Empire was lost without a sign of it left. Europe, Africa, and Asia Minor were converted to Christianity, by the dint of the sword.

After this, the conflicts between the Christians and others, and even among Christians themselves, were totally devoid of humanity and principles, in which cruelty was at its peak. Many pages of history remained blackened by the horrifying description of events in these conflicts.

Of the ways and means adopted to rid their lands of all non-Christian beliefs, one was in the form of Religious Courts (Inquisitions). These Inquisitions came into being on the express orders of the Pope of Rome. In these, the crimes that people were

---

[41] Mark Antony alone is said to have presented 200,000 books to this library alone. Vasius writes that 20 years later, one not totally afflicted by religious bigotry, seeing the desolation of the bookshelves, could not avoid the feeling of sadness and of hate and anger for the perpetrators of this wanton destruction. This incidentally is the same library that some Christian historians have accused the Muslims of destroying

[42] all the details are given in Gibbon's book, "Fall and Death of the Roman Empire"

tried for included heresy, blasphemy, Judaism, Islam, and mistreatment of the spouse. According to the law in force, the punishments for such crimes included, but were not limited to, burning people alive, cutting off the tongues, digging out the dead and buried, and casting their bones outside.

On account of these Inquisitions, in Spain alone, 340,000 people were put to death in various ways. Out of these, 32,000 were burnt alive. Apart from Spain, those who similarly lost their lives in Carthage, Sicily, Sardinia, Malta, Naples, Milan, Flanders etc., numbered no lesser than 150,000. (Encyclopedia Britannica, Arts, Inquisition)

This policy was the other result of the defective teachings of Christianity. The first result being that when the Christians initially started following the religion, they became too soft and tender hearted. Even when they had the ability to defend themselves, they tolerated cruelty and oppression. Thus, they continued tolerating the process of their extermination for about 300 years.

Subsequently, when times favored them, they gained power as a result of statehood being bestowed on them; they had to climb out of the narrow restrictions their religion imposed on them. Not finding the needed divine guidance and direction, they started following the dictates of their ego and subjecting humanity to all kinds of cruelty and oppression.

Occasionally, savagery did play its role in some of the Muslim wars. Muslims too can be accused of waging wars for territory etc., claiming these to be wars in the name of Islam. However, the basic difference is that for the excesses of the Muslims, Islam cannot be held blameworthy. The injunctions of Islam are in consonance with the need of the times and human nature. They are not unnatural that following them or remaining within their bounds would be quite impossible. Nor are they so permissive that they allow the human being to do what he likes, unquestioned. For this reason, all excessive behavior can be termed as unlawful. The law or rules of Islam cannot take the blame for such actions.

As opposed to Islam, Christianity has not provided its followers any set of rules as guidance for the actions and interactions of routine life. It has not guided them as to the means and ways they should adopt to gain strength and if they are in a position of strength, how their strength is to be used; on what basis and principles, treaties can be entered into with other nations; the permissible causes of wars; the code of conduct in battlefields, the treatment to be meted out to the fallen enemy, the concessions to be granted to people of other religions and if they are to be disciplined, the causes for which they can be taken to task.

Christianity, therefore, has to take part of the blame for excesses committed by its followers, both when they kept strictly within its bounds and while they were outside of them. It cannot stand blameless, saying that its followers deviated from the correct path they were instructed to follow, since there was no such path shown to them at all.

Christianity would have to adopt one of the standpoints. It would have to either declare all those Christians as sinners who accepted the office of running a state and its politics, even if the execution was fair and true or else declare all such rulers blameless, even if their conduct in that position was vicious and unrighteous. There is no third option for Christianity. Not having been instructed on the code of conduct, those involved were forced to do what appeared best to their own limited sense of discrimination between righteous and unrighteous behavior.

An Overview of the Teachings of the Four Major Religions of the World

We have discussed the aspect of war in the four major religions of the world. This presents to us two varied schools of thought. Two of these major religions consider war permissible. However, the extent of their permissibility permits them to wage wars in any cause their ego finds justifiable. Their causes have no bearing on righteousness or unrighteousness.

Neither an elevated aim is presented to man in their teachings nor is guidance provided towards the achievement of any ethical excellence. Rather, these religions permit their followers the freedom of indulgence in the natural desire to arrogate the rights of any and to usurp whatever they desire. Whatever progress these nations have made in the ethical sense is that they have laid down some rules for such adventures. They insist on their adherents that whenever they wish to go on a manhunt (war) they have to adopt certain methods and avoid certain others. Along with this, they have divided the earth into boundaries on geographical, racial, and linguistic basis. Some races have been granted certain privileges, of which, the rest of humanity have been deprived.

The other two religions do not consider the permissibility of human beings to arrogate the rights of others; while correct, this consideration takes them to the other extreme. They have progressed from fighting against conflict to fighting against human nature itself. They wish to totally destroy some of the capabilities and strengths God has granted man for the establishment of moderation in the world. On the other hand, they wish to impose certain other restrictions on human nature. The result is that those who follow their dictates find themselves in the pit of humility, humiliation, and disgrace. Those who are unable to follow their dictates and are obliged to undertake the duties of normal civic lives, do not find the light of guidance in any sphere of activity, with the result that these poor creatures have place their full dependence on their own faulty intellect and desires. They have to wander rudderless through the sea of life.

Between the two extremes of excessiveness and scant, Islam has shown a way of moderation. It puts forward a system that seeks satisfaction of human nature, desires, and wants. At the same time, it seeks the reforms of humanity. With the purpose of these reforms, it divides wars into two categories. One is fought for land, wealth, supremacy, and subservience of the enemy or for the satisfaction of the ego. The other category is of those wars that are fought in the affirmation of righteousness and for the eradication of strife and cruelty.

In the first of the two categories, Islam terms turmoil and tumult as strife. It declares such wars the worst of sins and is strictly against it. Conversely, if wars are fought only in the interest of righteousness and do not involve the ego, Islam declares these a supreme worship, a very sacred obligation and declares that there is no better service to humanity than participating in such wars. It lays down the bounds of even such righteous wars and the occasions under which they may be undertaken. It outlines the causes and purposes for which such wars become necessary and the ways and means to be employed in their pursuance have been outlined with clarity, so that this august institution is not exploited for satanic purposes and prevent egoistic desires from entering into the consideration.

The institution of war in Islam is governed by an elaborate and complete system and law, the like of which is not seen in any other religion. It is an undeniable fact that except Islam, no other religion has been able to keep war within its natural bounds and to raise it from the status of a savage conflict to that of respectable combat, from cruelty to the status of justice and from mischief to piety. By adopting its laws of warfare, the world can save itself from the curse of cruelty and oppression, as well as from the curse of being cruelly treated.

Chapter Seven

The Concept of Warfare in the Modern Times

Under this heading, we will examine the causes of war and its laws in the present day societies, to see their standing in the modern ethical system. (*Because the original book was written in the time period between the two world wars, the references are mostly from the First World War*)

The person going through our discussions cannot help saying that Isladid introduce some causes and ideals, which the popular religions and cultures of the time were quite unaware of. But today, after centuries of progress, when man's intellect has considerably matured and so has his thinking on war, the rules of combat that have taken birth now could be beyond comparison to those, in practice, when man's intellect was in its infancy. There is a need therefore, for another comparison between Islam and the modern laws, to determine which of the two is more correct, relevant, and beneficial today. Before we indulge in the comparison, however, we have to determine the references that have to be consulted, in order to find out the laws that govern the warlike activities of the West.

We can judge the conditions of beliefs in a society by three things: its religion, its literature, and its trends. Concerning religion, modern society has deemed it one's personal affair, and in the modern socio-cultural set up of the West, religion has very little effect on one's activities. Concerning literature, a huge treasure of it exists in the West. Western religionists and scholars have written a great deal on the subject of war and have discussed it from all angles. However, the works of such scholars and intellectuals, no matter how great an effect they may have had in the intellectual development of the society and no matter how great a part their thinking have had played in the enactment of laws, they do not have the zest or depth in their thinking, by virtue of which, they could be termed as representing that segment of the human race, entirely. Not even the best of them can claim that any of their sayings acquired the status of a principle or law. Though it may be true that under the influence of their teachings, some laws were enacted, but even these laws will not have the stamp of the influence of that particular author. The nation would rather say that these are laws because the nation chose them to be so. In any event, the banks of literature, produced as a result of the mammoth effort of Western writers and thinkers are of little value to humanity in general, where principled warfare is concerned.

The only source of divining the causes and reasons for war that the Western world considers valid are the agreements between the Western, civilized nations. These agreements are of two kinds, the written, and the un-written. The written agreements have acquired the status of international law, while the unwritten law prevails where common interests and interactions are concerned among the Western nations. Of the two, which is more dependable and respected? In case of differences between the two, on which is one to place one's reliance on? In addition, which has more capability of becoming the representative law of the West? These are some of the questions that have so far not been answered and Western scholars appear to be divided on these issues. However, we do not have to get involved in this particular discussion, suffice it to know that various aspects of war have been divided between the two. The ethics of war have fully become a part of the unwritten law, while its practical aspects have become a part of the written law. Therefore, leaving aside the question, as to which is the more superior in stature, we will discuss both aspects in isolation.

The Ethical Aspect of War

In our discussions on war, the ethical aspect has been and still is our foremost consideration. Before proceeding further, we have to see how war is viewed in the West; what status war occupies in its system of ethics, what in its consideration are the valid causes for war, and which causes are invalid for its undertaking, whether indeed it has some high and pure aims. If not, what is the status that its wars occupy in the world of ethics and culture. After coming to some conclusion on these questions, we will examine whether these principals continue to remain applicable in the modern scenario.

On the above questions, the modern Western jurist is completely silent, where in the past, the question of ethics of warfare were given due importance. The first person to invite universal attention to this aspect was Grottoes in his book, "De Jure Belliac Pacis." He has on several occasions tried to discriminate between the right and wrong of the causes of war. In modern times, however, the international law completely ignores the question.

Professor Lawrence in his book, "Principles of International Law," writes,

> "Modern international law is completely ignorant of these ethical problems. It does not say anything of these. In fact, it completely ignores them. In its view, whether or not war is justified, whether it is legal or not, in any event, it changes the relations between the belligerents, in a variety of ways. Therefore, the object of law is only to lay down the bounds and delineate the legalities of war. It tells us belligerency comes into effect and what the rights and duties of the belligerent parties are in regards to each other and to the neutral parties. The question of ethics, regardless of its relevance and importance are quite out of place in the book of international law, just as the discussion on the ethical aspect of marriage is out of place in the book of personal law."

A German writer, Eltzbacher, writes,

> "International law has always imposed only such restrictions on war, which without gaining ascendancy over the causes of war, are capable of being sustained and adhered to."

He has satisfied himself, by stating only that,

> "The enemy should not be made to suffer undue damage. That is, only such damage should not be inflicted on the enemy, which is not directly relevant to the attainment of the aims and objectives of the war, or are disproportionately exorbitant, as compared to the gains."

Professor Nippold writes,

> "The question of sin in war is not pertinent to international law, but to ethics. International law cannot discriminate between its righteousness and un-righteousness, because war is always undesirable in its view." [1]

We thus find that where written law is concerned, it does not discriminate between the rightfulness and un-rightfulness and between the righteousness and un-righteousness of wars. From these written laws it is not possible to determine, which of the causes of war it holds as righteous and which unrighteous. However, as Dr, Bye states, "There is, however, an informal and unwritten law as well and that in fact is the real law."

Now we have to see, how this effects the civilized and respected nations of the West, those nations, that are the "standards of modern culture," whose every trend today, founds a new culture, and whose every act and speech can be equated to a modern cultural basis. We have to find out that, when war is undertaken by these stalwarts of modern thinking and culture, what are the categories of wars they consider rightful and justifiable and what are their causes?

For the purpose of finding answers to the above questions, we will not consider the smaller conflicts that took place in the 19th and 20th centuries, because these cannot be termed as exemplifying the Western concept. Therefore, setting these aside, we will set our sights on the World War 1 of the 20th century[2].

World War I involved all the flag bearers of Western civilization and culture. The story of this war will clarify for us the Western, ethical standpoint on discrimination between the right and wrong of wars.

---

[1] Eltzbacher Nippold, Development of International Law, page 7-8.

[2] It may be kept in mind that this book was written after the World War 1, therefore the ethical aspect it discusses, pertains to that war. After this, the world witnessed another World War, the ethical aspect of which is even more disgusting and horrifying.

The Causes of World War

Although smaller nations took part in World War between 1914 and 1918 in one capacity or another, it mainly involved six powerful nations of the time. On one side, were Austria and Germany, while the other side consisted of England, France, Russia, and Italy. Internally, the member states of each side had historically not been on good terms with each other, but were knitted together out of necessity. France and England were old enemies; in 1899, they had almost gone to war with each other on the question of Sudan. Russia and England were not exactly friendly. In the beginning of the 19th century, England was always ready to oppose Russia's advances into India. France and Italy were in opposition to each other on the question of Tunis and for that reason, Italy had friendly relations with Germany almost until the beginning of the War. In the first decade of the 20th century however, they found some common interest, which united them and united they went on war with the other group.

On the other side, Germany was on friendly terms with England until 1904 and until 1914, it had formal relations with Italy. Russia and Italy were friends until 1908; in fact, the Czar and Ceazer were quite good personal friends, but for some reason this friendship turned to enmity. Germany then per force had to unite with Austria, an age-old rival, in order to meet the challenge of its new found enemies.

The Union of Nations

At first glance, it is difficult to fathom the causes for the disenchantment between the two groups of nations. Religion could not have been the cause, since all were Christian. It could not have been the defense of the homeland, since no nation attacked the other. There was also not the question of usurping of rights, since all were well capable of defending theirs. History tells us that the only reason for their conflict was that each wanted to grab a little more than its share of trade, industry and influence and each desired that the other be eliminated or otherwise forced to yield some of its share.

The first seed of discontent was sown in 1870 when Germany annexed the areas of Alsace and Loraine. Although all of Alsace and a large portion of the populace of Loraine were ethnically and linguistically German, France considered this a violation of its rights. It became a French preoccupation and obsession to cut Germany down to size and regain what it considered its lost territory.

This was the period in which Germany made great strides in trade and industry. Around the end of the 19th century, it had become the leading nation in these respects. In 1900, Germany came to the conclusion that England that had a monopoly on sea trade could not be deprived of its trade without a strong naval force. It started building a navy to match the English. England realized the danger and between 1899 and 1906, made every effort to befriend this growing German might. Mr. Chamberlain, Lord Denis, Down and others tried to woo the Germans but Germany was not ready to accept the monopoly of the English. It wanted the leading nation status in matters of commerce. Their opposition continued mounting.

On the other side, a great political revolution took place. Setting aside old enmities, France and England became friends. France accepted the English sovereignty over Egypt and England accepted French overlordship on Morocco. Both entered into a pact to look after each other's interests in future. In 1907, Russia too joined the pact. It had two objectives. One was the control of the Straits of thru Bosporus and Daniel pass. It had been trying to achieve these objectives for the past century and a half. The other was the total mastery of the Balkan region, so that it could gain access to the Aegean Sea and the Adriatic Sea (Bahar-al-Mutawassat). For this, both Germany and Austria were in opposition to it.

Germany wanted to establish a railway link from Berlin to Baghdad to enable it access to the markets of the east. For that purpose, it wanted the Balkans and Turkey free of Russian influence. On the other hand, Austria in its quest for territorial and commercial expansion could only think of one thing and that was the occupation of the Balkans, so that it could take advantage of the Aegean and Adriatic ports. With this objective, it formally annexed Bosnia and Herzegovina in 1908.

England had remained opposed to Russia, on account of political differences, until 1907. However, when England realized that it could not get to the jugular of Germany without Russian assistance, it extended its hand of friendship towards Russia, with the promise that it would assist Russia in gaining the Daniel Pass and the Bosporus.

In this way, by 1907, two very strong alliances had formed. One alliance consisted of England, Russia and France, while the other of Germany and Austria. The Objectives of the former alliance were territorial gain and furtherance of trade. For the purpose, it had to overcome the combined strength of Germany and Austria. The objectives of the German alliance were territorial expansion and the establishment of supremacy over world trade and economy. For this purpose, they needed each other's assistance. Italy, until that time, had not fully aligned with either of the two groups. Apparently, it was in alliance with Germany, but how it deserted its erstwhile friend and joined the other alliance, is a very strange tale.

Italy had maintained its relations and pacts with all five nations, in such a way that, for the occupation of Tunis, it could call for the help of Germany, and when it needed help for attaining certain areas of Austria, on which it had claims, it could call for the assistance of the other alliance. At the beginning of the war, it saw the English naval might was with the French and that Germany could not assist it in gaining Tunis, it changed its stance and showed its inclination towards the English alliance. It falsely donned the garb of righteousness, declared the cause of Germany and Austria false, and joined the alliance of the English, French, and the Russians.

Beginning of the War

In 1914, the murder of the Austrian crown prince at the hands of a Serbian anarchist provided the opportunity for the unleashing of strife that had been brewing for the past 44 years. For the Austrians, this provided the opportunity for advancing into the Balkans, which was their coveted objective, and for the achievement of which Serbia was the main obstacle. Germany too considered the exploitation of Serbia a situation beneficial for the furtherance of its ambitions. Therefore, it joined the Austrians in their cause.

Russia, on the other hand, considered Serbia its "younger

brother" and had all its plans in the Balkans tied up with its well-being. It was therefore its (Russia's) analysis, that if Austria was able to exploit the situation to its own advantage, nothing could stop it (Russia) from establishing its hold in the Balkans. It therefore stood up in favor of its "younger brother."

France feared that if Germany and Austria were able to overpower the forces of Russia and Serbia, their combined strength would increase to the extent that not only would it be unable to regain its cherished territories of Alsace-Loraine from Germany, its own existence will be in jeopardy. It therefore joined in the cause of Austria and Russia.

England, after its two allies had joined together against the German-Austrian alliance, found it quite impossible to remain uninvolved. This champion of righteousness had taken on so many ethical responsibilities of the world that fulfilling them was quite impossible without eliminating the German threat to the world's ethical well-being or rather removing from the queen of the seas, the threat to its sea trade. Therefore, it too joined in the Russo-French alliance.

The grand conflict that ensued among these stalwarts of righteousness, made the previous lesser conflicts between the unrighteous and unrespectable nations seem of little consequence by comparison.

The Aims and Objectives of the Participants

Each of the participating nations in this war vociferously claimed that they were fighting not only to defend its sacred rights, but also for liberating the weaker nations from the forces of coercion and oppression and establishing in their place, peace, freedom and tranquility in the world. However, during and after the war, the way these champions of righteousness divided up the nations and states between themselves and indulged in the barter of kingdoms, breaking integral areas and dividing people in the process, it amply describes what righteousness and rightfulness is in the perception of the Western Civilization.

In 1918, King Carl of Austria had tried to break off from his partners in war and enter into a separate treaty with England, France, and Italy. He started a dialogue with them through the services of Prince Sixte of Bourbon. He gives the details of his discussions with the allies, in his book, "Austria's Peace Offer".

England and France had sought Italy's participation in the war on the promise that it would be granted the southern part of Austria. For this reason, it was against any separate treaty with Austria. France, which wanted to isolate the Germans, was in favor of the treaty. However, Italy opposed the treaty with such vehemence that the threat loomed that if the treaty was proceeded with, it would break off from this coalition of the "righteous" and join the "unrighteous." Paul Combo, who at the time was the ambassador of France in London, says in one of his meetings with Prince Sixty, "Italy's greed can compel it to any mischief" (Austria's Peace Offer, page 103). He adds, "Italy has repeatedly stated that it had joined the war effort, only because it wanted to gain some areas of Austria." (Ibid, page 173)

Zhol Combo, Paul Combo's brother, who was the French ambassador in Berlin, opposed the talks, stating,

> "If a separate treaty was signed with Austria, within 48 hours, Italy would be in the German camp."
> (Austria's Peace Offer, page 28).

On a different occasion he states,

> "Italy will not do anything for us. It entertains the hope that when other partners are exhausted, at the end of the war, it would be able to gain the upper hand in trade and commerce."
> (Austria's Peace Offer, page 173).

Those were the conditions of the ones, who were in the alliance, fighting a war in the cause of righteousness and those were the opinions about such fighters.

When it was finally accepted that Italy would not forego its claims to a part of Austrian territory, it was proposed that Austria should give Italy the area it desired, for which the righteous alliance would compensate it, by giving it the German territories of Bavaria and Saluki, after conquering them. It is well known that people of the German descent inhabit the area and that the area is historically, ethnically, culturally and geographically an indivisible part of Germany. Yet, the "Righteous conglomeration" decided to hand over the people and area, as if it was their own or their looted property. Stranger still is the fact that the righteous Austria agreed amicably to part with its own territory and people, but refused the barter, not because the area belonged to an ally and friend, but because the area was not at the time in French possession and it doubted the Alliance's capability of conquering it. A search was mounted for other territories that could be given to Austria. Tripoli was considered first but Italy was unwilling to cede the area; it had its dreams of reincarnating the past glory of the Roman Empire and had its claims on the entire territory of Carthage.

Eritrea and Somaliland were next considered. None had objection to handing them over to Austria and Austria was also willing to accept them as compensation. For some reason however, the deal could not be finalized and at Italy's insistence, the talks were called off.

Secret Pacts

Another chapter of this dark and un-conscionable tale of the barter of lands and people is the one dealing with secret pacts made between the allies. This international tale of robbery of nations and kingdoms may have remained hidden from the world forever but for the fact that during the war the Russian revolution took place. In 1918, power was wrested from the Czar and in its place a Bolshevik government was formed in Russia. The Bolsheviks, in order to expose to the world the thinking of the capitalists, published the secret pacts that they had gotten hold of from the secret niches of the Czar. Thus, the dark diplomacy of the West was brought to light.

There was no clause in the secret pacts that did not deal with distributing some economic means or some territory that they planned to wrest from other belligerent or friendly nations during and after the war.

The first agreement was that the territories of Alsace-Loraine would be given to the French. The people living in the area were ethnically Germans and geographically as well, the area was more a part of Germany than of France. That area was being partitioned from Germany only because, earlier to 1870, it had been a part of France.

The second point, mutually and secretly agreed upon, was that all areas west of the River Rhine would go to France. This part of the agreement was kept a secret by the Russians and French, even from their ally England. It was only made known when after the war, in the peace council, the question of the distribution of the spoils, came under discussion.

The third agreement was about Morocco, which was until then under the French influence, would be declared French occupied territory. All other occupied territories in Africa, wrested from Germany, would be the lot of France and some parts of Turkey were also to be given to France. These were to be the portion of France, of the spoils of war, for its part in the "righteous" war.

Italy, which in the cause of "righteousness," had given up its alliance with its "unrighteous partners," it also had its rights on the spoils of war. It was therefore apportioned the territories of Thracia, Terrentino and south Travail. All ports on the Adriatic and its islands were allotted to Italy, as were some of the territories, to be captured from Turkey, were to be given to it as well.

Russia the flag bearer of righteousness could not be left out. The first agreement was about Poland. The gist of it was that in order to keep the aggressive nature of the Polish under check, Russia would be free to take whatever action it wished, uncensored, these were the same Polish people who had been promised independence, at the commencement of the war. Only on the insistence of Bolshevik Russia, first France and then England, accepted supporting it about the status of Poland.

The second agreement was about the straits and Constantinople. Six months before the commencement of the war, the Russian Crown Council had decided that there was no requirement of delaying the annexation of Bosphorus and Daniel Pass. The preparation for the purpose, were already under way. Therefore, at the commencement of the war, the immediate Russian consideration was the fulfillment of this "ethical duty." In 1915, in a secret agreement, it procured the agreement from the members of the alliance that out of the spoils of war, the Daniel Pass, the Bosphorus, Constantinople and the eastern territories of Asia Minor, would be its share.

In 1922, a Russian historian, Baron S.A. Karf wrote,

"In the secret agreements, the Othman Caliphate,

Austria and Hungary, were to be declared, spoils of war. These were to be distributed among the members of the French alliance. In this agreement, the Daniel Pass and Bosphorus were reserved for Russia."

England the chief guide of the "Righteous" group could not remain satisfied with its limited share of the German occupied territories in Asia and Africa. It opened another front, which speaks of its daring political approach. Five months after the war was declared on Turkey, it made a secret agreement with France, by virtue of which, Arabia was divided into two provinces. One was Syria and the other was Iraq. The first was accepted as the province under the influence of France and the latter, under the British. The success to the plan of was not possible until Arabs would give their full support to the war effort. It was also impossible that the Arabs after learning of the division of the area between France and England would continue aiding the effort. Therefore, they played a trick on the Arabs, in connivance with the allies. The Arabs were assured that they would be aided in overthrowing Turkey and an Arabic state would be established, consisting of all Arab areas that were under Turkish control, except for southern Iraq and a strip of Lebanon, along the sea. The dream of Arab state charged the Arabs with a new enthusiasm. They signed a pact with the alliance in October 1915 about nine months after the English and the French had their secret pact. Sir Henry McMohan represented the alliance, in the pact with the Arabs. By virtue of this pact, the entire Arab strength was on the side of the alliance.

After this pact, Sharif Hussain revolted and announced his independence from Turkey. Later, Iraq, Syria, and Palestine also followed suit. Soon it became apparent that the Turkish rule could not last long in Arabia. The Anglo-French plans were succeeding. Both, therefore, had another pact in Nov. 1916. This pact came to be known as the Sykes-Peco pact. In this pact, it was decide that Iraq would fully come under British rule, while Syria would be under the French. Palestine would remain an international area, with Haifa and its port coming under the British. The areas on the coastal belt between Iraq and Syria would be divided between the French and the English. In this pact, Sir Mark Sykes decided to give Mosul to the French. Since it had been decided that the areas of eastern Kurdistan, Armenia, and Turkey, which meet at Mosul, would go to Russia, and the English did not fancy having common boundaries with the Russians, they decided to have French in between. Mosul was highly cherished by the British nonetheless. While the Czarist threat existed, they agreed to the French occupation, but after the fall of Czar, the English, notwithstanding their friendship with the French, occupied Mosul.

The Distribution of Nations AMONG the Victors, After the War

These were the intents and plans with which the righteous West went into war. Let us see how they proved their righteousness after the war.

In the later part of the war, incidents took place, which compelled the members of the alliance to make major changes in the plans they had prepared as a result of the secret pacts between 1915 and 1917. One of these incidents was the entry of United States of America into the war; the other was the Russian revolution. The United States had entered the war, setting aside its policy of non-interference in the European affairs, because peace was a pre-requisite for the success of its trade and commerce. Its efforts therefore, were at ending the war as soon as feasible and that the post-war distribution of spoils, would not by itself become a cause of another war.

On the other hand, Russia had entered the war under an imperialistic government but the present Bolshevik state was viewed as a greater threat to their objectives by the rest of the members of the alliance, than Germany had ever been. Therefore, all the maps demarcating the Russian share of the territories had to be canceled and drawn anew. These would of course include the areas to be given to the U.S. as reward of its peaceful intents.

It has been stated that in a secret agreement with Russia, it was agreed that the areas west of the River Rhine, would go to the French, after their conquest from Germany. Thus, France was set on replying in kind, to what Germany had done to it in 1870. However, it well knew that both England and the U.S. would oppose this plan. France therefore kept this plan a secret. When at the end of the war, in the peace conference, it put forward its demand, as expected, both objected vehemently, and despite the French insistence, did not agree. Monsieur Clemenchieuv, the chief minister of France, proposed that as an assurance of prompt payment of the war damages and fine imposed on Germany, France be granted the fertile Rhine area, for a period of fifteen years. Many politicians, including the French, were unable to fathom the political wisdom behind the proposal. Clemenchieuv explained to the French parliament, that Germany would be deprived of the fertile area for fifteen years and so many fines would be imposed on it, that it would have to default on the payment of the fines, thereby foregoing its rights on the area to France. The entire house agreed with the wisdom of the scheme.

One particular remark of the chief minister is worthy of some thought. He said, addressing the French president:

> "Mr. President, you are much younger than I. I assure you that after 15 years, when you choose to grace my grave with your presence, you will definitely give me the good news, that we are still holding the Rhine area."

The ploy worked and France was able to get the approval of the rest of the alliance members for its proposal. France's desire was fulfilled and Germany was additionally deprived of the coal fields of Celesta, making it even more difficult to pay in 15 years, the ransom imposed on it, at Versailles.

The map of Poland was drawn in such a way that the eastern part of Prussia was cut from the rest of the country. The situation was so difficult that it could not be solved without Germany going to war with Poland, immediately after recovering from its post world-war problems[1]. Despite its problems, when in 1923, it became apparent that Germany would be able to pay up its ransom and recover the Rhine area, France decided on recommendation of Monsieur Derrick of its treasury committee, to attack and capture the Ruhr valley, on which area, much of German industry and economy depended. France sent its troops into the Ruhr valley in 1923.

The reasons for Monsieur Derrick's recommendations, in his

---

[1] This came true in 1939, when Poland became the first target of Nazi Germany in WW II.

own words, were that:

"In 1913, the coal extracted from German mines totals 191 million tons. Of this, 115 million tons are from Ruhr valley. Out of that about 55 million tons production was taken away, 10 million tons was assigned for gas production and another 45 million tons was for other extracts. Of other associated mineral extracts, of the total of 32 million tons obtained from German mines, 25 million tons were from Ruhr valley. Furthermore, during this period half a million ton ammonium sulphate was a by-product of the industrial usage of coal. In addition, 0.4 million tons of Bitumen was used to produce materials for dyes chiefly produced from ammonium sulphate, Ruhr valley is famous for its dyeing industry. Apart from this, perfumes medicines, dyes, and ammonium sulphate are the main products of German industry and these are all derived partially from coal. The only coal producing area left with Germany is the Ruhr Valley. Other areas have been lost in war. The same is the condition of the production of other minerals. Before the war, the total iron produced in Germany, was 19 million tons a year. Of these, 9 million tons came from the Ruhr valley. The other 10 million came from Sylessia and Loraine. Both these areas are not parts of Germany now."

From the above report, it is quite clear that the main objective of France was to deprive Germany of its mineral wealth and to economically destroy it. Not only would France gain its (Germany's) mineral rich areas but would ensure Germany's default of payment of its ransom. Thus after a period of fifteen years, the west of Rhine would also become French territory, permanently.

To fulfill Italy's greed, not only was it granted Thracia and Terrentino, but the southern regions of Tyrol as well. The inhabitants of Tyrol are mainly of the German race. Islands and ports of the Adriatic were also granted to Italy in the secret pacts, but the rise of Serbia as a sea power, became an obstacle in the fulfillment of the Italian plans. Further, the Adriatic was divided in such a way that it was neither beneficial to Italy nor to Yugoslavia. Therefore, there has always been a tension between the two and may one day become the cause of war between the two.

The major European powers of the time were not unaware of the dangers of this inequitable and illogical division of Europe. The British P.M., Mr. Lloyd George, sent a memo to the peace council, stating that, placing hundreds of thousands of Germans under foreign subservience is not wisdom and that such an act may draw Europe into another conflict soon. In his own words, it reads:

> "All inhabitants of Europe, from one end to the other are opposed to the present way of life and object to its politics, economics, and the collective life. …. The biggest danger is that they may opt for Bolshevism as a way of life and give themselves in the hands of the mentally unsound Bolsheviks, who dream of conquering the world by dint of the sword."

Mr. Lloyd was not a helpless journalist but the most influential member of the Peace Council. If he had so desired, he could have stopped this unjust division of Europe, but the greed or "righteousness" with which they had entered the war, led him into taking exactly those actions that would lead them into another war.

This was the demonstration of "righteousness" in Europe. Let us now examine the effects of this "righteous" war on Asia. The division of Arabia between France and England through secret pacts in 1915 and 1916 has already been discussed earlier. According to these, Iraq, Syria, and Palestine had already been divided between the two big powers. The Arabs, however, were kept ignorant of this division. They were constantly being led to believe that the war was for winning for them independence from Turkey and for establishing for them a great Arab state. On 11th March 1917, when he entered Baghdad, General Maude, made a general announcement saying,

> "We have not entered your city as victors, we are your friend, those who would win for you, your freedom, ---- and the people of Baghdad should know that it is not our intention that we rule them.

> Our objective is that the desires of the scholars and
> religious leaders be fulfilled; that their country is
> free again and that in it a constitution and law based
> on the dictates of the religious schools of thought
> and traditions is established."

At the end of the war, another declaration was made to the
Arabs jointly by the French and the English, which claimed in very
high-sounding rhetoric, the following:

> "This war was to protect people from German
> expansionism (not to fulfill our own expansionist
> desires). The only reason for involving the east in
> its dangers was because Britain and France sought
> to deliver the nations from the arrogance and
> brutality, that they had been the targets of under the
> Turkish rule, to win freedom for them and establish
> such national government and organizations in
> them, that were based on national inclinations and
> desires, in which no outsider interfered."

Notwithstanding these declarations, the Arabs noticed that the
French had taken up military positions in Syria, Iraq, and Palestine;
the English had consolidated their positions. They realized that
they had been hoodwinked and that their plan had been just to
create a rift between the Turks and Arabs, in order to grab Arab
lands. They therefore commenced their own struggle for freedom
and in Syria, established their own national government under
Amir bin Faisal.

Meanwhile, differences had arisen between the members of the
alliance on the question of spoils of war in the east as well.
According to the Sykes-Peco Pact, the areas of Mosul were to be a
province of France, but seeing the enormous oil-wealth there, the
British, out of their greed, occupied it. Palestine, it had been
decided, would remain an international area, not under any one
particular power's control. However, seeing the unease of Egypt
and fearing the loss of control over the Suez Canal, the British saw
it expedient to establish their sovereignty on the other side of the
Suez too and if possible, to establish another route from Haifa to
Basra. Therefore, it brought Palestine fully under its control as
well.

That Syria should be under the total influence of the French was not to the British liking. Britain was of the opinion that a national government of the Syrians under its influence would be most beneficial for it. Both partners of the alliance kept up their struggle for their purposes. However, when both noticed the rising tide of nationalism among the Arabs, they decided to face the danger, united. In April 1920, at San Remo, it was decide by mutual consent that Syria would remain under the de-facto control of the French, while Iraq and Palestine would be under the British. This distribution was not much different to the way robbers divide up their loot among themselves. However, the "righteous" robbers of the West sought to give even this the color of respectability and honesty. For that purpose, they made it known that the international council had put the area under their protectorate.

Although no international organization had any authority to distribute away countries like cattle or sheep, neither had any international committee met at the time, nor had any decision been taken on protectorate areas[1]. In any case, Syria became the property of France and soon afterwards, a 100,000 strong force of French soldiers, under General Gourd, landed in Syria. The same Arabs were forced into subservience who had been befriended four years earlier, in order to fight the Turks for them. The same people until two years earlier had been assured that they (the French and the British) had come to win them their freedom. Even after the war, they had been assured that they would have their own nationalist government.

The people of Iraq had risen in protest when they heard of the assigning of protectorate status. They were subdued, at the point of the sword. The British then brought in a contingent of 90,000 strong, where the Turks had never had more than a force of 14,000 soldiers. In this land, where the cruelty had never been the cause of

---

[1] On the question of protectorates, the Supreme council of the alliance had already reached their decision on 25th April, 1920, while the first meeting of the League of Nations was held on15th Nov. 1920, in Geneva. Protectorate here did not mean that on the request of the League, England and France would take over the guardianship of these underdeveloped areas. It in fact meant that England and France had already occupied the territories, prior to the birth of the League of Nations, prepared a declaration on its behalf and as soon as it was born, got its signatures on the declaration, thus having their occupation regularized. (End of note)

more than 200 deaths a year, the "righteousness" of the "liberators" claimed the lives of 10,000 Arabs in just one summer (1920). All this took place at the time that the Arabs were assured that the British "had not come here as enemies, but to win for you your freedom."

The British people had started showing their unease at the mammoth expenditure of ten million pounds a year in Iraq. In order to satisfy them, as well as to give an air of respectability to their presence there, the British thought it better than establishing their direct rule over Iraq, that they should install a puppet government, which in contrast to the declaration of General Maud, would act, not according to the wishes of the Iraqis, but of the British. With that objective, in the spring of 1921, it was announced that Iraqis would be permitted to nominate their own ruler. However, in actuality, Iraqis had no part in the nomination. Instead, Faisal bin Hussain, who had been deprived of his throne in Syria, was nominated for the Kingship of Iraq, not on the consensus of the Iraqis, but because he appeared more pliable to the British. The local protests were subdued forcefully. The influential Iraqi leader, who had been outstanding in his services to the British during the war, was arrested and transported to Ceylon as an exile. To arrest the growing dissatisfaction among the Iraqis, the coronation of Faisal bin Hussain was performed hurriedly - his throne was not ready and one had to be improvised, using wine kegs.

Thus, Faisal became the King of Iraq. However, immediately after his coronation, the British demanded of him the fee for his coronation. The fee they demanded was that Iraq would come fully under the sovereignty of the British Crown--the British would hence decide the lot of the Iraqis. The people out rightly rejected this agreement, but to convince the world otherwise, the British managed to get the stamp of the Iraqi approval in a very devious manner. One midnight, the members of the ruling council were rounded up from their homes and ushered into the council hall by a police contingent and their votes forcefully taken. It was then announced that the Iraqi parliament had approved the agreement.

The division of Turkey, as proposed and agreed to by the members of the Alliance, had to be annulled, on account of Bolshevik Revolution in Russia. A new division was proposed, whereby in place of Russia, Greece was made the beneficiary of the share that was Turkey.

To bring the scheme to completion, Greece attacked eastern Thrace and Izmir, depriving the Turks of a big portion of their country. Along with this, the combined force of Greece, France, and Britain, attacked Constantinople and occupied it. Turkey was also deprived of Daniel Pass and the Bosphorus, which were originally to be given to Russia. The Luzon Conference, however, disapproved this second division of Turkey. Righteousness and justice played no part in this disapproval. The fact is that the combined force and Greece in separation, could not withstand the determined Turkish defense, which ultimately forced Greece and its Allies out of Turkish territory. The Luzon Conference regularized the failure as the non-approval of the distribution.

The 'Rightful' Causes of War

These were the actions of those Western nations, who are the flag bearers of their civilization, whose culture is actually the Western culture. The fact is, that apart from a very few intellectuals and philosophers, the entire Western Civilization has been quite unable to influence the morality of their respective nations. The general populace of England, France, Italy, Germany and Austria cannot escape the responsibility for the actions of their respective states, since, without their tacit approval, a war of such magnitude could not have been undertaken. We are therefore forced to conclude that the vile actions undertaken by the Western nations, in the name of righteousness and justice, are in fact the exact reflection of the value placed on righteousness and justice in the West, in general.

The criteria that the West holds for deeming causes of war permissible appear to be Machiavellian. According to its criteria, the causes of war that are held permissible, as judged from the causes of WW I, are:

a) For furtherance of one's trade and commerce, gaining monopoly over the world's resources.

b) Crushing any nation that shows the capability of extending its own trade and commerce.

c) Bringing under its own influence, those nations, and

territories that fall between the mother country and far-flung areas under occupation.

d) Breaking up nations and states and gaining the subservience of weaker states.

e) If an enmity develops with another nation, trying the utmost to destroy it or at least breaking its strength.

The causes, termed as sacred rights by the West, need no further clarification or explanation. Individuals can decide on their reasonability and sacredness, or the lack of these, according to the dictates of their own conscience.

It is possible that some reader would term such analysis biased or prejudiced, but what else could be termed as Western culture, other than collective actions of the Western civilized nations. Religion could have been termed as the standard by which to judge the culture and value system, if it had any influence. However, neither the Europeans nations permit religion to interfere in their politics nor does the religion show much inclination to keep any links with it. Law and the judicial system could have been held the supreme authority in this context, but as explained, it is not interested in discussing the right and wrong of the causes.

After disregarding these two factors, we are at a loss to determine the source from which the values of the Western system can be determined. Should we tap the scholars of ethics, for the purpose? Or shall for the answer to our question, we lean on their thinkers who preach world peace? Or shall we count on the handful of authors and journalists, who pleasantly, sometimes indulge in the universal problems of humanity?

We have nothing against reaching out to them, but we need to be informed of the names of not a thousand or so of these, but just a few, who have acquired the classification of "totally correct", or "absolute authority" and on whose rightness, truth and authority, the entire West or most of it is in agreement. If none such are available on which there is a consensus in the West, we have no option but to base our study of the ethical beliefs on the subject of causes of war, on the normal actions of the West.

Establishment of Peace and Arms Reduction

In order to prove their peaceful intent and their sincerity, regarding reduction of conflict in the world, the West would be keen to point out their efforts towards trying to limit the usage of certain arms and ammunition and reducing or totally eliminating the war-like capabilities that are forever on the advance. However, if we look through their deception, it will become apparent that even behind such moves, the desire is not of decreasing the dangers of war, but increasing its possibilities.

The proposal for arms control was put forward for the first time formally in 1898. The Czar issued a circular to all big powers of the time, stressing the need for an international conference to discuss the problem. It reads:

> "The defense of peace is considered the main aim of international politics. In this, all-powerful nations are in agreement. For the insurance of this peace, their military strength has increased to the level never witnessed before. They continue to make further progress in this direction and are ready to make any sacrifice for the purpose. However, regardless of their efforts, their main and sacred aim of the exercise is still as evasive as ever.

Every day the wealth that would be better spent on normal and welfare activities is being diverted in the direction of increasing the war-potential. The labor, intellectual and physical efforts and the wealth of nations is being expended for the purpose, instead of in the right direction, is not yielding much. Tens of millions are being spent on modernization of weapons, which new inventions and progress in the field, soon renders obsolete.

Because of this arms race, progress and the ability to generate income have either been jeopardized or the progress has been negligible in these areas. Apart from this, the progress in the armament of a nation is directly proportional to the increase in remoteness of chances of achieving the national objectives of peace. The economic difficulties, that are a resultant of disproportionate increase in military strength, as well as the increase in potency and number of lethal weapons, are an unbearable burden on the society.

It is obvious that if the situation is allowed to continue unabated, it would drag the world towards destruction, even the thought of which is horrifying."

These were the thoughts expressed some three decades ago, by a kingdom, which was foremost in the world in its war-preparations and war-preparedness. When the world became aware of these thoughts, they were welcomed everywhere and many nations expressed their willingness to join the recommended International Conference. Consequently, within a year, in 1899, the first Hague Conference was held.

The first point in the agenda of The Hague Conference was the arrest of the increase in naval and military might of nations of the world. However, when it came up for discussion in the conference, it became obvious that no nation was inclined in the direction. Mr. Hollis, the American representative, understood the implications and hopelessness of the attempt, and stated in unequivocal terms:

> "Every person, who out of his simplicity, has faith in the proposals of disarmament, or the one who believes that an international court will be formed, with an international policing agency, and that its decisions will be imposed on the world, would definitely be demoralized later."

> (Times, dated 1st August, 1899)

The outcome of the conference was exactly as predicted. "Arms Reduction" or "Arms Control" were initially opposed, but on the greater insistence of some, the conference satisfied itself in only adopting a resolution, that reads:

> "This conference is of the opinion, that heavy military equipment is a burden on the world and reducing their numbers is the ethical and moral responsibility of all, for the betterment of humanity."

The value placed on the "suggestion" and the moral and ethical obligation can be judged from the fact that between the first Hague Conference and the second, no nation gave any consideration to the resolution and the war potential of nations continued growing. In 1907, when the 2nd Hague Conference took place, there was no mention of disarmament or reduction of arms. In contrast, it was explanatorily annotated that the subjects dealing with reformation of the military or navy should not be touched upon. To the resolution of the first conference, the following was appended:

> "Since there has been considerable increase in the armaments of nations, till then (till after the first conference), it is required that the nations reconsider the question seriously (of arms reduction)".

The object of this resolution was only that the Nations "reconsider seriously." The nations "reconsidered" very "seriously" and came to the conclusion that they needed to increase their military might, rather than decrease it.

Just prior to the WW I, the question came under discussion among thinkers as to what could be done to enforce peace in the world and to what extent would such actions be allowable in the considerations of international law. However, these discussions were still underway when the war broke out and humanity was deprived of the answer to the problem of its well-being. However, even then the intellectuals continued their discussions on "arms limitation" and "disarmament" and were thinking of ways and means of forcibly stopping the war. The defacto situation was a little different. The world did not have the time even to listen to their thoughts. America however, decided to give official cognizance to the movement.

On 22 January 1917, President Wilson wrote a letter to the senate, proposing among other things, the following:

> "The forces should be used with moderation. The military force should be used for the establishment of peace, not in the cause of aggression and cruelty. If the systematic establishment of the war industry continues, the realization of hope and peace cannot become possible among the nations of the world. The problem of naval and military strength is an important question and is closely linked to the well-being of humanity."

This was the second time that the question of arms reduction was officially raised by a Western nation since 1907. However, this time the proposal was more meaningless than before, because the sponsor himself was soon after involved in war, negating his own contentions.

The League of Nations

After WW I, the victorious nations, on the advice of President Wilson, formed an organization that was given the name of "League of Nations." Its first objective was the elimination of war and its causes. For the purpose, it established an "International Court of Law," which would decide between conflicting perspectives and claims of the world's nations.

A clause in its charter advises that the nations should try to solve their problems in a peaceful manner. If any nation chooses to take up the sword for the purpose, the other member nations would bring it back to the path of peace. Clause 16 reads:

> "If any member nation chooses to ignore clauses 12, 13 and 15 and wages a war, it would be as if it had waged a war against all member states. Members of the league hereby solemnly affirm, that they would then, sever all trade and economic links with the member violating the above clauses, and would stop all dealings between the citizens of their states with the rogue state. They would further make efforts that the rogue state citizens are prevented from having trade, economic and personnel links with other states, whether the latter are members of the league or not."

In the next clause, the executive council has been empowered to requisition the required military and naval force from the member states, in order to militarily resist the nation's warlike activities. The members were made duty bound to provide the military and economic assistance required by the league.

At first glance, this appears to be the most capable and faultless means of keeping all military conflicts under check. In actuality, however, it turned out to be a more respectable, more innocent looking and at the same time a more dangerous version of the groupings, on account of which, in 1914, the WW I took place.

Because the Europeans had witnessed the horrifying results of such alliances and held them responsible for all their woes, they were disinclined to become a part of such an alliance. They, however, realized that it would be quite impossible for them to realize their political aims and objectives without becoming a part thereof. No single state could have the military and economic strength to establish its supremacy over the world and realize its objectives. For realizing joint objectives, it was necessary that the big powers should make joint efforts and with joint effort make their grip firmer over the world.

A new countenance was given to the old alliance. This new organization, instead of openly declaring its alignment for military purposes, wore the cloak of peacekeepers and thereby lent it some sanctity. However, behind this sanctity, there was the same old spirit. Where there was a requirement to force smaller states, the league was a handy tool. If there arose a difference between say Greece and Bulgaria or there was a conflict between Poland and Lithuania, nominal military action or just the threat of it, would be enough for them. Thus not only could smaller conflicts be evaded but the greater advantage was that the world would be impressed by the leaders of the league. They could then, like the Gods of ancient Greece, attempt to run the system of the world. When they desired, they could make changes in the system, increasing or decreasing the strengths of the states that were popular or unpopular with them respectively, keeping the unpopular ones in fear. They had great ability to perform these functions when required, in relation to the smaller states. However, when it came to the more powerful ones, if they violated the charter, nothing could be done against them. Attempts in this direction were doomed to failure[1].

Suppose England chose to violate the charter and undertook some action, which had the potential of damaging the world peace. The league would call its general meeting and with the agreement of all the members, England would be warned to refrain. However, if it were to choose to ignore the warning, the league, perforce would have to request its members to break off all diplomatic and economic links with England and use their military might to bring England to book. The question would then arise, whether the members of the league, just on its instructions, would follow its

---

[1] Years after the writing of these words, when Italy attacked Ethiopia and Japan attacked China, and when Germany started swallowing up its smaller neighbors, the weakness of the organization became clearly apparent and was to become the reason for its ultimate demise.

directions. Would they be willing to sacrifice economic, trade and political links with such a powerful nation and forego all the advantages of such links? Can 4/5th of the world's population at one stroke, sever all links with the remaining 1/5th?

Could America and Europe come in conflict with this powerful nation, just on the instructions of the league and be ready to bear all the losses? Anyone with the slightest understanding of the world politics will reply in the negative. If the answer is in negative, we would have to accept that the League is powerless in dealing with its powerful members, but very effective against the weaker nations. Although the fact is that, the major threat to world peace is from the greed of these powerful nations.

This is not just a supposition and theory. It has been practically seen that in the past eight years, it has not once dared to question the acts of the powerful nations. In Damascus, France openly indulged in the slaughter of the Arabs, though the charter clearly mentioned that Syria had become its protectorate. France and England combined, slaughtered the small nation of Reef, but the League kept its silence. In the conflict between Italy and Yugoslavia, the League tried to interfere, but a threat from Italy was enough to keep it quiet. England caused massive bloodshed in Iraq, but there was no one to question it on its actions in its own protectorate.

Then again, whenever there has been a conflict referred to the League, where a big power and a smaller power were involved, the decision has always been in favor of the more powerful. It has never been seen that a smaller state has won a case against the superpowers. The problem of Mosul is another example. The area was segregated from Turkey and attached to Iraq to cater to the economic greed of the British.

From the above quoted incidents, it would become quite obvious that the League is just an alliance of the powerful states, to be manipulated to realize their own objectives. The weaker nations have shown their dissatisfaction and anger at the performance of the League. Now it is their desire to form such an alliance of their own, so that, when the united strength of these big powers chooses to oppress or suppress them, they may reply to this oppression and suppression through their own combined force.

Two such opposing alliances prior to WW I brought it about. If the envisaged alliances do in fact take place, we are in for witnessing another global war, perhaps of a much greater intensity.

Modern Suggestions of Arms Reduction

For the last several years (the period is between the two World Wars), the subjects of "Arms Control", "Arms Limitation" and "Global Disarmament" have been under discussion in the West. Many suggestions are being discussed in the context and the simple and believing public has hopes that may be this time around, these are based on good intent. The fact however is that these discussions are as far removed from sincerity of purpose, as they have ever been.

The common people of the West have been so long involved in wars that they have begun to crave for the atmosphere of peace and tranquility in which their trade and industry can prosper. Even false hopes are beneficial in order that some semblance of sanity may still exist in their midst; if not peace, an illusion of peace is their requirement. For this reason, they like to listen to the discussions, though they are aware that these thoughts have no possibility of reaching their logical conclusion. The fact is that in the past seven or eight years, the world's armament holding has risen phenomenally, to the extent that the armament holding of 1914, when the world was armed to the teeth in preparation of WW I, was much less in comparison.

After World War, in 1921, America once more raised the issue of arms control and under the auspices of the movement, a conference was held in 1921 in Washington D.C. The declared objective of the conference was the scaling down of the armament capability of the powerful nations. In fact however, the real intention of France, U.S., Italy and Japan, was scaling down the British Navy. The British ruled the seas and these powerful nations, whose trade was dependent on the safety of the sea links, could not feel secure in their trade. The age-old controversy was also the hallmark of the Washington conference. Every participant wanted to put some restriction on the other, but could not foresee any on itself. The result of this conference was that a proportional naval might was envisaged for each of the participants. The U.S., which had been the champion of the arms reduction, soon afterwards undertook the construction of five Dreadnaught class ships and rearming the Panama Canal with the latest weapons.

In the same conference, the question of submarines also arose. The state that was affected by the submarine threat the most was England, since its economy depended chiefly on sea trade and for the reason it had the largest number of sea-going vessels. During the World War, the submarines had virtually destroyed its sea-trade and had generally made life miserable for the mariners. Therefore, the Washington conference tried its best to declare submarine warfare, illegal. France opposed the motion, since its naval strength was much inferior to the British and for the defense of its sea-trade, it depended much on its submarine force. It declared that the submarine force was not for aggressive purposes, but for defense only and that those states that did not have the required surface naval force were dependent per force on the submarines, for the required protection. The U.S. proposed a moderate path, which was acceptable to all. That was, that during wars, use of the submarine force by the belligerents, for disrupting each other's trade, was declared illegal.

Another problem was of the use of poisonous gases as weapons of war. Earlier, in 1899 at The Hague Conference, it had been decided that the use of poisonous and suffocating gasses be banned. England had vehemently opposed the motion, but later it agreed at the 2nd Hague Conference of 1907. However, the U.S. continued its opposition, until the end. During the war, Germany and its enemies used war gasses to a great extent against each other, breaking all rules that they had themselves made.

Once again, in the Washington Conference, banning of war gasses was considered and a motion to the effect was tabled. No nation was sincerely in favor of the banning. The French representative, while signing the declaration, wrote a note stating,

> "It is not possible that the attempt to ban the use of gasess will succeed"

Mr. Balfour, the British representative, thought it politic to add,

> "Notwithstanding the security this agreement provides, it does not preclude the possibility that war gasses will in some occasions be used during

wars by some mischievous enemy."

The result of the reluctance of nations to sign the declaration was that the pact remains ineffective and a meaningless document. After the Washington Conference on April 1922, held on the call of Lord Lloyd George, a Pan-European conference was held in Geneva. The objective was to effect an agreement between European nations that they would not attack each other for the next ten years and all those who had been at war, would be provided relief in the form of reconstruction of the affected areas. America did not participate in the conference. France had earlier declared that it would not consider itself bound by the decisions of the conference, Turkey was not invited, and Russia was invited under so many conditions that it refused to participate. The result was that the conference ended in total failure and the preparations for war continued, unabated.

After Geneva, the 2nd Hague Conference was held, but it too met with failure as the Geneva Conference. Another international conference was held in London, but in this conference, a misunderstanding developed between French and English counterparts. It climaxed in Monsieur Ponkara walking out of the hall and returning to Paris.

In 1925, the League of Nations took over the question of arms limitation on itself. On its directive, the council, attempting to come up with a respectable way towards achieving a solution, formed a preparatory committee. This committee had on its agenda studying the overall context of the problem and devising such principles as would enable re-inviting the major powers for a meaningful dialogue. This committee was unable to undertake its work for a year. On 24th September 1926, the General Council recommended that the work of the committee be completed by 1927, so that the council could call the International Conference on arms limitation before the 8th meeting of the League of Nations. However, the committee was unable to complete its work within that timeframe. Until today (i.e. until the writing of this book), meetings were held off and on but without any result. Since the committee has not given any recommendations/comments, commenting on its performance would be a little out of place. Indications however, are that this effort would also meet the fate of earlier such exercises. If there had been any sincerity among the

Western states, they would have accepted the Russian suggestion on arms reduction, but none was ready to take the big step. The British representative, Lord Kushingdon had emphatically declared,

> "Total arms control, is in fact pushing a nation towards anarchy and revolution."

From the number of conferences held on the subject of arms limitation and the fate they met, outwardly apparent posture and the real hidden desire of nations become obvious. It is apparent that the Western nations are quite fed up with war and its effects that they have become of those who value peace from the heart. That they sincerely wish to give up this deadly drama of war and bloodshed, give up the destruction of humanity and now remaining within the natural bounds, concentrate on the well-being and meaningful progress of man.

That is what is apparent. However, the actual conditions are that within these nations, severe enmities and severe hatreds exist. Their military strengths and capacities are on the increase, their weaponry progresses by the day in lethality, and every nation is compelled by its desire to prove itself superior in might to the other in the next war, subduing all who oppose establishing its own supremacy. Seeing this, who can say that the nations, who oppose and hate each other, in fact entertain a desire to live at peace with each other and in fact regret their participation in the earlier wars?

In the memorandum of 1919 stated earlier, the British P.M. writes:

> "For the success of the League of Nations, the requisite is that between Great Britain and the republics of America, France, and Italy, there should be an understanding, according to which, all constructions of ships and increase in armed forces are arrested forthwith, pending signing of a formal agreement. If this cannot be done, the League will remain ineffective."

As predicted, the League has acquired a very ineffectual and an almost purely ceremonial status today (at the writing of this book). A full-fledged arms race is in progress among the nations. The West is fully committed to increasing its armed forces and its armory, and along with that, increasing the lethality of its weapons, manufacturing mammoth ships, destructive warplanes, poisonous gases and other destructive materials are of the quantum never before witnessed in any other period of history, not even in 1914, when Europe was arming itself in preparation for the Great War.

After considering these undisputable facts, clearly observable by all, it is not possible that anyone can be misled into placing any credence in the West's profession of its being peace loving, in their regularly held so-called peace conferences. That is just a false front, a hoax and a deception.

The Practical Aspect of War

Whatever has been said so far of Western wars has been from the ethical point of view. We have examined the ethical perspective of the causes of war and its objectives.

Regardless of the progress the West has made in worldly affairs, not much progress has been made in cultural affairs. The causes of war today are quite identical to the causes that were considered righteous among the unlettered savages of many centuries ago. Their materials of war have definitely progressed far beyond what the "savage" could have imagined. The excellence of training given to the soldier of today, the beautiful uniforms, their military excellence, and the eye-catching upkeep of their weaponry, would definitely impress all. However, even in this age, the spirit behind the warfare is the same as was in the age of tumult. The "savagery" did not decrease with the increase in means and progress, but continued increasing and just became "greater savagery." Like the savages of the past, these savages of today do not hold any elevated purpose or point of view, nor any high ethical motive, which would render one as ethically superior to the other. The same craving for the increase in land holding, wealth and grandeur and for furtherance of authority, that motivated the unsophisticated, unlearned and savage tribes of 4000 years ago, motivates even today's respectable and righteous nations to wanton bloodshed and killing.

The effects of culture, civilization and ethical well-being is hardly in evidence where war is concerned. If indeed there has been any progress, today for the fulfillment of petty and lowly aims, the force used is a thousand fold more destructive and terrifying. *(The invention of the nuclear bomb and its use in World War II, and later inventions, developments and stocking of more lethal weapons has raised the proportion to millions of folds.)*

Obviously when the cause is devoid of all righteousness and purity, then the methodology adopted in achieving it, no matter how elevated and pure, cannot lend it the degree of sanctity, making it worthy of any reward in the sight of the Lord. However, for the sake of argument we must see the laws the Western Civilization has enacted for the conduct of their warfare and how these compare with the Islamic laws.

The West claims that it has given war a new meaning. It claims that it has changed it from a savage conflict to a respectable struggle for achieving one's contested aims. The claims are made with such an air of superiority and while doing so, such grandeur and nobility are outwardly on display, that an uninformed and believing world is compelled to believe it. However, we wish to put it to an acid test in order to determine for ourselves what the actual truth of the matter is.

The Truth about International Law

The laws that govern the Western dealings and their war and peace have come to be called the "International Law." Scholars of jurisprudence have described these laws in different ways. The most accepted of these is,

> "It is a custom which respectable nations are compelled to follow."

This custom has not been imposed by any sublime authority that all nations would be compelled to follow and no one would be allowed to make changes in it. The fact is, that for the sake of convenience, the West imposed it upon itself and once implemented, it is their privilege that they mold it to suit their purpose and if necessary, cease following it. It will be more correct to say that international law follows their dictates, that they follow the dictates of the international law. The way they follow is for their ease, generally becomes law, and the ways they give up, no longer remain law. Similarly, the set of rules generally agreed upon by the Western nations is the international law. However, it is not necessary that today's law would also be a law tomorrow. Tomorrow, if the West abandons one rule and starts following another, today's law would stand canceled and the new principle and rules would acquire the status of International Law.

For this reason, some Western scholars of note state that calling these customs law is wrong. Austin in his book, "Province of Jurisprudence Determined," states,

> "International law draws its strength from general consensus; therefore it truly cannot be termed as law"

Lord Salisbury states,

> "No court of law can enforce it, therefore terming it as law can be misleading"

In 1871, the supreme court of the U.S. when passing judgment in a case, noted,

> "The Marine Law, like all international laws, is founded on the consensus of all respectable nations. It is implementable only because it has been accepted generally as a code of conduct"

Lord Birkenhead, in his book, "International law" writes,

> "The good health and firmness of International Law is dependent on three things:

a) The considerations of national respect, which are born out of international opinion.

(Although it may die out of the necessity of times)

b) Being ready to go for war, only for the most important causes and having enough restraint to avoid war on account of petty reasons.

c) The realization among nations that international laws are for their own benefit and it is in their own interest that they should individually try to follow them as meticulously as they can"

At a different place Birkenhead writes,

> "In principal, international law has nothing else to

back it up except general consensus of opinion and
the willingness to implement it, voluntarily."

From these quotes, it becomes evident that international law is
just a set of customs followed by a few nations and has neither a
strong foundation nor any legal worth.

The Composition of International Law

International law is composed of several components. These
components vary in value and importance. Some components are
such that they have only ethical influence on the law, while others
influence them in the material way only. Often, the ethical and the
material influences are found in contradiction to each other.

In order to understand the arguments that follow clearly, it is
necessary that we understand the sources from which these laws
have been adapted.

1. The first source of adaptation is the opinions of scholars.
The thoughts of all scholars of international jurisprudence are
available in books. Their contributions are considerable in the
making of international law. However, the only value of their
thoughts and opinions is that they have been referred to in solving
complex international problems, off and on. No law however has
been based on such opinions alone.

Lawrence in his book, "Principles of International Law,"
writes, "On different affairs, their opinions are given much weight,
but in no way are they the final decisions."

Birkenhead writes, "They do not make any law as such, but
only advise us of the factors on which statehood depends."

Justice Gray in one of his judgments, writes, "by quoting such
authors in courts, it is not intended that the court be informed as to
what the law should be, the sole intention is that irrefutable
evidence be put forward, stating what the law in fact is."

Chief justice Cockburn writes in one of his judgments, "the
opinion of the authors cannot author a law, but the general
consensus can make such opinions, law."

From the above quoted opinions of people of high repute, it
becomes clear that the renowned books of international law,
written by even the experts of international jurisprudence, have

very little practical significance.

2. The source is the international agreements. These agreements are of two kinds. The first are the declaratory types and the other, the non-declaratory types. Declaratory agreements are those that have the agreement of all or most of the members of the group and a modus has been set for following them. Examples of declaratory agreements are the Vienna Agreement of 1815, the Paris Agreement of 1854, the conventions of Geneva conferences held in 1854 and 1906, the London declaration of 1871, The Hague pacts of 1899 and 1907, the 1909 London Declaration, and the declarations of the Washington conference, held in 1922.

Staying within the bounds outlined, in such pacts and agreements, is obligatory on all whose representatives have signed them. However, they also have the right to extract themselves from these pacts, after informing the other members of the pact of their intention. It follows that such pacts cannot form the basis of any universal law. According to Lawrence, it cannot be said with any certainty that such pacts are legislative acts. Non-declaratory agreements are understandings not involving the powerful nations of the world, but between two or more smaller states, to further their own dealings or for the achievement of their own objectives. Lawrence says of these agreements:

> "These second type of agreements are not an indication of what international law is, but actually depict what is lacking in international law."

From the juristic point of view, both the types of agreements hold no significance, though some pacts and agreements do depict the principles of law. For example, in The Hague conference, the rights and duties of combatants and non-combatants have been specified. However, these legal principles depend on the co-operation of the states for their implementation. If one of the big powers or several smaller states violate the agreements or pacts, all others feel comfortable in violating them. In the end, nothing is left of the pacts.

3. The third component is the decisions of the international courts, the prize courts (dealing with spoils of war), and declarations made in the major international conferences. These decisions in fact do not make any law, but are the derivatives of the

law already in force, in cognizance of the existing circumstances. Therefore, at the maximum, they can be said to be explanatory or illustrative of the existing International Law. Certain honorable ones have, without doubt, adapted clauses of the existing law in dealing with particular problems of the current nature. For example, Lord Stowel, M Portilius, and Mr. Justice Stroike are included in those of high repute, who have explained and adapted the international law, as explained. However, even their principles and explanations had to bear the stamp of governmental approval, before acceptance.

4. The fourth component is the governmental instructions and code of conduct laid for armed forces of that country to follow. Originally, these instructions were given by a certain country to its soldiers, but later others accepted the principle as well and adopted them in their system. Gradually it acquired the status of an international custom. These instructions in their totality do make up a law, but it is not of international applicability and is only enforced because of the individual nation's appreciation of them. Every nation has the right to change this law in favor of another, if it so desires.

The Unreliability of International Law

The various components that make up international law have been described above. It has been shown that, in isolation, none of these components possess the binding quality of law. If the building of international law has such weak foundations, it follows, that the building itself will be weak. A detailed examination of international law would reveal to us many weaknesses and defects. In this law, every cause has been made dependent on the approval of nations who become subservient to it. The principle or rule that has consensus of the states is proclaimed as international law. The principle they do not approve of or after approving chose to abandon, is no more a law. In this way, this law has sunken to the level where it is but an instrument of the politics of powerful nations.

The promulgation, alteration and the utilization of the international law, according to their own requirements, has been left to the powerful nations and their wise men, who would quite probably be willing to use all means, fair and foul, to further their own cause. Then there is so much scope in it for delaying tactics, so much flexibility for differences of opinion, and so many ways to wiggle out of responsibilities, that member states may for their interest, whenever they like and with impunity, violate the law, yet the law will remain inviolate, as if the permissibility of violating it is incorporated in the law itself.

The fact that the exalted law is still in force is because the powerful nations want it to be so, for the furtherance of their own purpose. If per chance the law is utilized for the exalted purpose it was meant to be, in its full vastness and elevation, it is possible that it would not be allowed to exist anymore.

The Department of War in International Law

In this law, the part relating to wars, in reality has a weaker foundation than the part relating to peace. The Western laws of war are not based on ethical principles. Rather it is based on the fact that the states wish to protect their own citizenry from savagery and unbearable agony. For this reason, they got together and decided that if and when they are at war with each other, they would respect such and such principles.

In the 1907 Hague Conference, for example, an agreement was reached on the treatment of prisoners of war (POWs). By virtue of this agreement, the POWs were granted many privileges. The reason for this consensus among nations was not out of the goodness of their hearts; they wished to treat their very attackers well. Rather, the fact was that every country wished to ensure that when its own soldiers were imprisoned by the enemy, they would not become the objects for the enemy to vent its vengeance.

If today a nation violates the agreement on POWs and starts treating them as they had been treated in the 6th century by Rome and Persia, it is probable that even the most respectable of nations would not waste time in retaliating in kind, notwithstanding any agreement.

The condition is not different regarding laws dealing with aerial bombing, use of hollowed exploding head bullets, use of poisonous gases and respect for military-theater hospitals, the sick or wounded and other such affairs. All laws made and conventions agreed to regarding such matters are motivated by the fact that all nations wish to protect their armed forces and civilian population from undue destruction and death. If there is a contravention of these agreements, it follows that the other belligerent party would not consider itself bound by them either.

The True Perspective of the Conventions of War

The rules, which are termed as the conventions of war, are nothing more than agreements, which remain effective as long as the other party is known to be following them. Whenever a powerful nation or a few of the smaller nations, are known to be violating them, all respectable nations consider themselves exempt from their applicability. Such conventions cannot be termed as "laws." The true "law" can be defined as a set of principles that every individual is bound to adhere to, unconditionally. When one's adherence to a principle is conditional to another's, it is not "law," but an agreement or pact. Agreements or pacts, no matter how sanctified and exalted, can never lay claims to the reverence and respect of genuine "laws," because all agreements are based purely on selfishness and not on ethical excellence.

These thoughts are shared by some of the most eminent European scholars and political thinkers. Sir Thomas Bradley writes at the end of one of his essays:

> "The laws, relating to wars, should not be dependent much on the immediate requirements of war and the spirit and emotions always in attendance in wars, can compel violation of the best of rules, which diplomacy, using its most noble efforts and intelligence promulgated. These rules however, evince the general aversion that respectable nations have towards savage behavior and an attempt to arrest it." (Encyclopedia Britannica, Art, War).

A little before the World War I, Germany's Department of War published a book titled, "Kriegs Brauch im Land Krieg" (Instructions on Land Warfare). It began with these words:

> "Conventions of war are not any set of compelling rules that International Law has given birth to. They are just a mutual agreement on privileges and a

restriction on complete freedom of action, born out of the combination of customs, compromise, piety, and lies. But there is nothing to compel adherence to them, except fear of absolute retaliation." (Kriegs Brauch, page 2).

This fear of retaliation is in fact the basis of all European conventions of war. In the World War (WW I), when the emotions of revenge overcame the "fear of retaliation," some nations disregardful of retaliation, started acting in contravention of the rules and conventions agreed to in Hague and Geneva. The world then witnessed that all nations started considering themselves free of those restrictions. All sins committed by one, became a license for its enemy to commit similar sins against its people. Every law broken by the enemy became permission for the other belligerent to do likewise. All of Europe combined to tear up to tatters the convention Europe itself had agreed to, just seven years earlier. Had these laws been based on ethics, one wonders, if they would have met the same fate.

The Law of 'Imperatives of War'

After human nature has played its part, under the influence of anger, greed, and vengeance, whatsoever little vitality is left in the Conventions of War is sapped by the all-powerful, all-encompassing, and impelling law of "Imperatives of War."

In the battlefield, principles, conventions, and decisions of peace conferences always find themselves in conflict with the immediate requirements of the battle; principles and conventions have always come out the losers. Professor Nippold writes,

> "As compared to the other aspects of International Law, the laws of war contain more contradictions, because conflict easily arises between laws of war and necessities of war. Considering this factor, maintaining laws of war, within the overall structure of International Law, can only result in making the overall structure as unreliable as the laws of war." (Development of International Law after the World War, page 9).

On another occasion, he writes:

> "Under normal circumstances, conduct of war will always be subservient to the imperatives of the war and not to any other consideration. For this condition of self-sufficiency and self-provisioning, whatever rules are made, must take into consideration the limits to which they can be adhered to. If these limits are not considered, the probability is that they will be utterly disregarded. This contention has been fully illustrated in the World War. Therefore, the need is to pay special attention to this fact, when propounding the rules in future." (Nippold, page 112)

The Difference between Truth and Exhibitionism

When the conventions of war were being drawn up at The Hague Conference, European politicians were in a grip of an exhibitionistic culture. Without considering the actual inclination of their people towards war and war-like activities, such rules and conventions were tabled and agreed to that in appearance were very elevated, idealistic, grand, and humane in the extreme. However, the military was not willing to accept them. Marshal B. Burrnstein, the German military representative, had warned early in the conference:

> "The conventions of war that we wish to propound here should consist only of such clauses, following which would be possible under battle conditions too."

None paid heed to his warning. The result was that within four years, when opportunity put these conventions to test, in the campaigns in Tripoli and the Balkans, they were openly disregarded. Within the next one year, the onslaught of the World War (WW I), laid berserk, these conventions.

Seeing the conditions, realization dawned on the scholars and politicians of Europe that it is incorrect to make rules of war based on idealism and exhibitionism. Only after this, did the trend among the scholars change. A German scholar, Max Huber writes,

"In future it should be the imperative of International Law to clear the grounds of all idealistic and quixotic laws and impose bounds that are factually based. It should not happen that under the spell of desire for its own overall progress, international law should feel satisfied with conventions of an un-compliable and unbelievable nature. It should strictly erase all exhibitionism, that diplomacy in the interest of general good opinion, has cast a meaningless spell of progressive internationalism on law."

Professor Nippold had been so impressed by the failure of the conventions of war, that he fully recommended their expulsion from International Law. In fact, he totally disagreed with the fact that laws and agreements have anything to do with war, or that war can be kept within the bounds specified by them. He states,

"International Law has far extended itself in objecting to war. In equating war with laws, it has even had to accept that war is a form of legal institution and in arguing for this cause, it has ignored all ground realities. Those who favor its cause have failed to recognize that law can never be imposed on war nor in any capacity, can law keep it within its bounds. The plain fact is that war and law are a contradiction in terms. In war, no law but the imperatives of the battle in progress are the governing factor. It is also a fact that war is no legal institution, but an exertion for gaining what one desires, through might. It is an employment of brute force to establish one's claims. It is an exercise in self-provisioning and self-sufficiency. That is how war has been defined and International Law must make concessions to this correct perspective. Even if we choose to ignore the definition, it has become quite apparent now that war stands far out of the bounds of any legality. Although several attempts have been made to bring war within bounds, but the actual results remain as divorced from the attempts as ever." (Nippold, page 7)

Another expert on war, Howitz, writes,

> "International Law is so far removed from the law that seeks to put order in relations between belligerents that it is in fact anarchical. It is only an attempt at some mutual declaration." (Nippolod, page 8)

Max Huber is also in agreement with this and says,

> "Even before the World War, realization had started dawning, that war is in fact the relic of the age of savagery. The impressive advances made in establishing conventions and laws governing warfare, are nothing but impressionism and showmanship. They seek to keep us oblivious of the basic political fact that the only choices we have are that we stay peaceably within the bounds of law or be in the state, where lawlessness is rampant and use of force and might is the order of the day." (Nippold, page 8)

On a different occasion, the same author states,

> "Taking war to be a legal institution and dreaming of bringing its proceedings within the bounds of order is a mistake of International Law. It is a throwback on the thoughts of Rome and the middle ages." (Nippold, page 9)

These are the thoughts of some of the leading European experts in International Law. They must have been a little troubled and a little ashamed in accepting that the magnificent mansion of conventions they had constructed so painstakingly, turned out to be as fragile as a bubble. At the same time, they must have been stuck with the fearful possibility that this fragility of the laws of war may become a cause for the loss of faith in the entire set of International laws. For that reason, they had to accept that it was impossible to bring war within any form of law and order. There is contradiction between war and law. The actual laws of war are not those that are propounded in Hague and Geneva, but those that are established in the battlefields, through cannons and guns. This is the truth about the conventions of war, which are considered the respectable laws of the 20th century.

Differences between the Military and the Politicians

The reason for the difference between fact and exhibitionism concerning the laws of war is that there have always been two schools of thought. One school of thought is of the philosophers, scholars of ethics and law, and of the politicians. These, in the interest of exhibitionism and showmanship and petty impressionism, wish to bring war within ethical bounds, turning it into just a respectable contest. The other school is of the soldiers, who consider war an act of self-sufficiency and self-provisioning. Man indulges in it only after all attempts at solving particular problems through legal means have failed.

One school considers attaining the objective the true achievement. The other school wants the achievements to be secondary to staying within bounds of ethics and civilization. One considers breaking the laws, while staying within the bounds of law hypocritical, while the other group is of the conviction that law is a gift of civilization and even if it has to be broken, it should be done in an orderly manner.

The difference is not restricted to opinions only, but extends even to the sphere of activities of both groups. The legal and political group has the upper hand in international conferences and inter-group meetings. It is therefore capable of influencing them into enforcing restrictions on war and entrapping wars in the claws of idealism. However, it is not possible for this group to wield its influence in the turmoil of the battlefield and maintain its hold of idealism there. Military supervision, organization of the departments of war, instructions on conduct of battle, naval and air support, as well as the overall conduct of war, is completely the jurisdiction of the military group.

When in the state of war, the military group renders the entrapments of the idealists torn to tatters, and notwithstanding the dictates of the legalistic group in the world of reality, does all that the laws of Hague and Geneva forbid, but which the "law of Imperatives of War" holds permissible.

Obviously one has to base one's judgment on the actions of a group, not on its professions. Whatever one may profess, we have to see how one acts. In our view, the real laws of war are not what are written on paper, but the laws the Western Civilization follows when at war. For that reason, we do not hold the group of lawmakers dependable, but the military group that has the responsibility and capacity of action. We can judge the inclinations of the Western civilization from the views the military group holds in regards to the laws of warfare, and actually, only these are worthy of any consideration.

The well-known European expert on warfare, Clausewitz, in his book, "Yom Kriege," writes,

> "Rules of war are but self-imposed restrictions, almost imperceptible and hardly worth mentioning, termed as the usages of international law. For the lovers of humanity, it is possible to believe that it is possible to disarm and overpower the enemy, without any large-scale wastage of human lives; that this is the real objective of the science of warfare. However appealing, the thought is conceptually wrong, and the sooner we get rid of the thought, the more beneficial it is for us, for in such a terrible affair as war, if entry is granted to such emotions as kindness and spiritualism, the ills that are given birth to are worse.
>
> In connection with war, allowing such philosophies, as principles and restraint to hinder, is wrong. – War, in fact, is an act of force and self-imposition, which does not accept being subjected to any bounds." (Yom Kriege, Kap)

The German book of war mentioned earlier, while defining the "Imperatives of War," states,

> "A soldier should go through history. He will observe that certain hardships are unavoidable in war and often the dictates of humanity are that these should be utilized without hesitation." (Krieg Brauch, page 3)

In the same book, at another place, the respectable rules set forth in The Hague and other such pacts are described as, "humanitarian and wholesome emotions, which contradict the very nature and objectives of war."

Admiral Abbe, in one of his essays, writes,

> "War is described as an appeal of righteousness
> against a power that disagrees with this
> righteousness. It obviously follows that its objective
> is that the enemy should be hurt in any way that is
> possible. Since the resources and wealth of a nation
> are its main limbs, the use of everything capable of
> disrupting these wealth and resources, should be
> brought to bear." (Revue Des Deux Mondes, 1882,
> page 314)

From these quotations, it is obvious that the ethicists and
politicians, for the purpose of displaying to the world their
humanitarian and pleasing bent, have enacted such rules of war
that the group responsible for their implementation considers quite
meaningless. Adhering to them, despite the necessities of war, is
difficult, if not quite impossible.

Initially the group of jurists did struggle in favor of their beliefs
of humanitarianism and civilization, but during the World War
(WW I), when the military group established its supremacy and act
differently to what they prescribed. They (the Jurists), had to
swallow their pride and give up their contention and had to, per
force, accept the militarist's viewpoint.

We have seen earlier in this chapter how scholars of law, like
Professor Nippold and Max Huber, had accepted the failure of
their earlier concepts. Later, we will see how under pressure of
ground realities, the clauses of law were amended to include the
militarist viewpoint.

The Position in Principle of the Western Rules of War

Where principles are concerned, we have clarified the factual
position of International Law and its section dealing with war. We
have attempted to examine this law, what its value is as a "law",
what in its own view is the standing of the rules of war, to what
extent it has the ability to bring war within the bounds of ethics
and to what extent, it can succeed in bringing order in war

practically as well as perspective. In the foregoing short discussions, we have attempted to throw some light on the questions. Now we will examine, how this so called law has been able to lend order to the disorder of war, how the principles and rules that it lays down for the conduct of war, compare with those laid down by Islam, the difference between its exhibitionist rules and the defacto rules of war, how the intellectual progress it displays compares with Islamic thought, and how in actuality it has served humanity.

The History of the Laws of Warfare

Until the beginning of the 17th century, Europe was quite unaware of any rules of warfare. Both as a principle and practically, war was considered outside the realm of rules, restrictions, and the bounds of ethics. The belligerents had the unrestricted freedom to cause damage to each other as they desired, or had the ability to. From the conditions depicted in history of the wars of those times, it appears that when two nations were at war, they did not hesitate in committing the cruelest of deeds or in indulging in the most terrible of acts. Not only in practice, but even in principle and belief, there was no difference between combatants and non-combatants. The same was true even in the views of ethical jurists like Grotious, who states,

> "In principle it is permitted to kill all those found in enemy territory. Women and children are no exceptions. Foreigners, who do not leave the territory within a reasonable time, are also not exempt from the rule." (Lawrence, principles of International law, page 330)

This unlimited right was used with such freedom during the "30 year war," between 1618 and 1648, that the whole of Europe was shaken. An awakening arose among the thinkers that some kind of bounds should be placed on wars. This desire was first felt by Grotious of Holland. He was prompted into writing the famous book of history, titled, "De Jure Bellaic Pacis," which is considered the foundation of International Law. It was published in 1625 and was included in the curriculum of the Hiedleburg University. The book caused a general stir among the intellectuals of the time and was responsible for much progress in the field.

About half a century after Grotious, his student Puffendorf, published his book, "De jure Natura set Gentium." This book was followed by a series of such books on the ethics of war in Europe. This flood of writings finally resulted in the enactment of the International Law, in the 18th century. In 1780, the famous English jurist, Jeremy Benthem had christened it the International Law. It is still known to the world by the same name.

Practically, the effects of this progressive thought pattern were seen in Westphalia, when influential Europeans, after the "30 Year War" accepted Grotious's recommendations, that,

> "As a concession (not as a law), women, children, the aged, clergymen, agriculturists, traders and P.O.Ws, should be accorded safety from death and destruction." (Bernard, Paper on Growth of the laws of War, Oxford 1856, page 100-104)

This was the first ray of light, seen in the dark and dismal skies of Europe, in 1647 years after the death of Christ. After this, the savagery in warfare, as witnessed in the "30 Year War," began to pale. However, where the ethical acceptance and reforms of war were concerned, they took 200 more years to come into effect. Europe made no ethical progress in this respect until then. In mid-1857, during the "Indian awar of Independence" (also termed as the "Indian Mutiny" of 1857), the English forces committed such brutalities that human conscience shudders at their remembrance. As far as we know, until the mid-19th century there was no International Law in existence, which the nations had accepted, and was under implementation among the Western Armed Forces.

Among the Western nations, America was the first to take a step in the direction. In 1863, a manual of instructions was published for the armed forces. The aim of this manual was to consolidate the code of conduct for the armed forces during wars. After this, Russia, Germany, France, and England also started giving similar instructions to their armed forces. Gradually, all of Europe accepted following the same way, that a savage and unlettered nation under the guidance of its illiterate Prophet and his unlettered companions had implemented some 1600 years earlier in Arabia.

For the first time in 1864, an international conference was held in Geneva, Switzerland, to decide on an agreement regarding the war wounded, the sick, and the people of the medical profession. Later the rules were amplified and added to in the second Geneva conference, in 1868. However, Europe had to be satisfied with piecemeal provisioning of these laws. It remained deprived of a complete set of laws, until the convening of the 3rd Geneva Conference, in 1906 (Birchen head, International Law, page 207).

Until 1868, Europe had no rules or conventions governing the use of weapons or ammunition. This year an international conference of the military, in St. Petersburg recommended to the leaders of the Western group of nations, that the use of exploding projectiles, weighing more than 400 grams and exploding head bullets, that explode inside a man's body as well as exploding gases, be disallowed in military conflicts. On its recommendation, the group with the exception of the U.S. and Spain signed a convention, to the effect on 29th November 1899. After this, on the recommendation of Czar Alexander II, a conference was held in Brussels in 1864. In this conference, for the first time, rules of warfare were decided. However, no state was willing to ratify them. In fact, Germany and England outrightly refused to accept them. These rules remained unimplemented and unaccepted for the next 25 years. Then in 1899, on the endeavors of Czar Nicholas II, the first Hague conference was held. 26 nations took part. In the conference, rules of combat were discussed and the following conventions were agreed upon:

a) Attempts at peaceful settlement of international conflicts.

b) The Rules and conventions of war.

c) The approval that the applicability of Geneva Convention of 1864, regarding sick and wounded in land battles, be extended to cover sea battles as well.

d) Extension in the period of applicability of St. Petersburg Convention regarding explosive head ammunition. (They were initially approved for a period of five years.)

e) Extension in the period of applicability of the St. Petersburg Convention on explosive head bullets.

f) Extension in period of applicability regarding the St. Petersburg Convention on use of poisonous gases.

This conference was unable to complete its mission and for eight years, further enactment of rules was suspended for the period. In 1907, on the endeavors of President Roosevelt of the US and Czar Nicholas II of Russia, The Hague conference was reconvened. This conference gave to Europe, for the first time, a comprehensive set of rules and conventions regarding war. Apart from regularizing the 1899 Conventions on War, with some additions, others conventions were enacted. These were:

a) Limitation on the use of force for reclaiming loans.

b) The necessity of declaration of war before commencing hostilities.

c) The rights and duties of neutral states in a war.

d) The status of commercial shipping in sea-warfare.

e) Rules regarding conversion of commercial ships for naval use.

f) Rules regarding sea mines that explode on contact.

g) Bombardment by ships during war

h) Rules regarding arrest of ships.

i) The formation of the Department of Spoils of sea warfare.

j) Rights and duties of neutrals during sea-wars.

Although this conference was successful in compiling a very wide-ranging set of rules and conventions, it cannot be said that these were in anyway complete and all encompassing. Soon after this conference, the need arose to address the use of submarines, airplanes and for stiffening and further elaborating the rules, on the use of poisonous gases. This need was later overcome in the Washington Conference in 1922. At this present time *(referring to the time of original writing)* it cannot be said for certain, how many more conferences would be required to address other unforeseen contingencies and for those that will arise in future international conflicts.

From this brief description of history, it becomes obvious that not more than 60 years have elapsed since the West became aware of the respectable rules of warfare. In other words, if we leave aside the earlier period and consider just the period since the enactment of the rules and conventions, it can be said that, until 60 years ago, the West was ignorant of the ethics of war. As compared, it is clear for all to see, that such rules have been in existence in Islam for some thirteen and a half centuries and as far as principles are concerned, there has never been a need for any conference, agreement, or convention, to cancel, alter, or add to these rules. Despite this, the rules are not too different from the ones the West adopted in 1907. Yet there remain certain of these rules, the West has not managed to reach so far.

The Legal Standing of the League Hague Conference

It may be obvious from the above that in The Hague Conference of 1907 overrode and re-wrote all previous agreements, on the consensus of member states. Therefore, when one wishes to comment on the Western rules and conventions of war, commenting on the ratified rules of 1907, should suffice. However, before proceeding with the comments, one needs to ascertain the legal standing of the conference, the real value of the agreements and whether they can be rightfully considered laws at all. For this purpose, we would have to consult the conventions of The Hague Conference themselves and put our trust in the comments of the Western experts in law on the conference.

Before judging the legal position of these conventions, we have to first determine the extent to which the signatory states are bound to their adherence. It has been clarified in the conventions itself, that governments cannot be forced to follow them meticulously under all circumstances. Their only obligation is that the governments would ensure that these conventions are given due weightage in their individual rules of war.

In elaboration, the first clause of the 4th Hague Convention, states,

> "Signatories of this convention will pass such
> instructions to their armed forces that corroborate
> the rules and conventions regarding land and sea
> warfare, stated herein."

The second question that needs elaboration is the extent of applicability of these conventions. The Hague Conventions themselves clarify their position in this respect. It states that these rules are applicable to conflicts involving the signatories only. If one signatory is in conflict with a non-signatory state, or if in a conflict, one of the belligerents, has as its ally, a non-signatory, these rules and conventions become invalid. Clause 2 of The Hague Convention states,

> "These rules will be applicable, only to those conflicts, in which both parties to the conflict are signatories to the convention. If one of the parties is a non-signatory, these conventions will be inapplicable."

Such a clause has been kept as the last clause of each of the agreements. This conveys to us that all these noble rules and conventions have not been accepted as ethically compulsory law, but are only agreements between some nations. The basics of these agreements being that each agree to treat other with humanity, only on the condition that the other reciprocates in kind.

The third question is to the extent to which these conventions can ensure adherence of the signatory states, to the bounds they lay down. The Hague Conventions specify that no state is bound to adhere to these, always. They may, whenever they so desire, free themselves of its obligations after informing the Netherlands Government. The Netherlands Government has the obligation that as soon as such notice is received, it will inform the other signatories of it. The withdrawal from the agreement will come into effect one year after such notice has been received by the Netherlands Government. The implications of this clause are clear, but for further elaboration, we will copy Mr. James Brown Scott's treatise on the subject, put forth in his, "Collection of Agreements of Hague." Mr. Scott was the Director of the Department of International Law at Carnegie University and was considered to be an authority on law in America. He writes,

> "Hague Conference is often termed as the parliament of humans. However, this is not a correct description. It is not a parliament in the true sense of the term. It affects only those nations who participated in it. This was a one-time affair, as its name suggests, not a sitting parliament. Its contentions are just recommendations of the participating states, so that each state in accordance

with its laws, adopt them. ------- The signatures of the state representatives on any agreement in The Hague Conference do not hold the states legally obliged to follow the conventions set forth. However, since the representatives are officially appointed by the states, it does impose on them a moral responsibility, that the declarations and pacts are passed on to the relevant sections of the government and after getting their approval, they may be granted the authority of the state laws. The conventions will become obligatory after the formal ratification is received back at The Hague."

Professor Morgan in his book, "War, its Conduct and Legal Results", writes,

"It is absolutely clear that the applicability of The Hague Conventions and their vitality are doubtful and suspect. However, the conventions that all signatories have ratified can almost be considered as general rules of law and according to these, the signatory's war activity can be judged."

From these explanations, it is obvious that the conventions of war propounded at Hague, from their legal standpoint, bear no comparison to the Islamic rules of war. Adherence to the Islamic rules is absolutely mandatory for all Muslims. To stay as Muslims, it requires not to violate their bounds. It is possible that a Muslim abandons his religion and frees himself of the obligation of following its rules. It is not possible however, that one while remaining a Muslim, would be exempt from at least holding the belief of the sanctity of their bounds or be allowed to alter them on the plea of the requirements of the time or for his own benefit or abandoning them, adopting others and calling them Islamic.

Unlike the Western rules, the Islamic rules are not man-made, but have the authority of the Most Sublime and have been sent to the Muslims only to be adhered to. The Muslim has only two options open to him. One is that, if he accepts the authority of Allah, he has to accept the sanctity of the rules too. The other is that, he does not accept the sanctity of the rules, meaning that he does not accept authority of the Almighty. In this event, he is out of the pale of Islam. There is no third option for him.

On the contrary, the Western rules are made by the Westerners themselves. They therefore have the privilege to adhere to them as long as they wish to and to abandon them whenever they so desire and start following other rules. According to the law, whenever they want to abandon their rules, first, the rules will stand expunged and only then, new laws would be adopted. On the contrary, no matter if, a Muslim nation revolting against Islam expounds a thousand rules, none of them can become an Islamic Rule. The Islamic rules and laws will remain only those that Allah and His Prophet (SAW) have prescribed.

One other aspect in which the Islamic laws are superior to the Western rules is that they are not conventions and rules, but "laws." While adhering to the Western rules and conventions is conditional to the opposite member also adhering to them, Islamic laws of war are not conventions or agreements that following them would be based on reciprocity; they are defacto laws and following them is not an option or a matter of choice. They simply have to be followed.

Actually, when the Islamic laws were made, it was not possible that any agreement or deals could have been made with the non-Muslim powers. The fact is that the enemies of Islam, at that time, always fought Muslims with phenomenal savagery. The knowledge that Islam forbade the Muslims from following the savage ways had emboldened the enemies further. It follows that the Muslim "laws" have an ascendancy over others, that none can deny.

The Rules and Conventions of War

Leaving aside the principles of warfare, let us now examine the rules and conventions of war and their intended, practical usage in actual conflict. In this connection, we will try to examine the rulings of The Hague on the different aspects of war and the extent to which the West considers them practical and practicable.

Declaration of War

The foremost problem of war is how hostilities are to commence. Initially, it used to be general practice that before commencement of hostilities, messengers, or envoys gave the information to the enemies. Even at that time, jurists placed much importance on the declaration of war. Some even held the opinion that it was not right even to launch an attack before formal declaration of it. Later the opinion changed and declaration began to be considered unnecessary. (Lawrence, page 299). At this time, it became common practice for nations to start hostilities without notice. History tells us that between 1700 A.D. and 1872 A.D., 120 conflicts took place with only ten of them being commenced after formal declaration. (Birkenhead, page 191). Some of these wars were commenced even before formal severance of diplomatic ties. For example, in 1816, before breaking of ties, America arrested all those English warships, that were in its ports and without notice attacked Canada. Similarly, in 1854, England attacked the Russian Black Sea fleet and made it flee towards Svestopol, although their ambassadors were still at their places of duty. (Maurice, Hostilities before Declaration of War, page 44-48)

Towards the end of the 19th century, Europe reverted to the old practice and wars began to be commenced after formal declaration. Hence, the 1870, war between Germany and France, the 1877 war between Turkey and Russia, the 1879 war between America and Spain and the Boer war, were all fought after formal declaration. Again, in the beginning of the 20th century, the war between Russia and Japan started without declaration, when Japan attacked Russia without warning.

Until the beginning of the 20th century, there was no laid down rule for the commencement of wars. Sometimes, some nations would declare war before starting it, at other times the same nations or other nations would not. In 1907, at The Hague conference, it was decided for the first time that a methodology should be adopted for the commencement of wars. An agreement was therefore reached to this effect. It reads:

> "Clause 1: The conference affirms that there will be no war among the members, without prior and formal warning, the warning may be in the form of a formal declaration of war in which the causes for the war are enumerated or in the form of an ultimatum, which contains a formal declaration of war.

Clause 2: When the state of war has been entered
into, the neutral states be informed without delay.
Until the time a formal receipt of this information is
received (which should always be by telegraph), the
rules regarding neutral states will not be applicable.
However, the neutral state should not wait for this
formal notice, if they have become aware of the fact
that war has in fact commenced." (Hague
Conventions 1907) (111)

These formal conventions came into force in the West, only
about 20 years prior to the World War II. (However, it is a fact that
they were not actually followed. Hence, in World War II,
whichever side attacked the other, the attack commenced without
any formal declaration of war). This was just an agreement
between the participants of the convention only. In Islam, however,
such a rule has been in force for the last thirteen and a half
centuries (Referring to the time up to the writing of the original
book). The rule states:

"Do not commence hostilities with the nation, with
which you have a pact or treaty, unless it has been
warned that 'now, because of such and such act of
yours, our treaty stands cancelled. We are now your
enemies'."

The requirement of the above declaration is not conditional to
there being any sort of agreement with the enemy that neither side
would attack the other without warning.

(For explanation, please see chapter 5 of this book, under
heading, "Declaration of War")

Combatants and Non-Combatants

After hostilities have begun between two nations, the question
presents itself as to how citizens of enemy nations are to be treated.
Until the 17th century, Europe was unaware of the discrimination
between "belligerents" and "combatants." In its view, all
belligerency was a form of combat. Therefore, killing everyone
and confiscating or destroying their property and assets was a
permissible act, regardless of the fact that the victim was a woman,
child, or the aged, or belonged to the non-combatant community.

The 17th and 18th centuries gave birth to a school of writers of International Law that tried to establish the difference between the combatant and the non-combatant class of citizens. They failed however, to establish a consensus on the bases for the division of the society, which could be adhered to during wars. In the 19th century, the problem was solved, by dividing the community into groups. The groups that took part in activities connected with war were termed as Combatants and the rest of the hostile nation's citizenry were non-combatants, but this was not as simple as it looked, since activities of one usually overlapped the activities of the other, directly or indirectly. It was later decided that only the soldiery of the conflicting nation's citizenry would be combatants. However, this gave birth to other complications. Dr. Loveller states, "To deny citizens the right to defend his own country cannot be justified in any event."

The situation gives rise to the question of the status of those citizens who, out of patriotism, rise with arms and start warlike activities in an undisciplined manner as irregular forces. Should these be given the status of combatants and given the privileges that regular soldiers of the army are given or should they be included in the non-combatants and treated as common thugs, terrorists and pirates? The law in answer stated that the non-combatants who take part in warlike activities will be given the privileges of neither the combatants nor non-combatants. Meaning, that if he is taken prisoner and suspected of taking active part in the war, he is liable to be sentenced to death, if he is wounded, he may not be given the required medical aid and generally in accordance with the code of conduct reserved for regular soldiers. This clause of the law created extraordinary difficulties for those who were involved in independence movements or out of patriotism decided to contribute to their country's active war effort, without becoming a part of the regular armed forces.

In 1870, when France started recruiting civilians for an irregular army (Franc Tireurs) and Germany, its opponent in war, refused to concede to them the privileges due for the regular soldiers, only then did the full impact of the anomaly of the law dawn on the international community. In 1874, in the Brussels Conference, it was discussed in great detail and the rules for distinction between combatants and non-combatants were made.

According to these, only those would be considered combatants:

a) Who wore markings on their person, discernible from afar.

b) Who carried their weapons openly?

c) Who abided by the conventions of war during conflicts?

These bases of distinction were further ratified in The Hague Conferences of 1899 and 1907. In addition, The Hague conventions elaborated that:

> "If the citizens of some unconquered areas, upon the arrival of the enemy, rose and organized armed resistance, they would be given the privileges of combatants, on the condition that their resistance was declared and they abided by the conventions of war. In wars, the resistance can be comprised of both the combatants and non-combatants and in the event that either of them are taken prisoner by the enemy, they would be entitled to the rights and privileges reserved for prisoners of war."

By virtue of this ruling, one question was addressed while the other remained unanswered. It was not the independent states alone, which felt the need for armed resistance, but even the people of semi-independent and occupied areas who needed to take up arms to get some of their usurped rights. It is the right of every nation to fight for its freedom and independence and if for gaining the same and from forces of occupation, they have indulged in armed struggles, they cannot be termed guilty of any crime, by any means. The question is, if a nation is trying to cast off its chains of slavery, can the entire nation be treated as guilty and unrighteous? Should they be declared terrorists and robbers and punished to death, after being taken prisoners?

These questions were not addressed by The Hague and the general inclination of the West seems to be that such nations are neither deserving of the treatment reserved for members of the regular armed forces nor for non-combatant civilians. It is their lot that they should continue to be targets of guns and canons and should be victims of mass murders and that men should be hunted like animals and murdered. The brutalities of England in the Northwestern frontiers of India, of Spain in Reef and of France in

Syria, are all proofs of the fact that Western law does not recognize the rights of people fighting for their freedom.

The discrimination between combatants and non-combatants on the basis that those who do not take up arms during conflicts be declared non-combatants is also not totally correct. The West had been for a long time proud of the fact that they had limited antagonism in wars to the regular armed forces and the non-military organizations have been delivered from effects of war. However, today they have accepted the fact that their basis of discrimination has been wrong on principle and are practically impossible. In this connection, it is better than giving our own opinion, that we copy the opinions of the Western intellectuals and writers, who on the basis of their experiences of the World War (WW I) have realized how meaningless were the bases of differentiation, which they had so far prided on[1].

Professor Nippold writes,

> "Recent experiences have proven that in the present age of trade and commerce, when hundreds and thousands of people are spread in foreign countries and roam about freely, it is impossible that wars be declared only the realms of the armed forces of the warring countries. These experiences have left no doubt, that not only in the countries in conflict, but in the entire neutral world, no person can avoid being effected by any major war. The affairs of personalities and people of all walks of life have become so entangled that no one can hope to remain safe from the effects of such wars. For this reason, limiting these effects or preventing them from spreading, is bound to be futile. Therefore terming

---

[1] The only reason for the stress of the Western politicians on keeping the non-combatants safe from the effects of wars is that they are highly concerned of their own trade and commerce and wish to keep them continued in all conditions. For the reason, they had tried their utmost in The Hague conference of 1907, to establish the principle that during wars, "states should make all efforts to maintain all mutual trade and industrial relations" but the fact is, that this desire of theirs can neither be nor has ever been realized, in any war waged so far. The World War has proved that even Europeans themselves are not capable of giving their desires any practical countenance.

war as only the affair of the concerned states and all war efforts, the concern of the armed forces personal only, is meaningless. The fact is that in this era, war is the concern of entire nations in conflict, who pursue it to the fullest of their physical and economic capacities."

Later in the same book Professor Nippold states,

"The aims of wars are to vanquish the enemy. From this perspective, undoubtedly, all commercial activity not beneficial to the war effort must cease but one must not lose sight of the fact that the citizenry of the state does not comprise of the armed forces personal only, but of normal civilian citizens as well. Moltke has differed with the concept that the object of war is to weaken the enemy militarily only. He states: 'The nation at war has to exploit all its resources, including its economy, railroads, and even its moral influence. If war is indeed breaking the enemy's will to resist, it becomes not only a necessity but a permissible act that the nation uses its military resources not only against the enemy's armed forces, but against its economic resources too. Now, since the economy of a state is dependent on its manpower, it is necessary that the person himself and his property be targeted, to the extent necessary and beneficial for the achievement of the war aims.'" (Nippold, page 121)

Professor Nippold further adds,

"A nation should also protect its war resources in the economic war, as it does in military confrontations. In both cases, the resources that are liable to cause insufferable damage to the enemy must be brought to bear. For this reason, the economic war, must not be limited to action against the enemy trade but must seek to cause insufferable damage to its economic life as well. In the pursuance of this objective, causing damage to private enemy citizens (non-combatants) is unavoidable." (Nippold, page 122)

Professor Neimeyer states in his book, "Principles of Sea Warfare,"

"In sea warfare, it is necessary that life should be made very difficult for the enemy, even if it means using the most savage means."

Burkhardt writes,

"Holding the mistaken concept that war is but a struggle between armed forces only, which has no concern with the peaceful relations between the non-military people, is living in a fool's paradise. Neither can the armed forces hold themselves in isolation from the people, nor can the state isolate itself from society. Despite all such grand concepts, war is in fact fought between entire nations, since people from every strata of the society participate in it. Although the weapons in use of each are different, there is a deep relation between them in the overall pursuit of war by a state. There can never be any criteria for differentiation between the state and the citizens of that state. As war is a struggle between armies, it is also a struggle between nations."

On a different occasion, the same author writes,

"Sinking the enemy's trade to the bottom of the sea is far more humane than drowning human beings. In fact, a deeper analysis of the situation reveals that efforts to overcome the enemy's military are quite futile, when its economic condition is such that it actually has no real requirement for maintaining an army. For this reason, it is unavoidable that nations at war should seek to destroy the enemy's economy. The military capability of defense is so entwined in its economic capacity that separating the two is quite impossible. The economic well-being of a state is as necessary to the continuation of war, as is the life and well-being of its soldier. Hence, no nation can avoid offensive action against the enemy's economic resources. Subjecting the enemy to death by starvation, though extremely cruel, is not a prohibitive act of war." (Nippold, page 122)

On another occasion he states,

"Limiting acts of war to soldiers only, is a concept of dreamers. They wish that properties of civilians would remain safe that even among states at war, trade relations would continue unaffected and that war should be fought between opposing armed forces only, not between the total citizenry of opposing states. However, today no practical citizen is enamored of this concept. Not only because this concept is far removed from ground realities but also because it is a totally artificial and unnatural one. Apart from this, in areas affected by war, mutual trade has to be adversely effected to some extent. It is not wise to expect that a nation would stake the lives of thousands of its young men in wars against the enemy and at the same time allow the same enemy freedom to continue its trade in peace; that on one hand the nation would expend heavily in terms of men and precious resources in trying to bombard the enemy's harbors and anchorages, and on the other hand allows its imports and exports to continue unabated."

(Nippold, page 113)

Another writer Elzbacher writes,

"Since the enemy's military might is deep-rooted in its manpower, it follows that this resource needs to be crushed, using all available means. In consequence, the war that started as a conflict with the enemy's armed forces, soon acquires the enormity of war with its entire nation. When it assumes such immense proportions, International Law is forced to follow the conflict, not vice versa. It was the principle of yesteryears that wars were the realm of the armed forces and that the civilians would not become its targets. In the event that such becomes unavoidable, the extent and bounds of these actions should be pre-determined and agreed upon. The principle has been negated and put away as not practical and not practicable. It has not only been violated in individual cases, but has been discarded for good. In future wars this principle will not be taken into consideration, it is dead and will remain dead." (Nippold, page 133-134)

From these lengthy quotations, it may have become obvious that declaring the non-military strata of the society as non-combatants, keeping them safe from war effects and providing whatever relief that is reserved for the non-combatants, is not only practically impossible, but in principle, also very incorrect. Without doubt, specially targeting the civilian population and destroying their economic life are the objectives of war, but equally undoubtedly, they are also transgressions and equally transgress is the concept that the entire lot of normal civilian citizens of the state be declared non-combatants, though they provide aid to the enemy's war-effort, no lesser than soldiers do.

The line drawn between combatants and non-combatants by Western Jurisprudence is highly unjustified. On the one hand, it declares many groups as non-combatants and deprives them of the rights of the combatants, when they, in fact, deserve these rights. On the other hand, many are undeservedly given the rights and privileges of the non-combatants.

The Islamic criteria for differentiation between the two groups are different from the Western criteria. It is a path of moderation between the two philosophies of the Western intellectuals. It does not discriminate between the combatants and non-combatants, on the basis of their profession rather on the ability of the person to participate in wars.

Those persons of a nation at war, who actually take part in it and who possess the capability to take part in it, by virtue of their ability, nature, and inclination, are all declared as combatants. Those who by nature and inclination do not possess the ability to participate in wars are declared non-combatants. Examples of such are women, children, the aged, the sick, the disabled, the mystics etc. Anyone who approaches the Muslims, with the intention of fighting them, whether he be a part of the regular armed forces or not, he will be considered as a combatant and be entitled to all the privileges of combatants. The condition being, that he has not proven himself to be insincere and inclined to break his word.

The able and the able-bodied will have to undergo the rigors of the group of combatants, whether or not they actually take part in the war, out of the necessities of war. They will however be given asylum and safe conduct by the Muslims, if they seek them. If a person wishes to conduct peaceful commercial activity between the war zone and the Islamic state, he may be permitted to continue doing so, as a concession, provided he avoids participating in war-like activities and persists in honest trade, in ways not harmful to the Muslim war-efforts. He will be only conditionally, and as a concession, is granted the privileges of a non-combatant, though by status he will remain a combatant.

This is the only natural criterion for differentiation between combatants and non-combatants. It is also the only concept of moderation between the two afore-mentioned groups of extremists i.e. those that favor the unlimited concept of warfare and those who seek to maintain it within the bounds of law. This also is the only concept that possesses the possibility for a dialogue and a consensus between the groups with extreme views.

The Rights and Duties of Combatants

Among the warring nations, the two major groups, the combatants and the non-combatants are governed by two separate sets of laws; therefore, we will discuss each separately. We will begin by addressing the combatants first.

The need for internationally recognized rights and privileges for combatants had been felt much earlier and the concept had been a subject of discussions and parleys. In fact, some of the states had practically started according some of these rights to the combatants on their own; the concept was first given full recognition in the 19th century. Until 1829, the states were not ready to accept any of the comprehensive rulings on the subject. They considered it their right to deal with enemy combatants as they saw fit and their discretion to discriminate between the combatants and non-combatants.

The president of the U.S. had openly declared that:

> "A nation should decide for itself when it should grant those involved in wars, the rights of such, whether the belligerents are those fighting for independence from a power they consider cruel and oppressive or they are members of independent nations involved in war with each other." (Parliamentary Papers, North America (1872, No. 29, page 17).

It is highly improper that each nation should sit in judgment over its own actions. The only possible result following such concepts would be that the rights of warring nations would be fully violated and destroyed. This fact started dawning on the West and gradually it started accepting the principle that nations should, on the basis of reciprocity, grant some rights and privileges to the combatants, should they be involved in wars and that this decision cannot be left to the discretion of the belligerents themselves. The principal was agreed upon first in St. Petersburg. The declaration stated,

> "There should be just one objective of nations at war and that should be to weaken the enemy. For the purpose of pursuance of this objective, it is enough that efforts are made to disable as much of its manpower as is possible. Using such weapons that would unnecessarily increase the pain and discomfort of the already disabled or causing their death will be termed as transgression."

This was the first rule to be made in regards to the rights of combatants, in 1828. Later, in the Brussels conference, some rights and duties were also considered in this connection, but until the end of the 19th century, no law was made that the entire West accepted. At the end of the 19th century, in the first Hague Conference, some conventions were agreed on. It stated the following principle,

> "For nations at war, the right to inflict damage on the enemy is not unlimited." (Hague, Article 22)

Along with this, rights and duties of combatants were also decided. These are stated in article 23 of The Hague regulations, it reads,

Apart from prohibitions in specific agreements, the following acts are also strictly prohibited:

a) The use of poison or poisonous materials.

b) Wounding or killing the enemy through deception.

c) Killing an enemy who lays down his weapons or being weaponless, gives himself up to the enemy.

d) Making an announcement that asylum will not be granted to anyone.

e) Using such weapons or materials that cause extreme damage.

f) Using the flag of truce or the enemy's national flag or military insignia or uniform or the signs specified in Geneva, for specific purposes, in an impermissible manner.

g) Destroying enemy property, unless necessary for the pursuance of war.

From this declaration, we have come to know when and how the rights and duties of combatants were decided on. Now we will discuss some specific rights and duties one at a time.

Adherence to Conventions of War

The greatest stress that governments lay on is the adherence that combatants must adhere to the military regulations and on keeping in consideration the conventions of war. Almost every nation refuses to give rights of belligerency to wars that are unregulated and unbounded by any law or convention. The German law prescribes for those involved in such wars, a minimum punishment of ten years imprisonment, and a maximum of death. In the American law, section 4, clause 13, declares such people thieves and looters and prescribes for them the same punishment as prescribed for common criminals found guilty of such crimes.

Such people have not only been denied the rights of belligerency, but have even been stripped of basic human rights.

Hence, in the 1899 Hague Conference, Britain tried very hard that against "savage" nations, the use of Dum Dum bullets should be made permissible.

The British representative, Lord Lance Downe in his speech stated that in 1895, during the Chitral operations, ordinary bullets were unable to stem the tide of multitude of savage enemies attacking them. Dum Dum bullets, he stated, do not harm them much (Birkenhead, page 220).

These are the same Dum Dum bullets, the mere mention of which makes the common European shiver with the pangs of conscience. However, to quell the savage uncivilized people, involved in an unregulated and indiscipline war, the same were considered necessary and permissible by one of the most civilized nations of the West! It even refused to sign the declaration that made the use of such bullets illegal and later agreed to it, only when the declaration was made applicable to just the signatory states.

Asylum

The first and basic right of the combatants is that when they seek asylum from the enemy, they be granted the same. Until the 17th century, the concept of granting asylum to those of the enemy who sought it was not recognized. During the English wars, the parliament had absolutely refused to grant amnesty to Irish fighters. Until the end of the 18th century, the warring nations considered it their own right to either refuse or grant asylum to the enemy personnel. In 1794, the French convention had announced that no asylum would be given to English soldiers. In the 19th century, at last, the right of combatant personnel to asylum, when they sought it, was recognized. It was agreed that when the enemy soldiers sought refuge, hostile action against them would cease and they would thence be governed by the conventions regarding prisoners of wars.

These conventions regarding asylum seekers were only applicable to those who sought it in battle[1]. There was however, no

---

[1] The present law differentiates between "Battlefield" and "Battle" conditions, but we have used the term to denote both these conditions. Till today *(referring to the time of original writing)*, there is no specific law on the

rule laid down for those who were already in enemy custody or inside enemy territories, at the commencement of hostilities. There is still no such rule *(referring to the time of the original writing)*. Until the 18th century, the practice was that such people were arrested and kept imprisoned as common criminals, until the end of hostilities.

In 1756, England, for the first time granted concession to the French, who happened to be in English territories, when the Anglo-French hostilities commenced. They were given asylum, on the condition that they solemnly affirm that they would remain non-partisan to the French cause during the war. Similarly, in 1794, there was an agreement between the English and the American union, that both would grant asylum to the other's men, if it was sought. In 1803 however, when the truce of Amiens was broken, Napoleon refused to grant amnesty to the English, who were in French territory. In 1894, another way of dealing with asylum seekers was formulated and all three ways were simultaneously in vogue. In 1854, during the Crimean war, in 1897, between Turkey and Greece and in 1898, during the war between the American Union and Spain, the warring nations granted asylum to each other's enemy personal. But in the 1870 war between Germany and France, all Germans were expelled from French territories and in the Boer war of 1899, the two South African republics, expelled all Brits from their territories.

Until the 20th century, no clear rule could be made concerning asylum. In the 1904 Russo-Japanese War and in the Turko-Italian War of 1911, (for some time), the warring nations followed the convention of granting asylum to enemy personal. In the World War of 1914, however, England, France, and Italy allowed a certain time limit in which the personal belonging to the enemy nation could leave the country. After the time limit expired, those found still in their territories were arrested and put in isolation camps. Germany and Austria, on the other hand, evacuated enemy nationals, of military service age from their territories and put the others in isolation camps. Portugal too, followed suit. The U.S. and

subject. The trend of nations generally is to order evacuation of those, not of military service age and holding others in isolation camps. (Birkenhead, page 197-198)

Japan, however, granted asylum to all.

As opposed to this, a specific law regarding asylum to those who sought it, has been in existence in Islam for the past thirteen and a half centuries *(referring to the time of the original writing)*. It specifies that asylum would be granted to all those of the nation at war with the Islamic state who sought it. Those granted asylum, if they wanted to stay in the Islamic territories, they would be allowed to do so, in peace. In case they wished to return to their home country, they would be allowed safe passage out of the Islamic territories. Apart from this, wide-ranging concessions and rights have been granted by Islam to the enemy nationals and combatants, the wisdom of which is yet beyond the comprehension of International law makers.

(For details, please see chapter 5 of this book, under sub-heading, "Truce and Asylum")

Prisoners of War

The European laws regarding prisoners of war (POWs) are quite comprehensive. The reason for this, according to Professor Morgan, is that they are advantageous to all. Every state is desirous of the welfare of its own officers and soldiers; therefore, it treats the enemy POWs well, in the expectation of reciprocity.

However, these civilized laws are a product of the recent past. Until the 17th century, the common practice was of enslavement of POWs. Grotious raised his voice against this custom and advised the Christian nations that instead of enslaving and selling each other, they should accept ransom for the prisoners and release them. However, for a century, his advice remained unheeded. Only towards the beginning of the 18th century did the practice of ransoming prisoners became common and was adhered to till the end of the century. The pact of 1870 between England and France declared one pound as the ransom money for each soldier and 60 pounds or sixty soldiers as ransom for an admiral.

In 1799, Napoleon, the greatest general of civilized Europe, accepted the surrender of 4000 Turkish soldiers, on the condition that their lives would be spared. Later, however, he had all of them killed, just because he could not arrange feeding of all of them, nor could he arrange their transportation to Egypt. (Allison, History of

Europe, 111, XXV).

About a century later, another similar atrocity was committed. In as late as 1896, (only about 30 years before the writing of this book), the Cuban-Spanish Captain General Weyler declared the prisoners of war as traitors and had them slaughtered. He also imprisoned thousands of unarmed civilians and kept them in such horrible conditions that all of them died of hunger and thirst.

In any event, it is a fact that formal rules regarding POWs were made in 1874, in the Brussels conference. They were further elaborated in The Hague Conference of 1899 and only in the 2nd Hague Conference of 1907 were they finalized and approved as an international law. The conventions regarding POWs are given at agreement number 4 of the conventions. They read:

Clause No. 4: POWs will not be the property of the nations at war nor of the ones who takes them captive. They are to be treated with humanity. Except for horses, weapons and military papers, whatever is in the possession of the prisoners will remain their personal property.

Clause No. 5: Prisoners of war should normally be kept in isolation, but if necessary in the interest of safety, they may be kept in confinement.

Clause No. 6: The government, whose prisoners they are, may keep their status in consideration, may use them for labor. They will be paid for their labor, equal to which is paid to the local laborers of the imprisoning nation, for similar work. Officers however, will be exempted, on the condition that they are not made to labor beyond their capacities.

Clause No. 7: The nation that holds them prisoner will be responsible for their upkeep. Except under special conditions, the POWs will be given accommodation of the same level as provided for its own citizens employed in like rank or status.

Clause No. 8: Prisoners of war will be subject to the laws in force in the state that they are held. In the event of indiscipline, they would be liable to rigors that would disable the repetition of such conduct. Prisoners attempting to escape, if captured before they reach to their own forces will be liable to disciplinary action. If they are captured after they have reached their own forces, on a different occasion, they will not be held liable to the punishment for their acts during their previous imprisonment.

Clause No. 9: Every prisoner is required to give his correct name, rank, and number when required by the imprisoning authorities. If he resists doing this or gives wrong information, he is liable to have his concessions reduced.

Clause No. 10: POWs may be relapsed on their undertaking that they will not participate in the ongoing war. If any prisoner procures his freedom in this manner, it will be his duty to abide by his undertaking. His government will not force him to do otherwise.

Clause No. 11: No prisoner will be compelled to accept freedom on conditions given in clause No.10 nor would any government be bound to give prisoners freedom at his request on those conditions.

Clause No. 12: If a prisoner accepts freedom conditionally, as stated in Clause No.10 and latter is involved in hostilities against the state granting him conditional freedom, if captured, will be liable to be proceeded against legally.

Clause No. 13: Those non-combatants who informally join the armed forces, e.g. newspaper reporters etc. may be captured and held as POWs.

Clause No. 14: During war, every state will establish an information cell, which would keep available all information on POWs and would periodically keep the native governments of the POWs informed of their condition.

Clause No. 15: Committees formed in accordance with a nation's laws, for the aid of POWs will be entitled to all assistance from the conflicting nation; their agents would be permitted to visit POWs in their camps, in the fulfillment of their duties, on the condition that they abide by the instructions of the local government.

Clause No. 16: The information cell would be exempt from postal duty. Letters, money orders, valuable articles, and parcels sent to and from POWs will be exempt from postage charges. There would be no excise or railway duty levied on them.

Clause No. 17: Officers who become POWs, will be given the same pay, that capturing governments give to their employees of like rank or status. This amount will be paid back by the native government of the POWs in the end.

Clause No. 18: POWs will have the freedom to follow the rites of their own religion. Within the bounds of rules and regulations imposed, in the interest of discipline, they will be allowed to visit their places of worship.

Clause No. 19: Wills of POWs who die in prison, should be executed as wills of own soldiers are. In the event of their deaths, their burial rites would be carried out with the same honor and respect, entitled to own soldiers of equal rank.

Clause No. 20: After peace has been established, exchange of POWs will be affected as soon as possible.

(These conventions are only for the uniformed personal taken as POWs. It is still doubtful whether they would apply to civilian prisoners of war as well).

If these rules are stripped of minor administrative details and only their principles are examined, we will find that they do not represent any change from the Islamic rules.

(For a comparative study, please see chapter 5 of this book, under the title "The Civilized Rules of War," subtitle "Prisoners of War")

The Western Law seeks to provide its POWs the same facilities it expects for soldiers of equal status held POWs by the enemy. In contrast, the way of the Prophet Muhammad (SAW) and his companions was that they provided for their POWs had better keep than they could afford for themselves. In those times, Muslim prisoners could hardly expect enough food and clothing from the enemies and were sure to be inflicted with near unbearable physical hardships.

Western nations charge a large part of the expenses of maintaining the POWs from the home government of the POWs, although the Muslims expended on the prisoners held with them, even when there was little hope of an agreement with the enemies for re-imbursement.

The West agrees to free its POWs on the conditions of reciprocity, i.e. when exchange of POWs is agreed upon. Islam however, has often released POWs without exchange and in fact considers the act of freeing its prisoners an act of piety.

There are some concessions granted to the POWs that are in access of what Islam grants. However, before forming an opinion from this, one has to take into consideration, the fact that all concessions are granted on the condition that the other party in conflict would reciprocate them. In contrast, Islam has granted the concessions, without there being any pact or agreement with the hostile nation and without any hope of reciprocity from them.

After the first battle of Islam, the POWs that were held by the Muslims were treated with a very high degree of kindness and consideration, when scores of Muslim prisoners of war were made to suffer such unbearable tortures as being made to lie down bare-bodied on the oven-hot desert sands, the daylong. It was not possible that any pact or agreement could be established with the enemies at that time, the concessions granted by the Muslims, therefore, were the best that could be accorded. However, today, when a possibility for such agreements exists, Islam would not hesitate one moment in increasing the concessions it already gives, on a reciprocal basis. Islam permits any pact or agreement that grants any concessions on such bases.

The Sick, the Wounded and the Dead

Until the 17th century, there were no special arrangements for the sick and the battle-wounded. Around the 17th century, the first military hospital was set up and a system for recruiting doctors and surgeons to provide wounded soldiers with first aid was initiated. However, the concept of providing medical, surgical aid and hospital care to captive enemy soldiers was still far from a practical reality in Europe. The sick and the wounded were often just put to death or in grievous conditions, left to die on the battlefield. Hospitals and their medical staff were taken as prisoners with no special treatment or concessions allowed to them. Until the mid-19th century, there was a controversy among nations, whether doctors and nurses were to be treated as combatants or non-combatants. (Lawrence, page 348).

During the American wars, it was considered rightful by the

international community, that if the services of doctors and nurses were required during wars, they could be captured and forcefully put to work. In short, Europe was very unaware of any law regarding treatment of the sick and the wounded. The need for such a law was first realized when Henry Dunant of Switzerland, a lover of humanity, raised his voice against the savagery of the civilized nations.

In 1859, there was a conflict between the combined forces of France and Sardinia on one side and Austria on the other. Solferino was the site for a military action in this conflict. Apart from the other savage acts that were committed here, the treatment of the battle-wounded was of the degree of cruelty that left the European humanists shaken. Henry Dunant published a book on the subject in 1862, which compelled the European community to seek ending such savagery.

In October 1863, the Swiss government held an unofficial congress in Geneva, to study what all could be done for the safety of the sick and the war-wounded in future conflicts. On the recommendations of this conference, a second official congress was arranged in Geneva, the next year. After much discussion, an agreement was reached, which was signed by all the attending nations except the U.S., on 22 August 1864.

In the agreement, military hospital and their staff were declared neutral. The hospitals were granted immunity from military attacks and the staff from being taken prisoners of war. Impeding the work of caring for the sick and wounded was declared impermissible. Further, it was recommended that the facilities should conspicuously display the marking of a red cross on a white background. This should be discernible from afar, and no military action should be taken against buildings or vehicles that carried such markings. All parties involved in wars were required to have the wounded treated, without distinction, whether he was friend or foe. After his recovery, he was to be either released on the condition that he would refrain from taking further part in the ongoing conflict or he was to be taken as a POW.

This agreement had many flaws. The major ones being, that there was no recommendation to ensure that it was followed and not following it was not declared a punishable crime. In order to find a solution to this problem, another conference was held in Geneva, in 1868. In this conference, a supplementary agreement was reached. It had 14 clauses, five of which dealt with land warfare and nine with sea-war.

Among other clauses, the agreement recommended to the nations that conscious and purposeful violations of agreements regarding medical aid to the battle wounded and sick combatants should be declared a criminal and punishable offence. However, the member states did not agree to abide by such an agreement. The 2nd Geneva conference was therefore a failure.

The 1874 Brussels conference further pursued the problem, but with no better results than the earlier Geneva conference. Twenty-five years later, The Hague Conference of 1899, further expressed the need for a comprehensive set of rules on the subject of the sick and the battle-wounded. On its request, the Swiss government was requested to call a conference on the subject for the third time, in Geneva. Calls were sent out to invite the nations to the conference in 1901, 1903 and 1904, but received no encouraging response. At last, in the summer of 1906, the conference was finally held. On the 2nd of July 1906, an agreement was reached, which until today *(referring to the time of the original writing)* is the unwritten law for the West.

In The Hague Conference of 1907, another agreement was reached which sought to make valid all clauses of the earlier agreement, for sea-wars too. (Hague Convention, No. 10). However, 17 of the 44 attending members did not agree with its implementation. These included Britain, Bulgaria, Italy, Greece, and Serbia. For that reason, this agreement as well, was practically useless. The result was that in the World War (1914-1917), hospital ships were sunk with impunity (Oppenhiem, International Law, vol. V11, page 205).

The basics of all the agreements are that it was inhuman to inflict further injury on a combatant who had become disabled from further participation in the conflict by virtue of his sickness or wounds. The regulations made later at Hague and Geneva, have their basis on this very same principle. These conventions consist of practical details, which, with the changing circumstances, need to be revised. Only the concept needs to be kept in sight. This concept may be new for the Western World, but Islam recognized its sanctity some thirteen centuries ago *(referring to the time of the original writing)* and it was a part of the Islamic rules of war. The basic difference between the two, however is that the present Western conventions came into force when all the nations had agreed to following them, whereas the Islamic rules regarding the sick and the wounded were already under implementation, when there was no agreement with the non-Muslims, nor was there any hope for such an agreement. At that time, the Muslim war-wounded were put to death without the slightest hesitation. Islam instructed its followers under these circumstances, to treat all the wounded and disabled with kindness and compassion, regardless of the enemy's attitude and behavior.

The Use of Hazardous Materials in War

Since the time science has started making available more and more dangerous materials for use in weapons, Europe has started feeling more and more the necessity to limit their use in war. Seeing the ravages of poisonous gases, explosive bullets, incendiary weapons and other such war-materials that have the most disastrous effect on the human body, the Europeans started feeling the pangs of conscience. The group of intellectuals, with an ethical and humanitarian bent of mind, began making efforts to influence public opinion against the use of such inhuman materials in war and pressurizing politicians to prohibit or at least restrict their use. The military group however, seeing the immense help such weapons and materials provided in obtaining their war objectives, were unwilling to give them up. A struggle between the two groups has been in evidence for a long while now.

The politicians tried to solve this problem by keeping the ethical intellectuals satisfied through resounding speeches, highly charged with emotions and love of humanity, in international forums and prepare declarations to the effect. At the same time, they not only encouraged the militarist groups for use of such horrid weapons of destruction, but also permit and foster the invention of newer and more destructive materials. Some of the materials that apparently are savage and inhuman, the West has for a long time abandoned their use. Weapons dipped in poison have probably been out of use since the 18th century. The practice of filling canons with spikes, glass pieces, steel blades, and firing them towards the enemy has been banned for a century. However, many other materials, outwardly not so savage, but in actuality, much more brutal and hazardous are still *(author is referring to the time of the original writing, however, the situation is not much different even today)* in use and the more civilized of nations, are the more insistent on their use. In the conferences of 1868 and 1907, all attending nations accepted the fact that such actions against the enemy, which without aiding the achievement of war objectives, served only to increase the affliction of the enemy, to an unbearable degree, should be avoided. In pursuance of this principle, use of the following materials was forbidden:

1) Explosive or incendiary projectiles weighing less than 14 ounces.

2) Explosive bullets that explode and scatter inside the human body.

3) Poisonous and suffocating gases.

4) Bombardment with explosive bombs, by balloons or airplanes.

Of these, the fourth prohibition, no other accepted, except two nations and it died at birth. The third prohibition was initially objected to by the U.S. and Britain, but later violated by all. In the World War *(I)*, all nations flagrantly disregarded this prohibition. After the World War *(I)*, in the Washington conference, reaffirmation of the prohibition was attempted and a new draft was prepared to the effect, but till today *(author is referring to the time of the original writing, however, the situation is not much different even today)*, no nation has shown any inclination for accepting it.

Regarding the second prohibition, the definition of explosive bullets is not fully agreed on, by all. When the definition of a certain thing is not agreed on, its prohibition would mean different things to different people. In short, the prohibition would be meaningless. Talking of the first prohibition, it is only a paper exercise, with no connection to ground realities. After the freedom and impunity with which toxic and incendiary materials were used in the World War *(WW I)*, none would like to be reminded of the agreements of Hague and St. Petersburg, for fear of becoming a laughing stock.

(The use of the atom bomb, the ultimate in destructive weaponry, in World War II, emphasizes the value the West places on its agreements and the like.)

In this connection, Islam has not laid down any detailed instructions. The prohibition of a particular type of weaponry or war material is dependent on mutual agreement. If one party to a conflict uses a certain type of advanced weapon or material in a war, while the second party self-imposes a ban on such, it is putting itself at a disadvantage and is likely making arrangements for its own defeat. Islam has permitted Muslims the use of all currently available weapons and methodologies of war. At the same time, it does not forbid entering into agreements that forbid the use of particular weapons or methods in any particular conflict or series of conflicts, provided these are on a mutual or reciprocal basis.

Spies

No law grants sanctuary to spies and like other laws, the Western Law does not grant any status to the institution either. Clause 30 of The Hague Conventions, grants the concession that no government can punish anyone for the crime of espionage, without holding his formal trial. Another concession granted vide Clause 31 of the conventions, is that if after his mission, a spy is able to reach his force and is subsequently arrested while on a different mission, he is immune from prosecution and punishment for his earlier crime of espionage. Apart from these two concessions, The Hague conventions permit a government to award convicted spies what punishment they prefer.

The Islamic injunctions regarding spies are no different. Like others, it proclaim one as a spy, who infiltrates the enemy lines and then covertly seeks to learn its secrets or the prevailing conditions. The ones who try overtly to achieve the same ends are not termed as spies. The Western conventions however grant them more privileges than the Islamic rules do. However, the Western concessions however have resulted from mutual agreements.

All nations are involved in espionage activities and no nation would like its highly patriotic and dedicated men, who routinely risk their lives in the national cause, be left in the lurch. Therefore, they have reached the agreement, which concedes each other's spies some concessions. If such concessions are granted to spies of the Islamic state, it would have no objection to giving the same concessions to spies of other states as well.

Stratagem of War

Tactical deception is permissible in war. Frederick the Great states,

> "In wars, a person has to, at times, wear the skin of a lion and at other times the cunning of a fox is more successful than the brute strength of a lion."

There is however, a vast difference between stratagem and deceit. Sitting hidden in camouflage, leading the enemy into a trap and catching it unaware; deceiving it by feeding it wrong information; making the enemy falsely believe that one is retreating or advancing, thus inducing an error in its judgment; making the enemy believe one is retreating and then suddenly turning and attacking it and all such military maneuvers are included in the definition of stratagem. The enemy is duty-bound to be prepared for such tactics. In contrast, luring the enemy closer by showing signs indicating danger on one side and then attacking it, showing the white flag of truce and then launching an offensive against the enemy, donning the flag reserved for indicating hospitals over resting grounds of soldiers and over magazines, lining up women and children in front, in plain visibility, then cannonading the enemy from behind them and other such acts should fall in the category of the impermissible.

Apart from those mentioned above, there are still some acts, which cannot be out-rightly categorized as deceit or permissible tactics of war (stratagem). For example, wrongful uses of the national flag of the enemy or his uniforms have been held permissible by the scholars of International Law, but the militarist group holds it impermissible. The German law declares it an impermissible way of war and the American law describes it as such a deceit, that indulgence in it deprives the person or group of any concessions from the enemy. (The United States instructions of War, Clause 65)

In fact, no law can be made which covers all the circumstances when subterfuge and ruses of war may be employed. The use of these would depend on the level of military ethics of a nation. Every nation can decide for itself, which actions are in conformity with its notions of chivalry. The Hague conventions have not sought to clarify what ruses of war should clearly mean. They have satisfied themselves in stating that use of means to procure information of the enemy is permissible. (The conventions of Hague, Clause 24)

On this question, Islam is in full agreement with the West. It also declares the uses of stratagem (ruses of war), permissible and has left it for the scholars of the time to decide which act falls in the description of "ruses of war" and which in the jurisdiction of deceit.

Vengeance

The convention and laws of Hague and the earlier and later conventions have not gone into any great detail concerning acts of vengeance. No one from the West is able to inform us, whether taking revenge for a wrong or an atrocity committed against one, is permissible and if in the event it is, what is the extent of this permissibility? Perhaps, The Hague conference has on purpose left the answer ambiguous, since the militarist group, in this regards, wishes to keep all options in its own hands.

Some scholars have personally tried to lay down some bounds in this regard. Worth mentioning are the recommendations of Professor Holland through his suggested four-clause law. He states:

Clause 1: The crime, for which vengeance is sought, should be fully investigated first.

Clause 2: It should be undertaken only when no other way exists, by which, the damage done can be compensated, and there is no way in which the real culprit can be punished.

Clause 3: Only then, except under special circumstances, acts of vengeance will be undertaken and then only with the express permission of the supreme commander.

Clause 4: Vengeance should not in any event exceed in severity the original transgression. (Holland, "LAWS of War on Land").

However, these are just the personal opinions of some scholars of International Law, which the militarist group has never accepted anyway. The experience of the World War (I), however, tells us that the international inclination in the West is that any transgression by any one party to the conflict makes equal retribution permissible and legal, in the view of the other party/parties. For example, treating POWs with cruelty, attacking hospital ships, sinking commercial ships, subjecting undefended townships to bombardment, using poisonous gases and explosive bullets are not permitted by law, but all powers involved in the World War (I), freely indulged in these crimes, on the plea that their opponents had done so first.

In this connection, the injunctions of Islam are clear. It states:

> "If ye punish, then punish with the like of that wherewith ye were afflicted. But if ye endure patiently, verily it is better for the patient."
>
> (Al Nahal: 26).

> "And one who attacketh you, attack him in like manner as he attacked you. Observe your duty to Allah and know that Allah is with those who ward off evil" (Al Baqarah: 194)

> "Fight in the way of Allah against those who fight against you, but begin not hostilities. Lo! Allah loveth not aggressors" (Al Baqarah: 190)

In the above quoted verses from the Holy Qur'an, the acts of toleration and forgiveness have been declared to a very high degree of piety. If however, taking revenge is necessary, it is also permissible, but the degree of its permissibility is such that it should not exceed the damage or harm caused by the enemy. Even with this permissibility, it is necessary that piety be kept in view and all acts of vengeance are kept strictly within the bounds of what is permissible in Islam. By "keeping piety in view and keeping within the bounds-----", it is meant that the desire for vengeance and anger should not influence one to commit acts that have by themselves been declared impermissible. That is to say, if enemy soldiers enter Muslim territories and disgrace the women there or amputate the limbs of the dead, with the intent of dishonoring them, in revenge, committing disgraceful acts against enemy women and tearing off the limbs of their dead is held as impermissible as when such acts are originally committed.

To state another example, if during a war, the enemy chooses to murder Muslim women and children, the aged, the sick and the wounded, it is impermissible that Muslims indulge in similar acts in reprisal. As opposed to this, if the enemy chooses to use poisonous gases or explosive bombs against the Muslims, it is permissible that Muslims use weapons of similar nature and potency against the enemy.

Rights and Duties of Non-Combatants

After discussing the combatants at length, let us now turn to the non-combatants and dealings of combatants with the enemy non-combatants.

As stated earlier, the realization that enemy non-combatants were also entitled to certain rights and privileges and that they had certain duties, dawned on Europe very late in history. The concept took shape in the 18th century, but until the 19th century, there was no law that restricted action against them. The freedom and impunity with which general slaughter was resorted to by the French in Algeria, by the British in India, during the so called mutiny and in the Peninsular War, by the allied forces, reminds one of the darkest age of savagery.

Though since the time of Grotious, the scholars had recognized the need and were agitating for the rights of non-combatants in wars, but it was not until in 1874 during the war, that the work practically begun. The 1899 Hague Conference gave it a formal shape and only in The Hague Conference of 1907 was the work completed. Thus, we can say that the age of the law regarding non-combatants is no more than 45 years. In formulating the modern laws, the West has been quite generous to the non-combatants. However, along with this, the modern principles and ways of warfare preclude the possibility of distinguishing between them and the combatants. It is no wrong statement that the modern wars, as concerns the non-combatants, are far more cruel, savage, and dangerous than the wars of the era of savagery. The Western intellectuals recognize this fact as well. In this connection Birkenhead in his book, "International Law," writes,

"Unfortunately, the modern principle of distinguishing between the armed forces and the civilian population is on the verge of extinction."

(Birkenhead, page 205).

A big reason for this situation is the fragility of the foundation on which these laws of distinction and discrimination have been laid on. Garner in his book, "International Law and the World War," states,

"When we examine the happenings of the World War of 1914 - 1917, in the light of the clauses of Hague Conventions of 1907, it becomes necessary that we keep sight of the fact that all participants in the war were not signatories of the conventions agreed to, therein. It therefore becomes doubtful whether the conventions were applicable to all." (International Law and the World War, page 16-18).

However, the real reasons for the inability to distinguish between the two in wars were a little different. Professor Oppenheim writes in his scholarly book, "International Law," according to his research, the inclination of erasing the line between combatants and non-combatants, is based on four factors. These are:

- Conscription or the system of sending the able-bodied men to the fronts and leaving behind the unsound of bodies and the womenfolk to look after the war industry and to carry out other duties.

- Use of the airplane with its offensive not only limited against forts and other permanent military structures, but also against communication facilities and lines of communication. (Later during World War II, more than this, one of the objectives of aerial attacks was the destruction of the enemy's industry and economy. In the pursuance of this objective, large-scale bombardment of industrial areas and harbors were carried out and a large number of cities were flattened.)

- Freeing of democracies from the opinion and advice of the people, who in fact installed them.

- The stress that was being placed on burdening the enemy's economies to an unbearable extent and on the destruction of the means of national well-being (Lawrence, page 345).

The main reason for the non-preservation of the rights of non-combatants is not only the frailty of foundations of the conventions of war in the West, but the materials and methodology adopted in modern warfare, make this distinction quite impossible.

Nevertheless, despite these defects in the principle, we must examine the rights and duties the West has ordained for the non-combatants.

The Basic Duties of Non-Combatants

The basic duty of the non-combatants that every hostile nation insists on is that the non-combatants should take no part in wars. When hostilities begin, they should decide whether they want to take active part in the proceedings or to keep themselves away from it. In case, they decide on participating, they should join the regular armed forces. However, if they decide to keep away, they should continue with their normal business in a peaceful manner. If they were unable to decide and take part in the war on an irregular basis, they would deprive themselves of the rights of both, the combatants and the non-combatants. Meaning that they would not be treated with kindness, they would not be granted asylum and if they were captured, they would not be granted the rights of the POWs. (Lawrence page 345).

Islam is in agreement with the Western Law, that if the non-combatant takes active part in war he would not be entitled to the rights and privileges of the non-combatants. It however differs with the West, that they should be denied the rights of the combatants as well. Islam grants right and privileges of combatants to all those who take active part in wars, unless they are involved in acts of subterfuge and deceit. For example, if a woman adds poison clandestinely to the drinking water of the Muslims, she would definitely be put to death. Similarly, if a person, when in the asylum of the Muslims, seeks to harm them, he would definitely not be shown any mercy.

Some tribesmen of Ukhail and Uraina were granted asylum by

the Prophet (SAW), they murdered the camel herders with whom they were staying and made away with the camels in their charge. The Prophet (SAW) deprived them of the rights of both the combatants and non-combatants, declared them robbers, and gave them exemplary punishment.

One other duty of the non-combatants is that when an enemy force is passing through their area, if it seeks guidance as to routes, it should be provided the required guidance. If it seeks transportation, it should be provided the same and its activities pertaining to war, should not be hindered. If the non-combatants act, otherwise their enemy has the right to punish them severely. (Lawrence, page 345)

The Islamic and the Western laws are in consonance in this matter.

Honoring the Rights of the Non-Combatants

The basic right of the non-combatants is that they should be kept safe from death and destruction during wars. Despite this, it is impossible that it can be practiced on every occasion. For example, if an area is being cannonaded, it would be quite impossible that women and children in the area can be kept safe. In another example, if a train, on which non-combatants are also traveling, comes under enemy attack, it is quite possible that some of them would also be killed. However, such unintentional killing does not constitute the violation of their basic right. The law just requires that the aggressing force does not on purpose target the non-combatants and till the extent possible, they be kept safe. (Lawrence, page 345)

In this connection as well, the Islamic and Western laws are in consonance. Islamic law declares non-permissible an attack only on non-combatant civilians, on purpose. However, if some harm comes to them unintentionally, in the normal pursuance of war, the perpetrator is not to be held blameworthy.

At the time of the siege of Taif, when catapults were being used to bombard a fortress with heavy rocks in order to destroy its fortifications, there was a reservation among the Muslims that the non-combatant inhabitants of the city would also come to harm. The Prophet (SAW) ordered the continuation of the bombardment, since the prime purpose of the bombardment was the breaking up of the fortifications, not targeting those within the walls.

Bombardment of Unprotected and Undefended Buildings

After accepting the principle of security of the non-combatants, the question arises, as to how such security can be ensured during wars. On this question, there is a difference of opinion between the militarist and the jurist groups. The jurist's viewpoint however is being gradually overtaken and overpowered by the militarists.

If the combat is hand to hand or between the fighting armies alone, it is possible to keep the non-combatants safe and uninvolved. However, where the warring parties bombard each other when still miles apart and especially when the objective of one of the parties is the conquest of a city, there is not even the remotest chance of keeping the non-combatants safe from the effects of the bombardment and generally of the war. The group comprised of jurists holds that there should be some bounds placed on the bombardment of dwellings. The militarist group however insists that such bombardments should be unhindered by any consideration, except those of the war in progress. Until mid-19th century, it was a custom that the inhabitants of a dwelling which were to come under attack, were given time to vacate the area. In the 1870 war, Germany followed the custom at one or two places, but later the military groups mutually decided that giving such warnings was against the very aims of war. Hence, when the Germans started bombing Paris, no warning was given, and the Parisians were not allowed time to leave the city. They in fact declared that the presence of the non-combatants in the city was the very requirement for the bombardment, so that the opposing French would after suffering from death, hunger and disease, hand over the city to the Germans.

Soon afterwards, the well-known essay of an American admiral Ubbey was published. It was immensely well received by the militarist group. The essay stressed on the total destruction of enemy's economic resources. It stated,

> "In future wars, we must expect that the armed naval fleets would turn their attention to the towns

close to the shores. Whether or not they are fortified and whether or not they possess the means of defense, the fleet would burn and destroy them and would relentlessly hold them ransom."

In 1888, England held a large-scale naval exercise. One of the aims of the exercise was to practice the launching of attacks on shore-based townships and holding them ransom. Professor Holland severely objected to this and wrote several articles on the subject in the "London Times". These raised again the question of permissibility of subjecting the civil population to bombardment. The jurists and the admiralty were deeply opposed to each other on the subject. The Admiralty held that it was a totally permissible and rightful act, while the jurists held the opposite view. In 1889, a special committee, set up for studying the proposition, submitted a report, with complete consensus of all its members, endorsing the admiralty's concept.

The first Hague Conference of 1899 re-addressed the question. At that time, the jurists held sway over the conference and the militarists also held their peace, in deference to the political compulsions of their governments. For that, reason bombardments during land wars were placed under bounds. In 1907, these bounds were further extended to sea-warfare. The convention declared:

> "Bombardment of undefended cities habitations, dwellings and buildings and launching attacks against them by any other means, is prohibited." (The Hague conventions Clause 25).

> "The commander of an aggressing force is required to warn the authorities of the area, which is to be bombarded, to use all means for its defense, unless a surprise attack is necessary." (Clause 26)

> "During bombardment or when storming fortifications, every effort is to be made to spare the buildings that may be reserved for religious, educational or charitable services. Further, all possible measures are to be taken that historical monuments, hospitals and other places, where the sick and the wounded have been housed are kept safe and out of harm's way." (Clause 27).

As stated, these bounds were extended to sea-warfare as well. The 1907 Hague Convention number 9 lays down the following bounds on naval bombardment:

Clause 1: Bombardment from the sea of undefended cities, harbors, villages, habitations and buildings is prohibited. The presence of deployed, submarine contact mines around a harbor is not reason enough for the bombardment of the harbor. (France, Britain, Japan, and Germany objected to the last part of the clause.)

Clause 2: Military workshops, military or naval departments, armories, stores of military equipment, such workshops and engines that can be helpful to the enemy's land forces or fleet and ships anchored in the enemy's harbors are not included in the places and facilities against which naval bombardment is prohibited. The naval commander, after giving warning of the impending bombing or attack, can proceed with their destruction-- if the enemy chooses not to destroy them of their own accord. In this eventuality, the commander will not be held responsible for any unintentional damage.

If the imperatives of war dictate an immediate attack, efforts should be made to uphold the sanctity of the undefended parts of the city. The commander should however, try his best to cause as little damage to the city, as possible.

Clause 3: If in spite of the formal demand of the area naval commander, the required logistics and replenishment is not provided to him by the local authorities, he may after giving them fair opportunity, bombard any undefended harbor, city, village, dwelling or building.

Clause 4: Causing damage by bombardment of undefended and unprotected areas for the reason of non-payment of ransom is not permitted.

Clause 5: In case the naval bombardment of a city is undertaken, the commander of the invading force must ensure that as far as possible, no damage to buildings of religious, educational, charitable, historical significance is avoided. Special effort is to be made to avoid damage to historical monuments, hospitals, and places where the sick have been housed, on condition that such buildings are not being used for aiding the enemy's war-effort.

Clause 6: When a naval force bombards a city, it must ensure that no damage is done, as far as possible, to buildings of religious significance and those reserved for educational and charitable purposes, special effort is to be made to avoid such damage to historical monuments, hospitals, and places where the sick and the wounded are housed. The condition being, that these buildings and areas are not being used to aid the enemy's war-effort. Such buildings and facilities should have on prominent display, special markings specified for the purpose. These markings are big rectangular shaped, with a diagonal, that divides the rectangle into two triangles, the upper triangle being black in color, while the lower triangle, white.

Clause 7: If the military situation permits, the commander of the invading force, before commencing bombardment, should make all efforts to warn the area authorities of his intent.

These bounds are very defective in nature. The first of the defects is that the term "undefended areas," has not been defined properly. It just cannot be determined from the conventions, which qualities qualify an area for being termed as a "defended" area, and the absence of which qualities, makes them fall in the classification of "undefended."

The second defect is that the requirement of warning the targeted dwellings, cities etc., before commencing their bombardment has been left totally to the discretion of the commander of the invading force. This to the extent that he may give the warning only if he so desires.

The third defect is that, where the conventions accept the sanctity of buildings of religious and educational significance and of hospitals, instructing the aggressor to ensure their safety as far as possible, they also exempt them from this blanket of security, if suspected of housing activities in aid of the enemy's war effort. That means that the commander of the aggressing force has the option to bombard any area or facility, on the pretext that he suspected them of being involved in activities afore-mentioned.

The biggest defect of the conventions however is that the aggressing commander has been granted the right to bombard the dwellings and the areas that fail to provide it the required and demanded logistic and equipment support. This single clause has rendered the agreement meaningless. It is a simple matter for the aggressor to demand such logistic and equipment support that would be impossible for the already beleaguered area to provide. Then as a result of this non-fulfillment of the demands, he could proceed with the bombardment. It is mentioned in Clause 9 of the convention that the demands should be within the means of the area. The problem, then is, who would decide on the capability or incapability question. If in the opinion of the aggressor, the demanded substances and quantities are within the means of the area, while the local authorities hold that it is not, what the court would come to decide which of the two sides is correct?

Despite these defects, the fact of the matter is that the militarists openly refused to accept these conventions. In their opinion, giving warnings to the enemy that bombardment is about to commence and giving the residents time to clear out of the area, is indulging in unnecessary wastage of valuable time (Kriegsbrauch, page 19).

Demanding logistics support, fulfilling which would be within the means of the enemy areas, though conceptually very attractive, is unrealistic and impossible to ensure adherence to (Kriegsbrauch, page 62).

More than all of this, granting the non-combatants the concession before the bombardment, is not only unnecessary, but is in fact, a controversy in terms. Making the non-combatants the targets of such bombardment is the very object of this exercise. The militarists say,

> "At the time of the bombardment, the presence of women, children, and other non-combatants within the target area is a requirement from the perspective of war, because only in this way the besieging forces can put fear in the hearts of the besieged, compelling them to lay down their arms." (Kriegsbrauch, page 21).

These thoughts have not only been expressed by word of mouth and through the pen, but practically as well. The bounds of The Hague convention have been grossly violated. After The Hague Conference of 1907, the first war was between Italy and Turkey. In this war, the bombing of Beirut was commenced without any warning. A large part of the unprotected population was destroyed. The next war was between the allied nations of the Balkans and Turkey, in which the non-combatants of Macedonia and Thrace were openly slaughtered. Investigations revealed that in western Thrace alone, about 240, 000 Muslim non-combatants were put to the sword. (Bombay Chronicle, 31st July 1922, Introductory note by Mr. Pikthal)

Later in the 1914 World War, between the highly civilized nations of the West, all bounds were violated, as though they never existed. Birkenhead, in his book, "International Law," writes,

> "The distinction that had been created between the defended and undefended habitations, prior to the World War, was no more now, there was a difference in the description of the defended and the undefended and since the end of the war, no attempt has been made to differentiate between the two."
>
> (Birkenhead, page 226).

The factor most responsible for erasing the bounds demarcated by The Hague Convention was the use of the airplane as a war-machine. The airplane is not really the weapon of war, in the sense that it does not directly participate in the attainment of the aims of war. The real aims of the war are breaking the strength and will of the enemy to continue the war and capturing as much of the enemies area as possible. The airplane cannot on its own achieve these objectives. The only thing it can do is that it can rain bombs from the sky over populations, without distinction and destroying all, including women, children, the sick and the wounded. It destroys cities and districts, with its bombs and harasses the enemy nations to the extent that it (the enemy) loses all interest in the further pursuance of the war. In other words, its main utility is in breaking the will of the enemy.

Prior to the war, jurists held the conviction that this form of warfare was impermissible and sinful but when it became a norm in the World War, the Jurists themselves experienced a change in attitude and started accepting it as inevitable. Hence, Elthez Bacher writes,

> "Many acts of war are permissible only on the premise that their object is to destroy the bases on which the enemy's will and ability to wage war

rests (the bombardment of undefended shore based cities is one of this type of permissible acts). Because, by virtue of such acts, the enemy's economic life is disrupted and a special fear takes birth in the enemy populace. ----------- On the basis of this same argument, there should also be no restrictions on bombardment from the air.

In regards to such attacks, creating distinctions of defended and protected areas, is fruitless. The object of bombing an area, in most cases, is not its conquest, but only causing disruption in the enemy's economic life and to harass it, in an attempt to break its will for further resistance. This objective can only be achieved through those bombs that are cast over the undefended areas."

(Nippold, page 124).

After the World War of 1914, the necessity was felt to restrict aerial bombing through enactment of some rules and bounds. The public opinion in Europe and in the United States stressed on the need for such bounds. The 1922 Washington Conference formed a committee in which France, Britain, Italy, Holland, and the U.S. were represented. In 1923, it gave some recommendations, which briefly stated:

a) Bombardment by airplanes was only permissible if their targets were military areas. These consist of cantonments, defense industry, military stores, military departments, and their staff, the industrial areas, where weapons and other means of waging wars are being manufactured, routes, and means of transportation for war.

b) Bombardment of such military areas should be avoided which may be located in areas where it would be difficult to cause damage to them, without also causing damage to the civilian population.

c) Such habitations and buildings, which are within the war, zone, in which there is reason to believe that the enemy forces had gathered, is fair target for aerial bombing.

However, outside the war zones, bombing of populated

areas is prohibited. Hence, any bombing, the object of which is the harassing of the civilian population and destruction of their property, is impermissible.

d) Attacking the pilot, who has bailed out of an aircraft, to save his life, and is parachuting down, is impermissible (Birkenhead, page 226-227).

The recommended rules are yet just the ornamentations of the books of Hague. No nation has accepted them and included them in its war-books (Birkenhead, page 208).

It is even doubtful whether adherence to them is even practicable in future conflicts. Birkenhead, hence writes,

> "The virtues of rules, whose object is to place aerial bombardment within the bounds of certain rules, have come under much criticism. It is doubtful that even if they are accepted, whether they can be adhered to in future conflicts, where air power could be used to a larger extent than what could be envisaged in 1918."

From the foregoing detailed discussions, it must have become quite apparent that the distinction made between defended and undefended areas and the rights the undefended areas have been entitled to by the Western Law is just eyewash. The Western Law cannot lay claims to anything other than a vague concept, "that the life and belongings of the non-combatants are worthy of some concessions," where their defacto considerations are concerned, they are as far from being defacto as they were at the time of Grotious.

The Cities that Fall to the Enemy

The discussion of the rights of the non-combatants lead us to another question, that is, when a city falls to the enemy, after putting up a stiff resistance, what kind of treatment it should expect from the victors. In bygone days, it was considered the natural right of the victor, to put to the sword all inhabitants of cities that fell after resistance. Until recent times, this custom was prevalent in all Europe.

The revolt in Netherlands against Spain, of which it was a part and after that, the ensuing religious wars, in which each contestant entered the cities of others and indulged in general slaughter, is a prime example of the state of affairs. The European conscience finally woke up to the horrors of their undertakings after the 30 Year War, but until the mid-nineteenth century, no prohibition of its practice existed. In this context, the opinion of the famous Duke of Willington is that, if the defenders of the city have been overpowered, the city has no right to asylum. (Dispatches, 2nd series, 1, page 93-94)

In the peninsular war, on many occasions, France threatened the besieged cities that if they continued their resistance, they would be subject to mass slaughter (Bernard, Growth of Laws of War, Oxford Essays, 1866). Hence, when Cuidad Rodrigo, Badajos, and San Sabastian fell after resistance, there indeed was a mass slaughter and destruction in the cities. In 1790, in the war between Russia and Turkey, when the Russian forces entered Ismail, they put all combatants and non-combatants in the city to the sword. In 1837, when the Algerian capital, Constantinople, fell to the French forces, the French were busy slaughtering the inhabitants for three full days. In 1857, when the British gained control of Delhi, during the so-called "mutiny," they also slaughtered the residents, en masse. Even the honor of the royal family was not taken into consideration.

Until that time, no law existed in Europe that forbade such acts. The 1874 Brussels Conference had indeed passed a resolution that, after a city had fallen, the soldiers were not to be let loose to plunder and kill there, but no nation had been ready to accept and implement its resolutions. It therefore did not have the privilege of being part of the European law books. The first time the looting, arson and destruction of the conquered city was prohibited, was in The Hague Conference. Its Clause 28 spells out the prohibition. The evil practice has however not yet been given up fully. During the 1919-1920 war, under the sponsorship of the "most civilized nations of the world," the horrors committed by the Greeks, are proof that even in the 20th century, some relics of the age of savagery, still exist. In concept, Europe can be said to have received enlightenment as to the civilized way of conquerors for entering conquered cities (though the practice of doing so, lagged far behind).

In comparison, the Prophet of Islam (SAW), some 1340 years earlier *(referring to the time of the original writing)*, at the time of his entry into Makkah, after it had fallen to his forces, displayed in letter and spirit, the concept and the practice, the true meaning of which still evades the West. It indeed was not an isolated incident. Later, the pious caliphates displayed the same spirit, humanity, restrained and the truly civilized conduct, when Iran, Iraq, Syria, Egypt, and numerous cities of Africa fell to the Muslim sword.

Occupation and Laws

Occupation is a term of recent times. In the earlier times, when a country was conquered, it became the rightful territory of the conquering nation. According to Islam as well, the conquered territories entered the realm of Islamic territories, and its citizens thenceforth, became entitled to the privileges of "subjects" of Islam[1].

According to the current International law, the defacto occupation of territory does not make it enemy territory. It remains "occupied territory" under enemy administration, unless a formal treaty between the conflicting sides declares that the conquered territories have been handed over to the conquerors. Those living in occupied territories are citizens, neither of the conquering nation, nor of the conquered. They continue their existence as a usurped sub-nation, under the illegal occupational rule of a military clan.

The 1899 and 1907, Hague Conventions have not attempted to clarify the rights of the sub-nationalities under occupation, nor has The Hague determined the extent to which conquerors can exercise their rights on such people. Some laws have been enacted that throw some light on the rights and duties of the governments and people of the occupied territories. These are copied below:

When the reins of governance have been formally passed on to the occupational forces, they will, to the best of their ability, try to

---

[1] Jurists of Islam have made only this distinction, that if a territory is conquered during a war and it has not been decided yet whether the occupation of the area would be permanent or temporary, it would be governed by the rules specified for war zones, but, when the control has been consolidated, the area would have the status of Islamic territory and would be governed by general Islamic rules.

maintain general peace and security and would endeavor to maintain the laws that were in force, prior to their occupation (Clause 43).

This clause lays down a general policy for the occupational forces and is actually quite meaningless. The addition of the word "endeavor" to the phrase "to maintain the laws already in force" makes the clause confusing. It virtually provides opportunity to the forces of occupation to impose its own laws, just as if the territories had been annexed fully. The enemy can easily claim that it was not possible for it to maintain the laws of the past. For that reason, there is very little difference between annexed and occupied territories.

It is impermissible for a hostile nation in occupation of a territory, to force a citizen of such territory to provide intelligence of its own nation regarding its armed forces and their ways and means (Clause 44).

This Clause was not accepted by Germany, Japan, Austria, and Hungary, right from the beginning. The militarist group had serious objection to this clause, since it does not tolerate any restriction on its means of procuring information. The wordings of the criticism in the German war book are:

> "Forcing people to provide information on their own forces and their movements and their means is indeed very cruel. This act is condemned by intellectuals of all nations. However, despite this, no military leader can always avoid such acts. Without doubt, his indulgence in it would never be without remorse, but the necessities of war will often compel him to make use of this source." (Kriegsbrauch, page 48).

Later it is written again:

> "Forcing a person to provide intelligence on his nation's armed forces, is asking him to facilitate his nation's defeat. This is an extremely painful exercise, from the human point of view, but for a force in occupation of its enemy's territories, it is

extremely difficult to forego this available means of intelligence." (Kriegsbrauch, page 48).

These are not the views of the Germans alone, but the entire Europe holds the same and as far as we know, in no war has Clause No. 24 of The Hague conference been adhered to.

It is impermissible for a nation at war, to force the citizens of its occupied territories to participate in warlike activities against their own nation, though they may have been in its service prior to the war (Clause 23).

According to Professor Morgan, this clause just states a principle. The implementation, however, is left to the governments to decide. (War its Conduct and Legal Results)

It is obvious, when governments or rather the armed forces are given the freedom of action, the statement of principles is quite insufficient. The armed forces would obviously take actions that they consider useful for the achievement of the objectives of the war in progress. Hence, this freedom of action was exploited to its limit during the World War (I). The opposing forces utilized the enemy's citizenry, not only for obtaining information, but also used them for such military work as digging trenches and erecting fortifications, as well as for creating obstacles in the enemy's rear (Birkenhead, page 225).

The citizens of occupied territories cannot be forced to swear allegiance against their own nation.

It is imperative that family, honor and rights to the life and property, as well as the religious beliefs held by the people in the occupied territories, are given due respect. Confiscation of personal properties of such citizens is also prohibited.

Wanton destruction of materials and properties, per these instructions is prohibited.

If for monetary benefits, excise and taxation are imposed in areas under occupation, it should be that their valuation and payments are in accordance with the existing rules. The expenses of the occupying forces may be defrayed by these means (Clause 48).

If monetary contributions are to be taken from citizens of the occupied areas, other than the excise duty, such should be only to defray expenses of the occupation forces and for the administration of the area.

No contribution can be levied on the citizenry of the occupied territories, without an express written instruction, promulgated on the authority of the commander-in-chief. Such contributions may be levied, on the condition that they are in accordance with the existing tariff, and a formal receipt is to be given in each case.

Services or logistics support in terms of grains are not to be requisitioned from the municipalities or from ordinary citizens, unless the occupation forces themselves are in need for such. These demands should be such that they are affordable by the locals and they should not be such that fulfilling them would be, for the locals, tantamount to participating in war against their own nation. Where possible, such support and services should be paid for, in cash and a receipt to the effect is to be provided (Clause 52).

It is permissible for the occupation forces to confiscate only such property that belongs to the hostile government and which can serve the enemy in the furtherance of its war effort. However, all materials and equipment, which are used for the transmission of information, through land, air, or sea, or for transportation, all arsenals, and stores of military equipment, can be confiscated without hesitation, even if they are the personal property of an individual. However, it is necessary that they be handed back to the local government, after peace has been restored. (Clause 53)

An attempt has been made through these clauses, to keep the rights of the occupation forces to confiscate and utilize materials and equipment in occupied territories, within bounds. On paper, the occupied areas have been protected to a great extent from the possibility of transgression by the occupation forces. On the ground, however, the militarists are totally opposed to their adherence. They insist on exploiting all available means, which may help in the pursuance of their war effort. Their views are stated as follows, in the German war-book,

> "When required for the purposes of war, all confiscations, all exploitations, all usages, and all forms of sabotage and destruction is permissible."
>
> (Kriegsbrauch, page 53).

In reply to the recommendation of keeping the affordability and means of the occupied areas in consideration, the militarist's state,

> "This concept of moderation, though very noble, its practical implementation is quite impossible."
>
> (Kriegsbrauch, page 62).

Clausewitz's stated opinion, in this regard, is very popular among the militarists, since they as well hold permissible the exploitation of all means and materials that fall in the hand of the conquering forces. They do not consider compelling the authorities in the fallen areas ample enough. They would like to procure whatever they require, by force. Clauzewitz states,

> "There is no limit to this exploitation of this means, lest the occupied nation becomes bankrupt and incapable of paying even another penny."
>
> (Vom Krieg, kap 14).

In this case, too, the militarists have prevailed over the jurists. We see that in no war, have the civilized and highly elevated rules of occupation of foreign territories, outlined by Hague, have been followed[1]

Punitive action cannot be taken against the occupied nation as a whole, whether in the form of monetary fines or otherwise, in retaliation for acts of individuals. (Clause 50)

These bounds were routinely trespassed during the World War. The conflicting forces would often impose punitive fines on the entire occupied region and were more likely to do so, when unable to find the real culprit of an offence against them (Oppenhiem, vol. 11, page 170).

Wanton Destruction

In the 17th century, customarily when a force advanced in any foreign country, it would pillage and destroy all that came in its path. The enemy's right to do so, in those days, was unlimited.

---

[1]Seeing the actions of the U.S., Britain and Russia, in their occupied territories of Germany and Japan, after the World War II, none can say that these civilized nations are adhering to the very same rules that they themselves recommended in the first place.

Such wanton destruction was in evidence even in the 19th century. Many villages were torched by the American army in 1813 and in retaliation, the British destroyed many buildings in Washington. In 1857, the British wantonly pillaged, burnt, and looted large areas of Kanpur, Luknow, and Delhi in India. Before the Crimean War, in all wars, when the Russians advanced into Turkish territories, they would routinely pillage and destroy, as they advanced.

The realization of the need for some bounds in this respect had come in the 17th century. Groitus had clearly declared the concept, stating:

> "Lying waste an area is permissible only to compel
> the enemy to sue for peace, in a short span of time."
> (Lawrence, page 440 - 441)

Later, in the 19th century, Vatel put forward the idea that general terrorism and pillage in enemy territory is permissible on three conditions:

- When it is necessary to put an end to the savagery of a cruel and savage enemy.

- When it is necessary to make a route, in order to effect proper protection and security of own boundaries.

- When it is necessary for action on land or for a siege (Lawrence, page 441).

Towards the end of the 19th century, the Western thought made some progress towards civilization and made it a common rule that only that much destruction was permissible, which was unavoidable for the pursuance of war (Brussels Code, article 13).

The 20th century European intellectuals are of the opinion that pillage and destruction are permissible to the extent dictated by the necessities of war. Destruction for the sake of destruction, however, is not permissible. Lawrence in his book, "Principles of International Law," writes,

> "The laws of war hold permissible the destruction
> of the cities, so as to disable the besieged from
> taking shelter or so that the field of fire for artillery
> is cleared. For these reasons, buildings may be
> destroyed and trees cut down. In fact, in order to

clear the path for the advancing force, villages can be burnt down. These actions however, are justified only on the condition that they are necessary for the immediate objectives of the war in progress." (Lawrence, page 44).

Professor Westlake writes,

"In hostile lands, destructive action is only permissible, when the success of the current military action is dependent on it." (Principles of International Law, page 236).

The German War Book rules,

"Without necessity, even the minutest destruction is impermissible, but necessity makes the biggest destruction permissible." (Birkenhead, page 261).

Here, the Western laws bear a resemblance to the Islamic laws, but only to the extent that on such destructive action, the success of the ongoing military operation depends. The subject has been discussed in detail in chapter 5 of this book, under the sub-title, "Impermissibility of Wanton Destruction." There however is one aspect in which the two laws differ with each other. Islamic Law does not differentiate between the civilized enemy and the uncivilized one. In its view, the destruction of standing crops in the fields of an uncivilized enemy is as much a cruelty as when the crops of a highly civilized enemy are destroyed. In fact, at the time of the birth of Islam, there was no civilized enemy around. Each one was as uncivilized as the other. The Western Law does discriminate between the two. For it, the "bounds of necessity" are limited to actions against "civilized" enemies as regards the poor "uncivilized" enemies; there is no limit to the permissibility of the wreck and destruction they can unleash. Professor Lawrence clearly explains:

In wars against savage and semi-savage nations, Vatel's first rule applies. It is commonly believed that leading away the domestic animals of the savage and uncultured people, destroying their crops and burning their hutments and dwellings, leaves a strong and indelible effect on the psyches of these people. If this destruction is through cannon shells and if incidentally, many people are killed in the action too, the indelibleness of the effect and respect for the Whiteman's justice and power is likely to be much more pronounced (Lawrence, page 41-42) [1].

The Rights and Duties of Neutral States

The History of Neutrality

Among the Western nations, the concept of neutrality is fairly new. About two centuries ago, they had no idea of it at all. So much so, that there was not even a word in their dictionaries to express its true meaning. Grotious uses the word "Medii" to express the concept, while Boiker Schoek uses "Non Hostes" for the purpose. It was only towards the end of the 17th century, that the Germans started using the word "Noitral" or Neutral. Around the middle of the 18th century, Vatel made its use customary when he started using it in his writings of International Law.

During the 16th and 17th centuries, neutrality was considered dangerous and impossible to maintain and it was practically quite meaningless. Machiavelli of Florence, considered it necessary that when there is a conflict between two of his neighbors, a ruler must side with one. A century later, Grotious suggests about the same. He states that between two conflicting nations, a ruler of a third nation, must side with the one he finds in the right and oppose the one who he considers wrong. When, however, it is difficult for him to decide which one is right and which one wrong, both should be treated alike (Lawrence, page 475-477).

In practice as well, until the end of the 18th century, no rights of neutral states existed. Often in their fights, hostile nations would, without much ado, enter the territories of non-partisan states. The declared non-partisan states too, unhesitatingly aided the side they favored. The process of determining the rights and duties of neutral states was started in 1794, when the U.S. declared that, for its citizens, it was impermissible to take part for or against any nation in conflicts, which did not involve the U.S. itself. The process of law-making continued, till in 1818, a comprehensive

---

[1] It is interesting to note that the above has been detracted from the latest edition of Lawrence's book. Perhaps the realization of uprightness in the character of savages and humanity above all, has inculcated some shame in the Whiteman's character of late.

law was enacted, regarding neutrality. In 1819, Britain adopted the American example, and the laws of neutrality enacted by the congress were included in its books of law. Other states soon followed in the footsteps. In 1907, The Hague Conference made it an international law, when the group of Western nations reached a consensus as to the rights and duties of the neutral states.

The Present Concept of Neutrality

(The word 'Present' is referring to the time between World War I and II)

It is strange to note that neutrality, as a concept, was born in the twentieth century and in the 20th century itself, it went into its death throes. Hardly seven years had elapsed since the 2nd Hague Conference completed the task of formulating the laws of neutrality. When the World War *(referring World War I)* broke out in Europe, it tore to shreds the laws of neutrality, which were so recently legislated[1].

During the war of 1914-1918, there was not a single right of the neutral states that was not violated with utter impunity. Their ships were sunk, their commerce was ruined, and they were subjected to searches and were arrested. The fact of the matter is that they were treated no differently than hostile nations. The violation of their rights became routine so that it became doubtful whether such states possessed any rights at all. To aggravate the situation further, now wars do not remain solely conflicts between the armed forces of hostile nations, but became wars involving economies of nations.

The question now arises whether the state, which has economic relations with the enemy, provides logistic support and extends

---

[1] Whatever was remained of the laws, the 2nd World War destroyed it. In this war, the freedom with which, both parties to the conflict attacked neutral states, violated their frontiers, made passages through them by force and by force utilized their resources and wealth, leaves the concept of neutrality, quite meaningless. To top it all, when the U.S., Britain and Russia, declared their intention to keep intact, the system of international peace, they outrightly gave notice to all neutral nations, that if they wished to qualify for the system, they would have to declare war on Germany. If they failed to do so, they would be expelled from the brotherhood of "peace loving" and "civilized" nations.

help to sustain its economic life, can such states be termed neutral? Can it ask for freedom of action to continue such activities? Such questions have put the very foundations of neutrality in jeopardy. In fact, international law has so far been unable to determine, in the light of these newly surfaced problems, what rights and duties it can prescribe for the neutral states. This is not an exaggeration, but a mere statement of facts. The same thoughts are a source of unease for scholars of international law. Professor Nippold, in his book, "Advancements in International Law, After the World War" *(referring to World War I)*, has discussed the problem in detail in the light of the thoughts of renowned scholars of law. The thoughts of Elthez Bacher, stated in the book are copied below:

> "The present war has greatly hurt the position of the neutral states. Many of their rights have been trampled upon with such freedom, that one is put into doubt whether these laws actually exist in International Law. ---------- Since they have been violated so frequently, the chances are that they will not remain valid for long. The newer concepts of rights and justice have cast away the old ones; the breach created between the two can never be filled. The earlier laws, especially the Paris Agreement's Marine Law, Clauses 2, and 4, in the International Law, have been overtaken by an unwritten law, this law holds even severe infringements permissible into the lives of neutral states."

The same author writes at a later stage:

> "The era of large scale international wars has started and all big powers must be prepared to be dragged into these. After all, the International Law has been created on their desires and no international law can continue to exist without their express intent. Therefore in these times, when the inviolability of the non-aligned and neutral states is seen as a burdensome restriction by most of the big powers, their diminishing position even in International Law should come as no surprise." (Nipped, page 146).

From this statement, the present status of neutrality in the Western Law is made known. Let us now examine the details of the laws of neutrality and see whether it is a complete and viable code and how it compares with the Islamic Law on the same subject.

Duties of the Nations at War, Regarding Neutral States

According to Clauses 5 and 13 of The Hague Conventions, the duties laid down for the nations at war regarding neutral states, are as follows:

1. No warlike activity is to be conducted inside the territories of neutral states, by other nations who may be at war with each other.

2. For nations at war, it is prohibited that their forces or materials of war or support be routed through the territories of neutral states.

3. Neutral states cannot be made a base for preparations for wars. Arming/rearming, grouping/regrouping etc. of troops and other such actions are impermissible in such areas.

4. Intruding into neutral territories or waters, for the purpose of capturing the enemy or for attacking it, is an infringement of the rights of neutrality and must be strictly avoided.

5. It is the duty of nations at war to respect the laws that the neutral states make to enable them to fulfill their duties of neutrality.

6. If on occasions, intentionally or unintentionally, the rights of neutral states have been infringed upon, it is the duty of the transgressing nation to make adequate amends.

All these laws are just the manifestations. The main principle behind them is only one and that is, "The rights of the neutral states are inviolable and ought to be fully respected by nations at war." Such a principle is a part of the Islamic system as well. Out of the permanent clauses of the Islamic Law, one states that if a state has a treaty or accord with the Islamic state and does not take part in hostilities against Islam, then if an enemy, while fighting, enters the territories of such a state, it cannot be pursued therein nor can an enemy residing within such a state be attacked. In fact, the residents and frontiers of such states remain inviolable during war with other nations.

The Duties of Neutral States towards Nations at War with Each Other

The duties imposed on neutral states, towards nations mutually at war, by the International Law, are stated below:

Neither of the conflicting nations is to be provided arms aid and both or all-conflicting nations are to be treated alike.

This is the basic duty of neutrality and without its fulfillment, the concept cannot be complete.

Of the nations at war, neither/none can be provided weapons or instruments of war and monetary aid.

This means that it is impermissible that neutral states should sell arms and ammunition and other war equipment to nations engaged in wars. The full extent of the bounds of this law, however, is not clearly defined.

One means of selling arms and ammunition is that a state makes a deal with another for the sale. The other way is that the nation puts up its weapons stores for auction, in which the agents of either or both nations at war may also participate. The first method is obviously prohibited, while the permissibility of the second remains in doubt. There are examples where the big powers have maintained that it is permissible. In 1870, when Germany and France were at war with each other, the U.S. auctioned its stores of military hardware. In this auction, the agents of France purchased large quantities of weapons and transported them to France. These were used in the ongoing war. When objections were raised against the act, the U.S. senate formed a committee to look into the affair. The committee's report stated that it was an open auction and even if the chief executive of the government of France had been one of the bidders, selling him the equipment would not have been illegal. In an open auction, there is no discrimination between bidders. (Wharton, "International Law of the United States," page 391). The decision of the committee leaves very little difference between the allowable and the disallowed, leaving the law quite purposeless.

The second part of the duty is regarding fiscal loans or grants. Now again, there are two methods in which a nation can be given a loan/grant by another. One is that the neutral government itself gives a grant or a loan to another, while the other is that the citizens of a state give a loan/grant to another state, on a personal basis. The former method is obviously held impermissible by general consensus, but there is a difference of opinion regarding the latter. The general trend is that by the second method, the governments of states at war do procure large amounts of monetary aid. In the 1894 Sino-Japanese War, in the 1911 Turko-Italian War and in the Balkan War of 1912, the conflicting nations were able to acquire huge amounts of loans and grants from private citizens of neutral states, with ease.

In 1863, the British government enquired of the experts of International Law, whether it was a duty of the governments of neutral countries to prevent their citizenry from monetarily aiding the nations at war. Lord Lynhurst's reply stated that such an act does not comprise a violation of the laws of neutrality (Hallek's International Law, page 110 and 195-197).

In this way, International Law, making a distinction between governments and people, permits the governments to remain neutral, while their people have the option to aid either or both sides, in wars. Obviously, under the conditions, the laws of neutrality become quite meaningless. If a nation's wealth and resources are dedicated to serve the nations at war, its neutrality or partisanship hardly differs in meaning.

The nations at war are not to be allowed to transit through the territories neutral states. This duty for neutral states is a recent introduction in the International Law. Until the 19th century, both states and intellectuals were inclined towards considering it permissible. In the 17th century, Grotious wrote:

> "The nations have a right of way through neutral states, if this is denied to them without ample reason, the nation desiring to transit through, may acquire it by force."

The 18th century scholar of International Law, Vatel, writes:

> "Nations at war can ask for the right of way from
> their neutral neighbors, but without dire necessity,
> may not acquire the same through force. (Lawrence,
> page 525)

Wheaton, whose book, "International Law," was published in 1836, accepts this right, but does not consider exercising it rightful, without the permission of the neutral state (International Law, page 4-7).

Manning, whose book, "Law of Nations," was published in 1839, does not consider giving warring nations permission to transit through neutral countries, as contrary to laws of neutrality, provided this permissibility extends to both parties to the conflict (Chapter 11).

Hall, a writer of 1880s, holds it impermissible and other writers of the time are also in agreement with him.

The condition of the practices of nations in this regard is no different. When Austria attacked northeast France, it forcefully obtained the right of way through Switzerland. In 1827, the Mexican forces entered the U.S. to fight their enemies there the same year; Russia made an agreement with neutral Romania for the transit of its forces to launch an attack against Turkey. Hence, during the war, five hundred thousand troops transited through neutral Romania, using its rails and roads quite freely. (Wheaton, International Law, page 418)

The biggest example is of *this era*. During the 1914, World War, Germany forcefully acquired the right of way through neutral Belgium and despite opposition by Belgian forces, the German forces transited through it.

Although the last incident has been declared an outright violation of a state's rights, but such tendencies are indicative of the fact that when it is a question of a nation's survival, the stronger nation would always compel the weaker, neutral neighbor to provide it the right of transit through its (neutral neighbor's) territories[1].

---

[1] During World War II, Iran experienced the same difficulty. In order to

Neutral states should not permit states at war to prepare or launch invasions from their territories. Nor should their ships be allowed to be armed/rearmed, fitted/re-fitted from its ports.

This is a later addition to the duties of the neutral states and owes its birth to the Washington Agreement of 1871. Prior to this, examples of preparatory actions for wars being taken in neutral countries are aplenty.

Recruitment of its citizens, into the armed forces of nations at war is to be prevented by the neutral state.

This is also a supplementary duty of neutral states and is quite in conformity with the overall concept of neutrality. The realization of the necessity of including it in the laws of neutrality dawned fairly recently in the West. During the 1793 war between Britain and France, hordes of U.S. citizens went and enlisted themselves in the French forces. In the Greeko-Turkish war, hundreds of Englishmen, under Lord Byron, participated in the war against Turkey. In the 1876 revolt of Serbia against Turkey, thousands of Russian citizens went to fight against Turkey. Switzerland was, until 1859, a regular recruiting ground, from where nations at war could expect to obtain a large number of mercenaries.

It was only towards the 19th century that this aspect of neutrality was given a final shape. It was only then that the experts on International Law gave the verdict that recruitment from neutral countries was against the principles of neutrality.

This is the brief of the duties that International Law imposes on the neutral states. The weaknesses present in these laws have been stated in the foregoing pages. The underlying principle, however, is only one and that is, "neutral states should not aid any one side in a war nor should they undertake any action that may be construed as indicative of its partisanship of one of the parties to the conflict."

In spirit, this principle is embodied in the Islamic laws as well. Neutrality has been described in Islam as, "It (a nation) should not

provide support to Russia, the U.S. and Britain forced it to yield to them the right of transit through its territories and in fact kept a large tract of its territory under their military occupation for the purpose. The German aid any power in its conflict against us nor should it detract from any other of our rights." It can be deduced from this that any action falling within the meaning of mere exhibitionism and default is improper and its avoidance is prerequisite of neutrality[1].

---

[1] For details please see Chapter 5, under sub-title "Rights and Duties of Neutral States"

Conclusion

Before concluding this chapter, it is necessary that we cast a final glance at our previous discussions, in order to make a comparative analysis of the Islamic and the Western laws, to see how the Islamic laws are superior in stature to the Western ones. Therefore, bearing in mind the discussions in the foregoing pages, let us proceed with the comparison[1].

Firstly, the Western laws hardly fall within the description of laws at all. Their principles and implementation are totally based on the inclinations of the concerned states. They make or change the laws to suit their purpose and those, that all or a few of the big powers, do not find suiting their purpose, finally fail to attain the status of laws, or to maintain the status. Consequently, it is not the laws that determine the conduct of the nations, but rather it is the nations that determine what the laws should require and expect of them.

Contrarily, the Islamic laws are laws, in the true sense of the word. A Supreme Authority has ordained them and Muslims have not been given any authority to cancel them or even to make the slightest change in them. They have been decreed so that Muslims, without hesitation or ado, follow them in letter and spirit. Those who do not, are declared violators and transgressors. When Western nations violate any of their laws, it ceases to be a law anymore. On the other hand, even if all the Muslims of the world choose to violate the Islamic law, it still remains the only law for them and they become its violators.

Secondly, the section of the International Law known as the "Laws of War," is grossly less viable and dependable. These laws are always in conflict with the immediate imperatives of war and the latter invariably overwhelms them. Then again, the conflicts

---

[1] Violations are not quoted here, since the Western Nations are already in disrepute for violating all "civilized" laws, the trend continues even today (translator's/ Editor's words)

between the militarists and jurists serves to make these laws weaker. The jurists lay down a law and the militarists out rightly reject it; the jurists call for the implementation of a civilized and moralistic rule, which the militarists refuse to accept. Since the capability of the implementation of all laws and rules is in the hands of the militarists, the propounded law remains within the covers of the law books, while only those laws remain tangible that the military makes on the battlefield.

In contrast, the Islamic laws of war, like the totality of Islamic laws, are concrete, with no provision for altering or changing them. These laws have been made keeping in consideration the imperatives of war. They cannot be altered now. No military leader has the authority to make the minutest change in them.

Thirdly, the foundation for the Western laws of war has been laid on the mutual consent of the conflicting nations. A few nations decided by consent that if and when they were to fight each other, they would follow such and such rule. When these nations are at war with those who were not a party to the agreement, the rules would not apply. Even in the case of those nations who in practice abandon the agreements, they too would be out of the bounds of these rules and they would cease to enjoy the privilege of "civil" treatment by the "civilized" nations. Even from among those nations who are a party to the agreement, if any violates the rules agreed upon, the others would have the right to abandon the rules in a conflict with the violator. That is to say, that by virtue of such violations, the law of war itself, changes. This in turn depicts that the laws were to begin with not based on any ethical considerations, but rather on mutual consent and on exchange of concessions. Of the hostile nations, one does not treat the other humanely, because it should do so. Rather, it behaves so, on the condition that its opponent would also behave in a civilized manner. If one refuses to behave civilly, the other would have a right to behave in like manner.

The Islamic laws are not based on such mutuality. The laws made are of a strictly mandatory nature for the Muslims, under all conditions of the opponent's behavior. The one, who wishes to remain a Muslim, has to abide by the laws of Islam.

Fourthly, the civilized laws of the West are not more than half a century old, while the Islamic laws have been the flag bearers of humanity, culture and civilization for thirteen centuries *(up to the time of the original writing)*. In spite of such a vast difference in modernity, the Western laws have not been able to surpass the Islamic laws, one bit. Even in implementation, leaving aside the details, which temporarily bear relevance to changing circumstances and times, the Western laws do not show any improvement over the Islamic laws. In fact, there are aspects in which Islam still enjoys a supremacy over the Western laws.

Fifthly, the Western Civilization having decreed some pragmatic laws for man has left man free to wield his strength where he feels like and for whatever purpose he desires. It only demands of man that when he slays a man, he should slay him in a prescribed manner and not otherwise. Where the cause for such slaying is concerned, it shows no concern for its rightfulness or otherwise.

To the extent that the actions of the civilized Western nations depict, we learn that they hold permissible waging wars for the purposes of imperialism, sovereignty, expansion of trade, making gains in wealth and territory and for universal plundering. In fact, satisfaction of all animal desires is considered valid reason for wars. Islam, on the other hand, does not instruct its followers only on the civilized methods of fighting wars, but educates them on the validity and invalidity of the causes as well. In fact, it lays more stress on this aspect of wars. It has not left its determination to the discretion of man, but lays down strict bounds, which he has no right to violate.

These are the reasons on the basis of which it is claimed that the Islamic laws of war as compared to the laws prevalent in the West, are more virtuous, more correct, more beneficial, more logical and more viable.

A possible objection to the foregoing discussions could be that in the comparison where the West is concerned, we have taken into consideration only its actions, while where Muslims are concerned, not their acts, but their law has been considered. A little deeper contemplation of the discussions, however, will allay these objections. The fact is that Islamic laws and the actions of the Muslims are two distinctly different affairs. In the ordinance of Islamic laws, the actions of the Muslims or their inclination and choice have no place. Hence, where the morality or depravity of the laws is discussed, actions obviously have no place in the considerations. Contrary to this, the laws of the West and the actions of the Western people are not so distinctly different form each other. The process of law-making, not only the choice and inclinations, but even their actions play an important part. Where the Western laws of war are concerned, the actions of the Western people lead the way and the law just follows. We are therefore constrained to consider their actions when we discuss their laws.

Postscript

As it happens, in all works of translation, some of the charm and a little of the meaning of the original is lost, by virtue of the difference on stresses on words. So probably will be the case with this translation. If some of the magic of the original work is not discernible in this, it is absolutely without intent. I have tried my best to justify the confidence my little brother, Firasat Shah, has placed in my ability to undertake and bring to a conclusion, such an important and ponderous task. I wish him all the success in whatever he intends to do with it. I have the fullest confidence in his dedication to the cause of Islam and am proud to be of whatever little service I have been to his cause.

The Qur'anic translations that appear in this book are copied verbatim from Marmaduke Pikthall's "Meaning of the Glorious Qur'an", while words of the Bible, both from the Old and New Testaments, have been copied from, "Holy Bible-- New International Version", published by the International Bible Society. However, since the English versions of texts, pertaining to the Hindu and Buddhist religions, have not been available, the reader will have to rely on my understanding and translation of these.

All other quotations are translations from the original book, "Al Jihad Fil Islam."

Translator

Syed Rafatullah Shah

Glossary of Islamic-Arabic Terms

Amr: Command, order, establish

Ayah: Verse of Holy Qur'an

Fard: Obligation, further classified into: 1) fard ain an obligation for every Muslim, fard kifayah an obligation that is fulfilled for a Muslim community if some of the people from that community do it.

Fasad: Trouble, turmoil

Fe sabeel illah: In the way of Allah

Fitn: Arabic dictionaries describe 'fitn', a grammatical form of 'fitna' (translated here as strife), as determining the purity of gold through the process of heating it. The dictionaries also state its meaning as casting humans into fire. The Qur'an in describing the 'day of reckoning' also uses the word in that sense. A derivative of that is the term trial and tribulation. Or, 'that which puts man on trial'. Therefore, man's wealth and family have also been termed as 'fitna' (trial, strife). Use of the word in the Qur'an, in relation to wealth and family as such, is because these things put a man on trial, whether he holds truth or these dearer. Bliss and tribulations have also been termed as 'fitna' because in these conditions, man is also on trial. The revolutions and changing colors of history are similarly termed so, since whole nations are on trial at such times. Putting more loads than a man can bear is also a 'fitna', since it is a test of his endurance.

Fiqh: Islamic jurisprudence.

Haj: The visitation to the city of Makkah and performing certain rituals in and around the city at a prescribed time of the year, obligatory for healthy adult Muslims who can afford the journey.

Hadith: The recorded sayings, teachings, actions, approvals, and disapprovals of prophet Mohammad (SAW).

Hijrah: Primarily used for migration of the Muslims from

Makkah to Madinah, the beginning of Islamic calendar is also referenced from the same year and is called Hijrah Calendar. The concept of Hijrah is part of the Islamic teachings and its application is valid based on the severity of situation that Muslims may face in the land (country) they are living in.

Iman: Faith

Jazjya: Tribute or the tax levied on conquered non-Muslims who become protégés of the Muslim State, on the termination of hostilities, for the protection and security, granted to them by the state).

Jihad: Utmost struggle to establish peace and justice, including but not limited to fighting in the righteous cause, although the fighting is regarded as one of the highest degrees of Jihad. Jihad fe sabeel illah, the qualifier fe sabeel illah means in the way of Allah.

Kalimah: The proclamation that 'there is no god but Allah and Muhammad is His messenger', the declaration that makes a person Muslim.

Masjid: Place dedicated for worship in Islam (masajid, plural)

Mufsid: Troublemaker

Mujahid: One who struggles and fights in the cause of Allah.

Maroof: Virtue, It can also stand for 'that which is a fact', or 'that which is known to be correct, or the truth'. It can be used to denote that which human intelligence acknowledges as correct and what every person will feel is good.

Munkar: Vice or evil, it can mean 'that which is unknown or unfamiliar'. In usage, it can denote 'that action which is disliked by nature, which is considered wrong by human intelligence and which is disliked by normal humans'

Nahi: Prohibit, annul

Qasas: Compensation given to the family of one who is killed by the one who killed through the mutual agreement between both parties under the supervision of judiciary in the Islamic system.

Salat: A set of intention, actions, and uttered words (mostly from Qur'an) that constitute Muslim prayer, Obligatory prayer is five times a day for adults in normal conditions.

Surah: A chapter of Holy Qur'an

Ummah: Nation

Umrah: Visitation to Kaaba in the city of Makkah and performing certain rituals, not obligatory and can be performed at any time of the year.

Zakat: Yearly obligatory charity for Muslims.

Abbreviations of Arabic Terms:

A.H.: After Hijrah, used for Islamic calendar that begins from Prophet Muhammad's migration from Makkah to Madinah

SAW: (Sal Allaho Alyhi Wasalam), peace and blessings of Allah be upon him), used Prophet Muhammad (SAW).

AS: (Alayhi Salam), peace be upon him, used for prophets (AS).

RA: (Radi Allaho Anho), Allah be satisfied with him, used for the companions (RA) of Prophet Muhammad (SAW).

Names of Prophets in Arabic:

Eisa (AS): Jesus (peace be upon him)

Musa (AS): Moses (peace be upon him)

Yusuf (AS): Joseph (peace be upon him)

Dawood (AS): David (peace be upon him)

Yahya (AS): John (peace be upon him)

Solomon (AS): Solomon (peace be upon him)

Shoaib (AS): Jethro (peace be upon him)

Saleh (AS): Sale (peace be upon him)

Adam (AS): Adam (peace be upon him)

Uzair (AS): Ezra (peace be upon him)

61656066R00245

Made in the USA
Middletown, DE
13 January 2018